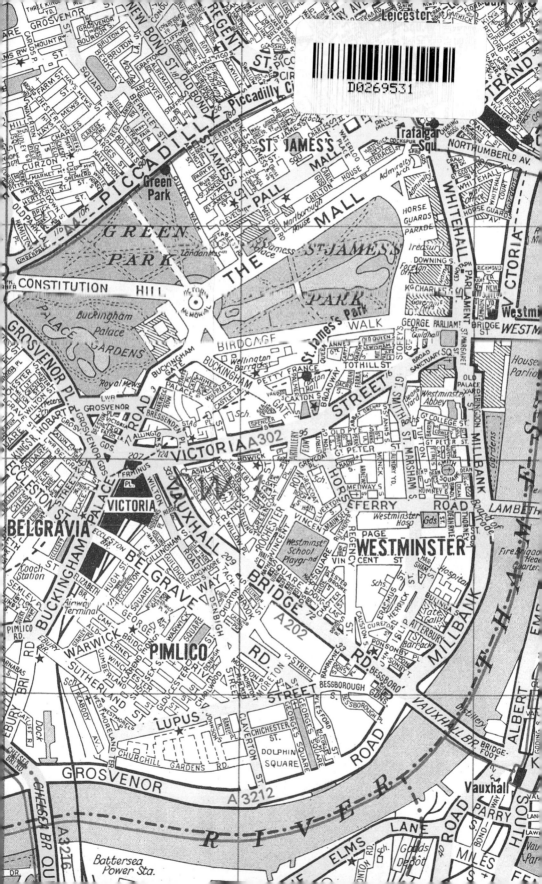

A DIFFERENT CLASS OF MURDER

Laura Thompson is author of Somerset Maugham Award-winning *The Dogs: A Personal History of Greyhound Racing* (1995), *Newmarket* (2000), *Life in a Cold Climate: A Biography of Nancy Mitford* (2003) and *Agatha Christie: An English Mystery* (2007)

Agatha Christie: An English Mystery

'Laura Thompson has certainly written the last word on Agatha Christie. Her book is a superb piece of biography.'
CHARLES OSBORNE, *Literary Review*

'This splendid account of [Christie's] life and work is unlikely to be bettered.'
MELANIE MCDONAGH, *Evening Standard*

'The best biographies are labours of love and this fascinating book is just that.'
JESSICA MANN, *Sunday Telegraph*

'Laura Thompson's outstanding biography... is a pretty much perfect capturing of a life.'
KATE MOSSE, Book of the Year, 2007

'A triumphant success.'
A. N. WILSON, *Daily Mail*

Life in a Cold Climate

'Well-nigh perfect.'
LADY DIANA MOSLEY

'A brilliant study, original, perceptive, passionate and very nearly as enjoyable to read as the subject's own novels.'
SELINA HASTINGS, *Sunday Telegraph*

'Thompson, like Mitford, writes in a witty, humorous and touchingly personal manner.'
Daily Express

A

Different Class

of

Murder

The Story of Lord Lucan

LAURA THOMPSON

First published in 2014 by Head of Zeus Ltd

1 3 5 7 9 10 8 6 4 2

A catalogue record for this book is available
from the British Library.

ISBN (HB) 9781781855362
ISBN (E) 9781781855355

Designed and typeset by Lindsay Nash

Printed and bound in Germany
by GGP Media GmbH, Pössneck

Head of Zeus Ltd
Clerkenwell House
45–47 Clerkenwell Green
London EC1R OHT

WWW.HEADOFZEUS.COM

To my family

Contents

'Law! What law can search into the remote abyss of Nature, what evidence can prove the unaccountable disaffections of wedlock? Can a jury sum up the endless aversions that are rooted in our souls, or can a bench give judgment upon antipathies?'

GEORGE FARQUHAR, *The Beaux' Stratagem*, 1707

INTRODUCTION

A Brief History of Murder, According to Social Class

'Anything a Wimsey does is right and Heaven help the person who gets in his way.'

DOROTHY L. SAYERS, *Strong Poison*, 1930

DO EARLS COMMIT murder?

It is an incendiary question, in a country obsessed with class. Why shouldn't a peer of the realm be a murderer, the same as anybody else?

Why not indeed; yet murdering is something that they seldom do.

They have slaughtered to achieve advancement, of course, since historically that is how advancement was often achieved. An example: Richard Bingham, a soldier of fortune whose descendants became the Earls of Lucan, defended Ireland for Queen Elizabeth I and earned a knighthood for his savage efficiency. Peers have also killed by the careless exercise of inherited power. During the Irish potato famine of the 1840s, for instance, the 3rd Earl of Lucan cleared his Co. Mayo estate of poverty-stricken tenants, serving 6,000 processes for eviction, and eventually caused the workhouse gates to close in their 'death like faces'.

But domestic murder: no.

In the last 500 years just eleven titled people* have been tried for murder in England, two of them twice. A twelfth person, the 7th Earl of Lucan, was named guilty in 1975 by an inquest jury.

Of the eleven who faced trial, six were convicted of murder, and four of manslaughter. All were tried 'by their peers'; meaning by other titled persons. This right continued until 1948, as did the tradition of the silken rope, with which aristocrats could be hanged more soothingly than with hemp. A further right was 'privilege of peerage', which could be pleaded by those found guilty of a first offence. It did not extend to murder, but it allowed a peer to walk free from a lesser charge.

---

* For further details of these eleven titled murderers, see Appendix I (page 377).

When, therefore, the 7th Earl of Pembroke was convicted of manslaughter in 1678, he got away with it. The Lord High Steward warned him that 'his lordship would do well to take notice that no man could have the benefit of that statute but once', but Pembroke carried on exactly as before. In 1680 he was found guilty of murder, and received a royal pardon. His status as an earl clearly brought him an outrageous degree of favour. This did not extend to every aristocrat: three have been hanged for murder in the last 500 years. Yet Pembroke's treatment was far more typical. So too was the nature of his crimes. Both the deaths for which he was indicted were the product of boredom, booze and a belief that he could do whatever he liked at any given moment and too bad if somebody got hurt along the way. This, in murder and in much else besides, was the aristocratic way.

Pembroke's sense of entitlement defined him. He lived within his own world, according to his own crazy code of conduct. So too did the 4th Baron Mohun, a posh thug acquitted of murder in 1699 after a drunken duel in Leicester Square; and the 5th Baron Byron, great-uncle to the poet, who in 1765 put a sword through his cousin's stomach and was let off with a fine. Later Byron shot his coachman. He did so in the manner of somebody taking a pop at a pheasant, just as Lord Pembroke, in 1680, had killed an officer of the watch who happened to be on a street where he was brandishing his blade.

It is unsurprising that the lower orders should have been so frequently the victims of aristocratic murder. In 1760, for instance, the 4th Earl Ferrers shot a man named John Johnson, a steward for his family estate. Ferrers was described as being 'of ungovernable temper, at times almost amounting to insanity', although this may, of course, have been simply a manifestation of extreme arrogance. It is very difficult to tell, in these cases, where arrogance ends and lunacy begins.

Ferrers was one of the few who did not get away with his crime. He was hanged at Tyburn, where he was denied the courtesy of the silk rope. This was the last occasion to date on which an aristocrat would be tried and convicted of murder in England. The excitable, damn ye sir passions of the seventeenth and eighteenth centuries had pretty much burned themselves out, although it was not until the last duel was fought, in 1852, that gentlemen would cease their particular kind of terrorizing street violence.

There had been innumerable deaths by duelling, very rarely resulting in any kind of prosecution. Of the handful that were charged, the last was the 7th Earl of Cardigan, who with his hated brother-in-law, the 3rd Earl of Lucan, would later preside over the hundred-plus deaths that occurred during the 1854 Charge of the Light Brigade in the Crimean War. Thirteen years earlier, Cardigan had been tried for shooting a fellow officer in a duel. 'I have hit my man,' he said. Yet in the House of Lords he was acquitted on a ludicrous technicality: his victim was wrongly named in the indictment, presumably in order to leave a loophole through which Cardigan could slide. 'In England', wrote *The Times*, 'there is one law for the rich and another for the poor.'

That same year, 1841, the right to plead exemption from justice for a first offence was ended, but nobody really believed that privilege of peerage did not carry on regardless. In 1922, for instance, the public was convinced that Ronald True, a former RAF officer, had dodged the gallows because he was the illegitimate son of an unnamed peeress.

The thirty-one-year-old True had savagely murdered a prostitute in her London flat. His defence of insanity failed, and he was sentenced to death. However, when further medical evidence was presented to the Home Secretary, True was reprieved and sent to Broadmoor; and the public went berserk.

The sense of outrage was class-based. Even as True's life was being saved, a pantry boy named Henry Jacoby, who had murdered his titled employer, was hanged despite a recommendation to mercy on grounds of youth. As it happened, True's peeress mother was a creature of myth. He had simply been lucky. Yet the rage against his 'escape' from justice, and the collective belief in the hidden powers of privilege, were intense.

The acquittal of Sir Jock Delves Broughton, tried for murder in Kenya in 1941, also tugged at the idea that posh people can 'get away with things'. Broughton was accused of killing the Earl of Erroll, the lover of his far younger wife. These three belonged to what was known as the Happy Valley set, a collection of beyond-bored white settlers, who slept with each other in between drinking themselves silly: symbols of the deadly decadence of lives in which nothing is earned.

Although Broughton's acquittal had not been a foregone conclusion, the idea that this man would hang – a baronet, an old Etonian – never seemed quite real. As the verdict was about to be delivered, the foreman of the jury winked at the defendant and gave him a 'thumbs-up' sign.[1] Not all the Happy Valley set had rallied to his defence, although generally it closed ranks. And the stepdaughter of one of Broughton's friends, to whom he confessed murder, kept his secret for almost forty years. 'I can remember having it drilled into me', she later said, 'that a man's life hung on it and that every time I spoke to the police I mustn't say anything that might hurt him.'

On 19 June 1975, Richard John Bingham, 7th Earl of Lucan, also 13th Baronet Bingham of Castlebar in Co. Mayo, also 3rd Baron Bingham of Melcombe Bingham and a baronet of Nova Scotia, was named by a coroner's court as the killer of his children's nanny. Mrs Sandra Rivett, aged twenty-nine, was bludgeoned to death in the basement of Lucan's Belgravia house on the evening of 7 November 1974. As there has been no formal sighting of the earl since a few hours after the murder was committed, he has never been brought to trial.

On the face of it the Lucan case followed a tradition of aristocratic murder, in that the earl was pronounced guilty of killing a servant. Except that this was not really the case, since Mrs Rivett was almost certainly not the intended victim. According to the 'official' version of events – the one propounded by the police, ratified by the inquest jury, and generally accepted ever since – Lord Lucan killed Sandra Rivett in error, believing her to be his estranged wife Veronica. In other words he had attempted to commit a classic domestic murder; which is something that earls do not do.

Of the eleven titled people tried by their peers, none was accused of a domestic killing. This kind of murder assumed ascendancy in the nineteenth century, along with the middle classes who specialized in it. In doing so they have, like the mad aristos, defined a certain kind of Englishness. The Adelaide Bartlett case, the Croydon poisonings, the cases of Charles Bravo, Madeleine Smith, Florence Maybrick, Dr Crippen, George Joseph Smith, Armstrong, Wallace:* these are murders redolent of the parlour and the suburb, of passion among the antimacassars, of small sums neatly folded into life insurance policies. Impossible to conceive anything more different from the flashing, dashing, devil-may-care behaviour of Earl Pembroke and his like.

Domestic murder was a careful little business, for all its terrible riskiness. It was madness, but it looked like sanity. It was murder under wraps, behind curtains, committed most frequently with poison: a secret stream trickled discreetly into cocoa or a tea-time scone. It happened in places like Pimlico and Balham. Unlike aristocratic murder, it was committed by women as well as men. And it was done, typically, to maintain appearances, rather than to wreck them. It sought to retain the status quo by removing the element that threatened it. The brief period in 1910, in which Crippen played happy house with his mistress while his wife lay in the cellar, cut into small and harmless pieces, symbolized the state of unassuming bliss to which the domestic murderer aspired.

Crippen's is a classic story because it centres upon something that everybody can understand: an unhappy marriage. So too does that of Edith Thompson and Frederick Bywaters. Their love affair culminated, in 1922, in the murder of Mr Thompson. His wife was

* For further details of these cases, see Appendix II (page 380).

7

almost certainly innocent, but she was hanged for complicity. A woman of unusual allure, eight years older than the boy who had clubbed her husband to death, she did not command the sympathy of the Old Bailey. The judge disliked her, on what he called principle. In fact the prejudice against her was atrocious; but it is hard for a courtroom to be free of prejudice. When Crippen's mistress Ethel Le Neve was tried as an accessory to murder, she was in a position very similar to Edith Thompson with regard to the facts, but her air of poor-little-me vulnerability did her no end of good.

What motivated these murders was an abundance of emotion. But what caused them was lack of money; and the need for it, to keep up a front. Money, in fact, is the key to domestic murder. Crippen could not afford to divorce his wife, so he disposed of her instead. Edith Thompson dreamed of leaving her husband, but did not dare because she feared the loss of respectability. So again the answer was murder. Murder, all too often, was what happened when alternative action was too expensive.

No such cataclysm was necessary when the future 2nd Earl of Lucan fell in love with the wife of the future 12th Duke of Norfolk, formerly Lady Elizabeth Belasyse, a daughter of the Earl of Fauconberg. Freedom, in such circles, could be bought. Lady Elizabeth obtained a divorce in 1794 and married the Hon. Richard Bingham that year; in 1795 he became Lord Bingham when his family was granted its earldom.

That is not to say that there was no scandal. Indeed the scandal was intense. The divorce was the eighteenth-century equivalent of a tabloid sensation, after 'an action for Criminal Conversation' was brought by 'Mr Howard, the presumptive heir to the illustrious house of Norfolk, against Mr Bingham, son of Lord Lucan'. Criminal conversation was a peculiarly droll euphemism, which in essence meant anything but conversation. *The Times*, nudging and winking like nobody's business, wrote 'that Mr. Bingham had paid his addresses to her Ladyship before Mr. Howard had, that she was extremely attached to Mr. B., and that a considerable time after her marriage with Mr. H. this unhappy attachment was again revived'. Lord Howard was awarded £1,000 in damages, but of course the defence could afford to pay. Bingham's family owned thousands of acres in Mayo; Elizabeth brought to the marriage an estate in Macclesfield.

They could also afford to brazen out the shame. It was not for-gotten, but it was absorbed into the sheer scale on which they lived. Nevertheless a criminal conversation action was a horrible business. Was it worth it? The Lucans themselves split after ten years. The earl, who again had the means to escape, moved to Bologna, and eventually married his Italian mistress.

In 1825 it all happened again, unbelievably, when the Lucans' younger son was named in a crim. con. action brought by Viscount Lismore. Out into the courtroom came all the sordid details: a servant of the viscountess testified to seeing the adulterous pair on a sofa, where 'their general appearances, and especially the disorder of their dresses, manifested unequivocally the guilty intercourse which had just passed between them'. And so the evidence con-tinued, damaging but not fatally so (Bingham went on to a career in diplomacy). Edith Thompson suffered in a similar way when her love letters were read out at the Old Bailey, but for her the stakes were immeasurably higher.

Bingham's older brother, the 3rd Earl of Lucan, would also later separate from his wife. He had married Lady Anne Brudenell, sister of the duelling Earl of Cardigan, in 1829. From 1854 they lived apart. Lucan maintained an establishment in Mayfair and at Laleham House, the family residence built by his father on the Thames, some eighteen miles from London. His countess, getting away as far as possible, made her home on the Isle of Wight, with six servants. Living apart could be a civilized business, if money eased the way.

The earl found his own amusements, meanwhile, and contin-ued to do so into old age. A codicil to his will, written when he was eighty-three, made provision for the children of an Elizabeth Anne Powell. And eleven years earlier, in 1872, he had given some intriguing evidence at the trial of Marguerite Dixblanc, a Belgian cook who was accused of killing her French mistress, Marie Riel, at a house in Park Lane.

The nineteenth century saw several cases in which the tables were turned, and servants killed employers. In 1840 a valet, François-Benjamin Courvoisier, was found guilty of cutting the throat of Lord William Russell, son of the Duke of Bedford.[2] In 1849 Sarah Thomas battered to death a mistress described as 'tyrannical, peevish, and violent'; petitions were made for mercy, but to no avail. Like Courvoisier, the girl was hanged. So too was Kate Webster, who in 1879 killed her mistress, Julia Martha Thomas, at a house in Richmond, dropping a box containing body parts from the nearby bridge.[3]

Webster was a career criminal. Nevertheless the murder she committed seems to have been born of passion, as surely as if the servant-employer relationship had been a marriage: a final, calamitous explosion at the end of a period of high tension, in which the mere placing of a tea tray with too defiant a 'clink' can seem like an act of dangerous rebellion.

So too it had been in April 1872, with Marie Riel and Marguerite Dixblanc. At the inquest for what became known as 'The Park Lane Murder', which bore certain resemblances to the crime of which the 7th Earl of Lucan would be accused, a doctor described finding the dead body of Madame Riel, a widow aged forty-two. There had, he attested, been 'a fearful amount of violence'.

At this time, and indeed until 1977, an inquest jury had the right to name a person whom it judged to be guilty, who would then be committed for trial. The 1872 jury showed commendable scruples before doing this, rather more so than would be shown 100 years later towards Lord Lucan. Eventually a majority verdict was delivered: 'Wilful Murder against the woman known as Dixblanc.' At her Old Bailey trial, Dixblanc testified that Riel had started an argument as she was cooking dinner, whereupon she had seized Riel by the throat. Issuing an instant dismissal, Riel taunted her: 'And what will become of you when you leave here; you will have to go upon the streets.' Dixblanc replied: 'I shall not be so long on the *pavé* as you have been': an interesting aside. The maid then battered her mistress to death, and hauled the body into the pantry in an attempt to conceal it.

Although Madame Riel's home, number 13, was relatively small (two servants only at the time of her death), it still seems quite remarkable that she should have been living amid the *richissime*, between the great town houses of the Earl of Grosvenor and the Duke of Wellington. She did, however, have a gentleman supporter living nearby, another member of the aristocracy: none other than the 3rd Earl of Lucan.

The earl's friendship with Madame Riel emerged in the most oblique and, in so far as was possible, the most discreet of ways. At the inquest, a maid gave evidence as to how, when her mistress had apparently gone missing, Riel's daughter had asked her to go for assistance.

The report in *The Times* continued:

> The CORONER: And you went?
> Witness: Yes, I went and fetched some one from 36 South-Street. When I got back with ----- (the witness here dropped her voice – she was thought to say 'friend' – and the question was not repeated) I heard of the discovery that had been made.

The census from 1871 confirms that 36 South Street, off Park Lane, was the home of the 3rd Earl of Lucan. At the age of seventy-two he was still in the market for 'friendship': his regime of one meal a day, which he insisted was all a man needed to keep himself vigorous, was clearly working some sort of magic. Lord Lucan was called as a witness at the Dixblanc trial, where he testified that having cashed a cheque for £80 (a huge sum, equivalent to some £10,000), he had given half the money to Madame Riel.

Lucan's evidence has a repressive air, as one who does not wish to give away too much. In answer to a question about Riel's character, he said: 'Like a good many French ladies, she was a little *vive.*

I hardly know an English word that would describe her better. She was hasty. I don't go beyond that.' One can see him standing there, grand but not entirely at his ease. The 3rd Earl was a man accustomed to uncomfortable public speaking; almost addicted, in fact, to going head-to-head with adversaries. In 1847 he had faced the House of Lords and stridently defended his conduct towards his starving Irish tenants. In 1856 he spoke at great length before the inquiry into the ill-conducted Crimean War, explaining his actions and shouting down censure. Nevertheless this was rather different, to have one's lady friend throttled by a servant and be obliged to discuss her in public: a bizarre situation.

Marguerite Dixblanc was sentenced to death, despite the fact that the jury found premeditation not proven. Her foreignness had created its own prejudice, as had her appearance. She was described as resembling 'the class of Irish coster-monger women who are almost daily charged with drunkenness and assault'. Away from the hothouse of the Old Bailey, however, justice prevailed: the sentence was commuted to penal servitude for life.

Of course the most fascinating aspect of the case was not, as the arguments in court had it, whether or not Dixblanc's intention had been to commit murder. It was the fact that this grim crime had taken place in Park Lane, of all places, in one of London's sacred postcodes. Death in a pantry, in W1: how was it possible?

Murder in such a setting was rare, almost as rare as murder committed by the aristocracy. The natural home of domestic murder was the suburb. Sex murderers operated in what were then the wilder frontiers of Whitechapel and Soho.

Yet in the mid-twentieth century a handful of murders took place on upmarket territory. They were domestic, in their way, although no mystery lurked within the human dynamic. In 1923 Marguerite Fahmy, a sumptuously upmarket adventuress whose ex-lovers included the future Edward VIII, was acquitted of shooting her husband, Prince Ali Kamel Bey Fahmy, in their bedroom suite at the Savoy Hotel. Her defence was that she had been subjected to violence and sadistic practices: the prejudice, in this instance, was fiercely against the domineering man. Whatever the truth of her story that she had fired in self-defence, Madame Fahmy played the feminine part of victim to perfection.

In 1932 Elvira Barney, the daughter of a rich baronet, shot her unfaithful boyfriend at her Knightsbridge mews. There are parallels with the Ruth Ellis case in 1955. Mrs Ellis had also been played for a fool by her lover, to the point where she eventually snapped and killed him; the extenuating circumstances were powerful, but she was hanged all the same. By contrast, Mrs Barney had an expensive and caring defence. She made a pitiful figure in court – 'Knight's Daughter Collapses', blared the headlines and she commanded public sympathy. It was as though nobody could quite believe that a woman who appeared in *Tatler*, and whose family home was in Belgrave Square, was capable of murder.

There was no such difficulty in the case of Arthur Robert Boyce, tried in 1946. The setting for this crime was 45 Chester Square, at the calm white heart of Belgravia, in a house rented by King George II of Greece. A housekeeper, Elizabeth McLindon, had been engaged; somewhat astonishingly, given the status of her employer, she was a former prostitute, but had got the job on the strength of some splendid references forged by her fiancé, Arthur Boyce. What Miss McLindon did not know was that the man she hoped to marry had a wife already, and had served time for bigamy.

In June 1946 the King of Greece paid a visit to Chester Square, and was surprised to find no housekeeper there to greet him. The police were called. They broke down a locked door on the ground floor, and found the body of Elizabeth McLindon seated at a table. She had been shot in the back of the head. Presumably she had discovered rather too much about Boyce's past, and become a nuisance. By a quite extraordinary oversight, Boyce had left some of his letters among her belongings. He was quickly arrested, found guilty at the Old Bailey, and hanged.

Chester Square leads directly off Lower Belgrave Street, where the murder of Sandra Rivett was committed on 7 November 1974. In fact Chester Square may have played its part in the events of that night. Although very little of what happened is corroborated fact, it is likely that the 7th Earl of Lucan rang the doorbell of 51 Chester Square at around 10pm, an hour or so after the murder. He had then – again this is only probability – telephoned the house and tried to speak to Madeleine Florman, an acquaintance, who lived there with her husband. 'Madeleine?' he said. 'I know you...' Then he hung up.

Just a couple of minutes' walk from what was then the Florman house stands 46 Lower Belgrave Street: the setting for the most famous of those rare murders committed behind London's serene frontages, in the postcodes of the rich. The house gives nothing away. It is tall, slender, restrained. To its left is Eaton Square, where the 7th Earl of Lucan lived as a boy. Behind is Eaton Row, the mews built for the horses and carriages used by the Lower Belgrave Street families, where Lucan's wife has lived since 1976. Everywhere is seemliness and symmetry: the clean lineaments of money. Belgravia is a place of order and grace, created in the late Georgian era when Thomas Cubitt laid the groundwork on some marshy meadows owned by Robert Grosvenor, later the 1st Marquess of Westminster. Once known as the Five Fields, the land had been a haunt of thieves, 'beloved by bull-baiters, badger-drawers, and dog-fighters'.[4] But this bloody history was subsumed into Cubitt's glorious dream of stucco. It became the home of prime ministers, of the aristocracy, of Alfred Lord Tennyson and Vivien Leigh: a white island untouched by the lapping tide of London.

Yet in the midst of it all is a house that stands not just between its similarly stately neighbours, but alongside 39 Hilldrop Crescent, in whose cellar Crippen buried his wife, and 85 Claverton Street, where Adelaide Bartlett's husband was filled with liquid chloroform. Like these, 46 Lower Belgrave Street is a totemic address in the history of English murder. The imagination seeks to penetrate the façade of these homes, to conjure the moment when the confusion of violence spilled over a lace counterpane or a kitchen floor. But what tantalizes is that the façade is maintained. Mayhem is screened behind the polite formality of door, brick and window. This is the paradox that enlivens English murder, and makes it the stuff of Agatha Christie and the Cluedo board: Lord Lucan, in the kitchen, with the lead piping.

And 46 Lower Belgrave Street has added totemic value, because its façade is all the more impenetrable, because it stands within the white island of London, because earls do not commit domestic murder. It is the place where the domestic murder became magnified, by contact with a world in which it did not belong.

Earl Ferrers, hanged in 1760, had killed with the open disregard for consequence that characterized the aristocrat. Nevertheless his crime had aspects of something more recognizable. At its roots lay two of the classic motives of domestic murder: a catastrophic marriage, and money.

The earl, who like Lord Lucan was aged thirty-nine at the time of the killing, was a gambler and a heavy drinker: also like Lucan. To some degree, Ferrers was mentally unbalanced; yet it was his countess, Mary, who was treated as a madwoman. This, it is generally claimed, was the situation in the Lucan marriage. Mary Ferrers had sought to escape her husband, and accordingly Ferrers held her prisoner at the family home in Leicestershire.

This situation was quite familiar in the eighteenth century, particularly among the titled classes, where pride and inheritances were at stake. While some husbands went down the 'criminal conversation' route, others took a different kind of vengeance. In 1700 the Earl of Anglesey tried to arrest his wife, as she went to and from the House of Lords in pursuit of a legal separation; in 1744 Lord Bellfield, suspecting his wife of adultery, held her at a house in Ireland for thirty years until her death. It could be dangerous to crave autonomy, or equality.

It was not until 1891 that the practice of wife-confinement (by then very rare) was ruled unequivocally illegal. Mary Ferrers was only released after a writ of habeas corpus was obtained on her behalf. She was examined by doctors and found to be sane. Eventually Mary was able to use her confinement as evidence of cruelty but, as was usual in these cases, Ferrers was not charged. The man whom he would later shoot, the steward John Johnson, had given evidence in Mary's favour.

There were no children from the Ferrers marriage; had there been, this would have meant another fight, since until 1839 the presumption under law was that the father got custody. There was then the question of money. Without a properly drawn-up separation deed, a wife was financially at the mercy of her husband, but the Ferrers estate, which was in trust and restricted the earl's hitherto hysterical spending, granted Mary an income. Johnson collected property rents for her.

Ferrers therefore seethed with resentment against his wife on two counts: her success in the case, and her claim upon money that he wanted for himself. She had won the day, in fact. An earl would behave like a gentleman if he lost to his friends at cards, but losing to a wife was another thing altogether. Perhaps Ferrers would have killed Mary, if he could have got his hands on her. Instead he did the next best thing, and attacked the servant who had taken her part.

The 7th Earl of Lucan, whom it is generally accepted had sought to kill his estranged wife, had similarly lost a court case: for custody of the three children from his marriage. He had also been preoccupied with money. His estate was held in trust, and supplied him with an income that had become grotesquely inadequate. After the Lucans separated, his wife had possession of the family home at Lower Belgrave Street, which he was obliged to maintain. He gave her an allowance, while also paying rent on a flat for his own use. He received around £12,000 a year from trusts, and at the time of the murder had debts of some £65,000.

Thus was set up a classic scenario for domestic murder: emotional motive, financial cause. If Lord Lucan had wanted to get rid of his wife, he could not, as his ancestors had done, simply throw money at the problem. He had none to throw. As with Dr Crippen and his class in the years before divorce on demand, so with a debt-ridden earl in the year of 98 per cent top rate taxation. Murder would have presented itself as the only option that would remove the disruptive element, and restore the status quo.

Nor could Lord Lucan claim any kind of privilege of peerage. Those days were over. Indeed one of the most striking things about the aftermath of Sandra Rivett's murder was that, in the court of public opinion, an earl was the worst thing that a murder suspect could be.

The Earl of Pembroke had got away with killing two men, simply because of who he was. He had sailed along in a world peopled only by his own kind, and if the lower orders raged or even knew about his doings, it was a matter of no importance whatsoever. Three hundred years later an earl no longer bestrode the airy spaces of his own life. The world had come to meet him. Lord Lucan was seen as representing the old ways of the aristocracy, and was judged according to the new mores of egalitarianism. Thus while justice was appallingly easy on Pembroke, it was especially severe on Lucan; for what he was, as much as for what he was perceived to have done. Prejudice, that inescapable irrationality, was against him.

The fact that the victim was a nanny – a servant – merely emphasized the lordly image. Sandra Rivett may have been murdered by mistake, but the connection was still there with those who had slaughtered the lower orders like so much vermin. What added a layer of murky paradox was the manner of Mrs Rivett's death. An earl, a man who thought himself better than the rest of us, hadn't even had the style to shoot or brandish like his swaggering forebears. He had killed, in fact, in a way strongly reminiscent of Marguerite Dixblanc: in a basement kitchen, with vicious blows. A master killing a servant, in the way that a servant had killed a mistress: it is hardly surprising that people should have been so shocked, mesmerized, sanctimonious and gleeful. Do earls commit murder? Damn right they do.

In 1974 the case was called 'The *Upstairs, Downstairs* Murder',[5] in easy reference to the then wildly popular television drama, set in the early years of the century, describing the lives of a Belgravia family and its staff. The series compelled millions, and forty years on nothing has changed: *Upstairs, Downstairs* has simply been replaced with *Downton Abbey*. Class does not go away. It is as though the British, or perhaps the English, feel that if they let go of their obsession they will have nothing with which to replace it. The sweetly naive may have believed that class was abolished in the 1960s, when Lord Lichfield became a photographer and rock stars pulled posh girls at Annabel's. Of course what really happened was that a pseudo-aristocracy began to grow, that of the rich and famous, while towards the old aristocracy deference segued into resentment. But the fascination remained, potent as ever.

The perception is still cherished that a posh accent is the voice of complete command; that David Cameron and his public school cabinet are, beneath their Boden, the representatives of the mad officer class who ordered the Charge of the Light Brigade. Possibly this is a safer belief than the admission that power today lies with the supranational class of the super-rich. The Duke of Westminster, who received an estimated £1,000 a day in rents in the 1870s, still owns much of Belgravia, but rows of stucco houses stand like so many bank-vaulted Picassos, the uninhabited acquisitions of foreign money. The only privately owned house on Belgrave Square belongs to the Russian oligarch Oleg Deripaska. The Clermont Club, where Lord Lucan gambled, is owned by a Malaysian conglomerate. Berkeley Square, where the club stands, belongs to a Middle Eastern sovereign wealth fund. Coutts and Co., which handled the Lucan family trust, is part of the Royal Bank of Scotland, whose hapless fiddlings in the global financial markets were revealed in 2008.

By 1974, the year of the Lucan murder case, it was perfectly clear that Britain no longer belonged to the aristocracy. It had been clear for years, in fact, but now the signs were positively blazing, to those who wished to see them. Oil money gushed freely over London, in what was described as an invasion by 'the white gowns of a new and suddenly universal priesthood of pure money'.[6] Crockford's gambling club established an 'Arab Room', for the people who were actually spending proper money. The Victoria and Albert Museum staged an exhibition entitled 'The Destruction of the Country House'. Union leaders, who had the upper hand in their death struggle with the government, were known as 'barons'. Len Murray, who ran the Trade Union Congress, had more power in his little finger than Lord Lucan ever wielded in his entire life.

And the murder of Sandra Rivett symbolized, with an absolute clarity, the collision of worlds. If Lord Lucan were guilty then he had killed with an aristocratic contemptuousness, but also with a desperate, secretive brutishness. If he had indeed made a failed attempt at domestic wife-murder, he had done so through lack of money. An earl without means, like the 7th Earl of Lucan, was a peculiarly vulnerable creature, naked beneath his ermine. But in the public consciousness his background became a confirmation of guilt.

For he had lived like a lord, even in 1974, traversing the terrain of Belgravia and Berkeley Square with all the old casual grandeur of his forebears. He had looked like a lord, although the pockets of his Savile Row suits were filled only with IOUs. Perhaps the difference between then and now is that, today, even the luxury of his aristocratic delusions would be impossible. He was the last of his kind. The murder of Sandra Rivett made that clear, too.

PART I

The Lucan Myth

'I met Murder on the way – He had a mask like
Castlereagh – Very smooth he looked, yet grim...'

SHELLEY, *The Mask of Anarchy*, 1819

THE FAMOUS MURDERS all become myths, and that myth is not necessarily a distillation of truth. It is, more precisely, a distillation of our perceptions. It has a different kind of truth, symbolic rather than factual.

The myth of the Lucan case is a parable about class: a tale of aristocratic hubris. Every element in the story has been seen through that prism. The myth contains some truth, of course, but it is not the whole truth. Indeed it is not above telling lies. This book will go on to tell a different story, because the myth can't be allowed to have things all its own way. Nevertheless there is nothing to be done with it. You can't kill a myth. It is the way that a story settles, and however much you shake it up it will always fall back into position. It is the favoured version, the one that people have decided upon.

Moreover, this particular myth has a tremendous power. Lucan symbolized the old and terrible ways, so casting him into hell was, and continues to be, a peculiarly satisfying act of national catharsis.

Forty years of newspaper articles prove as much. One can pick out the phrases at random, from any point between then and now: Lord Lucan was a 'murderous hooray Henry', the 'unacceptable face of privilege' who 'after a jolly night's gambling, bludgeoned his kids' nanny to death'. His 'eyes are arrogant and exude a dull-witted authority'. His victim, 'the Little Miss Nobody, was firmly kept in her lowly place'. His friends were 'an ugly bunch of right-wing boobies'. 'If that's how members of the "higher human strain" behave, thank God for the humble vermin.'[1]

Two weeks after the murder, this letter was published in a newspaper:

The ordinary people of this country are accustomed to being told how lazy and greedy they have become and how they must make greater sacrifices. If I were a miner, factory worker or railwayman and I had read of Lord Lucan's lifestyle (rise at noon, lunch at the Clermont, gambling losses of £5,000 in one afternoon) I would have said a few well chosen words when my alarm went off this morning.[2]

Them and Us, that great British theme, had found in the Lucan case a perfect conduit for its own expression. From the first, therefore, it has been almost impossible to question the Lucan myth without questioning the political orthodoxy that lay behind it. To suggest that the case might be a more nuanced business than it was perceived to be, that an earl is not evil merely because he is an earl, is a dangerous business. It is to become an implied apologist for the aristocracy, for the privilege of birth not merit, for the world before Attlee: all the wrong things. Meanwhile those who uphold the myth are on the right side, and can get away with prejudice because the prejudices are acceptable. It is entirely understandable, when one considers the centuries of dominance by men like the Earl of Pembroke, or indeed the 3rd Earl of Lucan. How to resist using the story of Lord Lucan as a means to balance those absurdly weighted social scales?

And Lucan was so earl-like: an aristocrat straight from central casting. He was screen-tested for the role of an archetypal English gentleman by the Italian director Vittorio De Sica, who had been struck by his remarkable presence and beauty in a Deauville casino. He failed the test, being too much the part to be able to act it.

At six feet two inches he 'stood like a guardsman, very stiff and upright'.[3] His face, a handsome shallow sculpture, wore its arrogance like a shield. His demeanour was impeccable. He was amazed, or thought that he should be, by the sight of a man in Annabel's wearing a pink shirt. On the London streets men not much younger than he were dressing as rock stars, with hair down to collars like the wingspans of model aeroplanes. But Lucan was contained within the structures of gentlemanliness, buttoned and tailored like a man who employed somebody to dress him, although he did not.

He presented an impenetrable façade; and, because murder is most fascinating when it wears a mask, this image of Lucan's became central to the myth. As with 46 Lower Belgrave Street, it seemed to magnify murder by its supreme incongruity. Unlike the classic domestic killers – Crippen and his prim detachable collar, Madeleine Smith and her rustling balloon of a crinoline – Lucan did not present an air of respectability. He went way beyond that, into the realm of the thoroughbred. Earls, after all, did not have to bother about being respectable, even though some of them were. They simply acted as they chose, and looked the way that they looked. In 1970s Britain, with its hippy-hangover fashions, its prime minister Harold Wilson doing his man-of-the-people act in a crumpled Gannex mac, this was a perpetual shock to the eye, a reminder of why Lucan must be hated.

So the myth begins and ends with class, as did the life of Lord Lucan himself. Both, in their way, were rendered incomplete by that strange and powerful nonsense.

Here, then, is the forty-year-old Lucan myth. It tells a simple story, as myths do: that of a man whose charmed life went wrong. The damage was self-inflicted, but the story is not a tragedy, because the man never had the capacity for greatness that a tragic hero requires. He was simply born lucky. He had every advantage, and he squandered them all.

Richard John Bingham was born on 18 December 1934, the second of four children. His father, although not excessively rich, was more than comfortable. The 6th Earl owned land in Ireland and on the Surrey–Middlesex border, and later set up family trusts that would ensure his son a substantial unearned income. Both he and his wife were Labour Party supporters, with the earl becoming Labour chief whip in the House of Lords. They were in tune with the times. Their son, flagrantly, was not.

As a child growing up in Eaton Square, Lord Bingham had, it was later said, a personal maid, as well as a nanny. During the

Second World War he was sent, with his brother and two sisters, to the safety of America. There he lived with the Brady Tucker family, awash with nineteenth-century banking money and owners of the last private house on New York's Park Avenue. Summers were spent on the family estate at Westchester, where the Lucan children had a house of their own. The future earl ate liberally from the fruits of near-infinite riches: the child's unquestioning familiarity with luxury would become, in adulthood, an insatiable yearning for it. 'He wouldn't have known how to be poor,' wrote Roy Ranson, the detective chief-superintendent who led the investigation into the murder of Sandra Rivett.[4] 'Lucan's trouble', says another former police officer who worked on the case, 'was that he thought he was entitled to things that he wasn't.'[5]

Lord Bingham attended Eton, completed his national service as a second lieutenant in the Coldstream Guards, and walked into a job at a merchant bank. In the innocent 1950s the City was full of well-born dilettantes, who took pleasure infinitely more seriously than work. Lord Bingham was the supreme example of the breed, with his bachelor flat near Regent's Park, his power-boating and bobsleighing, his Aston Martin. He owned racehorses: before 1974 his name appeared in the newspapers most frequently in connection with his runners at Newmarket. Although remaining semi-detached from high-society husband-hunters, he was an adornment at any party. He was astonishingly good-looking, as striking a creature as then bestrode the streets of London. And he led a playboy life: James Bond, without the spying. Indeed his acquaintance, Cubby Broccoli, considered Lord Bingham the very image of Bond.

He gambled, as his kind often did. Gambling, in fact, was the one thing that excited true passion in him. He was an immaculate fixture at the casinos of Deauville and Monte Carlo, and at the tables of his London clubs. Then he made a tentative entry into the set created by the young adventurer John Aspinall, who in the late 1950s began staging aristo-packed illegal gambling soirées. In 1962, two years after the Betting and Gaming Act liberalized the industry, Aspinall opened the Clermont Club casino at 44 Berkeley Square. Lord Bingham was one of its original members.

He also chucked his job. Although he worshipped wealth he had no desire to work for it in the normal plebeian way. After winning some £26,000 on chemin-de-fer at Le Touquet he conceived the idea that gambling could become a profession. He explained as much to the girl to whom he proposed in 1963: twenty-six-year-old Veronica Duncan, a pretty former art student. Veronica accepted the proposal, as well as Lord Bingham's theories of money-making. He was a remarkable catch, after all. 'I was looking for a god,' she later said, 'and he was a dream figure.'

In January 1964, just two months after the wedding, the 6th Earl died. The Lucans made their home at 46 Lower Belgrave Street, whose lease was acquired through a marriage trust fund. Between 1964 and 1970 they had three children: Frances, George and Camilla.

All should have been set fair. Behind the façade, however, life was falling steadily apart. Lucan's gambling grew ever more obsessive. One night he lost £8,000, another night £10,000, and so on. Other members of the club, such as King Fahd of Saudi Arabia or the businessman James Goldsmith, could sustain far greater losses with a shrug, but they represented the larger part of Lord Lucan's annual income. His countess accompanied him to the Clermont most evenings. There she sat alone, ignored, worrying herself half to death over the money that was scattering itself heedlessly across the chemmy table. 'But she had no business to come there,' John Aspinall would later say.[6] Most of Lucan's friends disliked her; they thought her socially beneath them, odd and difficult and not particularly attractive, unworthy of their precious earl. One evening Veronica threw a glass of wine over another of the Clermont wives. It confirmed, in the minds of the Lucan set, the belief that the countess was a strange little item promoted well above her station. She later retaliated by saying that they were the real social embarrassment: 'That is why they had to stay at the Clermont Club all the time.'[7]

As Roy Ranson would write, in the voice of egalitarian modernity: 'Veronica was an intelligent woman sentenced to a life as an upper-class bimbo.' She had no chance against the eighteenth-century allure of the Clermont, and could not break down the walls of Lucan's laughing, Stuyvesant-smoking, vodka-drinking, rigidly right-wing circle. They locked themselves together like a rugby scrum, like the bunch of public schoolboys that they were, and she was left outside, sitting on the 'widows' bench' beside the free-standing staircase at the Clermont, despairing at what her life had become.

Veronica had suffered post-natal depression after the birth of each of her children. In the late 1960s her husband began carting her off for psychiatric treatment. She ran away from two clinics although, wrote Ranson, 'in desperation she agreed to home visits from a psychiatrist and to a course of anti-depressant drugs'. It was a means to placate Lucan, who had told her that refusing treat-ment was the sign that one needed it. Like the smoothly sadistic husband in Patrick Hamilton's play, *Gaslight*, he was implanting in Veronica the idea that she was mad in order to make her so; like the 4th Earl Ferrers, he was exerting the cruellest form of control over a wife whom he believed to be unfit. After the birth of his son in 1967, he told his friends of his concerns about her mental state. Grotesque stories began to be spread about her. 'As far as I know,' wrote Ranson's chief-inspector sidekick David Gerring, 'not one of the rumours was true.'[8] Ranson, more forcefully, wrote that Lucan had lied to his 'young and vulnerable wife' about money; then, in the face of her anxious questioning, he had started a 'vicious and unrelenting campaign to brand her insane'.

For her part Veronica was telling people that Lucan was a violent, abusive husband. Lucan countered with a story that she had thrown herself against the furniture and threatened to accuse him of assault. 'The problem', wrote James Fox in a *Sunday Times Magazine* article about the Lucan case, 'was that from the moment of her alienation, her detractors had the monopoly on the gossip.'[9]

At the start of 1973, Lord Lucan moved out of Lower Belgrave

Street. Life there had become untenable: the Clermont was now his home. Veronica was taking a complicated cocktail of drugs. These encouraged paranoia and hallucinations, and caused her foot to tap uncontrollably on the floor beside the widows' bench. Not that she would be sitting there again. 'There was no attempt to work the problem through, to really sit down and sort things out,' was how Veronica later described the end of her marriage. 'He just said to the GP: "Is she fit?" and the GP said: "Yes, she is fit." And with that he just turned on his heel and went upstairs and began to pack.'[10]

Lucan first moved to the mews house at 5 Eaton Row, also owned in trust, directly behind Lower Belgrave Street. Then he went a little further afield, albeit still within the sacred precincts of SW1, to a flat at 72a Elizabeth Street. The idea of taking on this five-bedroom property was that it would be large enough to accommodate his children and their nanny. The idea, in fact, was to win custody.

In March 1973 Lucan made an application at the High Court to have the children placed in his care. This was granted, pending a full hearing. Accordingly he organized what would later be described as a 'kidnap'. When Veronica learned that her children had been seized, she became hysterical. She then spent eight days at the Priory clinic in Roehampton, in order that a report on her mental condition could be made, and prepared painstakingly for the High Court custody hearing in July.

Lord Lucan lost. Mr Justice Rees, who heard the case, thought him an arrogant liar with an outrageous lifestyle. Veronica supplied evidence that he was a sexual sadist. A psychiatrist at the Priory testified that Veronica had been cured by lithium. The judge decreed that the children should live with their mother, with a permanent nanny in residence.

Lucan had lost his children, and he had lost £20,000[11] that he did not have in paying for his wife's victory. Now Veronica was in control: living in Lucan's house, with his children, on his money. Again like Earl Ferrers, he had been bested by a woman who had proved her sanity in court; and his reaction would be very similar.

Between July 1973 and November 1974 Lucan hoped for a reversal of the High Court judgment. Escalating his former behaviour, he embarked upon a campaign of terror that 'made it clear that he was trying to drive his wife into madness or suicide'.[12] As he had done before the court case, he taped conversations between himself and Veronica. He began making anonymous telephone calls to Lower Belgrave Street. He paid private detectives to watch movements at the house, while he himself sat outside in his Mercedes, staring through dark glasses, a sinister and unignorable presence. His desire for custody is generally believed to have sprung from genuine motives, although Roy Ranson would later dispute this: 'I believe that, rather than the much quoted love of his children, it is his lack of money... that provides the key to this case.'

Indeed Lucan's financial situation, which had been worsening for some years, disintegrated after the custody hearing, and his gambling became concomitantly wilder. The absurd nickname of 'Lucky' Lucan, used by friends and subsequently embraced by the press, took on an ever-grimmer irony. He turned up at the Clermont with a dogged regularity, although the place had changed since John Aspinall sold it to the Playboy Club in 1972. 'Like many of his friends,' wrote James Fox, '[Lucan] resented the fact that any member of the Playboy could now come to the Clermont and dilute the exclusivity.'[13] The Clermont was about posh chaps together. Playboy was about bunnies and birds. That particular outlet for masculine boyishness held no charm for Lucan. He had a girlfriend of sorts, a pretty twenty-one-year-old named Andrina Colquhoun, but women were never really his thing. He was a man's man, through and through.

In between the unvarying meals of lamb chops (grilled in winter, en gelée in summer), the steady stream of booze and the berserk bouts of gambling, Lucan spent his time at the Clermont telling anybody who would listen about his wicked wife and what she had done to him. The wicked wife, meanwhile, was trying to cope with the procession of nannies that wandered in and out of Lower Belgrave

Street. In August 1974, however, a new candidate presented herself. She was Sandra Rivett: competent, pretty and good-natured. The two women, both separated from their husbands, became friendly. This was no mistress–servant relationship, but something more modern and enlightened. There seemed no possibility of Sandra leaving the position, as others had done. Veronica had established a status quo of her own. By the autumn of 1974, Lord Lucan was despairing of its reversal.

He wanted his children and his house, but he could not have these things because they now belonged to Veronica, and there was no money left to dislodge her. In every way, therefore, the scene was becoming set for a classic domestic murder. 'Lucan', it would later be said, 'wanted his life to continue as before, but without his wife. She had to be erased. It was a fantasy, and it required a fantastic plan of action.'[14]

The plan, in sum, was this. Lucan would kill his wife on the nanny's night off, when Veronica went downstairs to the basement to make her evening cup of tea. Some theorists posit that he paid a hitman to do the job,[15] but this suggestion was never seriously considered by the police and it does not explain why Lucan himself was at the scene of the crime. He would bundle Veronica's body into a sack, and either conceal it temporarily in the large safe that stood behind the basement stairs, or transport it directly into his car boot. Then he would drive to Elizabeth Street, change into his *tenue de soirée* and head for dinner at the Clermont, where he would assume his aspect of the guardsman who knew how to lose like a gentleman before disposing of his wife. With her body stowed in the car he would drive to the south coast and take a boat out into deep waters, where the body would be sunk.

Sandra Rivett, on her return to the house, would alert Lucan to the fact that his wife was missing. He would then make a concerned report to the Belgravia police. Veronica, with her history of instability, would be assumed to have wandered off; eventually, there would be a presumption of suicide. Veronica had disappeared before, albeit briefly, when she ran away from Greenways nursing home in Hampstead. 'It is possible', as was later written, 'that this incident gave Lucan one of his occasional ideas.'[16]

At some point before 9pm on the night of 7 November, Lucan entered the former marital home with his front-door key while his wife and children were watching television upstairs. Then he waited in the basement, lead piping in hand, in the expectation that Veronica would come down into the kitchen to make her tea. What Lucan did not know was that Sandra had changed her usual night off, and that she would be the woman who descended into the basement. Having removed the overhead light bulb in the kitchen, Lucan could not see that he was killing the wrong woman. It was a prolonged attack. Sandra Rivett's skull was split in six places. She died from bruising of the brain and inhalation of blood. Her body was then shoved into a mailsack. The basement area around the stairs was splashed and soaked with blood, as if a can of red paint had been emptied over the walls and floor.

Veronica would later testify that she had gone in search of Sandra, and that as she stood at the top of the basement stairs, calling to see where her nanny had got to, Lucan launched his second assault. The husband and wife grappled together. The piping landed at least four times on Veronica's head. Lucan then thrust gloved fingers down her throat and tried to strangle her. As they were rolling around together on the small square of floor, Veronica wrenched her husband's testicles and he released his grip. They sat together, breathless and spent, and Lucan confessed to having killed the nanny. Then they went upstairs to Veronica's second-floor bedroom. While Lucan was soaking a flannel in the bathroom with which to bathe his wife's wounds, Veronica escaped from the house and, at about 9.50pm, ran the short distance to the Plumbers Arms at the end of Lower Belgrave Street. There, after sitting silently for a few moments, she gasped out her story to the people in the pub.

As the ambulance and police were being summoned, Madeleine

Florman heard a ring on her doorbell at 51 Chester Square. Unnerved, she did not go downstairs to answer it. Not long afterwards she was phoned by a man whose voice she believed to be that of Lord Lucan. He also telephoned his mother at her flat near Lord's cricket ground, after which the dowager countess immediately left for Lower Belgrave Street. Both women told the police that they had heard no 'pips' at the start of these calls. This meant that Lucan had not used a public phone box, and raised the question – in those quaint pre-mobile days – as to where he did in fact make the calls.

Lord Lucan then drove to the home of his friend Susan Maxwell-Scott in Uckfield, Sussex. In her account, she stated that Lucan turned up unannounced at around 11.30pm and asked for her husband Ian (who was in London, where he worked as a director of the Clermont). Mrs Maxwell-Scott said that Lucan described the events of that night to her. His story was that he was walking past his former home and saw a fight going on in the basement between Veronica and an unknown man, who had already killed the nanny. Lucan intervened to save his wife, whereupon the assailant fled.

At about 12.15am Lucan telephoned a second time to his mother. He wrote two letters to his friend Bill Shand Kydd, the husband of his wife's sister. One of these reiterated the story told to Mrs Maxwell-Scott; the other contained directions as to paying off Lucan's creditors. He then wrote two letters to another friend, Michael Stoop, only one of which was shown to the police. According to Mrs Maxwell-Scott, Lucan left her house at around 1.15am. He had asked for something to help him sleep, and she had given him four valium.

At some point between 5am and 8am, according to witnesses who observed the road at those times, the Ford Corsair that Lucan had previously borrowed from Stoop was abandoned in a residential street in the port of Newhaven. When the police examined it on Sunday 10 November, they found smears of blood on the car interior. In the boot was a piece of lead piping, almost identical to the one found at Lower Belgrave Street.

Lord Lucan himself had disappeared. Newhaven, it seemed, was the journey's end.

The police had no doubt, from the very first, that the earl was their man. Veronica told them so, when they visited her at St George's Hospital at Hyde Park in the early hours of 8 November. Later that day she gave a full statement: some twenty pages of painstaking long-hand. According to Roy Ranson, she 'never varied from the essential facts of her account of that night – to my mind a clear indication that she had told the plain, unvarnished truth'. There were discrepancies between her statement and that of her ten-year-old daughter, Frances, who had been watching television in her mother's bedroom throughout this period; in Ranson's view, however, 'the evidence of Frances was always slightly muddled'. What was contemptuously dismissed was Lucan's own story, that he had entered the house to save his wife from an attack in the basement. As Ranson put it, Veronica 'stated, from the very first moment of the inquiry, that she had never set foot in the basement'. Blood from her group was in fact found there, but this was explained as accidental transference, from what Ranson described as 'the many movements of officers, dogs, scientists, fingerprint experts and undertakers'.

The newspapers, meanwhile, were going into paroxysms: understandably. Although Lord Lucan was not a well-known peer, he was a peer all the same, and earls do not commit murder. Yet it was beyond question that this earl had. The police and the press formed a close alliance, and from the first the papers were making clear not only who killed Sandra Rivett, but why she had died: the theory of mistaken identity was posited almost immediately. Sandra's mother, Eunice Hensby, stated in an interview on the 13th that 'Sandra and Lady Lucan looked amazingly alike'.[17] That same day, it was reported that warrants for Lord Lucan's arrest had been obtained at Bow Street Magistrates' Court.

But where was the man? Although a body was sought in the area surrounding Newhaven, the prevailing opinion, or perhaps the better story, was that Lucan was alive. 'World hunt for the Earl', ran a headline on the 14th. 'Detectives were posted to watch thirty homes in Europe, the USA and the West Indies':[18] houses belonging to friends of Lord Lucan. The following day it was stated that fourteen 'country estates' were being investigated. Almost certainly this is the only murder inquiry that has ever included a search of Warwick Castle, whose presiding earl had married Lucan's second cousin. Another powerful component of the Lucan myth was beginning to grow: the belief that his circle of friends had closed ranks around him. As a newspaper article would later put it: 'From the beginning, the police met nothing but obstruction from the circle of boneheads and gamblers who are friends of Lucan.'[19]

On the day after the murder, several members of the Clermont set had met for lunch at the Belgravia house of John Aspinall. It was speculated that they had concocted a plan to enable Lucan to flee the country. 'Men like Goldsmith and Aspinall saw themselves as outlaws,' it was said, 'and the murder of Sandra Rivett gave them a rare chance to live out that fantasy.'[20]

It was also said that the police encountered an unbreakable wall of silence when they tried to interview what they called the 'Eton Mafia'. 'All over London, Lucan's friends had begun to rally round. Their telephones were off the hook; no one was to be available until a plan had been formed.'[21] The nobs were sticking to their own kind. The fact that murder, and attempted murder, had been committed did not weigh in the balance against the necessity of protecting their friend, the earl. For Veronica, bandaged and doped in her hospital bed, there was no sympathy. She should never have aspired to marry Lord Lucan. In a sense, the whole sorry situation was her fault.

On 15 November an article was printed under the headline 'Anatomy of Honour', hinting that justice was being obstructed by a refusal to betray the old school tie. When Aspinall loudly proclaimed on television that Lucan was an 'old Roman', a man of 'dignitas and gravitas', this gave further credence to the notion that these were people who moved in their own sphere above the law, holding to an obscure code that set them above the ordinary people, who cared about dead nannies. No, that is not quite true: they did care, in their way. 'What a pity! Good nannies are so hard to find', was one woman's reaction, when told about the murder of Sandra Rivett.

The circle acquired an image of its own. It was the Happy Valley thirty years on, amoral and louche, shruggingly indifferent to a public that regarded it with disapproval, envy, downright amazement that such a set still existed. A woman who was a student in the early 1970s recalls: 'We had thought, I suppose rather naively, that sort of thing had had its day.'[22] The names of Lucan's friends became familiar: Aspinall, maestro of the Clermont, whose private zoos in Kent were dedicated to the rearing of the wild animals that he considered superior to humans; businessman James Goldsmith, whose showy love life included an eighteenth-century-style elopement with an underage heiress; glamorous society painter Dominick Elwes; racing tipster and *bon vivant* Charles Benson; Colonel David Stirling, who founded the SAS; and Greville Howard, who had worked as an aide to Enoch Powell. This close little bundle of posh boys huddled around the chemmy table while, in the world beyond Berkeley Square, people struggled with near-20 per cent inflation and IRA bombs shattered glass and limbs. They were throwbacks, clinging to the meaningless rituals of a vanished age, posing like waxworks in their exquisite bunker. They were immovably reactionary: as the former DCI David Gerring would later write, with regard to the circle's staunch defence of Lord Lucan, it wasn't as though he had done anything terrible, 'like voting Labour'.[23]

Small talk at the Clermont, when it was not about gambling or poor Lucky's frightful wife, was lamenting the dire state of 1970s Britain. Harold Wilson was a KGB plant, the workforce akin to the *sans-culottes* of revolutionary Paris. The only answer was to reclaim the country for its rightful owners. Stirling formed a *de facto* private army that would cross picket lines in the event of a Communist coup. Michael Stoop and Dominick Elwes joined up. MI5 observed with interest.[24] 'It was', a journalist later wrote, 'in the fetid, self-de-luding, pseudo-Nietzschean atmosphere of this set that Lucan's infamous plan to murder his wife was born.'[25]

The story of Them versus Us reached a climax in June 1975, at the inquest into Sandra Rivett's murder. The victim and her quiet, dignified relations were mere incidentals, bit part players in the tragedy. 'It was Lucan's aristocratic family and gambling friends who dominated,' wrote one editorial, railing against this 'ugly real-life performance of *Upstairs, Downstairs*'. Ranks were closed against Lady Lucan, 'who dared to accuse her husband, the 7th Earl of Lucan. Damned bad show, don'tcherknow.' Alluding to the fact that Bill Shand Kydd and his wife had gone racing on the fourth day of proceedings, the editorial concluded: 'What with the beastly inquest, into the bargain it was Ascot Week, too!'[26]

Opinion against the circle, already unfavourable, had further hardened in the days before the inquest, after the publication of James Fox's coolly persuasive *Sunday Times Magazine* article. This subsequently became definitive in its detailing of Lord Lucan's cold, aggressive behaviour towards his wife, her desperate isolation, the 'condescending, almost patronizing' attitude towards the investi-gation shown by Lucan's friends. It was said that people offered to meet the police for a chat 'in about three weeks, old boy'. Susan Maxwell-Scott failed to inform the authorities about Lucan's visit to her house: 'I had no reason to go to the police.' Madeleine Florman waited four days before telling them about the ring at her door-bell after the murder: 'It's the police's problem, actually. They're obviously trained to discern these things.'

At the inquest, the inhabitants of the Lucan world were paraded before the public gaze: his mother, his sister Lady Sarah, the Shand Kydds, the Maxwell-Scotts, Michael Stoop. People could behold, as it were in reality, the clipped restraint of their idiom, the untouch-able glaze of their appearance. One journalist who attended the inquest wrote:

The leading personality of that set, Lord Lucan, is in trouble. Wanted, dead or alive, on a warrant that alleges murder. Therefore, it is particularly important that his friends should put on the right show. That they should dress correctly, that they should behave with proud confidence, that every move they made during the long official proceedings should display that loyalty and show the importance for them of Lord Lucan's honour. So it comes down to a question of style. And if their style might not be to the taste of the rest, that was a matter of indifference. Proud, unbending and exclusive, they do not seem worried by what the world thinks of them.[27]

The world, naturally, did not like them one bit. They were as inimical to the British mood as the royal family would be twenty-two years later after the death of Diana, Princess of Wales. Sandra had died, but as the representative of normal human decency she had won the day, as surely as Veronica Lucan had won against her husband.

After the inquest, and indeed this has continued until the present time, the impression grew ever stronger that Lucan's set had enabled his escape. The coroner's jury had pronounced him guilty, and the next step was a trial. But the 7th Earl, unable to rely upon the beneficent judgment of his peers in the manner of the Earl of Pembroke, had found another way around the pesky legal system. The more that his friends and relations insisted that he had killed himself on 8 November, the more it was suspected that he had in fact scarpered.

After the inquest, Sandra Rivett's mother said: 'I like to think he is dead and rotting in hell.' Yet she spoke for the majority when she continued: 'Lord Lucan has so many friends. There is so much money around.' In other words, he had the means to get away with murder. That was what his kind did.

In her novel *Aiding and Abetting* (2000), Muriel Spark brought to glorious literary life the myth of Lord Lucan. The sections of the book that deal with the 'truth' about the case are based upon the story as above: Lucan treated his wife abominably, he killed Sandra Rivett in error, he was a 'sick' gambler, he lived on lamb chops, he had 'no imagination, or at least very little', his friends gathered together to bankroll his escape. 'Lucan is a friend of ours, he is one of us and you don't understand that people like us...'

There are two Lucans in *Aiding and Abetting*, both of whom are attending sessions with a female psychiatrist based in Paris. One of them (*bien entendu*) is an impostor. This uncertainty is a metaphor for the fact that Lucan's identity was a façade, an assemblage of earl-like attributes. It is also a creative expression of the doubt that infects Lucan's fate.

Disappearing is a rare trick. Marguerite Dixblanc tried to do it after murdering her employer in 1872, but she was quickly found in Paris. The Labour MP John Stonehouse tried to do it, just thirteen days after the murder of Sandra Rivett. He left a pile of clothes on a beach in Miami, then hotfooted it to Australia, where he was arrested on Christmas Eve 1974. His problems, like Lord Lucan's, were financial, and attention was first drawn to him because the Australian police had believed that he *was* Lord Lucan.

Agatha Christie also disappeared, in December 1926. She was found after eleven days, but then she had wanted to be. Indeed she had planned to be found almost immediately, by the husband who had recently asked her for a divorce: her intention had been to reclaim his love. Nevertheless she was one of the few people, at the time of the Lucan disappearance, who knew what it felt like to cease to exist. When she was nearing the end of her life, infirm and almost senile, she suddenly posed the question: 'I wonder what *has* happened to Lord Lucan?'

Lucan is undead: even in law. In 1992 the High Court made this declaration: 'Be it known that the Right Honourable Richard John Bingham, seventh Earl of Lucan, died on or since the eighth day of November 1974.' Yet in July 1999, even as probate was about to be granted on Lord Lucan's estate, his son was refused permission to take his seat in the House of Lords, there being reasonable doubt as to whether the earldom was his to assume. A statement was issued, 'that the Lord Chancellor did not authorise the writ of summons to George Bingham on the ground that he was not satisfied that his case had been made out'. Now, forty years after his disappearance, Lucan is seventy-nine years of age, and could feasibly be alive: technically, if in no other way, he is Earl of Lucan still.

This non-existent status has, over the years, become the most insistent aspect of the myth. The vanishing earl is part of our col-lective consciousness. It is, in fact, a kind of joke. An impossible occurrence is deemed 'about as likely as seeing Lord Lucan riding Shergar'. Lucan was named as the vicious killer of a young woman, and the Derby-winning racehorse Shergar was wickedly spirited away by the IRA, but the evil of these events has become absorbed into the kind of ironic bad taste upon which the British pride them-selves. Sometimes Lucan is alluded to with a lighter touch, also very British, as displayed by the jockey Stan Mellor on the occasion of the last National Hunt meeting at Nottingham racecourse. 'I rode a double for Lord Lucan there, but I'm not looking for him. He paid me.' A Lucan lookalike described an occasion when he was driving along the Mall in London, and the chauffeur of an oncoming car leaned out of the window and shouted his cap-tipping, deferential encouragement: 'Good luck, sir!'

Undead as he is, part-Dracula, part-Scarlet Pimpernel, part-monster, part-folk hero, Lucan floats like another figure of murderous myth, Jack the Ripper, who although quite obviously dead still hovers in his cloak of unpenetrated identity. Even if Jack the Ripper were definitively named, the myth would endure.[28] As with Lucan, it is now too bound up in cherished perceptions to be abandoned. It has acquired the power of fiction.

If Lord Lucan is dead, then the most likely explanations are that he jumped off a ferry from Newhaven to Dieppe, or killed himself some-where in the undergrowth of East Sussex. There is, however, the question of habeas corpus, or lack of it: no body has ever been found.

And there are other theories, some not entirely sane. Lucan was shot by the IRA, to whom, with his residual acres in Co. Mayo, he was a landowner enemy. He was disposed of by a friend who had abetted his escape, to whom he later became an embarrassment and a financial drain. He was killed by the army, which feared the disgrace of seeing a former officer stand trial at the Old Bailey. He was murdered because he owed money: Sir Rupert Mackeson, who himself disappeared for three years to evade debts of £100,000, told the police in 1980: 'I vanished because my life was threatened. Two thugs in London told me: "We've killed Lord Lucan and you will go the same way unless you keep your mouth shut."' He was shot by an unknown assailant in the drive of the Maxwell-Scott house, after his visit to Susan on 8 November. He committed suicide at John Aspinall's private zoo, Howletts, having requested that his body be fed to the tigers.

Against all this is the belief that Lucan did not die after the murder. The main theories as to his escape are that he sailed to France, or was flown out of Britain. He then made his way through Europe, and moved from country to country. He was given money by friends, who possibly also paid for plastic surgery. He remains the subject of an Interpol red notice, issued for restricting the travel of dangerous criminals. Since 8 November 1974 Lord Lucan has been seen, or rumoured to have lived, in almost every country in the world.

In the year following his disappearance, a thousand-plus sightings placed him in numerous different locations simultaneously. Lucan was road-painting in Spain; drunk-driving on the M1; travelling on a train to Edinburgh; buying flowers in Piccadilly; disguised as a policeman in Whitehall; hidden in a Midlands nursing home; enjoying dinner with a girl in Guernsey; stranded with a broken-down car in Colombia; and using the public baths in Finchley. In late 1974, an Iranian student, travelling on a bus in Hove, was formally cautioned as Lord Lucan. A boilermaker named Kenneth Knight, who had disappeared from his home in Kent, was arrested in Sydney, Australia. On seeing his photograph Mrs Knight said: 'That's not Lord Lucan, that's my Ken, that is.'

In June 1975, the police and press made a mass excursion to Cherbourg, where the earl was said to have been staying at the Grand Hotel. He was then seen in a casino at Saint-Malo, before apparently travelling to the Riviera. The *Daily Express* asked his wife to comment: '"I find that impossible to believe," sighed the Countess of Lucan, sipping one of France's better burgundies in her Belgravia home.'[29]

In 1975 Lucan was also in Mozambique. A Welsh GP called Brian Hill 'met a tearful Englishman weeping over his prawns. After a number of beers the tall, dark stranger confessed he longed to go back to England but could not because he was Lord Lucan, and wanted for murder.'[30] In 1980, corroboration of the Mozambique connection was seized upon when a former Guards officer and Clermont gambler, David Hardy, was killed in a car accident. In his address book, the police found the entry: 'Lord Lucan, c/o Hotel Les Ambassadeurs, Beira, Mozambique.' It was subsequently reported that the hotel register for 1975 included the name 'Maxwell-Scott'.

From the first, Africa has been the most consistently favoured location for sightings. Directly after the murder Lucan was reported to be in South Africa, and in 1976 he was there again, seen at the Café Royal in Cape Town by a woman who knew him from the Clermont. 'His hair was blond and fringed and he had shaved off his moustache.'[31] He has been sighted in Zimbabwe and Zambia;[32] he is rumoured to have seen his children, albeit at a distance and without their knowledge, in Kenya, Gabon and Namibia.[33]

In 1994 the former detective Roy Ranson travelled to Johannesburg, where he was told that Lucan had been posing as the boss of a South African clothing company. Throughout the murder investigation Ranson always claimed that Lucan was dead, but in his book about the case he executed an agile *volte-face* and stated, with absolute conviction, that the earl had escaped to Africa and was based in Botswana. This is the country most frequently cited as Lucan's hiding place. In 1976 a former inmate of Leeds jail saw him there, playing craps in the casino of the Gaborone Holiday Inn.

In 1990 two British engineers saw him, again in Gaborone, at the bar of the Cresta Botsalo Hotel, without his moustache and with a 'neatly-trimmed grey beard'. Twenty-two years later one of the men recalled: 'There had been talk for weeks that Lucan was around – he had links to Botswana. The instant he walked in I said to myself, "That's him." He was with about six people and had a very noticeable military bearing. His accent was so upper-class English that it cut the air and turned everyone's heads when he spoke.'[34]

In the 1990s, according to Ranson, Lucan was living in Botswana's vast, secluded, residential Tuli Block. A woman named Janice Main, who 'moved in the upper social circles of white Botswana', had encountered him on a street and looked straight at him. 'Lucan, in safari shorts, strode to a waiting four-wheel-drive vehicle and drove off. She never saw him again.'

In 2012 Lucan's younger brother Hugh, a resident of Johannesburg since 1975, took part in a short BBC documentary in which he declared his belief in his brother's innocence. Subsequently it was reported that he stated, off camera: 'I know for a fact my brother died in 2004 and that his grave is in Africa.'[35]

Lucan has also been seen in:

Scotland, 1979.[36]

Trinidad, 1982.

South America, 1982 and at other times.[37]

Perth, 1987.

Goa, 1991, where he was mistaken for the pot-smoking, bare-chested, shorts-wearing Barry Halpin, a former folk singer who addressed his friends as 'old cock'.

Brisbane, 1992, where he was identified as a manic depressive with memory loss, a butcher by trade, attending a group of recovering alcoholics.

New Zealand, 2007, where he was mistaken for a man named Roger Woodgate, who lived in the back of a van with Camilla, his goat. 'I am not Lord Lucan,' he told the press.'[38]

Undated rumours and sightings are as follows:

Mexico, on James Goldsmith's estate. In 2004 a man named Piers Dixon, who 'shared a godson' with Lord Lucan, stated: 'Lucan spent the first few years under the wing of Jimmy Goldsmith. It is more than a feeling – I know it to be true.'[39]

America, specifically San Francisco, where Lucan was said to be working as a waiter.

Canada. Lucan was said to have been a warehouse worker in Ontario, and to have been seen sobbing in a changing room at the British University of Columbia gym in Vancouver.

Japan.

The Philippines.

Madagascar.

Hong Kong.

Macau.

The Bahamas.

An unnamed Pacific island, close to Guam.

Wales.

And so on.

The strangest thing about a myth is that it makes the real seem surreal. It becomes extraordinarily hard, in the face of this vast mesh of collective perceptions, to realize that at its heart is something that *happened*, that was actual. One walks down Lower Belgrave Street, coming upon it from Eaton Square, with a sense of sudden trespass, as if one's thoughts were about to traduce the innocent present. Then imagination tries to conjure it all. The blue–black November sky, the discreet movements of traffic, the presiding calm before the brick–and–white symmetry was flung out of joint; the wrench of the stately front door and the footsteps clattering along the pavement; the little white-faced woman, her head full of clotting blood, scurrying and tumbling into the warm–lit pub; the man, heavy-footed, heading toward the dull white gleam of Chester Square; the girl bent double in the sack, her small black shoes beside it. One slides guilty eyes towards the basement: the steep steps down to the outside door, the small barred window with the sink, and behind it the dark hint of the indoor staircase; none of it giving anything away — just a formal London basement, like its neighbours — but holding the memory of that moment in time.

And that moment is unknowable, the mystery within mysteries. Of course murder can be described, and is rendered so frequently as to make it commonplace; nevertheless its truest depiction comes in the 1960 Powell and Pressburger film *Peeping Tom*, when the murderer attempts to film his victims as they die, and at the last moment the camera goes blank.

Twelve years later, a film by Alfred Hitchcock offered a complementary view. Hitchcock, whose fascination with murder was as great as anybody's has ever been, had the genius to render the greater part of its reality. He would have done an amazing job with the Lucan case. In *Frenzy*, released two years before the death of Sandra Rivett and set in contemporary London, he shows a murder so graphic as to be barely watchable, which is truth of a kind, but later in the film he does something much more insightful. Another victim is strangled in a flat above the old Covent Garden fruit market. Nothing is seen of the act. What is shown, instead, is the girl and her killer walking up the stairs to the door of the flat; as they enter, silence falls, and the camera shifts to an exterior shot of the flat's window; then it pans out, and out, and out, until it touches the merry bustle of the market; the window grows ever smaller and less significant, and as it does so becomes ever more resonantly the heart of the shot. Behind it, behind it: that is where the focus lies. And time, and life, move on.

This, then, offers the other side of the story: the context of murder, the backdrop, the world in which it takes place. The hushed rustle of Victoriana is necessary to the stories of Charles Bravo and Adelaide Bartlett, just as the post-First World War illusion of female liberty surrounds that of Edith Thompson. The early 1970s setting of the Lucan case, in which Lord Lucan himself was as out of place as a grandfather clock in a Wimpy bar, is the final component of the myth.

The era in which Sandra Rivett died carries its own imagistic power. Strikes; states of emergency; a three-day week; astronomical taxes; astronomical inflation; power cuts: these were the stuff of daily life. Did the lights go out at Lower Belgrave Street? They must have done. And at the Clermont Club? Did chemin-de-fer by candlelight merely add to the fun, the illusion? Men would have played that way in the eighteenth century, after all, and that was the spell that the club sought to cast.

In the real Britain beyond, the Conservative administration of Edward Heath tried and failed to assert itself against the unions. 'Who governs?' Heath asked, to which the implicit answer was 'Not you'. He had offered the Trade Union Congress a seat at the table to plan the national economy, and was turned down. In October 1973 OPEC announced a 70 per cent rise in the posted price of oil. On the first day of 1974, the brief era of the three-day week began. In February, the miners went on strike. An election was called, resulting in a hung parliament. Harold Wilson, who had become leader of the Labour Party in 1963, when Lucan's father was its chief whip in the Lords, led a minority government. In the autumn of 1974, he won a narrow victory.

Labour, with its 'social contract' between government and unions, opted for propitiation. When Heath's policy of wage controls ended, unions demanded rises and Wilson gave them, which at least got the lights back on. Public spending for 1974–5 increased by 35 per cent. The top rate of tax rose to 83 per cent. To those paying the surcharge on invested income, the rate was 98 per cent. By the end of 1974 inflation was heading for 20 per cent.

A Budget took place the week after the murder at Lower Belgrave Street. 'Don't squeeze too hard,' begged a *Daily Express* editorial, as cars queued to fill their tanks before petrol rose by 8½p per gallon. The plea was in vain, as such pleas always are. 'Everyone', wrote the newspaper, 'is condemned to four years' hard labour.' Once again, the unions raged and threatened. There was an argument for saying that Lord Lucan, wherever he was, was well out of it.

The *Wall Street Journal*, which called Britain 'the sick man of Europe', wrote: 'The British government is now so clearly headed towards a policy of total confiscation that anyone who has any wealth left is [taking] any chance to get it out of the country... Goodbye, Great Britain, it was nice knowing you.' There were fears of a return to a 1930s-style depression; of a Communist takeover; of totalitarianism.

Then came the IRA bombing campaign, reaching a climax of short terrible bursts during the dark autumn of 1974. On 5 October five people were killed in a pub in Guildford. At 10.17pm on 7 November, as the first detective was about to enter Lower Belgrave Street, an IRA bomb exploded at a pub by the army barracks at Woolwich in south-east London. Two people died. Later that month twenty-one people were killed in a single night, from two more pub bombs in Birmingham. Irish pubs were attacked in retaliation. The National Front gained popularity; in June 1974 it clashed with the International Marxist Group of Students, and a student was killed. To both left and right militancy was on the rise; the opposing factions were equally violent, equally voluble, and extraordinarily similar.[40]

And in the midst of it all was the Clermont Club, an impregnable place of safety with its gentlemanly excitements, its sublime wines, its promise of untaxable winnings. Yet on 22 October 1974, its walls were metaphorically shaken when an IRA bomb exploded at a fellow gentleman's club, Brooks's in St James's Street. Three staff members were injured. Reality, hitherto kept courteously at bay, lurched up to the Clermont door, although entrance was denied. The façade remained of a different Britain: an England, as one might say.

Neither the Clermont, nor indeed Lower Belgrave Street, nor of course Lord Lucan, looked anything like the Britain that they inhabited. They all looked old and remote and solid. The Britain of the early 1970s looked almost deliberately ersatz, with its leatherette and Formica, its linoleum floors and skimpy patterned curtains; its hefty dial telephones; its cars with their juddery gears and alligator-head bonnets, Marinas and Cortinas and Corsairs; its food, which knew little of pizza or artichokes or olive oil, which served prawns in a glass full of pink sauce and grilled its grapefruits; its pub drinks, Babychams, Cherry Bs, or a frothing cocktail known as a Snowball, which mixed yellow Advocaat with Schweppes lemonade and topped it off with a cherry; its pubs, which were plentiful and fuggy, and sold Golden Wonder crisps instead of tapenade and grissini; its cigarettes, Embassy and Player's and Senior Service, which were smoked on trains, in offices, at the cinema; its cheap-looking fonts and colours, its cheap-sounding pop music; its flapping collars and flares and hair. Then there were other things, which provoke a more complicated breed of nostalgia: evidence of a different kind of engagement with life, communal and consoling within the chaos. Everybody used the same incompetent GPO telephone system. Everybody, including Veronica Lucan on the night of 7 November, watched the same television programmes at the same time as everybody else. Nobody used computers, or clutched smartphones like talismans, or had headsets in their ears as they walked the streets; and the streets themselves were different, not just because they were free from CCTV, from Starbucks, from beggars at every turn. As Martin Amis would later write, 'one humble and unsonorous adjective comprehensively described the London of 1970. Empty.'[41] This was the Britain before mass immigration, before globalization, before privatization and deregulation; when people still talked of the recently dead shillings and sixpences, when the Second World War was a more recent memory than the case of Lord Lucan is now. And, like Lucan's world, this Britain with which he collided was a dying place, although at the time it did not know it: it had scant notion of the changes that would soon be wrought upon it.

Not that everything has changed. Forty years on here we all are again, indebted and ill-at-ease with ourselves, debating austerity versus borrowing, in fear of bombs and street violence, watching a television programme about posh people and their servants. Rage and ridicule and death warrants have been thrown at class, yet still it stands there in its shallow mystery, to be obsessed over anew; like its infamous representative, the 7th Earl of Lucan.

PART II

The Story

'The Lucan myth? That's the tragedy of it, really.'

DR JANE GRIFFIN, ELDER SISTER TO LORD LUCAN,
IN CONVERSATION WITH THE AUTHOR

The Lucans

*'Lavinia did not come from a particularly distinguished family –
her father, Lord Lucan, was a mere Irish peer...'*

Amanda Foreman, *Georgiana, Duchess of Devonshire*, 1998

IF THE 7TH Earl of Lucan had not disappeared on or around 8
November 1974, and if he had inherited the family tradition of male
longevity, he might now be contemplating the prospect of his burial
at All Saints' Church, Laleham.

The Lucan memorial in the churchyard holds the remains of
the 3rd, 4th and 5th Earls, together with their countesses. Earlier
ancestors are interred in the Lucan chapel, and the family name of
Bingham recurs on the list of war dead at the entrance to the church.
Lord Lucan had inherited the right to appoint the All Saints' vicar.
His parents did not choose to be laid in this ground, but unlike them
he prized the notion of earldom; although it is probably true to say
that he didn't know what to do with it.

There is nothing grand about All Saints': no pomp or circumstance. Twelfth century in origin, it stands on the corner of the road,
a little red building with a low tower shaped like a brick chimney.
It is quietly, comfortingly English. Even the tumultuous 3rd Earl,
whose grave is marked by the tallest cross in the churchyard, seems
becalmed in this setting. The Lucan memorial has that sense of
rightfulness which comes when centuries of the same blood are
gathered together. Here, it seems to say, order remains for all time.

The manor of Laleham was bought in 1803 by Richard, the 2nd
Earl of Lucan, who paid £22,000 for the greater part of the village.
He built a family home, a creamy neoclassical box with marble

floors and a giant Doric porch, fronting on to a narrow stretch of the Thames at the point where Surrey meets Middlesex. In the grounds, beneath some cedar trees, the 3rd Earl buried two horses that he had ridden in the Crimea. The 4th Earl lived there in considerable state, with nineteen servants that he could not really afford.

The earldom, however, was Irish. The Lucans owned an estate in Co. Mayo, some 61,000 acres by the nineteenth century, and lived in the county town at Castlebar House. Yet the Bingham family is as English as they come. Its Saxon roots run deep through the West Country. In 1228 Robert de Bingham became Bishop of Salisbury, and is buried in the cathedral.[1] The family lived peaceable centuries in its country paradise, marrying the daughters of local baronets, weaving itself into the faded fabric of domestic history. It was not so much grand as profoundly assured. So the lord only knows what happened to turn that first famous Richard Bingham, Dorset-born in 1528, into the fearless mercenary who would end up as Marshal of Ireland; but from somewhere he acquired a raging fire in his belly. Perhaps it was simply that he was a fourth son and needed to make his mark. Meanwhile Robert, the eldest, carried on the Dorset line; the estate remained in the family until 1900.

Richard Bingham was a force, albeit not a moral one: an adventurer with an eye for the right adventure. Today such men rarely rise from the comfortable bed of Western Europe, although the 7th Earl of Lucan had a couple of them in his circle of friends. Ireland, so dangerous to England with its alien proximity, let loose Bingham's ruthless gifts. He quashed rebellions and cut the throats of Spaniards washed ashore from the Armada. In 1584 he became Governor of Connaught, fighting off the local chieftains to acquire the nucleus of the Lucan estate, and received his knighthood. At the age of nearly seventy, still putting down rebellions with his sword aloft, he became General of Leinster and Marshal of Ireland.

He died in Dublin in 1598, at the height of his tainted glory. As he had no son the line continued through his brother, whose heir was created the 1st Baronet Bingham of Mayo in 1634.[2] By degrees the Binghams became that body of people who would be loathed by the Irish: the Protestant Englishmen who owned the better part of another people's country. And yet there was, within the Lucan earldom, a very real Irish connection. The 5th Baronet, born in 1690, married the grand-daughter of a man named William Sarsfield.[3] In 1691, the deposed King James II created William's younger brother, Patrick, the 1st Earl of Lucan.

The Sarsfields were an ancient Anglo-Norman family. They belonged to the ruling class in Ireland, yet had become almost pure native: Catholic, intermarried with the great Gaelic families. Nobody was ever more fervently Irish than Patrick Sarsfield, born in 1660 in Lucan, which stands south of Dublin on the River Liffey. There was once a Sarsfield Castle at the edge of the town. In the eighteenth century it was replaced with Lucan House, whose circular dining room is said – perhaps truly – to have inspired the Oval Office in the White House.

Patrick fought fiercely for the Jacobite cause, and won Connaught for the deposed King James II. In 1693, when he was fatally wounded in the service of Louis XIV, he watched his blood spill and said: 'If only this were for Ireland.' His son James, six months of age, became the 2nd Earl of Lucan. He died without issue, and the Lucan earldom died with him.

But it was restored to life, as earldoms can be, in the form of his great-nephew: Sir Charles Bingham, 6th Baronet, who in 1795 became the second incarnation of the 1st Earl of Lucan. Thus the title was a union of both the Irish sympathizer and the Irish conqueror, the man who brought Connaught to a Catholic king and the man who had ruled it for a Protestant queen. But the conqueror, for a while at least, would win out.

The Lucan myth has it that the 3rd Earl – 'great exterminator' of the Irish, buffoon of the Crimea, self-righteous attacker of absolutely anybody who questioned him – is the true and typical representative of the family. Indeed the 3rd Earl is immensely convenient to the myth. How like him the 7th Earl must have been! How easy to strip the side-whiskers from the taut, glaring face of the 3rd Earl, whose portrait hung in the dining-room at 46 Lower Belgrave Street, and to see the resemblance to that later Lucan. And how inconvenient, therefore, to consider the five earls before and between, who were not like that at all.

The 1st Earl, for instance, who enjoyed the title for only four years before his death in 1799, was far from being a monster of arrogance. He was a prominent Whig, a distinguished follower of Charles James Fox, and he had the wit to marry a talented woman: Margaret Smyth, a fine painter.[4] Two of Margaret's miniatures are displayed at Althorp, childhood home of Diana, Princess of Wales. This was by way of keeping things in the family. In 1781 the Binghams' daughter Lavinia married the future 2nd Earl Spencer: a remarkable coup, given that she had nothing to offer beyond a conventional pretti-ness, and indeed she seems never to have relaxed into her elevated role. Perhaps she remained fidgety with the knowledge that an Irish baronet – as Lavinia's father then was – was as nothing compared with the Spencers, their fabulous houses, their powerful alliances.[5]

And this, really, is the thing about the Lucan earldom. For all that the myth portrays it as some sort of aristocratic archetype, in fact its holder was a 'mere Irish peer'. Grand as hell, of course, but only relatively so.

Laleham, the 'country seat', was nothing more than a large and well-placed house, although it was distinguished by the 2nd Earl's taste. Like his parents, and notwithstanding the early scandal of the 'criminal conversation' action, Richard Bingham was a cultured, intelligent man. When he and his wife separated in 1804,[6] and he began the continental wanderings which took him to a life in Italy with his mistress, he became a patron of the arts. The National Gallery of Washington now owns the three exquisite marble busts of his daughters that he commissioned from the Danish sculptor Bertel Thorvaldsen. 'The thought of him in those days,' says his great-great-great-granddaughter Jane, 'travelling to Rome, finding this brilliant sculptor – not just a common or garden sculptor, he found the best.' Jane's brother, the 7th Earl, sold the busts in the 1960s.

The 2nd Earl was one of the original twenty-eight representative peers for Ireland in the House of Lords, a position that was held until his death in 1839.[7] His son also became a representative peer, although in no other way did he resemble his father. A portrait of him at the age of fourteen shows a fine, cold-eyed, rather brutish-looking boy with a dead rabbit slung casually over his shoulder. If one is seeking to understand his character through heredity, one can only look back to the soldier Richard Bingham; but that, as ever with such explanations, tells a partial story.

George Bingham was born in 1800, just as the 'United Kingdom of Great Britain and Ireland' was established. Two years earlier the Lucans' original home in Mayo, Castlebar House, had been destroyed and pillaged in an anti-Protestant rebellion, and they were obliged to rehouse themselves. It would not be long before the fire of Irish violence blazed again, its flames fanned no end by the future Earl.

He was no adventurer like his Elizabethan forebear. He had no need to be. The Lucan title was starting to hit its heights. George could afford to buy commissions in the army through the 'purchase' system, an absurdity intended to preserve the gentlemanliness of the officer class.[8] By 1826, having bought his way through the ranks, the young Lord Bingham became a lieutenant colonel in the 17th Lancers. But by the time he inherited his earldom, in 1839, he had turned the grim force of his attention away from the military, towards Ireland, where his 61,000 acres now housed some 100,000 tenants.

The 3rd Earl's tenets were industry, economy and good husbandry: remarkably unlike his great-great-grandson. He wanted to reform the farming of his Co. Mayo estates, which was the right idea in principle. In practice, it meant that many of his tenants would be evicted. The indigenous southern Irish lived on and from the land. Pitiful smallholdings, planted with their staple crop of potatoes, were subdivided over and over again.[9] And so when famine came to

Ireland in the 1840s, the effects of these land 'clearances' would be appalling: a tragedy of the type that would now be associated with the developing world.

The potato crop failed in 1845–6 and 1848. The country was said to have turned colour overnight, from green to scorched black. Ireland became a mass grave; but Lord Lucan did not falter in his programme of reform. He served an estimated 6,000 processes for eviction. Fifteen thousand acres were cleared, entire small villages replaced by fields and, in one case, a racecourse. A dairy farm was built using stones from the walls of demolished streets. And Lucan's desire to improve his estate grew ever more justified, in his eyes, by the fact that his tenants were unable to pay their rents yet refusing to leave. In every way, clearance was the answer.

The death of around one million people was certainly one way of clearing Ireland. Another way was emigration: one and a half million left the country. For those who stayed, the workhouse was a theoretical safety net, but in 1846 the Castlebar workhouse in Mayo was declared to be out of funds. Lord Lucan was chairman of its board of governors. From his London house at Hanover Square, he wrote regretting the situation and complaining that as he had received no rental income he was unable to subsidize the estab-lishment further.[10] The workhouse doors were closed. Families lay outside, beyond hunger and hope, their children with 'death like faces and drum stick arms that seemed ready to snap'.[11] Priests gave the sacrament in doorways, by roadsides.

It is easy to say that Lucan was deliberately cruel towards Ireland, although he did not see it that way; but he also seems to have been powerfully irritated by the place.[12] It did not fit with his vigorous, humourless, frighteningly single-minded personality, which con-sidered that certain things had to be done so there was no point in arguing about them. Certainly he was prepared to defend himself, with the utmost stridency. In February 1847 he took to the floor of the Lords, contesting the assertion that he had closed the work-house. In March he rose again to state that there had, undeniably, been processes served for rent, but that only people who did not understand Ireland would confuse these with evictions.[13]

Two years earlier, *The Times* had published a letter from a man who had observed the unspeakable situation in Mayo. This gave Lord Lucan credit for being 'one of the few landlords left in the west of Ireland who reside on, and perseveringly endeavour to improve their property'. Despite being called 'a great exterminator', he had at least 'looked the matter in the face'. It was a bravely argued case, in its way, but its logic collapsed against this simple statement from an English engineer sent to work in Ireland. 'If only', he wrote, 'the people had been treated with a little kindness.'

The 1851 census found the population of Ireland to have fallen by almost two and a half million in a decade. It also recorded that the Earl of Lucan, together with his wife, four daughters, and fifteen servants, was living at Laleham House, by now a treasure trove of precious marbles. The previous year a strange event had occurred: a man named Charles Holden confessed that, twenty years earlier, he had killed a prostitute with a blow to the head, and buried her in the grounds of the house. He had dug the grave with a spade taken from Lord Lucan's toolshed. When the case was heard at the local Petty Sessions House, where Lucan was one of the magistrates, Holden suddenly admitted that the supposed victim was alive and well 'in a public-house in Chertsey'. The identity of the body in the Laleham House grounds remains a mystery.

This was the kind of event that punctuated Lord Lucan's long and complicated life. Obviously the skeleton in the garden was nothing to do with him, any more than the 1872 murder of his lady friend; nevertheless he did seem to attract the most remarkable controversy. Now, in the 1850s, he was raring for a return to military action. He applied for a post in the Crimea, and became a lieutenant general with command of the cavalry division.

The Crimean War, an inconclusive campaign fought by Britain and France to halt Russian predations into the collapsing Ottoman

Empire, is best known for two things: the activities of Florence Nightingale, who organized the first base hospitals of modern times; and the Charge of the Light Brigade, a cavalry attack during the Battle of Balaclava in October 1854, during which almost half the brigade of around 660 men were killed, injured or captured. Half the horses also died, cut down from under their riders. A surviving officer said: 'Through God's mercy I have been saved from one of the most horrible engagements that ever British soldiers were sent into.'[14]

Although some historians now attribute a certain strategic value to the Charge of the Light Brigade, it was regarded at the time, and indeed for many years thereafter, as nothing short of a shambles. Among its casualties was the 3rd Earl of Lucan, who in a report to the war office described the charge as 'very brilliant and daring'. He was reported to have been 'wounded slightly', although this did not take into account the injury to his reputation.

The order for the charge had come from Lord Raglan, commander of the British forces. Unfortunately it was made upon the wrong guns. The intended target was a retreating Russian artillery battery. What was actually attacked was a battery that was fully prepared and armed. Why this happened is still unclear, although it was hardly helpful that the man in command of the Light Brigade, Lord Cardigan, was on non-speaking terms with the man in command of the cavalry, Lord Lucan. The unbelievable silliness of this meant that the order could not be properly assessed by the two men who had to enact it. It also meant that everybody, afterwards, could try to pass the blame on to somebody else.[15]

Lucan, severely criticized by a panicky Raglan, was recalled to England in February 1855. In September both he and Cardigan faced the censure of the Crimean Commissioners' inquiry.[16] It hardly needs saying that Lucan went berserk. He would, he said, tear to pieces those parts of the report that affected the cavalry. *The Times*, which now took an almost daily pleasure in teasing him, wrote that 'Lord Lucan, with his usual discretion, has hit upon the notable plan of abusing the Minister of War, the Judge-Advocate, and the

Chelsea Court, by way of bettering his case'. In December he sued the *Daily News*, which had referred bluntly to 'the Lucan–Cardigan scandal', but lost the case. 'Did not he and Lord Cardigan', asked counsel for the defence, 'behave more like two great schoolgirls than Generals?' Nevertheless, and despite the apparent frankness of the inquiry proceedings, the Chelsea Report itself was a white-wash. Cardigan and Lucan had been protected by their own kind.

Some 120 years later, a spectator in the House of Lords shouted an accusation at a peer who was speaking on a housing bill, whom he had mistaken for the 7th Earl of Lucan. In fact the speaker was Lord Raglan, who replied: 'Right battle, wrong man.'

In 1881 it was reported from Ireland that the 3rd Earl had sent a boat to the island of Inishturk and had its twenty-two families transported at gunpoint to the workhouse. He was still fighting his battle against his tenants, and still failing to realize his vision of a wondrously transformed estate. But by now the Irish were retaliating in a more organized way. The Land League, which sought radically to change the system of land ownership, was at its height, as was violence against the ruling class. When Charles Stewart Parnell, president of the League, spoke out against the evictions from Inishturk, the name of Lord Lucan was greeted with hisses. He got off lightly, in the circumstances.

Had he been born a century earlier, in a time arguably more fitting to him, the 7th Earl of Lucan might well have become a cavalry officer in the Crimean War; but he would never have embarked upon that death struggle with his Irish tenants. In no way was that his nature. As it was, he simply accepted the rents from the Mayo estate, which have not been paid since his disappearance. 'De Valera told us not to pay ground rent to absentee landlords,' said one of his tenants in 1994, 'and they don't come much more absent than Lord Lucan.'

According to the myth the 7th Earl shared with his great-great-grandfather an unwavering faith in his own righteousness, a belief that what he wanted was what mattered, and hang the collateral damage. Thus the same blinkered urges that caused the deaths of thousands in Ireland also led to the attempted removal of a vexatious wife. This, of course, comes back to class: the notion of *droit de seigneur*. Both the 3rd and the 7th Earl of Lucan had something of this in them, but it manifested itself in very different ways. For one thing, the 3rd Earl could never resist pleading his own case. When the 7th Earl was called upon to defend himself, to the police and the law, he did not do so. The 3rd Earl would have relished a trial: he would have been arguing with the prosecution, proclaiming that he had been falsely arraigned, almost enjoying himself; he did not shirk life.

Not that he would ever have been in such a position. He had simply walked out on his wife, in that decisive way of his, and taken up with other women as he pleased. He had the money to do it, of course. And, despite his obsession with bending public opinion to his will, he had a paradoxical disregard for it: he lived as he chose, and he had the courage of his choices. The 7th Earl merely believed that he lived as he chose. In fact his choices became illusory, circumscribed.

So for all that the Lucan myth takes the 3rd Earl as a kind of ancestral template for the sins of the great-great-grandson, there is in fact scant similarity between the two. Unless, of course, one believes that both were similarly, brutally, arrogantly violent.

Charles George, the 4th Earl, who succeeded to the title in 1888, marked a return to those earlier, civilized Lucans. He pulled off no small feat in mending relations with his Irish tenants. His father, naturally enough, had a low opinion of his tenure as MP for Mayo.

In 1859 he married a daughter of the Duke of Richmond, which meant that the 7th Earl was twice descended from illegitimate children of Charles II.[17] ('And you've been right royal bastards ever since,' said his friend Dominick Elwes.) Socially speaking, George represented the high point of the earldom. And he lived, accordingly, in a lordly style.[18] The Lucan wealth, never vast but capable of providing every usual comfort, was irrevocably diminished by the 4th Earl. Many years later, the 7th Earl would write to his uncle, saying: 'Nothing has been ventured in this family since our great-grandfather ran up a grocer's bill of £4,000.' In a way it was these two Lucans who most resembled each other. They would probably have been friends. Both were *bon vivants* and sporting gamblers, both had a conviction that life should be lived in luxury, and neither had a strong sense of how to pay for it. Where they differed was in their marriages, and in the 4th Earl's capacity for contentment. But then, he lived in an age when the worries of aristocrats were more easily forestalled.

Yet in 1906 he admitted to his son that he had lived in fear of bankers for fifty years. Twice he came close to being declared bankrupt; a fate that would be realized in 1975 by the 7th Earl. He died in 1914, aged eighty-four, just two months before the outbreak of war: in every sense, he had calmly absented himself from the approaching carnage.

It was his decent, dependable heir, George, who had to deal with it all. He had taken control of the estates in 1900, which saved his father from his first threat of bankruptcy. At first George must have thought that all was well: in 1901 he was living at Gorhambury, near St Albans, with his wife, his two-year-old son, and nineteen servants. Four hundred years earlier, Gorhambury had been home to the daughter of Sir Richard Bingham, conqueror of Connaught. Now it was rented from the Earl of Verulam, who could no longer afford to run it. Twenty years later George Lucan would be in the same position, frantically trying to let Laleham House.

The following year the house was put up for auction. Laleham, said the advertisement ominously, was 'purchasable on favourable terms'; its 83 acres represented 'ripe building land'. In July 1922 the bidding opened at £7,500.[19] There was no response. Nevertheless in August the 5th Earl, gamely keeping up appearances, staged a large party in its grounds for the Laleham Regatta.

The Lucans were far from alone in this need to sell off their money-eating houses. The late 1870s had seen the upper class at the tranquil zenith of its fortunes, sitting among the ancestral portraits as if all had at last been achieved. Seven thousand families owned four-fifths of the British Isles. Two hundred and fifty families had 30,000 acres or more. The Lucans were among this number, although they did not compare with those, like the Dukes of Westminster and Devonshire, whose wealth was near limitless.

Decline began in the 1880s, although it did not immediately show its inexorable face. It was propelled by the forces of democracy: the doubling of the size of the electorate meant that the social status quo could not hold. The 1881 Irish Land Act gave far greater rights to tenants. The 1909 'People's Budget' imposed British land taxes. When the House of Lords made trouble over it, Lloyd George simply took them on and cut their powers. 'Oh these dukes,' he said, 'how they oppress us.' The cry continues, although it no longer has meaning.

Aristocratic life, which had seemed so gloriously spacious, was becoming hedged in by reality. In 1913 the Duke of Bedford was glad to take £2 million for his Covent Garden estate. The First World War killed more aristocrats than any conflict since the Wars of the Roses. It was said that 'the feudal system vanished in blood and fire, and the landed classes were consumed'.[20] This was true in a way, yet in another way the aristocracy *en masse* were survivors; they would face facts and do what needed to be done; although among them there would be those, like the 7th Earl of Lucan, who would remain preserved in the ancestral amber, rigid as fossils.

The untrammelled life had also been an insular one, in which a country house, filled with the accretions of generations, was the centre of the known universe. Now the world was suddenly bigger. International trade brought down the prices of all that could be grown on British land, a quarter of which was sold in the years around the war. Upper-class families sought to save themselves by marrying American heiresses. Men who understood money, like the

Rothschilds, became the source of true power. In 1924 the newly ennobled soap magnate Lord Leverhulme, born the son of a Bolton grocer, bought Grosvenor House on Park Lane, where as recently as 1887 the Duke of Westminster had paraded his Derby-winning horse at a garden tea-party.[21] Small wonder that Nancy Mitford, daughter of the impoverished country squire Lord Redesdale, took consolatory delight in conjuring, for her 1948 novel *Love in a Cold Climate*, the unassailable wealth of the Montdore family: a Mayfair mansion, two country castles, its 'acres, coal mines, real estate, jewels, silver, pictures, incunabula, and other possessions of the sort. Lord Montdore owned an incredible number of such things, fortunately.'

Fortunate indeed. Elsewhere, the scale of territorial transfer was comparable only with the Norman Conquest. What happened to the Lucans was entirely typical. If the 4th Earl had done a bit less spending in the good times, the family would have had more resilience in the bad; but they were also carried along by forces beyond their control. In 1895 Earl Lucan sold the family's Macclesfield estate, using the £42,000 proceeds to reduce his mortgages. His son sold off great chunks of Mayo, again to pay off debts. By 1914 the rental income had fallen to a bare £3,336. For in Ireland an even greater set of external pressures was being exerted, culminating in the 1921 treaty that established the Irish Free State in the south. As the Act of Union was being severed, so it was estimated that more than three-quarters of the land, previously in the hands of the Protestant Ascendancy, had been transferred to tenants. The Lucans had been absentee landlords, of course, and this was just as well. In the end, Castlebar House was donated by the 5th Earl to an order of nuns, who converted it into a girls' school. In 1933 it was burned to the ground. The 3rd Earl would have been spinning and sparking like a Catherine wheel in his Laleham grave. He may have won his grisly war with Ireland, but what had it all been for? By the time that his great-great-grandson assumed the title, his 100,000 tenants had been reduced to 600. The former Lucan rent house became an arena for a different kind of conflict: Castlebar Boxing Club. The most secure and peaceable legacy was the family cricket ground, given to the town by the 5th Earl and still used by the local club.

At Laleham, meanwhile, land was sold off bit by bit. In 1966 the 7th Earl disposed of one of the family's last possessions in the village, the seventeenth-century house that stands beside the church and was once home to the Lucans' bailiff. By the time of the earl's disappearance, little more than the 100 acres of the golf course remained ('Not', says his friend Bill Shand Kydd, 'the road to riches'). Laleham House, which back in the 1920s had taken six years to sell, was eventually also acquired by nuns for use as a school. In 1981 it was converted into flats by Barratt Homes. A community of sleek gated houses stands on the site of the Lucan stables, where the 3rd Earl's Crimea horses lie buried beneath the immaculate courtyard.[22]

Having done his duty by the family finances, the 5th Earl went on to do it in every other way. He was the model of the great and good, irreproachable and respectable, the lifelong cricketer who always played by the rules. 'A long career of public service', was the un-arguable heading for his obituary in *The Times*. Born in 1860, he went to Sandhurst and, like his forebears, retained close links with the military. He became chairman of the City of London Territorial Army in 1912, holding this position until 1947, just two years before his death. By this time his life's work was symbolized by the veri-table alphabet of letters that had accumulated after his name: C.B., K.B.E., P.C., T.D., D.L., J.P., G.C.V.O.[23]

As Lord Bingham, he was Conservative MP for Chertsey. As Lord Lucan, he served diligently as government whip in the Lords from 1931 until 1940. After Irish independence, peers had lost the right to sit formally in the House, so in 1934 the 5th Earl was created the 1st Baron Bingham of Melcombe Bingham, after the calm Dorset village from which the family had sprung.

As befitted his courtly rectitude the earl also served upon royalty, both George V and VI. In 1929 he was appointed 'Captain of His

Majesty's Body Guard of the Honourable Corps of Gentlemen at Arms'. When a visiting monarch or statesman arrived in Britain, it was the 5th Earl who was sent to do the infinitely polite greeting at Victoria Station. At the coronation of George VI in 1937, he was there in his Gentlemen-at-Arms role, his own coronet carried by his page, Viscount Althorp, into whose family his great-great-aunt had been slightly grudgingly accepted. The following year he became a Privy Counsellor. More so than any other Lucan, he was Establishment: but he had all the sense of responsibility, and none of the arrogance, that this implies.

He also had none of his father's inconsequentiality, nor of his grandfather's lethal fire. When he was obliged to appear in court as a plaintiff, the judge commended him for conducting his case 'with great tact and ability and good temper'. Anything less like the 3rd Earl could hardly be conceived. Nevertheless he resembled him in other ways: his staunch tirelessness, his determination to live a life publicly, in the sphere of activity. In 1939, at the age of seventy-eight, he fell in the wartime blackout as he left the House of Lords. The Lords lamented, with evident sincerity, the 'dreadful accident which had deprived them of the services of Lord Lucan'; but he was soon limping back to work, broken leg braced in a support, dogged in his refusal to give in to age and injury.

The same year, he attended a ceremony at the parish church of Wilton. Robert Bingham was commemorated by a statuette on the façade of the church where, in 1229, he had been consecrated Bishop of Salisbury. A memorial tablet was also unveiled, dedicated to two Robert Binghams: the thirteenth-century bishop and his descendant, the twentieth-century American ambassador. Thus nineteen generations of the family were brought together, in quiet ceremony, in an ancient English chancel. It was the sort of occasion for which the 5th Earl was beautifully suited and, in its way, it too represented a high point of sorts for the Lucans.

Yet at the same time, and after a fashion, the earl and his countess, Violet, were homeless. Without Laleham, some of whose furniture was sold in 1938, they moved from house to house in London, staying for a time in Gloucester Place, where the future Veronica Lucan would live in a bedsit before her marriage. Eventually they took a flat behind Selfridge's department store. Violet lived there until her death in 1972, thirty-three years after her husband. The earl himself died at the Clarendon Hotel in Eastbourne. He was eighty-eight years old, and had gone there to convalesce in the soft sea air. His hotel stood just a handful of miles from where the Ford Corsair borrowed by his grandson would be found, abandoned, at the port of Newhaven.

John Bingham

'He should have had a trade, a profession. The calling of a gambler is madness. Being an Earl, full stop, is madness.'

MURIEL SPARK, *Aiding and Abetting*, 2000

IN OCTOBER 1934, the future 6th Earl of Lucan and his wife were involved in a road accident in Essex. George Patrick Bingham, known as Pat, had stopped after a collision, and was talking to the other driver when they were knocked down by another car. Both men suffered head injuries and were taken to hospital in Romford. Lady Bingham, who had remained in her husband's car, was apparently unharmed by the first collision, although later she was found to have a blood clot on the lung. Although Kaitilin Bingham was the kind of stoical, resilient woman who would, as far as was possible, have taken this in her stride, what made it peculiarly disturbing was that she was heavily pregnant at the time of the accident with her first son, Richard John. He was born on 18 December. A telegram of congratulations was sent to the Lucans from Buckingham Palace.

Pat was then based in Colchester, at the White Lodge army quarters. Like all the Lucans, he served in the military, in his case with high distinction in two world wars. Born in 1898, at a house in Mayfair close to where his great-grandfather had lived in old age, he attended Eton, then Sandhurst. During the First World War he was commissioned in the Coldstream Guards. He was wounded in action, and in 1918 awarded the Military Cross. In the 1920s he was aide-de-camp to the governor general of South Africa, where his eldest son would later be so frequently sighted.

During the Second World War, as colonel, he commanded the 1st Battalion of the Coldstreams. He then moved to the Air Ministry, before retiring from the army in 1947. Three years later he became captain of the King's Bodyguard of the Yeomen of the Guard, who in July 1950 were reported as parading before King George VI at Buckingham Palace in their bright Tudor outfits. 'King's Bodyguard, Hats off. Three cheers for his Majesty the King,' ordered the new Lord Lucan, as the king looked on in his naval uniform. Inspection over, crimson standard fluttering in the sun, the yeomen marched through the garden to their quarters at St James's Palace.

It was all very nice, very pomp and circumstance; and very unlike Pat Lucan. The previous year, on inheriting his title, he had taken the Labour whip in the House of Lords. 'My father', says his daughter Jane, his eldest child, born in 1932, 'was a political person after he retired from the army, and when his father died he could take up the politics.' If one sought to write a concise history of the Lucan earldom, its thesis might be that each peer behaved, in some fundamental way, in reaction to his predecessor. So where the 1st Earl was uxorious, the 2nd preferred the conquest to the comfortable fireside; where the 2nd Earl was refined, the 3rd burned with aggression; where the 3rd Earl was combative, the 4th was emollient; where the 4th Earl was carefree, the 5th was careful; and where the 5th Earl held, with a benign tenacity, to the values of the past, the 6th believed in stripping them away. That, along with social rise and financial decline, was pretty much how the story went. Interesting, but not atypical; until the 7th Earl, partly in reaction against the 6th, took the story in a direction so extreme as to lead to its abortive, final chapter.

Although Pat Lucan resembled his father in his powerful sense of public duty, his move leftwards was as striking a turnabout as if Carol Thatcher had gone CND marching with Michael Foot. 'It certainly distressed my grandparents,' says Jane, sister to the 7th Earl, who has lived for many years in New York and shares her parents' political affiliations, 'and the rest of the family. My grandfather was absolutely establishment. And his wife.' It was unusual, but not unknown, for aristocrats to support a system that would, logically, lead to their obliteration. This was particularly true after a war that had laid Britain bare, when the Labour minister Herbert Morrison could speak of what he called the 'genuine social idealism' emerging from the carnage: 'a revolution of outlook, shifting from the values of private enterprise to the values of socialism.' But the 6th Earl of Lucan and his wife had been Labour sympathizers as early as the mid-1920s, when the party had a brief shot at minority government under Ramsay MacDonald. The decline of the Lucan fortunes, the sale of Laleham, would have seemed to Pat not a disaster but a corrective.

Like his father, he believed in *noblesse oblige*; yet at the same time he did not, because being an earl meant nothing to him. This is easier said than lived. Even the least pompous aristocrats cannot help, on occasion, but remind one of who they are. And they enjoy being who they are. They prefer being Lord Venison of Deerpark to Mr Butcher: many people would prefer it, if they were honest about it, which of course they are not. Certainly all the Lucans enjoyed being earls, except Pat.

His forebears were earls by profession, as one might say. Because they were earls, the Lucans were also in the nature of things representative peers for Ireland, the 5th Earl being one of the very last of these. They had land, tenants, responsibilities (even the 3rd Earl would have thought in this way). They were officers, MPs, leaders of men. One could keep quite busy, merely by being an earl. Yet by the time of the 6th Earl, after two world wars, a social semi-revolution and the election, in 1945, of a government dedicated to principles of nationalization, the entire notion of what an earl *was* had come up for question. What was an earl for? What did an earl do, that could not be done anyway, or indeed not at all? And as soon as such questions are asked – What is the House of Lords? What is a Lord Chancellor, or a Black Rod? What is tradition? – then it becomes hard to answer them, other than by saying that this is the way that things have evolved, and that Britain is probably better at being inexplicable than at being logical.

As is all too apparent today, the class system did not disappear. When Pat Lucan inherited in the middle of the twentieth century, an earl was still a figure to be reckoned with. But something had been lost, the belief that aristocracy had an intrinsic value. Now its value came extrinsically, with the way in which it justified an un-justifiable position.

Pat Lucan, a man in tune with his time, was an earl ahead of it. He not only saw the direction the world was going, he approved of it. Physically less imposing than most of the Lucans, with the hand-some face of his son rendered ordinary by humility, he looked more like a decent, slightly worried chief constable than the inheritor of a venerable but bloodied title. He was described as 'quiet, unassuming, gentle, and kind': a good man. Although it was fashionable among thinking people to support the left, sometimes a kind of snobbery in itself, Pat actually meant it. He would have agreed without a qualm with this respondent to Mass-Observation,[1] replying to the question of what changes would be needed after the war: 'There'll have to be more equalness. Things not fair now. Nobody can tell me they are. There's them with more money what they can ever use. This ain't right and it's got to be put right.' After Pat's death in January 1964, another member of the House of Lords said: 'He was always for the under-privileged. If there was a question of a minority being bullied by a majority he was there to speak for them. Wherever there seemed to him to be injustice he was against it.' Pat would never know that his son, overprivileged in every objective sense, would also come to represent a minority under siege; that the first principle of justice, innocent until proven guilty, would be rejected by the majority in the case of the 7th Earl of Lucan.

It was Kaitilin who had to live with that irony. She was the person who first raised her husband's political consciousness, a woman of character, two years his junior, whose upbringing had encouraged independent thought. She was not high-born in the manner of her husband's grandmother, a daughter of the Duke of Richmond; nor did she belong to a family like her mother-in-law's, the status quo-affirming Spender Clays. Kait's father, the Honourable Edward Dawson, was a naval captain. 'The word', says Jane, 'was he'd run away to sea at thirteen. And she was the only child, and she was taught to do all the boy-type things as a little girl. She loved it. And while being brought up in a very unconventional way she acquired a wonderful education, even though she didn't go to school, of course, because in those days girls didn't.'

Yet for all that she was not raised to be a simpering debutante, Kait's grandfather was the 1st Earl of Dartrey, and her mother had been a lady in-waiting to Queen Mary, wife of George V. Meanwhile one of Pat's sisters, Margaret, married Field-Marshal Alexander of Tunis. His other sister, Barbara, married Colonel John Bevan; her memorial service in 1964, held at a church in Chester Square, was attended by the Duke and Duchess of Richmond and the Countess Spencer. The old family connections held firm, keeping the Lucans in the social stratosphere. But the 6th Earl and his wife breathed less rarefied air.

Pat made the clearest possible rejection of his aristocratic past when he gave access to family papers, concerning the Irish famine and the conduct of the Crimean War, to the author Cecil Woodham-Smith. This was an act of remarkable openness, one might even say atonement. Woodham-Smith's Crimea account *The Reason Why* was published in 1953, followed nine years later by *The Great Hunger: Ireland 1845–49*. The 3rd Earl of Lucan came out of both books, especially the second, very badly. 'It is almost impossible', wrote Woodham-Smith, 'to picture the deference, the adulation, the extraordinary privileges accorded to the nobility in the first half of the 19th century. A peer was above the law which applied to other men.' The 6th Earl, in helping these histories to be written, was placing himself firmly in their author's court.

His political career began under Clement Attlee, as an under-secretary of state in the Commonwealth Relations office; although, political new dawn notwithstanding, he was shunted into opposition when Churchill regained power in 1951. In fact Pat never served in government: he died just a few months before Harold Wilson won the 1964 election. But he did honourable service for his party. Some of the causes that he espoused, such as the integration of foreign students into British society, the 'tragic' paucity of affordable London housing, and the need for oil companies to respect the environment when laying pipelines, are notably contemporary. Together with other members of the opposition, including its leader Hugh Gaitskell, he sent Christmas cards to anti-apartheid activists kept under house arrest in South Africa. In late 1954 he was appointed opposition chief whip, a post in which he was praised for his 'spirit of reasonableness'. He held the position until his death, after which Lord Carrington, paying tribute, said that 'he knew of no one in any quarter of the house who did not regard him as a personal friend'.

His wife remained a member of the Marylebone Labour Association after the disappearance of her son, during the campaign for the 1979 election won by Margaret Thatcher, indeed until the end of her life in 1985, when she was given an unceremonious, non-Christian burial near her eighth-floor flat in London's St John's Wood. Her political beliefs were less compromising than her husband's. Kait was a great scatterer of pamphlets, a dinner-table debater. Neither her son nor his circle shared her views, but it is quite untrue to say, as it has been, that she was an embarrassment to Lord Lucan, and that his friends regarded her socialism as some sort of personal tragedy for him. 'She was the most lovely woman,' says Christina Shand Kydd, sister to Veronica Lucan. 'Lovely. She had the most incredible gift of being able to disagree with you about politics without there ever being any sign of it becoming an argument. It was always, merely, a good fun discussion. And it's a really great gift.' Bill Shand Kydd says: 'You couldn't help but love her.' One of Lord Lucan's oldest friends remembers her as 'rabid Labour, and charming. She was so nice, Kaitilin.' He also recalls how Lucan bought his mother a car for the 1959 general election: 'And he had it sprayed red. So she could go canvassing with a, you know, proper vehicle.' Lucan's sister Jane says: 'My mother and John would have good, intelligent discussions. But I think it always kept within bounds – I don't remember any real bad arguments. They could talk about politics in a sane way, and she could kind of bring him down off his pedestal, and say now, don't you really think this, or something... I know he was very fond of my mother – actually everybody was very fond of my mother. Wonderful eccentric lady.' The only person who admitted to open disputation with Kait was her future daughter-in-law, Veronica. They first met in September 1963, at the time of Veronica's engagement to the then Lord Bingham (John). 'We went to dinner at the Arts Theatre Club and had the most frightful political row. His father [Pat] sat at the other end of the table, looking horrified. John just stayed silent and let us continue fighting. The extraordinary thing was that she was wildly left-wing – I, the non-Countess, the conservative.'[2]

At the age of eighty Kaitilin took an 'A' Level in Russian ('getting ready for the revolution,' as Bill Shand Kydd puts it: but as a joke). This did not necessarily mean sympathy with communism, although there probably was a bit of that. She had grown up in a time when the creed attracted many highly intelligent idealists. Kait Lucan's relentless denial of the world of privilege extended to her appearance: she was described as 'wearing worn-out sandals and awful baggy trousers', as driving a clapped-out Land Rover, as having hair that looked as though 'someone had stabbed a sofa'.[3] It could have seemed like deliberate oddity, but it was born of a true conviction that other things mattered more. She was not, by her own admission, an especially good mother; at least not in the modern, hands-on, everything-stops-to-take-the-children-to-oboe-lessons sense. For all her kindness she had a definite touch of *Bleak House*'s Mrs Jellyby about her, being at least as engaged with her political activities as with her offspring. Nevertheless nobody ever had a bad word to say about her, except those who took her daughter-in-law's side in the aftermath of November 1974: the police, Veronica Lucan's counsel at the inquest, certain chroniclers of the Lucan myth. Kait, who would have been appalled by the suffering of the Rivetts and was as vehemently disapproving as anybody of her son's behaviour, was unflinching in his defence to the end.

But even left-wing aristocrats remain who they are, and through-out their happy marriage the 6th Earl and his wife lived in a kind of rackety grandeur. They were far from poor, however much the Lucan fortunes had diminished since the days of Laleham House and its nineteen servants. 'I know', says Jane, 'that between them my parents had quite a lot of money at the beginning. But they didn't care about it. They gave it away or spent it.' In Essex they owned for a time a large house, Wakes Colne Place, near Braintree. In London, where they moved just before the outbreak of war, they remained within the sacred postcodes: Cheyne Walk, on the Thames at Chelsea, then Eaton Square. 'I can vaguely remem-ber the house looking on to the river,' says Jane. 'John [the future 7th Earl] and I went to a little school in Tite Street. But then the house was bombed.' The four Bingham children – Jane, born 1932; Richard, always known as John; Sarah, or Sally, born 1936; Hugh, born 1939 – were evacuated. The Lucans themselves did war work in the fire service.

Jane says:

Eaton Square I don't remember before the war but we came home afterwards to dustcloths, and crazy furniture. It had a huge drawing room, and my father put a hook in the ceiling with a climbing rope through it that we could all climb. And they did things with us like carpentry, and making chocolates... I suppose they were trying desperately to get to know their children.

But the house was not fancy at all, even though there was a cook in those days – she had lived through the war with them. In fact they were all in Eaton Square during the war, because we came home and they had taken the windows out. And my parents had insisted on continuing to sleep on the second floor, because they didn't want to go down in the basement – which I guess every normal person did. As you may have gathered they were not a normal couple.

It was quite normal, however, to send one's children out of London at this time, when death by bomb was a very real threat. The Binghams went first to Wales, then Canada *en route* to America. 'It was a very quick decision that was made in England, and they had apparently forty-eight hours to decide, my parents, whether they would accept the berths that were available on the ship. And they sent nanny with us – Flora Coles.' Nannies, too, were a natural fact of life, although there is no evidence to corroborate the story that Lucan also had his own personal maid.

The four Bingham children arrived in Washington in 1940. They had no definite place to stay. It was all very ad hoc, rather terrifying. The policeman, David Gerring, who later described this flight to America as '*Gone With the Wind Up*', was really quite wide of the mark. Perhaps what had inspired the sneer was the fact that when the children did acquire a home, it was as different as could be from the usual evacuee billet. In the mysterious way that the upper classes have of knowing people, the Binghams found themselves living with the Brady Tuckers, one of the richest families in the US.

The Brady Tuckers had made their money in finance at the end of the nineteenth century. In good Edith Wharton style, they used this very modern fortune to recreate a kind of European ideal of bygone living, of gentility untainted by commerce. Having the children of an earl to stay with them did no harm to that image. Essentially, though, they acted out of benevolence; they were, says Jane, 'fabulous, wonderful, generosity-unbounded people'. Jane, who qualified as a doctor and married an American, has remained close to the family. Much later, the then Earl of Lucan would appeal to the Brady Tuckers in his custody fight with his wife. When Marcia, the matriarch, died in 1977, her will was found to contain a $15,000 bequest to Lucan. 'She was', says Jane, 'our sort of fairy godmother.' She was also as grand as any English duchess. Every morning she would dictate orders to her private secretary, who then delivered them to her enormous staff, some of whom were employed simply to walk around her giant estate and scare away cats. At the same time she lived in a way that was somehow very American, utterly free from that fear of vulgarity that so cramps the English style. Comfort, luxury and opulence were there to be had, so why not have them?

The Brady Tuckers had, as Jane puts it, 'three major houses'. They lived like Astors, spending the winter in their home on New York's Park Avenue. In summer they used their beach property in Florida or, in the main, enjoyed their estate at Mount Kisco in Westchester. The splendour of this place was almost unreal. 'We lived with everything – swimming pools, tennis courts, the whole nine yards.' The family also had homes in Washington and Maine, as well as an ocean yacht, *The Migrant*, requisitioned by the US military after Pearl Harbor. Twenty years later John Bingham would name his own powerboat *White Migrant*. This tribute to the Croesus-like benefactors of his childhood strengthens the idea that the five years with the Tuckers represented a kind of nirvana. The golden ease of wealth; how it garnished every separate moment with something beautiful or special that other people did not have; how it spread itself across every problem, smoothing away heat, cold, boredom, a cat on the estate, four children with nowhere to stay... 'I think the USA remained with him,' says a former police officer who investigated the case. 'Battalions of servants and all.' That, says the myth, was the dream of living to which the future Lord Lucan would always, fatally, aspire.

'But John was miserable!' says Jane.

Miserable. I think the Tuckers thought that they would do what would be normal for a little English boy. They sent him away to school, and he hated that. Really hated it. Tried to run away. So that was the first trauma. Then they sent him to a summer camp [at Adirondacks]. Then they tried another school – and he really was not happy at all. I think he tried to damage things.

The problem was mysterious. Certainly it was not with the Brady Tucker family, even if they had got it wrong by sending John Bingham away to school when he was already away from home. The sense of displacement was intense. It could be called homesickness, but it seems to have been something more, a kind of wrenching out of roots. Both the Lucans wrote regularly to their children, Kait with affectionate emotion, Pat more formally, and Jane recalls that one of Kait's uncles, an admiral, 'came over during the war when they were collecting boats from America, and he came to visit us in Westchester. At the request of his niece, I'm sure.' And of course John Bingham would always have been sent away from home, to school, although perhaps not at the age of five. But his sister, at a distance of more than seventy years, remembers his unhappiness in America with extreme clarity, and implies that something of the trauma remained with him. 'I think', she says obliquely, 'that's when it all started.'

The children and their American governess returned home by ship, arriving in Liverpool in February 1945. 'It was perfectly apparent by then that there wasn't going to be an invasion,' Kait later said, 'and Pat and I thought they would feel bad if they hadn't seen anything of their own country.' At a time when millions of children had died, or been orphaned, or were without a home at all, it is hard to say that there was anything very terrible about coming back to live in Eaton Square. Yet it must have been bewildering, after the land of plenty. A ten-year-old would not yet know that there was a Britain beyond Belgravia. And the house was cold and white as a ghost with its empty rooms, its knocked-out windows, its natural beauty rendered incongruous by the giant, levelled-out bombsite that London had become. This was a strange homecoming, another displacement.

It was in fact the return from America, rather than America itself, that infected John Bingham with his driving urge to find pleasure in life. 'Too many people say that money isn't everything,' he would write to his uncle, John Bevan, ten years later. 'It can't buy happiness, and all the usual patter. But this is either sour grapes or stupidity.'

His parents thought very differently, of course. A complexity of reasons had begun to drive their son away: not from them, but from their beliefs. As Jane puts it: 'He was going to do everything opposite to the homeland.' If he had felt an obscure resentment at being sent to America, he may have felt it even more against the home to which he returned. Why was his father's mansion interior-designed as if by a squatter? And his mother: he adored her, but why did she dress like a bag lady? Why did the family car have a leaking roof? Why could these people not live in a manner appropriate to who they were, the Earl and Countess of Lucan?

At first John Bingham attended Arnold House prep school in London. A fellow pupil was Jonathan Miller, later to be a star of *Beyond the Fringe*, a doctor, a theatre director, a ragingly brilliant polymath of a man whose own politics were very much in the Kait Lucan camp. At the age of eleven, however, he was immensely friendly with the 'intriguingly exciting and excitable' Lord Bingham. The pair would slope off to watch films in the West End, such as Powell and Pressburger's *A Matter of Life and Death*. They were, recalled Miller, 'equally delinquent', although his friend 'turned out, in the end, to be much more delinquent'. Miller was fascinated by the objects in the Eaton Square house, 'leftover uniforms from his grandparents, from the Light Brigade. I remember sometimes we used to let ourselves out of the sixth-floor window, on these fire escape ropes that would let you down into Belgrave Place.'[4] 'They had a great time,' says Jane. 'I remember one instance when my mother and I came back to the house one night, and John was in bed swaddled in bandages because he and Jonathan had had some failure with a chemical experiment.'

The cleverness of Miller, whose prodigious mind would already have been in evidence, makes these two seem unlikely companions. In later years it would become usual, or perhaps safe, to say that Lord Lucan was utterly brainless: Muriel Spark called him 'a stupid gambler', and the 8th Earl of Warwick recalled that 'the first boy I met at Eton was my cousin Bingham, who was very stupid'.[5] Yet those who knew him better disagree. His oldest friend, who was also at Eton,[6] says: 'People say he was not intelligent – he was very, very bright.' And Stuart Wheeler, a Clermont gambler who also played bridge with Lucan at the Portland Club, says: 'I don't think he was stupid. I think you can have the gambling bug, and be quite illogical about that, without being stupid. Silly, perhaps, is a better word.' According to his sister, who describes herself as the 'serious student' of the family:

> He was smart as a fox – very, very intelligent. Probably the brightest of all of us. He had other sides – he loved music, Bach. He took my mother to the opera. He taught himself to play the piano. He was hugely good at everything he tried. And yet he didn't put it to good use, which was so sad.

He continued, says Jane, to be restless and troubled throughout his childhood years in London. The conflicts in his upbringing, which some children could have weathered (his two sisters, for instance), seem to have weighed on him; he had persistent headaches and took large quantities of aspirin. He looked like an immensely confident person. In some ways he acted like one. In fact he was anything but.

In 1949, when his father inherited the earldom, his parents decided to send him to Eton. This may seem surprising given their political persuasion, although the Labour Party has of course never abolished private education, and indeed Attlee himself was perfectly comfortable with having attended the public school Haileybury. But the intention was that John Bingham should attend only for a short time. Jane says:

> They thought that Eton would give the extra attention needed – because he was showing signs, and I'm not sure what those signs were, of needing extra help. Not academically, but psychologically. I'm no psychiatrist, but I think it well could have been to do with

the separation from home at a young age, because I know for a fact that he was very, very unhappy.

The possibility of psychotherapy was even put forward, which may have been Kait's modern idea of how to deal with an apparently intangible misery. 'Lonely,' says his sister-in-law Christina Shand Kydd. 'It was a lonely childhood.' And Eton, as it happened, worked a kind of magic. For the first time John Bingham was somewhere that suited him. It affirmed who he was. It gave him his first real place of security. And it offered the first taste of the gambling that represented a kind of liberation. 'At Eton he got into this world, which was exciting,' says Jane. 'He would go and gamble on the dogs, horses. I have always blamed Eton, the fact that he started his gambling there.' From this point, certainly, John Bingham's life was taken down a path to illusory pleasure. But it might have happened anyway.

Eton, more than any other school, is more than a school. It is a totem, charismatic to some and repellent to others; rather like the aristocracy. It is probable that if prime minister David Cameron had gone to any other school, even Harrow, he would not receive the level of 'posh boy' abuse that is frequently hurled his way. Such is the symbolic power of Eton. With its 'beaks' and 'bobs' and 'Pop', its wall game, its tailcoats, its *Floreat Etona*, its fantastically beautiful buildings, some dating back to the fifteenth century, that loom on every side of the little town close to Windsor, it has the aspect of a small separate world, standing casually impregnable beside the Thames. And its boys, almost all of whom are covered with a cool sheen, a smiling haze of confidence, seem never quite to leave that world. They are always Etonians; even the ones who turn against the system tend to let people know that they went there. As one of Lord Lucan's gambling circle now puts it: 'People talk about public schools, but it's Eton and the rest.' There is nothing parochial about the place; its cosmopolitan aplomb is what sets it apart. The idea that Kait Lucan would have been an embarrassment to her son, turning up to the Fourth of June in her Aldermaston-marcher clothes, is nonsense. As Jonathan Miller put it, she 'would probably have shocked only the *parvenus*. It would probably have been more shocking at Radley than Eton.'[7]

Eton's alumni include James Bond, Lord Peter Wimsey, Princes William and Harry, nineteen prime ministers, Lord Lucan and several of his Clermont Club set – James Goldsmith, Charles Benson, Daniel Meinertzhagen – although those friendships came later. His oldest living friend, who became a successful and esteemed man, who gambled in a far merrier, less destructive way than the Clermont circle, was a contemporary of 'Bingham', as he still calls him, and their closeness began at school. 'I don't know why he became such a friend of mine, but he did. I think we sort of had the same attitude to getting by at Eton. I suppose we were out to enjoy it. And enjoy it in spades. Racing was obviously a component part...'

Windsor racecourse is very near to Eton, one might say dangerously near. 'Windsor, yes. We usually saw a master in the distance – had to duck out of sight, you know. But I think our respective housemasters thought we were quite sort of amusing. We weren't dull. Bingham was very good value. He was game for anything.'

He became the school bookmaker. In other words he ran a book, taking other boys' bets, which would then be relayed to 'the town bookmaker, a slight hero of ours'. These were the days before betting shops, legalized in 1961 under the same law that allowed John Aspinall to open the Clermont; the days of bookies' runners, who would go into pubs and factories and collect people's fancies; the days of on-the-hoof betting, when bookmakers were not allowed to have offices, although of course they did. Gambling was not illegal in itself, only gambling premises (the intention being to shoo it on to racetracks). It must have been much more fun before it became what it is now, a cautious corporate business. And John Bingham wanted fun. 'We had a very good time.' He played cards, smoked, drank gin: 'He was much more adventurous than me,' says his friend. 'He would go up to London, and go to a nightclub or whatever.'

But he stood out against getting involved in a sweet coupon racket, planned, in the dying days of rationing, with the dogged precision of Just William and his gang. 'Bingham never thought it would work. He thought we were vulnerable. It was about the only wise thing he ever did.'

Notwithstanding his activities, for any of which he could have been expelled, John Bingham became captain of his house. He had entered a world where a different code applied: where gentlemanly style was the best card in the pack, the one that trumped all his parents' values. As the 11th Duke of Devonshire would later recall, describing his father's complaints about his poor Eton school reports to a fellow company director: 'The man said: "But you surely wouldn't like your son to have good reports, would you?"'[8]

So Lord Bingham stood very firmly against his parents' efforts to remove him from Eton after a year, and send him to a local grammar. From their point of view he no longer needed to be at the school, as he was obviously no longer unhappy; but the reasons for this buoyancy had started to make the Lucans feel that he should leave. 'They were sort of wringing their hands,' as Jane puts it.

Kaitilin, in particular, was fiercely opposed to gambling. It was something for nothing: a reprehensible thing in her eyes and, of course, much of the appeal in a gambler's. Another attraction for John Bingham was the fact that it *was* so reprehensible to his parents. 'And yet he was very fond of them,' says Jane. 'They just disagreed, violently.' His rebellion was not intended to hurt, but it became absolute when his own creed proved to deliver such an intensity of pleasure. Eton had revealed itself to be where he belonged; far more than in that peculiar family house, now replaced with a flat in Regent's Park, but still bustling drearily with Labour Party activity. Gambling was bound up with this rebellion. It was glamorous, anti-socialist, a symbol of life as something thrilling and theatrical, rather than earnest and real. The driving principle of his parents' existence was public service. So John Bingham rebelled against that too. He turned away from his father's conscientiousness, from his grandfather's godly sense of duty: from *noblesse oblige*. His driving principle? 'Well, money, I think. He really wanted to be rich. To do the lovely things of life.'

Before that there was National Service, a duty of a kind. The service had become law in 1948, a *de facto* conscription for all fit young men; it was 'like the steam train, the Teddy boy, and *Mrs Dale's Diary* [an omnipresent radio programme], simply a part of the fabric of everyday life'. A standing army was deemed necessary, given that the Second World War had been instantly replaced with the Cold War, and the still enormous British Empire was revving up fractiously for independence. Every eighteen-year-old, unless in an exempted profession, had to join up for a period of two years. The last of them did not leave until 1963. Youth crime immediately increased; this led to a call for the restoration of National Service that has never quite gone away.

It was said that 'basic training was a great, if short-lived, equalizer of young British males whatever their social origin. It was designed to be "intentionally brutal" for eight to twelve weeks',[9] the usual drills and plank-like beds and gratuitous abusive shouting. John Bingham, accustomed to boarding school, bred into the military, probably found this easier to take than some. Anyway it was a given that the War Selection Board would very soon deem him officer material. While some public schoolboys refused to put themselves forward for elevation, on the grounds that the whole system was ridiculous, he was not of their number. He strode, with his guardsman's bearing, into his father's old regiment, graduating in 1953 from the officers' training school at Eaton Hall in Cheshire (the Duke of Westminster's property) as a second lieutenant in the Coldstreams. He was then posted to Krefeld in West Germany, where the British Army of the Rhine was stationed as a defence against the Soviet threat.

He also played a great deal of poker in the officers' mess. He joined the bobsleigh team. For the first time he went to casinos, which were legal in Germany. A fellow officer recalled:

He was always getting dressed up for dinner and going out to the best hotels when really the rest of us were quite happy to stay in and eat the most filthy food. Quite often he'd hire a car – it was the sort of thing that only John would do – and insist that we all put on our dinner jackets and motor down to the casino at Bad Neuenahr. On one occasion he actually hired a little plane and took three of us to the casinos at Trouville. There he was: sort of devastating to look at and always immaculately turned out.[10]

One of the most superficial, but in fact most important, things about John Bingham was becoming ever more apparent by the mid-1950s: his looks. It is hard to emphasize enough what a determinant factor these were in his life. That formal, well-grown, highly masculine handsomeness may not be to contemporary taste, which prefers the idiosyncratic, the feminized, the wafts of hair tumbling over puppy-dog eyes. Nevertheless he was, objectively, a remarkable physical specimen. As his future wife Veronica would later put it: 'When he woke in the morning and shaved, he must have looked in the mirror and thought: "I am vastly good-looking and I am a Peer of the Realm."'[11] 'Impressive,' says his Eton friend. 'Impressive fellow.' A girl who worked as nanny for his friends, the Maxwell-Scotts, in the late 1960s recalls: 'I thought he was extraordinarily good-looking. He was striking. He looked really scrubbed up all the time, and he was attentive and he gave you eye contact. He stuck out. Not in a sexual way, but I just thought he was a really attractive man.' His looks were already on the turn by the time of his disappearance: men of nearly forty did not, in the 1970s, seek to resemble teenagers, and the boozy, smoky, sedentary lifestyle did not help. In youth, however, he must have been extraordinary to behold. The Lucans are a handsome family, but with the 7th Earl all the elements came together to create something unusual, one of those rare people who look as though an invisible line has been drawn around them, marking them out as unnaturally perfect. That was why the film director Vittorio De Sica saw him instantly as an image on the screen, why Cubby Broccoli saw him as a natural James Bond. 'He really was Marcello Mastroianni,' says his sister, 'he looked seriously like him.' Mastroianni with the Italian filtered out, replaced by essence of earl.

But the looks, which gave John Bingham style, assurance, an awareness that he could attract, a separateness that intrigued both women and men, also worked against him. They made him seem far more profoundly confident than he was. They made him seem arrogant. Later, they would make him an object of loathing.

In the 1950s, however, Lord Bingham could bestride the world of pleasure, living the kind of life of which people feel that they should disapprove, but which few young men would not want to have: *Made in Chelsea* for the Macmillan era.

To his uncle John Bevan, a stockbroker, he wrote:

> I am perfectly happy now (this is to say I am not unhappy), but I know that with £2 mil in the bank I should be happier still (who wouldn't?). It wouldn't be a case of 'buying happiness', but motor cars, yachts, expensive holidays and security for the future would give myself and a lot of other people a lot of pleasure. These are some of my carrots, and I'm certainly not ashamed of them.

As it was, these things had to be paid for, and for the one and only time in his life he had a proper job. His future wife, Veronica, later said that the intention had been to send him to Oxford, 'but his parents were only going to give him enough money to go through university as an average student... so he decided against going there'.[12] This statement is unconfirmed. What definitely happened is that Kait Lucan pulled some strings, desperate to jerk her son back to the path of righteousness, and in 1955 he began work at William Brandt's, a small merchant bank in Fenchurch Street. He wrote to his uncle:

> I have come into the City in an attempt to make my pile. I don't know whether I shall succeed because, in my opinion, it's not just a

question of staring at ledgers. In my opinion the formula for success is as follows:

a) 60% luck
b) 20% industry
c) 20% Gambling ability

Mr Niarchos [the oil magnate] does not agree with me: he believes his success is only 40% luck and 60% hard work. Obviously, there are other requirements, such as an ability to get on well with people, honesty, trustworthiness and all the usual virtues. But taking these for granted, all I ask now is ten times my ration of good luck! It's impossible to qualify for this unless full use is made of (c) on the 'nothing venture, nothing win' theory. Nothing has been ventured in this family since our great-grandfather ran up a grocer's bill of £4,000.

There is something faintly silly about this letter. There is also a kind of uncertainty beneath the pompous, jocular tone: a suggestion that John Bingham is trying to defend what he knows to be folly.

A view of his three-year career at Brandt's, expressed in 1975, by which time people were being as rude about him as possible, was that 'he believed that through eugenics he must be a success, but in fact he was rather a failure. He had, of course, no economic training, but in those days there was some pretty low-grade thinking in the City.'[13] Actually John Bingham had a flair for banking. His uncle, who observed him with fond but clear eyes, thought he could have made a success at it. Even his use of language at Eton, his assessment that the sweet coupon racket was 'vulnerable', implies a financial brain. He would have needed that in gambling, otherwise he would have got through his money infinitely more quickly than he did: folly though it may be, it requires quite a lot of brains. Gambling is all about calculation of risk. Banking is all about gambling. Economic training, as has become grimly clear in the last few years, is not always enough.

His friend from Eton was in the money markets at the time, 'went round to all the banks with my top hat on', and the pair would meet once a week at Fuller's, next door to Brandt's.

> We talked about everything under the sun. He had endless schemes, some of which were good, some of which were not. And he talked about things like cornering the silver market. He thought he could do that. He knew a lot about silver. In fact I used to get him to lunch to talk about silver, he was that good on it.
>
> He was intensely amusing, he was very bright, he knew about markets – I mean, what else do you want, to make it in the City? He had it all. But anyway, he threw all that away...

Before he did, however, he used his £2,500 salary to enjoy himself. And what the patrician Lord Bingham liked more than anything was to go greyhound racing at Harringay. The dogs, popular in the mid-twentieth century to a degree that can hardly now be conceived, was fundamentally a working-class sport, but never only that: the Duke of Edinburgh owned a dog that won the Greyhound Derby. In fact it attracted all classes (not so much the genteel middle), who mingled with a worldly ease that horse racing, ever self-important, has never quite managed. Greyhound racing at the old Olympic stadium at White City was as smart as you like, run by ex-military types, commanding an implicit respect. It was fun, it was adult; and it was gambling, of course. The Clermont regular Charles Benson was at White City all the time in the 1960s and 1970s. Ian Maxwell-Scott, a director of the Clermont, backed himself to win an alcohol-fuelled race around the dog track. John Bingham went occasionally with his Old Etonian friend.

By contrast, the Harringay track in North London was majestically downmarket: a purposeful spotlit theatre of punters clasping their snippets of inside information, fences sidling up to racegoers and offering a glimpse of the diamond in their pocket, bookmakers with country houses in Totteridge, villains drinking convivially with a couple of Scotland Yard policemen. 'Harringay was our place,' says the Eton friend. 'We went there Mondays and Fridays, then worked on Saturdays – the banks were open on Saturday in those days. There was a bloke called Trevor, he was a tic-tac man,[14] and he used to give us a lift home.'

> Bingham had a couple of dogs, as did I. Anyway, one night, we had three runners between us. I had a very good railer, you know, liked the inside of the track. That won at 6/4. He had a hurdler, that won at 11/4. And then we had his dog Sambos Hangover. I remember it was 963 yards, a marathon – the dog was 100/7. And our trainer, Morse, said: 'The favourite in that race has just been given a bucket of water, and has absolutely no chance. And therefore, you know, Sambos Hangover might get a place.' So we did a win treble with Croydon Turf. And we made 300 and something pounds, which was big money in the middle fifties. We were very, very excited. And I remember John going up and being cheered by the bookmakers, you know – it was an absolute skinner for them – and just sort of bowing, left and right, taking the applause.

This was a very long way from Belgravia: not merely in mileage. It was further still from the serious-minded Lucans, with their pamphlets and causes, and further yet from the unbelievably correct 5th Earl of Lucan, whose idea of a decent bet was probably half a crown on Jack Hobbs to get a century at The Oval. His wife Violet, the dowager countess, summoned her grandson to her London flat to deliver a lecture. Yet one has the powerful sense that this was the future Lord Lucan at his happiest: carefree, comfortable with himself, surrounded by people who demanded nothing from him, Sebastian Flyte cut loose from Brideshead Castle. 'We had no money,' says his friend, 'and we had great fun.' The acquaintance who subsequently said that Lucan 'wanted to save England for grouse moors and stately homes' should have thrown in Harringay as well.

After he left Brandt's in 1958, his life became more glamorous, which he also craved; but the tension between duty and pleasure had gone, and with it the necessary sense of structure that he had found at Eton. It was claimed by the former policeman Roy Ranson that John Bingham resigned because 'one of his closest office rivals was promoted over his head'. This is corroborated by John Bevan. There is no evidence for Ranson's assertion that 'the bank's management were worried about [him]'; he would not have been the only posh young City boy whose attentions wandered from his work. Nevertheless he had, as Christina Shand Kydd says, quite quickly become 'bored out of his mind'. He had gone in to make his pile. Where was it? Two thousand five hundred pounds a year was a very good wage in the 1950s, the value of an average house, but he wanted more. Certainly he wanted a more than average house. He wanted Eaton Square, but with proper furniture. His father, with his refusal to manage his money properly, to avoid the earl's curse of death duties, seemed unlikely to deliver. But gambling? That held any and every kind of promise. 'The sort of gambling we're talking about was tied up with an easy life,' says Stuart Wheeler. 'Very different from going into a betting shop, you know.' Lord Bingham became friendly with the stockbroker Stephen Raphael, an older man who, says Christina, 'became his mentor. He very much took John under his wing. And taught him everything he knew about how to gamble.' This was fatal, really, since it gave an appearance that gambling could be managed, manipulated; which it can, but only up to a point. 'It became his job,' says his sister Jane. 'I don't know that he knew it was ridiculous. I think he was very confident of his skills.' He was a modern figure, in a sense: in search of instant gratification, excitably bypassing the processes of cause and effect. In another sense he was as modern as Stonehenge. The paradox therein would eventually prove impossible to reconcile.

It is usually claimed that he left his job because of one, incredible win of £26,000, but this merely confirmed a decision that had already been taken. His Eton friend recalls:

> He said, 'I can make £2,500 every night, or lose £2,500 every night
> – there's absolutely no point in going on working for William

Brandt.' We tried very hard to persuade him not to leave. But he couldn't see that any of us would get to the top, in the City. Least of all him. The City was very difficult to break through, but so is everywhere. You've just got to be patient, find a way. He thought it was not worth it. He thought that he could outwit the competition at gambling instead. I just think he was very short-sighted. Because he had the whole world at his feet, really.

In the five years between leaving his job and his wedding, John Bingham lived like the young lord that he was. He had humour, vigour, a straightforward joy in his youthful existence. No money: boundless hope. If his parents 'wrung their hands', there was absolutely nothing that they could do. 'I don't know', says Jane, 'how many long and hard discussions there were about it. I'm sure it was an issue, because they were so totally on the other side. But they would have said, probably, if it makes him happy...'

What was important was the sense that the times were with him then, as they would not be later. The cloak of austerity had been cast aside, the Conservatives were back in government, the heavy shadow of the atomic bomb gave a *carpe diem* edge to pleasure. The 1960s, with its skimpy finery, its knock-kneed nymphets and pill-popping mods, had not yet replaced smartness, suits tailored to the last eighth of an inch, 'model box' handbags, Terry-Thomas dashers and Kay Kendall girls. Fifties socialites looked like adults and behaved like hedonists, but hedonists who followed certain conventions: their spiritual home remained the Royal Enclosure at Ascot. The threat of levelling tendencies, the encroachment of Lucky Jim Dixon and Arthur Seaton, would not have impinged. *Look Back in Anger* would have been a fashionable, perhaps slightly boring couple of hours within the evening – 'Went on a bit, didn't he, that chap?' – cleansed away by a supper on the King's Road and some jovial barking among one's own kind.

The summer Season, which today has become italicized, even ironized, by self-awareness, was a simple fact of life. The coronation of Queen Elizabeth II was an intensely serious business. The last debutantes were presented in 1957, but the girls in white dresses had gone out in high style; the novelist Angela Huth, one of the penultimate group of debs, recalled that 'in those three months I went to ninety-six balls in the most beautiful houses, where fortunes were spent on flowers – £1,500 at one house – so I will never forget the scent of gardenias. It was wonderful fun... We gave lots of dinners at our house – Lord Lucan was one guest...'[15]

John Bingham was firmly in the eyeline of any mother looking for a catch. Nancy Mitford's Lady Montdore, obsessed with marrying off her daughter, would have noted his louche tendencies but still have put him near the top of her list. 'He had', says his Eton friend, 'a lot of very nice girlfriends in those days. Platonic, you know. People like Caroline Hill [sister to his friend Robin, the future 8th Marquess of Downshire]. They were so fond of him, in a platonic way. You trusted him, and he was fun, one of those sort.' He was said to have been bedazzled by Lady Zinnia Judd, whose magnificent looks were a match for his own, but marriage was somehow never a likelihood; not with her, nor any of the well-bred fillies who trotted his way. He could have found a conventional *Country Life* girl, or a staggeringly gorgeous girl, or a girl so rich that he need never again go to work at Harringay dog track. But he didn't. 'He was a bit of a loner, really,' says Christina Shand Kydd. Later he was called a 'playboy', but that is not quite accurate. He was also said to have been part of a 'Chelsea set', a bunch of self-conscious young fortune-hunters who longed to be seen as cads, like Kim Waterfield, owner of the first 'mobile' telephone, perched massively in his car and with the call sign HEIRESS. But that was not Lord Bingham's thing either. He did his own thing. He was, in fact, what the cads yearned to be.

Heir to an earldom, after all. Pat Lucan may have disguised himself as a civil servant but his son assumed the façade of what he actually was: an aristocrat. It was rebellion against his parents again, albeit of the perverse kind that sends the rebel strutting defiantly

93

into White's. In the face of Pat's exposure of the iniquitous 3rd Earl of Lucan, his son displayed a certain proud pleasure in his ancestor. 'We had a bit of the Crimea, the six hundred in the valley of death, we had a bit of that,' says his friend.[16] Yet there was something else to this resumption of the nobleman's mien. Nobody, but nobody, ever looked more like an earl than John Bingham. So he lived up to his own image of what an earl was, in an age when an earl was no longer really anything. To do otherwise would have been a waste, a folly, like running a thoroughbred in a donkey derby. Appearance was destiny.

Obviously he did not consciously think this. But the way in which he was treated, the frisson that he created when he walked into a casino, the endless stream of tributes to his looks, could not have left him unaware. In 1966 he got the call from De Sica to star in *Woman Times Seven*, a sophisticated sex comedy whose male cast would eventually include Peter Sellers and Michael Caine. His friend recalls:

> One day he rang me up and said, I'm going to Paris. What are you doing in Paris? He said, well, I'm going to star in a major film. So I said: Elaborate, please. He said, Shirley MacLaine is the star, and it's the seven men in her life, and I am the archetypal English gentleman. And it'll probably be a very large fee. Anyway, I'm looking forward to it.
>
> So he rings up a few days later, and I said how did Paris go? He said: Disaster. I sat on a sofa, with Shirley MacLaine, and I couldn't speak. He was very funny about it. Very disappointed, he'd been keen to do it, but amused. He just knew, from the moment he sat on the sofa, that it was no-go.

Nevertheless, to have been asked in the first place, and by a man of refined visual taste, who had directed the classic film *Bicycle Thieves*, was an extraordinary thing. It says everything about how John Bingham, by then Lord Lucan, must have looked.

In 1960 he left his parents' home and took a flat in nearby Park Crescent, the creamy curving Nash terrace opposite Regent's Park.

He drove a drophead Aston Martin coupé – 'He was a very fast driver, and totally unflappable,' says his friend – which in those days, in the London before road restrictions at every turn, was a buzz in itself. He motored down the west coast of America. He skied and bobsleighed at St Moritz. He did the Cresta Run, rather well. He travelled to the glittering casinos of Deauville and Monte Carlo, but his gambling was not yet confined within the walls of a club. For all that John Bingham called himself a 'professional gambler', it was a role that he was playing as much as a reality. When one is very young, and healthy, and on good terms with life, one does tend to play roles, shedding the consequences as if they were costumes. The fact that a role may become a reality does not occur.

Gambling was an adjunct to pleasure, not pleasure itself. His friend recalls:

> He told me that I was looking incredibly pale. This was late 1958. He said you've got to come out with a group of us and get some sun, and do the Cresta, and that we could finance the entire venture by playing ping-pong in the Palace Hotel. He said, what you have to do is to play badly for three or four nights, and then play well. Unfortunately the Italian fellow we decided to take for a ride – he was doing exactly the same thing. And we got conned. And quite right too.

The naivety, of thinking that he could pull off this classic sting, that the other fellow wouldn't have thought to do it also, is typical. For all John Bingham's apparent cool, he was very much an innocent abroad. His hapless boyish exuberance was later hidden beneath a hardened veneer, but in fact remained oddly intact: he was always there to be taken for a ride.

On another occasion he went out to America and backed himself at golf. His grandfather had played into old age, and he himself had a handicap of fourteen.

> He thought that he could get out of a bunker, and chip the ball, and guarantee to get down in two. I mean, world-famous people can't

do that. But he went off. He had lent me £1000, as I was pushed for cash. And he sent me a telegram after about three weeks saying 'Things have not worked out as expected. Please if convenient, but only if convenient, credit my account in Old Broad St with £1000' ... I mean, another financial disaster.

But perhaps his greatest passion was powerboat racing, physically exhilarating with the speed, the bash of hard salt spray, the ozone and the danger circling one's head. 'He was absolutely convinced he was going to win the *Daily Express* powerboat race.' This was a 170-mile contest from Cowes, on the Isle of Wight, to Torquay.

It was going to cost £7,000 to build the boat, which was a lot of money in those days [1963], and so he said to me, how can I raise £7,000? I happened to know a man at the National and Provincial Bank, and he had lent me some money, unsecured. I said, it's worth putting this proposition to him. Anyway he raised £10,000.

The boat, *White Migrant*, was built by Bruce Colin Campbell, who was based at the Hamble near Southampton. John Bingham ran the boat from the marina at the Hamble and, it was later said, from Newhaven.

And when this powerboat race took place, I went to Lord's for the day, and on the placard for the *Evening Standard* at lunchtime it said 'Surprise Leader in Powerboat Race'. The stop press said that Bingham was leading, quite comfortably, in a high-class field. And he led for four or five hours. And then sank. I came out of the cricket about 6.30 and it said: 'Powerboat Sinks'. Well I didn't even have to look to see...

White Migrant had overtaken the rest at the start, like a superior car in a Grand Prix. It sank just west of The Needles. John Bingham and his boat-builder were picked up, unhurt, by a retired boat.

They marked where he went down with a buoy, and the next day, when the insurance assessors sent their person down, there was no trace of the boat. They looked around the whole area and they couldn't find it. Wasn't a trace of it. And they said that the cross currents there, and in many places in the Channel, are so strong that they destroy anything.

And therefore I'm convinced that he went over, into the sea. After the event, you know.

The powerboat race had ended for John Bingham on 8 September 1963. Twelve weeks later, on 28 November, he married. On 21 January 1964, aged twenty-nine, he became the 7th Earl of Lucan. His gambling, from this point, grew ever more remorseless. The carefree life was over.

The Clermont

'It's a pleasure to lose it, by God!'

GEORGE PAYNE, EARLY NINETEENTH-CENTURY GAMBLER,
AFTER LOSING £40,000 ON THE ROLLS OF TWO DICE

IN FACT IT was quite natural, traditional, for earls to gamble. In the days when they had everything, only gambling represented a challenge: the thing that would not yield to their touch. It was this aristocratic ideal that John Aspinall sought to reconstruct at the Clermont Club, which opened in 1962, with John Bingham as one of its founder members.

The club was at 44 Berkeley Square, where had once stood the house of the 1st Earl of Clermont. He, like Lord Lucan, was a gambling earl, although the age in which Lord Clermont lived was far more suited to the breed. During the eighteenth and early nineteenth centuries, much of the aristocracy moved between horse races and gentlemen's clubs as if under a spell, hypnotized into a desire to squander all that they owned. 'Society', wrote the historian Trevelyan, 'was one vast casino.' On Newmarket Heath, then the open-air playground of the nobility, the equivalent of millions was gambled on match races between two horses. In 1757 the Earl of March, later the 4th Duke of Queensberry, rode his own horse and backed himself to win £1,000, rather as Lord Bingham would later back himself to win a bobsleigh race (and fell flat on his face ten yards in: 'He came back grinning from ear to ear,' his friend recalls). In the same era the 3rd Duke of Grafton gave the fullness of his attention to racing, and was prime minister on the side. He procured a pension of £500 per annum from the Treasury for a friend who had lost his fortune on the horses; the code of the club, applied to the country. Earl Ferrers, the last aristocrat to be tried and convicted of murder, owned a racing stud and gambled heavily. In the 1780s Charles James Fox, the most gifted politician of his age and a friend of the 1st Earl of Lucan, set up a stable in Newmarket with a friend who lost £100,000 on the enterprise. Fox himself pulled off one giant win of £16,000, which he instantly gambled away. By the end he had squandered a vast inheritance, and half-ruined the friends who had loaned him money.

The betting book at Brooks's, the club that 200 years later would be bombed by the IRA, records a succession of gentlemanly equivalents to the cockroach race across the floor of a prison cell: '50 guineas that Mlle. Heinel does not dance at the opera house next winter...' Ian Maxwell-Scott, a close associate of John Aspinall and actually a worse gambler than his friend Lord Lucan, would bet in that way, on two flies on a wall, two raindrops on a window. 'He was a chronic gambler, he really was,' says his then driver. 'I can remember being at that house one day,' says the former nanny to his children, 'when he won £127,000 on the horses, and we had jam for tea. But I can also remember being there when he lost huge sums of money. And Susie [his wife] screaming at him one night, why the fuck don't you just play backgammon?'

But to win, and to lose, was the mark of a gentleman. In the 1770s a man left Brooks's with £12,000, not realizing, or wanting to realize, that he was meant to stay and get rid of it. Beside his name in the club book was written: 'That he may never return is the ardent wish of the members.' Men of the proper kind did not slope off smugly into the night with full pockets. 'Who *was* that chap?' the 18th Earl of Derby would later say at the Clermont, after losing £200,000 to the Fiat boss, Gianni Agnelli, who had 'cut and run'.

Charles James Fox was the greatest casualty of gambling, in that he had the most to lose; not just money, but the life of achievement that he never quite fulfilled. There were others, however, like the Honourable Berkley Craven, who lost heavily on the 1836 Derby. A contemporary account described how he 'returned to his house in

Connaught Terrace, flung himself on a sofa, and later shot himself with a duelling pistol. His liabilities, about £8,000, were trifling [sic]. His friends would have paid them, had they known.'[1]

When, in the early hours of 8 November 1974, Lord Lucan's mentor Stephen Raphael heard that the police had broken into his friend's home, his immediate thought was that Lucan had killed himself because of gambling debts. In fact one never really had to pay up, except under threat of moral dishonour (in other circles there would have been the threat of physical harm, but that didn't apply at the Clermont). There was nothing in law to say that a gambling debt was enforceable; the Gaming Act of 1845 actually specified that it was *not* enforceable. This did not change until as recently as 2005, which means that throughout the whole of John Aspinall's career, when he was acting as Lord High Executioner to the aristocratic bank account, nobody need ever have paid him what they owed.

One evening in the mid-1960s, a Clermont regular, who was then in his twenties, was playing chemin-de-fer with a friend. John Aspinall and Ian Maxwell-Scott were also at the table, together with Aspinall's mother Lady Osborne, 'the Chancellor's granny,[2] who was as bent as a corkscrew. She was bliss. She always wore a wig, and when she got smashed, which was most nights, the wig would always go off at one side.' The chemmy game began:

> And suddenly my friend and I were down £100,000. It goes up very quickly – £8,000, £16,000, £32,000 – you only have to run about eight times. The whole thing happens in seconds. I lost £50,000 in one night, which in those days would buy a street in London – I hadn't got it. And I practically became suicidal, and I went for a walk down by the Thames and thought of throwing myself in. I got rescued by Andrew Parker-Bowles [former husband of Camilla, Duchess of Cornwall] at about six in the morning, which was very nice of him. And what was quite amusing, my friend and I had both lost a fortune, and all that my friend said was, How very tiresome, let me write you out a cheque...

But my father went to see Aspinall after I lost, tried to negotiate with him. If I'd had half a brain I would have just said to him, fuck off. You can't, though...

People paid, just as their forebears had paid. Aspinall was prepared to wait, because he too was a gentleman, but when a young aristocrat went to the club with a gang of heavies, saying he refused to settle a debt of £28,000, Aspinall coolly faced him down.

'One nice man lost a wonderful estate,' says the Clermont gambler. 'He owned one of those big estates in north Yorkshire, and his father had made it over to him a year or two before. It was a proper stately home – they had lived there for generations. Anyway he blew the lot. I mean, it was just awful. There were people wiped out, totally wiped out.'

The gamblers of the Georgian and Regency years, who lost the equivalent of hundreds of millions in a night, had done so with a kind of fine, hilarious flourish. Their behaviour was stark staring mad, but they had enjoyed it in their way, just as Lord Bingham had enjoyed standing on the stone steps at Harringay dogs, beneath the warm creamy lights of the stadium, amid the infinite vitality, the jabbering of '9/4 the field', the frenetic clockwork arms of Trevor the tic-tac man. 'It's a pleasure to lose it, by God' could have been his battle cry, as he chucked carefree fivers into the hands of the bookmakers. There was a lonelier, grimmer determination about his later gambling, as there would be in a particular aristocrat of the later nineteenth century.

Lord Hastings lost £120,000 on the 1867 Derby, and got no pleasure from it at all. In order to pay the debt, and the £79,000 that he had lost in one night at cards, he had to sell his Scottish estate. Yet after the Derby he had been the first to pat the winning horse, Hermit, on the neck. 'Hermit fairly broke my heart,' he said as he was dying, 'but I never showed it, did I?'

Never show it: that is the code. As important, or more so, than paying up. There was no surer sign of breeding than to maintain one's insouciance with the hounds of hell nipping at one's tailored shoulders. Lord Lucan, it was later said by the 11th Duke of Devonshire, also a Clermont gambler, 'had the most beautiful manners when he gambled at Aspinall's. He never showed emotion at any time.'[3] Thus the aristocratic façade became, by degrees, a mask. It was better that way. When Lord Hastings lost a further £50,000 at Newmarket in 1867, his knees visibly buckled; he pulled himself together immediately, but in that brief moment of collapse the whole mighty edifice of illusion had been threatened.

Through 1868 Hastings flailed like a man in quicksand, just as Lucan would a century later: pawning, mortgaging, selling, borrowing from a moneylender. He was hooted as a defaulter by the bookmakers, to whom he owed some £40,000. It was said that 'the once magnificent plunger could not now go beyond a pony [£25], and even when he ventured that modest sum he was brutally told by the bookmaker with whom he made the bet, "Now, mind, I'm to be *paid* this."'[4] Hastings died at the age of twenty-six, cause unknown. One could only say that gambling had killed him, and that he had somehow wanted it to do so. The embodiment of etiolated aristocracy, he seems to have felt that nothing was worth pursuing except the end of everything. It was as though he did not know how to live up to what he could have been. So he played the endgame of gambling what he did not have. It was an escape: from everything. Although it took all that he had, in a strange way it demanded nothing from him.

Gambling is not, of course, merely an aristocratic pleasure. Nor is there necessarily anything louche about it; to many people it is a perfectly normal thing to do, something that puts a bit of savour in the stew of life. There are many ways of being a gambler, just as there are of being a drinker. And not all gambling is foolish, by any means. A person who can assess risk, or better still has inside information, is as likely to win at gambling as at many other kinds of financial scheme or job. When Lord Lucan's old friend says that 'he thought he could outwit the competition', there is a kind of logic to that idea. As Dostoevsky wrote in *The Gambler*: 'One must win at gambling if one can only remain calm and calculating. That's all it is. If one does that, then one cannot lose – one has to win.' Not win every time – that isn't possible – but win overall. The passage continues, however: 'But how can the person who knows this secret find the strength and understanding to use it well?' And therein, for a gambler like Lucan, lies the problem.

Gambling does not have to be an addiction, any more than drinking does. It can be a habit, but a harmless one; as drinking can. It is perfectly possible to gamble every day, even to lose every day, and, so long as this is affordable, there is no issue. It is merely a pleasure, incomprehensible to some; like drinking. But what begins as pleasure can become, for those whose personality is made that way, an addiction of a different kind, what a racing man of the nineteenth century called 'the pace that kills'.

Gambling *is* a pleasure. There is no feeling quite like it. Even the hard-headed, the people who will restrain themselves to one enormous as-near-as-dammit-certainty bet in a year, are doing it for the pleasure. There are different ways of feeling this: some like the conviviality, some the self-absorption, some the simple fun. Some are entranced by the atmosphere. Some are showing off. Some enjoy the helplessness, the sense that fate is carrying them away from the responsibility of living. Any of these can be part of the pleasure. Always, though, a gambler is making a secret communion with the future: treating the future as something that they can manipulate, a moment that they can control and own. Beneath it all, this is the real joy of gambling. The future becomes yours. You make of it your own plaything. You feel it becoming a possibility, then – the purest sensation of all – feel the smooth little slip in time when you know that possibility must become certainty. When the other cards are being played and you know that your own must be the winner. That is what John Bingham would have felt, in the merry-making days at Harringay, when he watched a dog come round the bend, paws outstretched lovingly towards him; when he had asserted the belief that something would happen, and it did. Such power! Such happiness!

But the superman surge of strength has its opposite: the sensation of weakness, manifested physically by Lord Hastings in the stands at Newmarket, when the future doesn't do what has been asked of it. Then comes danger. This is the moment of crux. The desire to recapture strength can become a need. In Lord Hastings it was more powerful than his desire to live. Unless a gambler can accept the natural to-and-fro of win and loss, addiction will follow: addiction of the gut-gripping kind. Equally dangerous is the fact that, for a gambler of the besotted kind, every day is a new day, in a way that it isn't quite for other people. Every evening begins a new story. If it ends badly, another one will start tomorrow. So there is no need to stop, because there is always a new beginning. Anything could happen. Anything is possible. It is delusional, and it is also true.

A professional, which is what John Bingham decided to become after resigning from Brandt's, is a subspecies of gambler. Although there are people with the self-restraint to make a success of it, they are rare. More usually the delusions are strongest with this type of gambler, because he believes that he is in control.

In fact John Bingham could never have become a professional gambler. That was not the aristocratic mindset that he had chosen to enter. It would have been too much like the man who left Brooks's with everybody else's £12,000: bad form. As Stephen Raphael had taught him, he did have control when he played bridge at the Portland Club, or poker at the Hamilton Club. When he played blackjack, which he believed gave the best odds of success, he had a degree of control. When he climbed the golden staircase at the Clermont to play chemin-de-fer, a game of almost pure chance, with an incredibly high return and an equally high risk, he had scarcely any control at all.

The only truly 'professional' gambler is the connoisseur of probability, who makes a few per cent per annum, never loses more than he has chosen to lose and walks away when he has won. Calm and calculating, as Dostoevsky had it. Of course his gambler, like Dostoevsky himself, is the very opposite. This is Alexis Ivanovich playing at roulette, the least controlled game of the lot:

> I think about four hundred *friedrichs d'or* came into my possession in some five minutes. I ought to have left at that point, but a strange sort of feeling came over me, a kind of desire to challenge fate, a longing to give it a fillip on the nose or stick out my tongue at it. I staked the permitted maximum – 4,000 gulden – and lost. Then, getting excited, I pulled out all I had left, staked it in the same way, lost again, and after that left the table as if I had been stunned. I could not even grasp what had happened to me...

And then Alexis needs to win. Has to win. And that, for the gambler, is the most dangerous state of all. All gambling is working at play, but gambling to win is work, pure and simple. Eventually Lord Lucan would realize as much. By then he would be trapped, at the Clermont, in the aristocratic ideal of the gambling earl: a pointless way of being what had become pointless.

Happily for John Aspinall, who gathered in the greater part of the wages that Lucan worked to earn. Aspinall began life as a gambler, and understood the breed as well as he understood the tigers that he would rear at his private zoos in Kent. Tigers, although vulnerable as a species, are predators, and Aspinall understood that too. At the same time one has to say that he didn't force anybody to gamble their money away. The choice was theirs. But Aspinall knew how to make that choice seem a desirable, even an inevitable one.

With the Clermont Club, which he opened in 1962, he created a world unto itself where, as he himself put it, 'gentlemen could ruin themselves as elegantly and suicidally as did their ancestors three hundred years ago'. It was fantastically clever. In an age that threatened egalitarianism, he created a kind of superb bunker against the times. He also, more subtly, created a stage set. He understood that too much reality is bad for gamblers, and that what they crave is a deliberately heightened atmosphere: an objective correlative, as it were, to the tumult within. Most of the Clermont regulars, who were far from stupid, would have realized perfectly well that John Aspinall had created a construct, a fine replica of the eighteenth century, where the ghosts of the Earls of March and Barrymore (who squandered a £300,000 inheritance) could rise into the air and command them to lose like gentlemen. But that was how they liked it. As surely as racecourse gamblers thrill to the sounds of hooves and bookmakers, so the Clermont gamblers swooned a little as they stepped into the entrance hall, and felt the onrush of that sublime dramatic tension.

Aspinall, born in 1926, was of uncertain origins, conceived out of wedlock under a tamarind tree in Uttar Pradesh. 'You must be one of Polly's' was his father's greeting when Aspinall tracked him down. Although his mother later married a baronet – Lieutenant Colonel Sir George Osborne – there was perhaps a sense in which Aspinall relished both joining, and undermining, a class slightly higher than his own. His confidence was immense, but also aggressive. He felt most comfortable with the fabulous wildlife that he bred at Howletts and Port Lympne zoos: tigers, gorillas, black rhinos, elephants, cloudy leopards. There have been five fatalities at the zoos, but there is no denying the immense value of Aspinall's conservation work, nor his extraordinary bond with some of these magnificent creatures.

His passion for wildlife has been deemed to sit alongside a contempt for people, or at least those people who did not, in his view, match up to the splendour of animals. It probably did give him a kick to suck money from the foolish rich and recycle it into Bendicks mints for his gorillas ('If I give them cheap chocolate, they know'). But the connection between his zoos and his casinos was simpler, really. Both needed a man of his boldness behind them. He was a force, an adventurer. There are still men in this country like John Aspinall, but most of them were born somewhere in the former Soviet Union.

His charm is rarely disputed. He was great fun. Nevertheless, says one of the Clermont gamblers, 'Aspinall was a completely amoral man. He really was, by definition.' 'I sort of *quite* liked him,' says Stuart Wheeler. 'He was an amusing character and everything, but people say he was very ruthless about allowing young men to gamble far more heavily than they could afford, on the basis that their parents would cough up.'

He was William Crockford, in fact, the man who established London's first gaming club in the 1820s, where the Duke of Wellington was a founding member. Crockford's later moved to Carlton House Terrace, behind Pall Mall. Lucan would sometimes attend with his friend from Eton, who says: 'I was never trusted to gamble at the Clermont [Aspinall knew exactly what every member was good for]. Crockford's was a smaller market – relatively small. Huge, from my point of view. My salary was £750 a year in the 1950s – not really even a living wage. So the gambling had to be kept under control. But in John's case it just wasn't kept under control.'

Crockford, the son of a fishmonger, collected debts with the glee of an illegal car clamper, and cheated with a bare-faced rapacity. He was despised by the aristocracy, but in the late Georgian era he held them in his thrall. So too, in the 1960s, did a villain called Charlie Taylor. He would spend evenings collecting clueless young lords for his own games, rounding them up from the chemin-de-fer table at Crockford's, where, as his grand-daughter later wrote, 'he had already nobbled the croupier (a batch of cards was inserted into the dealer's shoe, who then dealt them in the order in which Charlie had memorised them). Unsurprisingly, Charlie kept winning, thereby dragging his upper-class marks into his debt. They didn't care...'[5] William Crockford would have approved. Taylor was a man after his own heart. Many years later it was alleged that John Aspinall had, throughout the 1960s, played a similar ongoing trick at the Clermont. His former associate, an Irishman called John Burke, claimed that the cards in the chemmy games had been minutely bent by a machine.[6] The bends denoted whether they were high or low, a key factor in a game where the winning card is the one closest to a value of nine ('*J'ai neuf*' is the cool cry of triumph). Readers trained in spotting the bends were then seated at the tables; although the scam was not flawless, the bends being so tiny, it was said to have given the Clermont a 60–40 edge. It was also said that on the first night it was tried, it earned a clear £14,000 for the club.

The man who in the mid-1960s lost £50,000 in one night at chemmy, ten losing hands in succession, says:

> I'm not saying that game was fixed, because I was a very small
> fellow. But when I went in that night I'd had twelve winning nights
> in a row. So I had accumulated quite a bit of money. I went in, and
> they hadn't started the game – and it was interesting, because Ian
> Maxwell-Scott was sitting at number one, which he never did nor-
> mally, Aspinall was at number two and Lady Osborne was at number
> three or something. And when I sat down, I thought to myself, I've
> never seen you all congregate like this... So I did wonder if that was
> a bent shoe. And when Andrew Devonshire and John Derby and Bill
> Stirling were playing for megabucks, it looked very much as though
> they were taken for a ride. And we all thought so at the time, that it
> was very odd how they would consistently lose.

Conversely Lady Annabel Goldsmith, whose second husband James was a Clermont gambler, firmly denied the allegations against Aspinall.[7] And Victor Lownes, head of the British arm of the Playboy business that bought the Clermont in 1972, says: 'I'll tell you, nobody ever said anything against his operation to us when we inherited it. I sent people over from the Playboy to run it – but we kept most of the staff on, and nobody ever told us anything about any bent cards or anything.'

John Burke's story of Aspinall's 'Big Edge' therefore remains uncorroborated. In a sense one might say that Aspinall had no need to do it, because as everybody knows the house always wins. Yet he most definitely cheated on one occasion, during a 1967 chemmy game in which the players included James Goldsmith, Cubby

Broccoli, the 18th Earl of Derby, Lord Lucan, Bill Stirling (brother of David) and an American billionaire named Emmett Blow. This time the cards were falling the other way, with Lord Derby up by more than £1 million. Suddenly Blow blew: he vomited prodigiously over the table. As cloths were wielded the players sat stunned, waiting to recommence, when Aspinall marched towards them in the manner of Marcadé at the end of *Love's Labour's Lost*. Blow, he announced, was dead. The game was *fini*. There was nothing to do but descend the little spiral staircase at the back of the entrance hall that took one down to Annabel's nightclub, and obliterate thoughts of the splendid game cut down in its prime. On the handkerchief-sized dance floor at Annabel's was Emmett Blow, jigging away in the fullness of health. Aspinall was superbly unabashed. 'When a man is down £1.5 million, he must take desperate measures,' he declared.[8]

It was, of course, the other players who owed Lord Derby: Lucan had retired owing £15,000; Blow himself owed £100,000. The point was that they would not have to pay immediately, and Aspinall would. And it was not so easy, he would have said, holding on to cash. He could not take a cut of the game unless he himself won (later it became illegal for proprietors to play). He could only charge a 'table fee'. Furthermore his earnings were taxed, as they had not been in the fiery, pre-Gaming Act days, when he had amassed great mountains of unkoshered notes by staging chemmy games in private houses.

It was in the 1950s that Aspinall changed guise from gambler to ringmaster. At Oxford he had cut his finals to attend the Ascot Gold Cup, at which he won, but having lost £300 at his first evening of chemin-de-fer he realized that the surest means to riches was to run the game himself. He wasn't the only person doing this, but nobody did it better. The then Lord Bingham was not a *habitué* of Aspinall's illegal parties, although naturally he knew about them. He was busy bobsleighing and boating, out in the good fresh air. Only later did he fully enter that closer, closeted world.

The chemmy evenings began at the Ritz, where Aspinall was living hand to mouth with his fellow Oxonian Ian Maxwell-Scott.

The first proper party, at which Maxwell-Scott provided the booze and Lady Osborne ('Al Capone with a shopping basket'[9]) cooked game pie, was held in a Brook Street flat with a Canaletto on the wall, hired from a nearby gallery: such was John Aspinall's chutzpah. The parties quickly became the hottest ticket in London. The way to evade the 1845 law against 'gaming houses' was continually to move venue, so Aspinall and his friends would dash from place to place (always within the sacred postcodes), just as people today would use social media to dictate where, on a given night, a club will be enjoying its brief, bright, firefly life as the acme of hipness. There was a sense of being in the know that was quite irresistible, and that Aspinall would have got an irresistible buzz from controlling. One can imagine the ringing phone, the self-important hushed delivery of the message – 'Aspers is at Sloane Court West tonight' – and then the descent of the gorgeous prey into the hands of their shaman. Did Lord Derby and co. know about the dark underside of these gambling evenings? Aspinall himself was prey to protection racketeers, who hovered around the stately venues with their glinting grins and their 'Now then, Johnny boy, let's have a little bit of what you're having...' Men like Charlie Taylor and the Krays would have respected him; they had seen the same gap in the market, after all. Aspinall was no upper-class mug, to use gambling parlance. He was as tough as they come. If the story of the 'Big Edge' is true, then the idea was given to him by Billy Hill, one of the worst mobsters in London. So Aspinall would have known that there was no defence against men of this kind, who had high-end police in their pockets. Anyway he could afford to spare them something. In three nights of parties he earned £20,000, and moved to Eaton Place with a tiger, a Himalayan bear and a capuchin monkey. In 1956–7, he made £350,000, and opened his first zoo at Howletts.

Then he began staging parties at his mother's flat at Hyde Park Street. This was a mistake; it lay within the jurisdiction of the Paddington police, less inclined to turn a blind eye than their counterparts in SW1. Or perhaps Aspinall didn't care. In January 1958, he was finally caught in the act by an inspector who had 'clung to the grille' outside the dining-room window, there to observe the cards rippling sweetly from the chemmy shoe. The policeman accused Aspinall of keeping a 'common gaming house'. Aspinall replied: 'What right have you to come breaking in here like this and start searching people?' His mother, still more in character, suggested that there had been nothing common about the house until the inspector arrived. Among the guests present – 'all intimate friends of mine,' declared Aspinall – were a young scion of the Hoare banking family, a relation of the Devonshires, Lord Willoughby de Eresby, John Burke and Aspinall's stunningly beautiful model wife, Jane (whom he would later divorce, alleging that she had made free with one of his chimpanzee keepers).

After the bust, sixteen people were bound over. Aspinall, his mother and Burke were committed for trial. With a straight face, their QC proclaimed: 'There is no shred of evidence to suggest that anybody even played a game of patience.' At any rate there was insufficient evidence of illegality. The case was dismissed. The law, it was tacitly admitted, had become an absurdity. It had been that, really, from the first, as evidenced by the 1868 prosecution of a book-maker for using a position beneath a tree in Hyde Park as his 'office'. If gambling was legal, then gambling premises had to be legal also. If Aspinall could be arrested, then so too could the organizer of a church-hall whist drive with a ten-shilling kitty. From the moment that his trial ended, the 1960 Betting and Gaming Act was inevitable. It was known, colloquially, as 'Aspinall's Law'. The Clermont was not the first casino – that was in a boat on the Thames – but for the next ten years it would be the best, and for that reason the most dangerous. 'Aspers', one of his club regulars would later say, 'did more damage to the landed gentry than Marx and Lenin put together.'

Today, forty years after the disappearance of its most notorious member, the Clermont is seen through a haze of excitable puri-tanism; as a dark and disreputable vortex of sin, where rich people behaved with the unaccountable carelessness of an age that was past, but not yet dead. It is all part of the Lucan myth, that aristocratic murder should have brewed and been concealed within that sinister palace. It is not quite the truth, of course.

After all, rich people still gamble in casinos, although both the people and the casinos are now very different. The gamblers are mostly foreign. The casinos are, on the whole, quite wilfully dull, their atmosphere remarkable only for being atmosphere-free, like boardrooms full of business people who have taken the Trappist vow, so must conduct their affairs through a minimalist sign language. Nobody drinks or smokes or does anything to break the metronomic click-and-flip of chips and cards. This shows gambling at its truest, perhaps, as an activity of deadly pointlessness. Yet the Clermont, tricked out with all the loveliness human beings can devise – art, amusement, women, food, wine – could create an illusion that gambling was the best possible way of spending one's life.

It is this, the fact that the Clermont lent so much glamour to vice, that now makes it seem peculiarly pernicious. It was a very beautiful place. It still is. The house was built in the 1740s for Lady Isabella Finch, a daughter of the Earl of Winchilsea (as she was unmarried there was only one main bedroom, with a mirror placed precisely so that she could see the arrivals in the hall below). The architect, William Kent, created something Italianate, a neat *palazzo* painted in reds and pinks, a gilded jewel box hidden inside solid London stone; as if, when the great black front door opens, one might see Lady Isabella revolving to the sound of a spinet. It is infinitely civilized, as the eighteenth century could be. Opulence, restrained by good taste. The rooms are shaped with absolute refinement. Downstairs, a small lobby leads to a bar on the left. To the right is the golden, fairy-tale, freestanding staircase down which Aspinall once led a pet tiger cub, which then roamed around the gamblers, purring with all the fearsome amiability of its owner. Beyond are the 'light' gambling rooms, relaxed and easeful, for games like backgammon that do not take away a man's fortune. There is the restaurant, red-draped and intimate, where Lord Lucan sat at the far corner; like Lady Isabella, he had a perfect view of who was coming in. Outside is a small flagstoned garden, with the sounds of London close by yet irrelevant.

It was upstairs, in the cube-shaped saloon, that the chemmy table stood beneath lofty ceilings with painted panels and a chandelier of immense, gorgeous, weighty complexity. Lives were wrecked in this room, yet no malaise hovers. The surprising thing about the Clermont is that it feels uplifting rather than doom-laden. More miniature Brighton Pavilion than Hellfire Club. It is not hard to understand why people wanted to go there. It feels like a house, still: a house belonging to a wonderfully rich friend who has welcomed you in to play your favoured, adult games, and who, so long as you remain inside, will protect you.

But to describe how it really was is near impossible, because people perceived it differently. One knows that everybody drank and smoked and looked smart as paint. This was the 1960s, but most people still used the legal high rather than the illicit, and dressed like adults rather than Jimi Hendrix. One knows, too, some of the things that John Aspinall did there. He had extraordinarily good food and wine, and in the days before it became illegal would encourage his gamblers to drink hard at the tables: 'He liked you to get lit up,' says a Clermont regular. His staff were among the best in London, and one who remains at the club is extremely loyal to what he viewed as a very decent employer. He held parties that were bacchanalian, as if devised by Nero. One night he threw a 'barbarians' party' for King Fahd of Saudi Arabia, with fifty midgets and everybody eating with their bare hands. Apparently Fahd loved it. He created an air of lustrous, smooth perfection, shot through with the throb of unpredictability. One went in there to win, but of course one might lose.

It was a man's world, no question. Men showing off to each other, really. Buccaneering, not with swords but with money. Behaving as they are no longer supposed to do. Not as badly as they did in the eighteenth century, when a woman would have taken her life in her hands if she had walked into a gentlemen's gambling room, but still with a *Mad Men* swagger that has them condemned (possibly secretly envied) today.

There were some amazingly attractive women around: Sally Crichton-Stuart, who married the Aga Khan; Min Musker, Aspinall's second wife; Zoe Peto, a seventeen-year-old model then married to Greville Howard; Christina Shand Kydd; Lady Annabel Goldsmith, who went gambling on her wedding night with her first husband, Mark Birley, and made the mistake of drawing his attention to herself rather than the game: 'You never interrupt a man who is running a winning bank,' she later scolded herself.[10] But the wives were beautiful incidentals, part of the theatre in their long sleek column dresses, there to adorn and charm and send a sweet stream of Shalimar into the Stuyvesant. Some of the men were womanizers, which can be another form of showing off to each other. James Goldsmith, who attacked romancing with the speedy force of a fly-half, had three wives, plus adjuncts: he conducted an affair with Lady Annabel when married to Ginette Lery, and took Laure Boulay de la Meurthe as his mistress when he married Lady Annabel. Ian Maxwell-Scott, who lived at the club during the week, was said to have played away from his devout Catholic wife, Susie. 'All I want is for him to be here,' she told her children's nanny, 'and he has these popsies hanging round the Clermont.' Inevitably there were a few upmarket tarts. Veronica Lucan later claimed that the gamblers wanted to plant one of them on her husband. She was said to chafe bitterly against the sidelining of women, from her position on what was known as 'the widows' bench' beneath the staircase. Yet to her sister Christina, whose husband Bill gambled occasionally at the club (one night winning and losing £70,000), the Clermont was straightforwardly enjoyable: simply the nicest place in London. Christina says:

> It was a very, very glamorous place, no question. Full of friendly, amusing people. Of course it was a man's place. I mean there weren't many girls gambling – mainly John Aspinall's mother. But

they'd always break for dinner, there'd be a really good dinner party in the middle, but normally the wives would go home after dinner and the men would continue into the night. The gambling would start, and the wives might stay for half an hour and watch, but then they would leave. And the men would go on until two or three in the morning.

Stuart Wheeler recalls:

It was all very friendly. If you didn't gamble upstairs [at chemmy], they didn't bother you. You could play backgammon downstairs in considerable comfort, and a lot of people would be doing that. I think their feeling was that, if they allowed people who liked gambling very much to have a good time and so forth, in the end they would go and gamble at the casino games, and in the end they would make money out of it. And it probably worked, I should think.

Aspinall was very good at making everybody feel they were his best friend, and the atmosphere was as if you were in a very important place. It might have been unnerving to an outsider, but if you were part of it, it was very relaxing, actually.

Daniel Meinertzhagen, the youngest of Lucan's gambling circle, who lunched with him most days after his separation from Lady Lucan, went to work at the Clermont soon after coming down from Oxford. At university he had become a gambler: 'I remember one morning, in the early hours, carrying my roulette paraphernalia from Trinity to New College, walking past the Dean...' Then he met a relation of Aspinall's and the die, as it were, was cast. 'It was an extravagant, decadent atmosphere – far and away the most exciting of the casinos. And I was a little scrubber from Oxford, and I walk in and there's King Fahd, Onassis, Niarchos, Andrew Devonshire. A bit intimidating, yes. But it could turn a young man's head.'

In 1972 the Clermont was sold to Playboy and Victor Lownes took over. His wife Marilyn, the former centrefold with the goddess body, worked occasionally on the club reception.

What was fascinating about the Clermont for us – there were five of us bunnies, on reception – it really was like a gentleman's club. There was this old man, Tom – oh my goodness, he was their butler. When you walked in, the gentleman's cloakroom was on the left. Tom used to shuffle in – he had dark trousers and a waistcoat – and they'd say Tom, can you get me this, get me that... He was in service. That was the mentality. He'd shine their shoes, he had all the brushes to brush down their coats, cologne – and he would go out and get a certain paper that they needed, or he would tell Billy Edgson, on the door, to get it. So they treated him almost like their butler. And that's why they liked going there, because they could still be those people with servants. It's like all of us, we go where we're comfortable and where we feel at home.

Victor Lownes has a similarly benevolent, faintly baffled take on the club that he acquired for just £500,000. The ludicrous price, which Playboy recouped in just three months (not three nights, as legend has it), is further evidence that the Clermont was only intermittently profitable for Aspinall, although he was also impatient to turn his attentions to his nobler enterprise of wildlife conservation. 'He only really wanted the British upper classes gambling there. He filled it with his friends, and he'd tapped them out. Once he'd busted them out, they didn't have any more money to gamble. We took our highest rollers out of the Playboy, who had never been admitted to the Clermont under the old regime, and we took them over there immediately.'

It was later said that the club changed, lost its cachet, after the 1972 sale to Playboy. It was even said that Lownes employed bunny girls as croupiers;[11] this is untrue. To all intents and purposes things went on much as before, including Tom the butler and Billy the linkman. The girls at reception wore normal clothes, with not an ear or tail in sight. 'Playboy followed a successful formula,' says Daniel Meinertzhagen, refuting the myth that the old guard was muttering Blimpishly into its martinis about the new ownership. 'It didn't change as much as you'd think.' It is true that a craps game was established upstairs, and that this was regarded as slightly *infra dig*. It is also true that the little staircase that took the gamblers straight down to Annabel's was sealed off by its owner Mark Birley, denying instant access to the *jeunesse dorée* below; but that had happened already. In fact the change had begun before John Aspinall sold the Clermont. Outwardly everything stayed the same, but the living, breathing club was slowly becoming a facsimile of itself. How could it not, when the shadow of uncertain times was falling upon it? Money was evaporating, draining away; unless it was oil money. Even Aspinall, who still showed his face regularly after selling the club, would lose his lot when the stock market more than halved in value in the early 1970s. 'Nice person, Aspinall,' says Lownes.

> I had no problem with him. And his mother – she used to bring a chimp in a carrycot, and leave it with reception while she went in and gambled. She was a very interesting person. Nice person.
>
> The Clermont guys were part of the atmosphere. They were a bit like schoolboys. They were pleased to be welcome there, even if they weren't gambling. I was comping them all meals and stuff. And hundred-year-old brandy – they were happy to be drinking from this wonderful liquor cellar that I got from Aspinall. And we were bringing over these Arabs and whatnot, and we wanted *them* to see that they were in with the British aristocracy. They liked that. Of course!

A year or so before the Playboy takeover, Lord Lucan took his sister, Jane, and her American husband for dinner at the club. Her reaction was different again. It would surely have been her parents' reaction also:

> I thought it was a nightmare. Such an unreal and distasteful world to me. I have one visual memory of sitting at the Clermont – there was a very nice sitting-room area [beside the staircase], and we sat there I think with Veronica, and John was somewhere at the table.

I never saw him at work... It was just being around the great and wealthy and all was always slightly distressing to me. But that was my hang up, as they say nowadays.

This, indeed, is what the Clermont was: a place where the privileged would assemble. In its glory years of the 1960s, it had a name that signified. There was a dazzling completeness to it, a theatrical gleam, as if one could walk in and be absorbed into another world. Every night was like an opening night, prickling with the sense that this was the place to be. Whether one liked it or not, and of course not everybody did, it was infinitely more than a repository for aristocratic throwbacks. Frank Sinatra went. So did Elizabeth Taylor, Lucian Freud, Ian Fleming, the American philanthropist Paul Mellon, the racing driver Graham Hill, Mick Jagger (Aspinall – who really was Jagger's 'man of wealth and taste'– hollered across the dining-room: 'Good to see you here, Mick. Glad to see you've joined the middle classes. Why do you put on that ridiculous voice when we all know you're a perfectly good middle-class man like the rest of us?'[12]). John Betjeman went, because he was in love with the building. The French novelist Françoise Sagan went. She was a heavy gambler, but the dangerous allure of the Clermont almost did for her.

> Someone brought her a little pile of chips in exchange for a little piece of paper which she happily signed. To her left there was talk of horses, to her right of regattas. Meanwhile her little pile of chips disappeared, one after the other. Hardly had one pile vanished than a splendid valet would place another on a silver tray in front of her and she would sign another piece of paper...[13]

After a while she asked how much she actually owed, and John Aspinall wrote it down on another little piece of paper, brought to her by the valet. Her debt was £80,000. Being a true gambler, Sagan stayed. By the end of the evening she owed £50. 'It was a great pleasure to have you at my tables,' said Aspinall, exerting all his lupine charm as she paid the cashier, 'especially since the French are generally so lacking in *sang-froid* when gambling.'

Within this assorted crowd of the famous, the onlookers, the upper classes, the grand old ladies who wore hats at the tables, were the people who would later become known as the Clermont set. In fact they were only a part of the whole, but what united them was that they were friends of Lord Lucan. John Aspinall himself, James Goldsmith, Charles Benson, Daniel Meinertzhagen, Ian Maxwell-Scott, Stephen Raphael, Michael Stoop, Dominick Elwes: the set, the inner circle, as it is perceived to be, that stands at the imagistic heart of the Lucan myth.

These men have been written about repeatedly, perhaps more than any other aspect of this story. The gamblers who protected Lord Lucan, the Happy Valley set transported to the darkened brick of Mayfair; indifferent to the world outside, applying the code of the club to the rest of life, as the 3rd Duke of Grafton had done when he gave a Treasury pension to a broke gambler. Muriel Spark rendered them in *Aiding and Abetting* with vast dollops of Scottish contempt. Her admirer Evelyn Waugh would have dealt with them more equivocally. One can imagine the elliptical conjurings: 'Lucky' Lucan and his lamb chops, the dull-eyed assemblage around the chemmy table muttering '*banco*' and '*suivi*' and '*neuf*, old boy, do forgive', the hovering sense of cosmic boredom, the bass notes of falsity within the image of antiquity. Liberal-minded writers have described them with a kind of horror. 'Casinos should be the preserve of the rich: it keeps these people away from the rest of us.' They were an 'overbearing, disdainful cast of characters', atrociously right-wing, 'a group distinguished by its wealth, arrogance, misanthropy and, ultimately, murder'.[14] The police, succinctly, called them 'the Eton mafia' (although only half of them actually went to the school).

At the heart of it all is Lord Lucan, seated at the table that came to comprise his life. Lucan, whose personality was subsumed into his obsession, whose habits became as addictive as his addiction:

119

the same meal, the same vodka martini, the same gambling. The aristocratic ace in John Aspinall's hand, a waxwork created to embody the lifestyle that led to nowhere. A figure from Hogarth, subject of a series of tableaux entitled *The Gambling Earl* that took him from chiselled dreamboat of Le Touquet to puffy-eyed bankrupt of Belgravia.

Lucan could sit in his tight little circle of players, within the constrained little circle of his mind, and outside the world could change as much as it liked. The pickets could rant and the bombs could explode, but the Clermont would still enclose the players in its velvet grip. Meanwhile his countess sat downstairs on her bench, abandoned and afraid, as her husband steadily disposed of his birthright, in the company of the men who would shield him against her with their silence.

This, then, is the myth. Is it the truth? No, not quite.

Walking through the same door every day, sticking together around the same tables; there is, undoubtedly, something silly about this. It does, indeed, make these men seem like the scions of privilege that they were, joshing together about the night when so-and-so threw such-and-such at backgammon, gasping in appalled admiration when old Lucky loses yet another three thousand that he doesn't have and doesn't bat an eye (there's breeding for you). It takes the concept of men showing off to each other to a parodic level. Surely there was more to life than this? Yes, but there had been more to the Clermont too.

In so far as the myth is true, it portrays the club only in its darker, declining years. In its golden heyday the Clermont was about far more than gambling. It was cosmopolitan, alive: like all the best clubs. What is rarely acknowledged is that it was *fun*. And the Lucan set were fun, some of them. They attacked life with a kind of laughing vigour. They didn't fret about alcohol units or body mass index or midlife crises. 'They were manly,' says Marilyn Lownes, and one knows what she means. 'Some of them were amazingly funny,' says Stuart Wheeler. 'They could be terribly witty. It was a gang. Not a violent gang – on the whole. I enjoyed all those people, enjoyed being in their company.'

Certainly the mythical image of the reactionary group in their Mayfair fortress, wallowing in their 'fetid, self-deluding, pseudo-Nietzschean atmosphere', makes little sense when applied to the Clermont as it was in the 1960s, when (in a manner of speaking) everybody went. It is quite true, however, to say that by the early 1970s the Lucan set had begun to turn inwards. The state of the nation had infused them with fear, and they used the club to keep it at bay. 'There didn't seem much point in any form of economy,' says Daniel Meinertzhagen, meaning that gambling made as much sense as anything else at the time. But the set was not alone in feeling alarm. So did most people. And one must be honest: how in heaven would contemporary Britain cope with the three-day week, the six-month wait for a phone connection, the sudden power failure cutting off *Grand Auto* mid-*Theft*? Thirty-three per cent basic rate tax? Inflation moving towards 20 per cent? Good God, we would all be looking for somebody to sue. In the everyday world, life went on stoically amid the financial Blitz, but the 'mustn't grumble' phlegmatism was, in its way, as much a façade as the gamblers' mask. Beneath both lay volatility. The IRA's bombs were an external expression of that fundamental disorder. Rightly or wrongly, logically or illogically, there was a sense that the future might drag the country, corpse-like, to extreme left or right, and rip its serene, flawed, ancient traditions to shreds.

From the Clermont viewpoint, there were insults on top of injuries. The top rate of tax, 98 per cent in 1974, was 75 per cent even under the Conservative administration. (No wonder they all liked gambling so much: tax-free!) There was the spectacle of the union 'barons', men with giant sideburns and faces like weapons, wielding the power that had once belonged to their kind; backed by that class traitor, Tony Benn, 'the most hated man in Britain',[15] the former Viscount Stansgate who sought a joint government by the Labour Party and the trade unions. There was the prime minister Harold

Wilson, suspected of Communist leanings. This was not mere Tory romancing: MI5 had opened a file on Wilson as early as 1945. Lord Kagan, one of Wilson's own set, was close to a KGB officer at the Soviet embassy. Peter Wright, the author of *Spycatcher*, suspected that Wilson was a KGB plant.[16] James Goldsmith, honoured in the same 1976 resignation list as Kagan, thought so too. 'Jimmy never had any judgment politically,' Woodrow Wyatt later told Annabel Goldsmith. '[He] was always writing me daft memoranda saying in ten years or five years, or whatever date he had chosen, the apocalypse would come, chaos and anarchy would reign...'[17]

But this, sane as it sounds, was said in 1986. Thirteen years earlier things were rather more hysterical. A group called Unison, which could not know that its name would later be given to Britain's largest trade union, was set up by a former deputy director of MI6. It was a vigilante organization, designed to protect the country against a Communist takeover or a general strike. Unison was joined by an ex-NATO commander, General Sir Walter Walker, who then formed a group of his own. He claimed to have some 100,000 members, and was openly supported by the Admiral of the Fleet, several former MPs and the former Goon, Michael Bentine. In an interview, he stated that Britain 'might choose rule by the gun [i.e. a military government] in preference to anarchy'. Utterly absurd though this now seems, the fact that it could be said at all suggests an acute, pervasive level of anxiety. Then came Colonel David Stirling, Clermont gambler and founder of the SAS. Stirling formed GB75, a patriotic group that again would act as a private army in the face of civil unrest. The virulent right-wing views of some of his followers made Stirling uncomfortable (according to the myth, he would have concurred in them), and he disbanded the organization. Nevertheless he did seek to infiltrate the trade union movement, hoping to destabilize it from within. This operation was backed and funded by James Goldsmith (the knighthood from Harold Wilson was truly a superb irony).[18] The private army, with which Stirling's brother Bill was also involved, was joined by Dominick Elwes and by Michael Stoop, who was soon to lend his battered Ford Corsair to his friend Lord Lucan.

What the other members of the Clermont set thought about the Stirling army is not known. Doubtless they were in favour, in principle. 'It was that moment, when everything was really going up the spout,' says the then girlfriend of one of the set, 'and there was that sort of talk, a lot of Harold Wilson was a Communist. And the country was absolutely going to the dogs, there's no doubt about it. Anybody who was successful at all either paid 98p in the pound or left.' The plan for a private army, albeit that it was abandoned, certainly supports the idea that the set harboured extreme views. So too does the fact that Greville Howard, who was on the fringes of the circle, had gone to work as Enoch Powell's private secretary. (Later he worked for Goldsmith; his politics moderated thereafter, although remaining on the right.) But resentful murmurings and alcohol-fuelled rants, which were the more usual thing, do not equate to neo-fascism. At a time when government ministers themselves were in a state of high alert – 'I know we are heading for catastrophe,' wrote Roy Jenkins, the then Home Secretary – it would have been amazing if the same apocalyptic prophecies had not been made at the Clermont.

The truth about the myth is that it only describes a part of the Clermont set. What is meant by 'the circle' is actually John Aspinall, James Goldsmith and Lord Lucan. The rest are caught up in the image of blistering upper-class arrogance. When they are seen as individuals, the story changes.

Aspinall and Goldsmith were arrogant, beyond doubt. They were the successes. They embodied the ethos of the Clermont as described by Dominick Elwes, being 'concerned with power and success and to a certain extent survival. Anybody who has fallen by the wayside is dismissed.'[19] And it was quite true that Aspinall and Goldsmith eventually left the rest behind. They had first met in Aspinall's lodgings at Oxford. Goldsmith, aged sixteen and just out of Eton, having won £8,000 at Lewes racecourse, marched into a chemmy game brandishing fivers. That set the tone: here were the two alpha males, the two great stags clashing antlers. They recognized each other as such. When Aspinall lost his fortune on the stock market in 1973, Goldsmith bailed him out, exacting the price of his friend's art collection. They opened a new casino in 1978, in the former Curzon House Club, and this time Aspinall made real money. The business was floated in 1983, and sold four years later for £90 million. Aspinall used his realized holding, some £20 million, to start a trust for his zoos. He lost a vast sum, again, when he backed a couple of Goldsmith's failed takeover bids. So in 1992 they opened another casino, again on Curzon Street, on the site of the old White Elephant where Lord Lucan, twenty-five years earlier, had celebrated the birth of his son with Charles Benson. ('He was happy as Larry,' Benson later said.)

Adventurer men are arrogant, perforce. They are not 'nice': how can they be? Success of that kind goes with ruthlessness, a near-excess of personality, an almost manic energy. When Aspinall was in hospital, fighting angrily against the cancer that would kill him in 2000, an exhausted nurse said to his third wife: 'Lady Sally, I feel that Mr Aspinall would make a speedier recovery at home.' It also goes with a kind of chippiness, which both men had. 'Jimmy thinks every morning he has nothing,' said his sensible French associate, Madame Gilberte Beaux. The Goldsmiths were Frankfurt bankers, regarded as poorer cousins to the Rothschilds, and the sense of this ancestral inferiority drove him to the wild frontiers of capitalism. He also saw himself as a stateless, rootless person; half German Jew, half French Catholic. On Coronation night in 1953, the twenty-year-old Goldsmith fell madly in love with Isabel Patiño, the daughter of a Bolivian millionaire. Her family objected to the marriage: 'It is not the habit of our family to marry Jews.' Goldsmith replied: 'It is not our habit to marry Red Indians,' then eloped with Isabel to Scotland. They married in 1954. Five months later his sweetly pretty wife died of a brain haemorrhage, hours after giving birth to a daughter, and Goldsmith fought a long battle for custody of the baby. One might say that this incident hardened him there-after. 'How long does it take to get over it?' asked a friend. 'I don't think you ever do,' he answered. Yet even before this Goldsmith had shown his venomous toughness. At Eton, where he had staged his first coup by selling off an entire stock of Latin cribs at double the price, he offered a selection of records as a leaving present to his loathed housemaster, then smashed them all in front of him.

He was a brilliant businessman, worth some £1.5 billion when he died in 1994. He took over companies with heedless, untrammelled vigour. He offered to buy the infamous Slater-Walker Holdings when his friend, occasional Clermont gambler Jim Slater, lost almost everything in the early 1970s; yet Goldsmith himself was more than an asset stripper, as Slater had been. His career zigzagged like a dodgy ECG, but his triumphs were always greater than his disasters. His Cavenham Foods business was one of the world's largest companies before he liquidated it in 1987, having seen the great market crash rolling tsunami-like towards him. Almost in passing he bred one of the best racehorses of the early twenty-first century, Montjeu, named after his Burgundian château. He wanted power as well as money, however. Above anything, he longed to own news-papers. He tried to buy the *Observer*, then the Beaverbrook empire. He started a magazine, *Now!*, but this collapsed after two years. Woodrow Wyatt had asked him what *Now!* was going to be like. 'And he produced a copy of *L'Express* which he owned and said, "Like that." I looked at it and said "But this will never do, Jimmy. It's all in French." For some time he didn't understand the joke...'[20]

Perhaps his yearning to be a press baron, to control the show, was connected to his apparently paradoxical hatred of journal-ists. He launched an extraordinary series of libel actions against *Private Eye*, which in December 1975 cast aspersions on his deal-ings with Slater-Walker and, more damagingly, suggested that he had 'obstructed' the course of justice in the Lucan affair. The case, which could have resulted in jail for the magazine's editor Richard Ingrams, lasted several months. 'From time to time,' wrote

Ingrams, 'he looked across at me, nodding and grinning, as if trying to convey a message of some kind.' Eventually Goldsmith withdrew the charges: 'He was advised that if he wanted to be a newspaper proprietor, it didn't look good to send editors to prison.'[21] *Private Eye* paid costs of £30,000 over ten years, which might just about have kept Goldsmith in socks.

There was something of the 3rd Earl of Lucan about James Gold-smith: that relentless insistence on his own righteousness. Strictly speaking, he had had a case against *Private Eye*, which had made unproven allegations of aiding a criminal (as the inquest into Sandra Rivett's death had judged Lord Lucan to be). But he pursued it with an unseemly ferocity. He was prescient in his misgivings about the anti-democratic powers of the European Union, but the Refer-endum Party that he formed shortly before his death in 1997 (for which Aspinall stood as a candidate) conducted its business with alienating aggression. His private persona was not very different. At dinner in the Clermont one night, he grew impatient with the waiter who had delayed (probably about two minutes) bringing his smoked salmon; Goldsmith fetched the whole fish himself, then gnawed it from the bone, very much like one of Aspinall's wild animals. He would walk into the club, see up to eight people playing back-gammon and declare: 'Right, take you all on.' 'I knew Jimmy quite well,' says Stuart Wheeler:

> He gambled in his business life tremendously, and very success-fully. We didn't meet very often – but there was he, extremely rich, and me not at all at that time, and he would toss a coin and I would call. If I got it wrong, I'd pay him £1,000, which was much more in those days than it is now. And if I got it right, he would pay me £1,100. So it suited me, because I was getting the right odds, and it suited him because he enjoyed seeing me scrabble on the floor to see if I'd won or lost, knowing it was quite important to me. He liked that kind of thing. He had this place in Mexico – it amused him to offer somebody £1,000 to swim across the river that had crocodiles

in it. That sort of thing would amuse him. I don't think anyone did it, but...

'He was a bully,' says Marilyn Lownes. 'But he was the richest. They looked up to him because he had the money – they bowed to Jimmy.'

'Of course I was terrified of Jimmy Goldsmith,' says the then girlfriend of one of the Lucan set. 'He was very, very scary. I mean, if you went to dinner he held court. I wouldn't have dared say anything, I don't think most people would. He had a court, definitely. There were all these funny people, sort of hangers on... And a lot of people wanted to be friendly with Jimmy Goldsmith. He had money, and I imagine a lot of people at the Clermont didn't have much money.'

Yes, indeed: what wouldn't Lord Lucan have done for Goldsmith's kind of money? What wouldn't most of the Clermont set, for that matter? Several became 'house players', perforce, sitting in on a game in order to attract the real gamblers: working for Aspinall, in effect.

It is interesting that the mythical arrogance of the circle was displayed, most potently, by the two members who clung only tenuously to the upper rungs of the social ladder. Theirs was the arrogance of money, of course. So much more real, by this time, than that of class. The arrogance of class was bred in the bone, but it was also on the defensive; it could not afford to swagger like Jimmy Goldsmith; it had to charm and cajole and self-deprecate. It certainly could not, as Jonathan Miller did, make casually snobbish reference to the 'parvenus' who would have been shocked by Kait Lucan. The liberal intelligentsia could get away with this kind of thing. The Clermont set would have been slaughtered for it. Of course these gamblers probably all were arrogant in their way, shuddering when somebody wore brown shoes in town or something, but then the intelligentsia would shudder at Mantovani or the suburban mindset, so that was really no different. Outside Aspinall and Goldsmith the arrogance of the set was a powerless thing, a function of words and attitudes.

And it did not equate to some nameless ancestral evil: Lord Lucan aside, the men were public schoolboys, not aristocrats (although in some cases they were related to them). What is extremely telling is that, as individuals, they are always portrayed quite favourably. Only as 'the set' do they become something ghastly. Daniel Meinertzhagen, a charming and courteous man who lost an inheritance from the Lazard banking family, is rarely mentioned at all. Michael Stoop, a man in his fifties with a fine war record, was complimented in his 2012 obituary for being 'less cliquey' than the rest (whoever they might have been). Stephen Raphael, also older and very close to Lucan, almost a replacement father figure, was a family man. Charles Benson, 'always spectacularly broke',[22] worked for the *Daily Express*. Not long before the murder of Sandra Rivett he became 'the Scout', the paper's racing tipster, and in the week of the inquest gave four winners on the first day of Royal Ascot. 'Hats off to the Scout!' proclaimed the front page of the *Express*, alongside the headline 'Contract to Kill: Inquest is told of claim by Lady Lucan'. Benson was a hugely convivial person, with a circle of friends stretching way beyond the Clermont (it was he, for instance, who invited Jagger). Bill Shand Kydd, on the outside of the set but a good friend of Lord Lucan, is held in the highest general esteem, not least for the way in which he coped with the fallout from the death of Sandra Rivett: 'Bill was fantastic in the aftermath,' says Lucan's Eton friend. He took on the welfare of the Lucan children, and later showed staggering, good-humoured courage in the face of a 1995 riding accident, in which he fell on his head 'like a dart' and was left paralysed. ('When they told me, I turned to my wife and said "Well, I've never done anything by halves, have I?"'[23])

Dominick Elwes, who took a fatal overdose of Tuinal in September 1975 at the age of forty-four, is always favourably portrayed. It was said, for instance, that he was sent by the set to visit Veronica Lucan in hospital because he was 'the nicest person present'.[24] Elwes was a painter, the son of a painter, and the nephew by marriage of Nancy Mitford. He is mentioned occasionally in her letters; she saw in him a resemblance to her feckless husband, Peter Rodd (Prod). She also contradicted the view of Elwes as a wholly likeable character. In 1952 she wrote to Evelyn Waugh:

> Dominick Elwes came to see me – it all took me back to my early married life – the looks, the get-rich-quick line of talk. Only whereas old Prod is good at heart I feel this boy is really bad. I took very much against him... I skilfully parried the question of an advance, which loomed throughout the interview. Got a gushing letter thanking me for my 'hospitality' (a glass of Dubonnet if that) & promising to come again very soon. He doesn't know how thoroughly inoculated I am!

Later that year, again to Waugh, she wrote:

> I'm frightened of Dominick Elwes. I see him as one of those youths who murder old ladies (me). He met an old pal of mine the Marquis de Lasteyrie & talked a great deal about his darling aunt & then said 'I want to go to Venice, do you know anybody there?' to which Lasteyrie, who saw through him like a glass, replied 'Is not Venice itself enough without knowing people?'

In reference to the death of Elwes's cousin Saul, who killed himself in 1966, she wrote: 'I ran into Dominick Elwes in the street & he said: they drove poor Saul mad (he said with a wealth of feeling) by finding him jobs. Of course one quite sees that would drive D. mad...' Yet to her friend Raymond Mortimer she described Elwes as 'that super crook (for whom I have a slight weakness)'.

Elwes had any amount of attraction, and was outlandishly funny, which went a long way with Nancy Mitford. Like James Goldsmith, although unlike him in every other way, he staged a highly public elopement. He ran away with eighteen-year-old Tessa Kennedy in 1958, marrying her in Havana in defiance of a High Court injunction, which he was obliged to purge with two weeks in Brixton jail. This was typical: a rush of excitement draining away in sad and pointless solitude. He lived a kind of high-end vagabond life, moving from place to place, seeking who-knew-what. He was wanted everywhere, including the Clermont, because he was so amusing. He wanted to be there, not so much for the gambling but because he was dependent on the comfort of friends. He was also restless and indebted and rather unhappy. 'He was warm, friendly, sexy, clever – and drunk,' says Marilyn Lownes. 'Alcoholic I think. He must have been depressive – you don't kill yourself in life because of one thing.' At the inquest into his death, like the Sandra Rivett inquest held at Horseferry Crown Court, Elwes's brother said that he was 'an extremely extroverted character, and like many extroverts always had a depressing [sic] side to his character'.

As Stephen Ward had been the sacrificial victim in the Profumo affair twelve years earlier, so Elwes would become the Clermont set scapegoat after the Lucan case. He was Lord Balcairn in *Vile Bodies*, who put his head in an oven after being cast adrift from aristocratic society. That, at least, is the myth. Elwes had spoken to the *Sunday Times Magazine* for its incisive, coldly damning account of the circle, published in June 1975. He was paid £500, which he no doubt needed, for his somewhat caricatured portrait of the club members.[25] He was also said to have handed over holiday snaps to illustrate the article, including one (cleverly cropped on the cover) that appeared to show Lady Annabel Goldsmith cooing lubriciously into the face of Lord Lucan. In fact the pictures had been lent by Veronica Lucan, who on subsequent occasions would reveal more photographs to the press.[26]

Goldsmith, predictably, went berserk. Annabel's son Robin Birley wrote to Elwes, accusing him of selling the photographs. Robin's father Mark banned Elwes from his two clubs and issued spiteful writs for two small debts. In other words, the angered parties were Annabel's relations. John Aspinall had covered his own back and humoured Goldsmith in his rage, but that was all. Nor was Elwes banned from the Clermont, which anyway was now owned by Playboy. His ostracism, therefore, was not exactly from the Lucan set. Two of its members, Benson and Meinertzhagen, believed his denials and staunchly took his side in the affair. His suicide note specifically read: 'I curse Mark and Jimmy from beyond the grave. I hope they are happy now.' Many years later, in a typical conflation of the circle and its individual members, an article about Elwes stated that 'a friend who considered him to be close to a nervous breakdown sent him abroad to recuperate. When he returned in August, he found the Lucan set implacably turned against him.'[27] Yet the 'friend' had been Meinertzhagen: one of the 'Lucan set'.

Of course none of this – not the *Sunday Times Magazine* article, nor the furore over the photographs – would have happened had Sandra Rivett not been murdered. Nor would Elwes have given another interview in late June 1975, this time to the *Daily Express*. It was headlined. 'Lucan, Please Call Me'. Elwes talked with the same lack of self-awareness as he had shown with the *Sunday Times*; one can picture him getting carried away in the presence of a sympathetic listener, rather than telling them to get lost as he ought to have done. This time, however, he sounded semi-hysterical with nerves. 'I am one of Lucky Lucan's best friends... Why, oh why, doesn't he get in touch with any of us? We are all prepared to accept his alibi and help him in any way possible.' Then he added: 'This is a ghastly business with police asking me questions all the time.' Elwes was weak, and it wasn't just Goldsmith and Birley who sensed it. The police and the press did too. They were probing away at him like a tongue at a sore tooth. They knew that they could get him to talk. Among other things, he told the police about the lunch held at Aspinall's house on the day after the murder. This did not lead to his ostracism. Yet it may have led to the belief that he had given the photographs to the *Sunday Times*; that he was unsound. And the relentless, cumulative pressure upon a lightweight but sensitive person became scarcely tolerable. In that more nuanced sense, therefore, Dominick Elwes was indeed the scapegoat for the Lucan affair.

At his memorial service in Farm Street, his friend Kenneth Tynan lamented his 'pathetic adulation of a worthless group of people'. John Aspinall's address, which contained the very true remark that 'modern society does not repay someone like him', was rewarded with a punch on the jaw from Elwes's cousin, Tremayne Rodd: 'That's what I think of your bloody speech, Aspinall.' Tynan, and possibly Rodd, blamed the set directly for Elwes's death, and the belief has persisted, although it is only part of the truth.

Shortly before he died Elwes had written a letter to Aspinall, in which he referred, somewhat heartbreakingly, to 'the incredible, wonderful times spent, more often than not, with you, Aspers'. Yet the irony is that if anybody blabbed to the *Sunday Times Magazine*, it was John Aspinall himself. He said far more than Elwes, and it was infinitely more damaging. When, at his first wedding in 1956, a group of bailiffs seeking him out served writs on Elwes by mistake, this had been a small prefiguring of what was to come.

In the *Sunday Times* article, Aspinall spoke in his usual florid vein, describing Lord Lucan as 'a leader of men', extolling his 'loyalty, honesty, reliability'. Aspinall was not stupid; he must have known how this would sound in the context of a young woman's murder. His final remark, quoted at the very end, was: 'Of course, out of politeness one says it's very tough on the nanny.' If anybody damned the set to its eternal perception as the symbol of a dying, unlamented world, it was he, its architect.

The members who remain to be mentioned are Ian Maxwell-Scott and Lord Lucan himself, who visited the Maxwell-Scott house on the night of the murder. Although Maxwell-Scott is rarely mentioned as an individual, he did indeed display all the arrogance of the Clermont myth. He was, in truth, what Lucan is said to be: a mad gambler and snob who treated his wife appallingly.

'Oh no, not the Ritz,' he had whined to the young John Aspinall, who in the early 1950s had found him sitting alone in an unspeakable slum of a flat, clutching the *Greyhound Express*, and had offered a stay at the hotel (where the pair remained for seven months). 'They don't know what they're doing with their wine.' Maxwell-Scott certainly did understand wine, and created a fabulous cellar at the

Clermont. Aspinall also employed him as a director of the club. For a compulsive gambler this was a dream job, although a Balliol man might have been expected to do more with his life. 'The fellow is not to my taste,' said Sir Andrew Clark, who refused to attend Maxwell-Scott's wedding to his daughter Susan. 'He has no proper job. He is a gambler. I prefer the man who does an honest day's work to any amount of nobility or family names.'

Maxwell-Scott, a Roman Catholic like his wife Susie, was a relation of the Duke of Norfolk. His mother, Ferga, was a descendant of Sir Walter Scott. She lived in an annexe of Grants Hill, the beautiful house in Uckfield bought with the payout received when Maxwell-Scott insured against his wife having twins, who were born in 1966. Ten years later Maxwell-Scott appeared before magistrates, threatened with jail over a £301.49 rates bill, which was paid at the last minute. He had been living on social security for the past five months. After this the Maxwell-Scotts moved to Wales, and effectively separated. The house was sold by mortgagees, the means to maintain it frittered away.

Maxwell-Scott gambled like a Lord Hastings: incessantly, joylessly and obsessively. 'He couldn't help himself,' says his then driver:

> At the weekends I used to take him to Brighton dogs. Dogs on Saturday, church on Sunday. And he'd come into the betting shop on Saturday, place a cash bet, because he'd probably exceeded his limit with his phone account. He had two cars, a Jensen Interceptor and a Bristol, and one day I was passing the car showroom – and Ian's two cars were in there. I said, what are they doing here? Oh, they said, we had to go and collect them...

His marriage, too, was an unhappy one. Susan Maxwell-Scott was a highly intelligent woman, a qualified barrister, stuck in a life that frustrated her, finding a release in alcohol and occasional flashes of temper or bizarre behaviour (as when the Lucans stayed for the weekend with their children and Susan scrawled on a wall, in shoe polish, 'Don't let Lord George fall down the fucking stairs'). Her former nanny says:

> Susie had all these children, six of them, and she said to me all I want is to be in London with Ian. She used to go to bed on Monday, and stay in bed till Thursday, when she'd get ready for his coming home. She was drinking, and then she would have something called Fernet Branca – she drank that to sober up quite a lot. And he would arrive on the Friday, and then they'd have a huge row – it used to be such a huge build-up. Often I'd get up the next day and he'd be asleep at the dining-room table.
>
> One night she got drunk with a lot of people from the pub. So I went up to my room and phoned the Clermont and said Ian, you've got to come home. Which he did. He came to my room, and I said to him this is untenable, all she wants is to be with you. And he said, but I cannot have her in London. She lets me down all the time. I said, but she loves you. He said I don't know what to say to you, but I cannot tolerate her behaviour. He and Susie weren't very well suited, but I don't know what would have been suited to him.

A friend of Marilyn Lownes, a former bunny who also worked as a lunchtime receptionist at the Clermont, remembers the regular gamblers as 'gorgeous, some of them. But Ian was a pompous ass. He was got rid of by Playboy. Good riddance.'

Lord Lucan, on the other hand, she recalls as 'very pleasant'. As Christina Shand Kydd says, 'All the staff there liked him, the doormen absolutely adored him.' The Maxwell-Scott nanny supports this. 'Some of those people would come for weekends, for Glyndebourne. John Aspinall came. I remember him with his new wife, and we all had to forget about his old one... I liked Lord Lucan the best of all the houseguests we had.' The receptionist remembers him bringing in boxes of shirts to the linkman, Billy Edgson, who would then take them to be laundered. By this time, Lucan no longer lived at Lower Belgrave Street, and the Clermont had become his *de facto* home.

It had been that way for some time, in fact. It had become an alternative life, an alternative to life. The reasons for this lay in his gambling, of course, but they also lay in his marriage. If the Clermont Club is the imagistic heart of this story, then the real heart lies in that complex alliance with Veronica Lucan.

Marriage

THE ENGAGEMENT BETWEEN Lord Bingham and Veronica Duncan was announced in *The Times* on 14 October 1963. 'He rang me up one weekend,' says his old Eton friend, 'and he said, I thought I ought to let you know, I've decided to get married. I said, what do you mean, you've decided to get married? Who's the lucky girl? He said, she's a very nice girl. But he was sort of matter of fact. The most unemotional conversation. It sounded as if he thought it was the right thing to do, at his age.'

He was almost twenty-nine years old, his fiancée twenty-six. Today that still seems very young, but fifty years ago men typically married at twenty-five, and women at twenty-three. When John Bingham's friend, Bill Shand Kydd, whom he had first met at St Moritz, married Veronica's younger sister, Christina, in January 1963, they were precisely those ages. It was through this marriage that John Bingham met Veronica, some three months later. She was, as it were, thrown his way at the Shand Kydd home, Horton Hall in Buckinghamshire, where he would sometimes spend weekends. 'Bill and Christina were partners,' says his sister Jane, 'and he was going around with them, in and out of their house, and there was Veronica – alone.' One particular golfing weekend, throughout which it rained incessantly, 'I told him to come down and stay here,' says Bill, 'and bring a bird. And he said – well, what about your sister-in-law?' 'He obviously fancied her,' says Christina. 'She was exceptionally pretty.'

She was doll-like with her extreme smallness, her air of break-ability, her white china face tilted up towards the splendid, sculpted height of Lord Bingham. As they began going about together he talked to Veronica about his views, his ideas, his belief that he could make his way in the world as a professional gambler. She listened and nodded understandingly. A few months later, at an engagement dinner at the Mirabelle, Stephen Raphael asked her if she minded her husband-to-be's habitual gambling, and she replied that he could do whatever he liked. 'He was absolutely straightforward with her,' says Christina. 'He said this is my life, this is how it will be. And people mustn't come into my life if you feel you can't do this. And she said she could do it.'

Naturally, he was quite a catch, after all. Breathtakingly handsome and heir to an earldom. Gambling, in such a context, could surely be put up with. Cynical to say, but marrying a catch – a millionaire, a celebrity, a looker, an aristocrat if that takes your fancy – does tend to entail putting up with things. In Agatha Christie's worldly little novel *The Hollow*, John Christow is a rich and brilliant doctor, desperately attractive, and an incurable adulterer. The implicit message is that this is only to be expected; one can't have everything. Today the *Pride and Prejudice* myth is the prevalent one: just by being herself, a girl can spear the catch of the season, ten thousand a year and a husband who will never put a foot wrong. No wonder the book, or at least this simplified version of it, has acquired a whole new non-readership.

Veronica Duncan was far more intelligent than that. She surely did not think that Lord Bingham would become a put-the-cat-out husband as well as a supremely debonair earl. Nevertheless reality does not obtrude at such times. Her own life had not always been easy. Her father, Major Charles Moorhouse Duncan, who received the Military Cross in the First World War, died when she was two years old. His first marriage, to the daughter of the 6th Baron Castlemaine, ended in divorce; he had two daughters with his second wife, Thelma, who died in 2012. After his death Mrs Duncan married James Margrie, and from 1947 the couple ran the Wheatsheaf Inn, near Basingstoke in Hampshire. One of Lord Lucan's friends apparently referred to Veronica as coming from 'that place on the way back from Ascot'; an insult convenient to showing the friend in a snobbish light, although geographically the remark makes little sense. But a policeman who worked on the case remarks: 'I'm a Countess of the Realm, she used to say – she loved that phrase. She only lived in a pub!'

Certainly the Wheatsheaf Inn is some metaphorical distance from Goodwood House, for instance, where the 4th Countess of Lucan had grown up as a daughter to the Duke of Richmond. Veronica had little in common with the Lucan wives who had gone before: the cultured Margaret Smyth; the grand, reckless Elizabeth Belasyse; the high-born Anne Brudenell and Cecilia Lennox; the fabulously correct Violet Spender Clay; the warm and charming Kait Dawson. Kait argued about politics with Veronica, as she did with everybody, but from their first meeting at the Arts Club the usual good humour was lacking. Violet, by this time in her eighties and about to lose two children in quick succession,[1] treated Veronica with semi-cordial *froideur*, rather as the Spencer family had treated Lavinia Bingham back in the 1780s. Yet Veronica, in the early days at least, was as carefully conservative as Lavinia had been. She was not the sort to declare open war on snobbery. She wanted to enter this world. When invited to meet Violet at the Portman Square flat, she did not wear a skirt two inches above the knee and start a prurient little chat about the Profumo affair. She smoked, which Violet didn't like, but that was not the real problem. Quite simply, Violet thought that her grandson was marrying beneath him. Not so much in pure class terms; there was, after all, the Baron Castlemaine lurking in the background. Anyway Violet herself had been a step down from her husband, while Kait Lucan was a downright flaming Red. But Kait was assured and frank and bursting with personality. This silent young woman would not, in Violet's eyes, cut it as the Countess of Lucan. Clearly her grandson didn't see it that way. Whether Veronica did is another thing altogether.

As a child she had lived in Uckfield, the quiet East Sussex town that recurs in strands of this story: John Aspinall spent some boyhood years there before attending Rugby school, Lord Lucan spent time there on the night of the murder. Then the Margrie family moved for a while to South Africa. The girls were sent to boarding school: 'We genuinely were tormented and bullied there,' says Christina. 'Our English accents, you know... Veronica couldn't handle it. But then we went to Grahamstown day school, and there were no prob-lems.' Nevertheless, and in an odd echo of Lucan's own childhood unhappiness, Veronica had already been seen by a psychiatrist. She had suffered from meningitis, a sometimes fatal trauma, and it had left her fragile.

On the return from South Africa, the Duncan girls were sent to St Swithun's school near Winchester, which again was a perfectly happy experience. Veronica had a good brain, and St Swithun's, which her own two daughters would later attend, is an excellent school. After this came perhaps the best time of all, when she studied graphic design in Bournemouth, and performed with the local dramatic society at the Palace Court Theatre. Veronica, who is still remembered at the society, cut an intriguing little figure on stage. 'She was', says her sister, 'a consummate actress.'

Then came London, and those strange, meandering years that most girls lived through while waiting for somebody to marry them. The 1950s did not expect its young women to make careers, although some did; it expected them to become wives, whether or not this was the right thing for them to do. Marriage was simply what happened. The walk up an aisle was, for good or ill, a slow glide toward destiny. Choice was theoretically, but rarely practically, available. 'I would have loved to read history at university but my family didn't have the money and there were no grants,' Veronica was later to say. 'I did what was expected of girls – marry as high up the social scale as possible.'[2]

In fact, like her future husband, she should have put her intelli-gence to use in a profession. Instead she took a job as a house model and helped to run a company that printed stage scripts. She lived in a bedsit in Gloucester Place. It sounds lonely, and probably was. In 1957 her mother asked Christina to give Veronica a room in her own newly rented flat, on Melbury Road off High Street Kensington. There Veronica would lie in bed, rocking herself for comfort.

She had, as it happens, already been thwarted in her female destiny: she had fallen in love with an older man, and suffered the shock of reading in the paper that he was engaged to another girl. She had two more particular boyfriends, one of whom remained very fond of her. But through no fault of her own it was an incon-clusive, unstable life, drifting through Holland Park without aim or anchor. She was now in her middle twenties. In those days the pros-pect of 'the shelf', and being deemed to be on it, carried a very real humiliation. Yet she would probably have married soon enough, and perhaps that would have been a success.

Instead a very different series of events was set in motion, when another girl living at Melbury Road began seeing a rich man named Hans Heyman, whom she later married. Heyman was a friend of Bill Shand Kydd: also rich (from the family wallpaper business), dynamic and shrewd and sensible, a dashing amateur rider and a damn good catch in his own right. In January 1963, after a short courtship, he married Christina at the church of Holy Trinity, a sober building at the end of a leafy lane leading off the Brompton Road. Veronica was chief bridesmaid, trailing like a demure little girl in the wake of her sister. She would hardly have been human if she had not taken pleasure in entering the same church just a few months later, wearing the diamond tiara of the noble Lucan family: walking slowly towards her fate, her happy ever after.

It is very easy to see why Veronica Duncan wanted to marry Lord Bingham. Why he wanted to marry her is harder to explain. There is a no mystery quite like a marriage, and often the mystery begins with why it happened in the first place. One could ask the same question about any of the marriages that ended in mayhem and catastrophe: why did Dr Crippen marry his wife, or Edith Thompson her husband? Did they not foresee the potential for unhappiness? But with the Lucan marriage it is different, in that the young Lord Bingham was so absurdly eligible. 'He had', says Bill, 'a lot going for him.' How many potential wives did he meet in the course of his carefree twenties? Hundreds, surely. Yet when Veronica came into his life, something about her made him say yes, I'll have this one.

It was later said that he had no real interest in women, which was true: his was a man's life. It was also said that he didn't like women. That is untrue. Public schools can nurture an inability to see women as people (although that mindset is more widespread in society at large than anybody cares to admit), and a man of Lucan's type would tend to commune obliquely, through charm or contempt, because oblique communication is what men like that do. Nevertheless there is no substance to the idea that he saw women 'as an inferior race':[3] a later description highly convenient to the myth. Christina Shand Kydd, Caroline Hill and her sister-in-law Juliet found him extremely good and courteous company. This was in contrast to Veronica's later remark: 'If your husband is someone who only knows how to talk to men, everything goes wrong.'[4] Greville Howard's then fiancée, Zoe, says: 'He was very sweet. We all went on a boating holiday, before I got married, and I remember John saying to me you really mustn't marry a gambler [sic]. He meant that gambling wasn't a good thing, and we should try and steer Greville off gambling. Which was quite interesting. He was very nice, always, to me.' Lady Annabel Goldsmith stayed in Mexico with Lucan in 1973 (the holiday that provided the snapshots for the *Sunday Times Magazine*) and spent hours talking to him. She later wrote: 'I gradually discovered the gentler side to Lord Lucan. By the end of the holiday I had found a new friend.'[5] Lucan was at ease with these confident women, more so than with girlfriends. 'The police asked me, "Was John a crumpet man?"' says Daniel Meinertzhagen. 'I mean to say... But the answer is no, he was a type more suited to men's clubs. He was impeccable in his behaviour towards women, but he wasn't a ladies' man.'

If he had been, he would not have contracted a marriage in the almost desultory way that he did. He had to marry, to get an heir. The time had come. But because he didn't really want to do it, he did the next best thing and chose a girl who, pretty though she was, looked as if she was hardly there.

Some years later, Veronica suggested that the then Lord Bingham had proposed because he associated her with good fortune. 'He'd sometimes phone me late at night and say, "Wish me luck, I'm about to plunge into a game." For a gambler to ask one particular person for luck was a great compliment. It meant since he'd met me he had been winning. Otherwise I don't think he would have asked me to marry him.'[6]

At least as reassuring, however, was the fact that Veronica was Bill Shand Kydd's sister-in-law. She was in the family, so to speak. Later still she offered a different view of his proposal, saying that Lucan married her because he 'was always on the lookout for rich connections. He was always looking for people [i.e. Bill] who might underwrite his precarious financial position.'[7] But Lucan himself had perfectly good expectations at the time, and anyway it is frankly incredible that he would have viewed Bill as that kind of touch. He looked up to his friend; he viewed him as strong, relaxed and resilient, all the things that he himself longed to be. It was to Bill that he would turn, on the night of Sandra Rivett's murder. If Bill had chosen Christina as a wife, that would have been the right thing to do, because Bill did everything right. Therefore the sister, by implication, would be all right also.

Yet it was, as his schoolfriend says, 'a very odd choice'. In fact Veronica was nothing like Christina at all. Very possibly this glamorous younger sister, with her open manner and easy self-assurance, was part of the problem. 'I don't know whether she was jealous. Perhaps – because I was happy in my life. And had always been happy. As a child, I was the happy one and she was the troubled one.' Even Christina's height would have been an issue, as Veronica was said to believe that her own smallness was a sign of inferiority.

But this air of acute vulnerability probably led John Bingham to believe that she would never pose any threat: neither to his elected lifestyle, nor in any other way. 'I think we as a family thought he felt sorry for Veronica,' says Jane. 'I think that can happen. People were surprised at his choice, that's very true. Maybe he just felt he needed a wife. But I can't explain it any more than that – he was sorry for her.'

Why, though, did he need to marry a woman for whom he felt sorry? Why do people marry, not the person who might augment their life, but one to whom they feel comfortably superior, or who will impress others, or any of the reasons that lead to disaster?

'I've always thought', says Christina, 'that he saw in her something of himself. He also had had quite a lonely childhood, and Veronica came across very much as a waif and stray – very shy, slightly sort of a loner. And I think he felt that they had that in common.' One is reminded a little of the young Lady Diana Spencer, fixing doe eyes upon the heir to the throne, flattering his sense of his own position while appearing to divine, as nobody else could, the real man within. 'There was a deep feeling between them,' says Christina. 'There definitely was, and not one that you and I can possibly completely understand.'

It is an unrecognized truth about Lord Lucan that he had little self-confidence. His noble demeanour somehow bespoke uncertainty. His arrogance was worn like a shield. He was, as Bill Shand Kydd later said, 'cripplingly introverted'.[8] Behind the façade was a lack of assurance; that was why the façade was so perfect. The life of a young lord had been glorious fun, but it was defined by youth. It could not go on indefinitely. As he reached his thirties he could still have made a productive future for himself. He was not yet an addict. He could have chucked what Bill Shand Kydd calls the 'lunatical' notion of gambling professionally, and done it for fun instead. As Veronica herself later said, 'if he had put the same energies into any other profession he would have been very successful.'[9] He had a decent brain, good friends, humour, looks, style: the absolute lot. Yet in the space of a couple of months, between his wedding in November 1963 and the death of his father in January 1964, he took a wrong turn that would never thereafter be righted.

Of course very few people get all that they should from their lives. It needs some luck, for one thing (he would have known about that). But there was such a disconnect, in this case, between what could have been and what was. 'If he gave me advice,' says his old friend, 'it was very good'; John Bingham would not have been the first person to see another person's life more clearly than his own.

It was a kind of inadequacy, really, that made him try to recreate the world of his forebears while shirking what underpinned it. He had been insecure since childhood; it made him feel good to stride into a casino and be fêted, to know that he would be missed if he did not turn up at the Clermont. ('No Lucky tonight? Not the same without him, eh?') 'He was terribly well treated there,' says Bill Shand Kydd. 'Aspinall thought of him as a very valued asset.' And it made him feel good to marry a woman who would, or so he believed, feel grateful to him. Her social 'inferiority' made him feel that he had something worth having. Other women, who had more in their own right, might have demanded more. She would not. She understood him. With her, he would be free to live the life that he wanted, rather than the one that he could have had.

He was right, and also very wrong. There was far more to Veronica than that, as the people around him realized. Her fragility was not merely that of size and shyness; its roots were deep. Ten years after the wedding, in a letter to his wartime American benefactress Marcia Brady Tucker, Lucan referred to 'Veronica's psychiatric record going back to 1962', although in fact it had begun much earlier. He probably did not know this; it is unlikely that the couple compared notes about their troubled childhoods. 'But', continues Christina, 'it wasn't particularly fair of us to put him off in any way, or vice versa, because she was very happy. It was a wonderful thing, really, because she had been very lonely and unhappy, and he came along and it seemed like a dream come true.' Veronica herself would later say 'I lost most of my friends when I married',[10] but it is hard to think that she had any such regrets at the time.

On her wedding day, in her doll-size wild silk dress, she looked as sweetly delicate as a Lladró; her husband looked impressive, as always; yet the pair have an air of Gainsborough's *Mr and Mrs Andrews*, a dead-eyed embodiment of immaculate Englishness.

'I don't remember much about the church,' says Jane, 'except that I was very pregnant.' Her parents had only been given the briefest notice of the engagement to Veronica. 'And I don't know what miserable thoughts they had, because we didn't in those days talk that openly – and by then I was living in America. But my mother was very good with everybody – she would put on a good face, and be as nice as possible, in order to try and make her son's life easier.' After the ceremony the couple drove in a blue Bentley coupé to the Carlton Towers hotel, where the reception party guests included Lord Bingham's uncle by marriage, Earl Alexander of Tunis, and the Duke of Gloucester's wife, Princess Alice. Among the four small bridesmaids was a descendant of the 3rd Earl of Lucan's loathed brother-in-law, Lord Cardigan. For their honeymoon, the Binghams flew to Paris and caught the Orient Express to Istanbul.

Just two months later, on 21 January 1964, the 6th Earl of Lucan died. He left an estimated £50,000 (the equivalent today of around £1,000,000) together with trusts that would supply his heir with a guaranteed income, some £12,000 a year by the time of his disappearance (today around £125,000). There was another trust for an heir's school fees, and a marriage settlement, again controlled by family members. Pat, putting personal considerations above political principle, had taken the decision to secure a financial bulwark against his son's own nature. As had been done in the case of Earl Ferrers in the mid-eighteenth century, the ancestral legacy was tied firm to its moorings; or so Pat would have hoped.

It was a peculiarly unlucky blow of fate that killed Pat from a stroke at sixty-four, an age so much younger than almost all his forebears. His good, useful life was over, which was a waste in itself.

And the inheritance would be wasted by a man who knew how to live up to what it signified, but not the thing itself. If the money had come to the 7th Earl a few years later, he might still have been forced to earn a proper living. Instead it poured into his hands just as the Clermont Club was getting into its glittering stride, and over the next ten years it would be turned into its equivalent in gambling chips. The idea that a flight from reality meant freedom would prove the greatest illusion of all.

Whether Lord Lucan would have visited the Clermont (and other clubs) with such obsessive regularity had he married elsewhere, is a question central to this story. The answer, almost certainly, is no. Part of the mystery of marriage is what it does to the characters of those involved. If a good marriage brings out the best in a man and woman, then it is also true that a bad one brings out the worst. That, by degrees, is what happened to the Earl and Countess of Lucan. Their alliance was an extreme example of a familiar phenomenon, in which two people who, if they had never met, might have led perfectly reasonable lives, together set off a malign chemistry that in the end destroys them both.

'It's obvious that they should never have got married,' says Stuart Wheeler, who observed the couple at the Clermont and took in their situation with shrewd eyes. 'I think we all felt exactly that,' says Jane. 'It was a tragedy.'

In the myth of the Lucan marriage, Veronica is unequivocally construed as the victim of her husband. He tried to send her mad, he badmouthed her, he was violent towards her, he kidnapped her children, he plotted to kill her, he attacked her. She was an entirely innocent party, like the poor pale wife in *Gaslight*, like the incarcerated Countess of Ferrers; and like them she survived, as the good should do, to testify against evil.

For forty years Veronica's version of the Lucan marriage has been the accepted one; to question it is to ally oneself with the powerful, the arrogant. Nobody objects to the idea that Dr Crippen had a difficult marriage, even though he too was a killer. But Lord Lucan? No. If the marriage was problematical then that was his fault, just as it was the fault of Prince Charles, or any other apparently domin-ant male with a wife who can command sympathy. In truth it is rarely quite that simple. In the case of the Lucan marriage, it was very complicated indeed. And the real myth, according to Christina Shand Kydd, 'is that he didn't love Veronica. He did. But he was increasingly unable to cope.'

Lucan's sister Jane sees him clearly; she is not deluded about his flaws, nor about the inherent difficulties of having to live with him. She was supremely unimpressed by his lifestyle, his materialism, his stubborn refusal to make the most of his qualities. Nevertheless she says of his marriage: 'It was awful to see him take the wrong path.' In the spring of 1964 the Lucans went to New York and stayed with Jane (by then a doctor) and her husband. She recalls:

> They came over for the World's Fair. We have a tiny apartment, very unlike what they were used to. And I can see Veronica ironing her wig. In those days people did iron wigs [they also wore them more habitually than today]. But they had to come home from the fair in a taxi – couldn't take the subway because she was claustrophobic or something.

A couple of months earlier, Lucan had spent a long weekend at Miami Beach with Bill Shand Kydd, to see Sonny Liston fight Cassius Clay (later Muhammad Ali). 'And Veronica came to stay with me,' says Christina, who then goes on to describe an incident in which her sister took exception to a remark made by the family nanny.

> There was the most appalling scene... Veronica stormed out of the house, and walked home to Park Crescent. I pleaded with her not to go, and not to be so silly, but that was the sort of thing that, you know... And when the men got back, I told Bill what had happened. John came round that evening, and absolutely flew at Bill, saying I won't have your wife belittling my wife because she's jealous of this,

that and the other. And when he'd finished, Bill looked at him and said OK, John, now it's my turn to come round to your house and tell *your* wife what I think of *her*. And there was a slight silence, and then John said, Oh, I don't think that would be a very good idea. And they sort of made it up. Between the rest of us it did last, for a longish time, until we went to do a power boat race in Miami in April [Lucan's new boat failed when in second position, and he gave up the sport thereafter]. Veronica treated us as if the row had never happened.

But John was fiercely loyal to her, at first.

The title, of which Christina was allegedly 'jealous', was deeply treasured by Veronica. 'I had a handle to my name,' she was still proudly declaiming twenty years after Lucan's disappearance. When a £19,000 lease was taken on 46 Lower Belgrave Street in July 1964, the countess life began in earnest. Veronica redecorated the house repeatedly over the next three years, very nicely (her graphic design training), with heavy reds in the ground-floor rooms, blues and pale yellow in the marital bedroom. A portrait of the 3rd Earl of Lucan glared across the drawing room. There was also a painting of Lavinia Bingham, wife to the 2nd Earl Spencer. Later these would hang in Veronica's mews house at Eaton Row behind Lower Belgrave Street, along with the portrait of the 7th Earl in his ermine robes, painted by Dominick Elwes.

A landscape attributed to Van Goyen would be sold in 1977 for £9,000, as part of the discharge of Lucan's bankruptcy. Also sold, for £520, were his robes and coronet, the aristocratic regalia that had been made for his grandfather.[11] These were kept in Lucan's ground-floor study. So too was the ivory backgammon board that had been his wife's engagement present, and a nineteenth-century desk, rosewood and tulipwood, sold by Veronica for £13,200 in 2009. 'That was my father's,' says Jane. 'Veronica sold some lovely things that we used to slightly weep over.' Even after the bankruptcy discharge a certain amount remained, such as paintings, jewellery and items of furniture, although Lucan himself had sold a good many things along the way: notably the precious marble heads commissioned by the 2nd Earl of his daughters. By 1974 Lucan would be placating his creditors with a promise to sell 'the family silver', a loss as wrenching as that totemic phrase implies, although he may have been beyond caring by that point. The collection included forty-eight George III plates, kept at the St James's Club and occasionally used for formal dinners; a decorated field marshal's baton presented to the 3rd Earl by Queen Victoria in 1887; and a truly magnificent William IV candelabrum, a giant thing with nine lights, again inherited from the 3rd Earl: 'presented to Lieutenant-Colonel Lord Bingham by officers of the 17th Lancers on his retirement from the command of the regiment as a testimonial of their respect and esteem.' This piece sold for £6,050 at Christie's in 1976, when the 102 items of silver together made £30,665 (around half the total of Lucan's debts). Many of the auctioned items were bought back anonymously, by friends, on behalf of his children. A further sale took place in Geneva.

In October 1964 the Lucans had their first child, Frances. A photograph by Lenare shows a wide-eyed Veronica with her baby, an intensely touching image of the happiness that might have been. An older woman named Lilian Jenkins was employed as the first Lucan nanny, and stayed with the family for eight years, through the births of George in 1967 and Camilla in 1970. Later Veronica would claim that she had not wanted a nanny at all. When she sacked Lilian Jenkins in late 1972, very much against her husband's wishes, she was said to have been asserting both her autonomy and her status as a mother.[12] However, given that she had suffered post-natal depression with each of her children, help was clearly desirable, as well as being the upper-class norm.

Throughout this period Veronica rarely rose before midday, and lived in as sybaritic a way as her husband had done in his twenties. Lucan was a very generous man. As gamblers do, he would chuck Veronica a gift whenever he had a decent win: usually a piece of jewellery. There were also lunches at San Lorenzo; dinners at the Mirabelle; hair at Carita in Knightsbridge; dresses from Bellville Sassoon; food account at Harrods; golf lessons; hunting with the Whaddon Chase; standing on racecourses in the hallowed square of turf that marks the owners' and trainers' enclosure, watching the two horses that ran in her name; attending the Cresta Run and its fabulous ball; staying with the von Furstenbergs, with the Aga Khan; summers in Monte Carlo, Italy, the south of France. It was a holiday life, punctuated by holidays. A lot of women would give their right arm for it. 'We were a beautiful couple,' Veronica was to say, 'and our marriage had its good times.' It doesn't sound as though there was much to bitch about.

Yet the bitching did come, increasingly so, and it was related to the thing that Veronica had previously agreed to accept: her husband's gambling. 'She'd said she didn't mind John gambling,' as Stephen Raphael put it, 'yet her chief complaint throughout the marriage was that he gambled.'[13] But really the complaint was about something more than that. The gambling became a symbol of a more diffuse sense of marital dislocation. Veronica did not fit into Lucan's world, and his reaction was to bury himself within it.

Today we would say: why *should* she have fitted into his world? Why should she have enjoyed the Clermont, or become friendly with Kait Lucan? A nice mother-in-law, one would have thought, but she wasn't obliged to agree. Indeed the police accounts of Veronica do present a modern, almost feminist heroine, standing up for reason against the brandy-soaked buffoonery of the 7th Earl and, by the end of this story, emerging the victor in every respect: destroying the man who had, according to myth, sought to destroy her.

Three cheers would be the modern response to this. Veronica as the voice of the put-upon woman, like Diana, Princess of Wales chatting away and stirring the dirt on *Panorama*; the only problem being that Veronica freely chose to marry Lord Lucan, she was bright enough to know what he was like, she absolutely loved having a title, and therefore, it would seem, the problem was not so

1. The 7th Earl of Lucan in 1973.

2. Laleham House, built by the 2nd Earl of Lucan in 1803, sold by the 5th Earl in 1928.

3. The 3rd Earl of Lucan.

4. The Lucan memorial in the churchyard
of All Saints', Laleham.

5. The wedding of Lord Lucan's parents, December 1929: Kaitilin Dawson walks up the aisle of Southwark Cathedral to marry George Patrick Bingham.

6. Lord Bingham, the future Lord Lucan, at St Moritz: early 1960s

7. Lord Bingham at the helm of his powerboat, *White Migrant*, 1963.

8. Lord Bingham and Veronica Duncan, newly engaged in September 1963.

9. The wedding of Lord Bingham and Veronica Duncan, November 1963.

10. John Aspinall (left), his associate John Burke and his mother Lady Osborne arrive at court in 1958. Aspinall was accused and acquitted of keeping a 'common gaming-house'.

11. Dominick Elwes and Tessa Kennedy, with whom he eloped in 1957.

12. James Goldsmith, 1954: during an interval in a court hearing in Paris concerning his four-month-old daughter, Isabel.

13. Lady Lucan with her first-born, Frances, in 1964

14. The exterior of the Clermont Club at 44 Berkeley Square.

15. Christina and Bill Shand Kydd, 1971.

16. Lord Lucan and Zoe Howard, wife of Greville Howard, on holiday in Portofino, 1968.

17. Lord Lucan at a London gambling club, 30 April 1973.

18. The mews at 5 Eaton Row (yellow door). The house backs almost directly onto 46 Lower Belgrave Street, whose garden lies behind the brick wall.

19. 72a Elizabeth Street, where Lucan took a ground-floor flat after the breakdown of his marriage in 1973.

20. Andrina Colquhoun, the debutante with whom Lucan formed a friendship in 1974, photographed in Hyde Park.

much that she wanted to set herself apart from his world, more that she wanted to belong to it and didn't.

It is said that Veronica, despite her dislike of the place, was obliged to go to the Clermont every night, otherwise she would never have seen her husband. This is something of an exaggeration: there were the social events, the private planes to go racing in France (which Veronica herself refused to do), the weekends away, the evenings in restaurants. They spent Sunday evenings with Zoe and Greville Howard at a club in Mayfair. Lucan's old friend from Eton would also meet them for dinner: 'She was never a real friend, you know. But I got on with her perfectly well. She wasn't that easy. You wouldn't think, after having supper with them, that it had been great fun. It had been OK – just nothing, really.'

But after a year or so of marriage, gambling did begin to assume a greater importance in Lucan's life. It is a familiar scenario. Going to the tables became the aristocratic equivalent of having a few quiet pints down the pub with the boys. It was an escape, or seemed to be one, even though it was also work. Money had to be acquired, despite the safety net of the trusts. Lucan dealt in casual thousands: £8,000 could go out on a bad night, but in the 1960s, when he still maintained a degree of control, it would come back in again. He had considerable success at cards and backgammon. 'He wasn't *supremely* good at bridge, but he was quite a good bridge player,' says Stuart Wheeler; overall he won more than he lost at the Portland bridge club. At backgammon he won the St James's Club tournament and became the champion of the West Coast of America. He also made money at poker, which he learned at the Hamilton Club and at which he was very good indeed (the façade being what it was). 'He kept on having these big wins,' says Bill Shand Kydd, 'which kept him afloat. He'd get a couple of grand, and squirrel it away.' The gambling took place at various venues, as did socializing; there was a communal dinner every Monday at the Portland. But it was the atmosphere of the Clermont that had begun to embrace him.

'It was', says Jane, 'a home from home. That was where he spent so much time, and Veronica would be there too. I can still see the rocking, actually...'

As Veronica sat in her finery, she would rock back and forth on the 'widows' bench'. 'On one occasion,' it was later said, 'she became distraught and sat constantly pulling her hair.'[14] It was only fair that she wanted to go there with her husband. Yet her presence became a clamp upon his mood: although she took up very little space, one was always somehow very aware of her, a tiny white figure amid the merriment.

The myth has it that Veronica had a singularly terrible time at the Clermont, sitting alone on the widows' bench while her husband gambled with his chuckling, braying circle of friends. 'Can you imagine?' says a detective who worked on the case. 'If *my* wife had to sit there like that she'd have plenty to say about it.' And that, certainly, is a point of view. Some of Lucan's friends shared it: the myth that they had no sympathy with her situation is much exaggerated. 'His wife would have had a rotten time, I think,' says Stuart Wheeler. 'I get the impression that she was very lonely there.' Lucan's schoolfriend says: 'I think she had a rough time, in that he pushed off to gamble at all hours – she sat in the corner at the Clermont club, sat on her own while he gambled. Not the whole time, of course. But that can't have been very easy for her.' Nick Peto, who later married Zoe and was then a Clermont regular, concurs. 'Veronica must have had a miserable life, sat there, doing nothing.'

After Lucan's disappearance, even John Aspinall conceded that Veronica had not had much fun at the club. 'She would sit down on the banquette and hardly speak to anyone. But she had no business to come there.'[15] That last sentence is nonsense, of course, typical provocative Aspinall; but the first does give pause for thought. Although it is always said that Veronica endured agonies at the Clermont, nobody ever really asks *why*. There were other women there, who coped with it happily enough. Was it really such hell, sitting in that beautiful, bustling house? One can think of worse fates. The Clermont had life, style, a sense that one had traversed the VIP rope. It was, at the time, the place to be: a Studio 54 where the drug of choice was gambling. If it required a bit of effort, a bit of social toughness, then so do most things. If it was boring, then so is sitting at home. Of course to the modern sensibility the club does cause a dutiful shudder. It was manly, showy, posh, celebratory of wealth: all the contemporary sins. Fifty years ago, however, and despite the distant rumble of the tumbrils outside, places like that were not merely acceptable but desirable. If one didn't like them, as members of Lucan's family most certainly did not, then one might think that the answer was to stay well away from the kind of man who did.

'If I'd been married to a gambler,' says Christina Shand Kydd, 'if Bill had been like John and gone there every night – I suppose I would have gone two or three nights a week, and other nights gone to a movie with a friend or whatever. Or Veronica could have come and had supper with us – but she wasn't like that. At all.' As Stephen Raphael said: 'She didn't create a life of her own.'[16] For a clever woman this should have been easy; there were alternatives to the charity ball circuit, which would understandably have bored her. No marriage requires its parties to be conjoined. Veronica's unusual persistence in shadowing Lucan made him more obstinate in turn. Again it was a familiar situation: that battle of wills – whether it be your mother or mine for Christmas, or who empties the dishwasher every night, or who can sulk for longest after an argument – which to an outsider seems so absurd, and within the marriage assumes a devouring importance.

And it now seems untenable that a man should go out gambling and a woman be expected smilingly to endorse it. Again, fifty years ago things were very different; it is impossible to apply retrospectively a feminist agenda; equal partnerships, marriages that are also friendships, are too rare today for us to start berating the past about its lack of them. Most of the Clermont women had married a place in the world, as much as a man. This still happens. There are still plenty of women who endure tedious dinner parties sweet-talking their husbands' business associates, or who maintain strenuous regimes of beautification, in order to justify their place inside architect-designed houses in Ladbroke Square. It is a choice. It is not our ideal of marriage, but it can succeed as well as the more romantic kind, as long as expectations are managed.

Veronica had, undeniably, got what she wanted from Lucan. She herself would later say: 'Right from the start I realized that if I were to marry him I'd have to fit in with his life.'[17] Why, then, the open discontentment, when the man behaved much as he had said he would, in a place where being an earl and countess still signified? 'It's very difficult to describe,' says Christina.

> She was very remote... I don't think that John didn't want her there. At the start anyway. But I mean she wouldn't make any attempt to make friends with anybody in his life, or any part of his life. She probably felt that she should go. But then when she got there she'd just sit.

Christina also says that Lucan's set 'tried hard with Veronica at first – particularly Zoe Howard'. Zoe, by then married to Greville Howard, became a good friend for a time.

> I was very fond of Veronica, else we wouldn't have had our lunches at San Lorenzo [then an intensely smart restaurant in South Kensington]. We used to have lunch quite regularly. She was always saying to me, you're very lucky to be married to a Howard, because your name is in Debrett's. And I'm not like that. I didn't know what Debrett's was! I wasn't into it at all.

Zoe would sit alongside Veronica and watch their husbands as they played backgammon. So the image of persistent loneliness is a little misleading, although the impression is definitely that Zoe, just seventeen at the time and full of sweet good nature, was the only woman whom Veronica found unthreatening. 'I don't think she had many friends. She wasn't over-friendly herself. I talked to other girls too, that were waiting, and they were quite fun and jolly. They were all very beautiful women – all smartly dressed. Some were mistresses of course, not all were wives. Everybody was always nice to me.'

It is said that Veronica was far too bright for most of the people who went to the Clermont (in fact several of Lucan's friends were Oxford graduates; whether they put their brains to good use is another question). She was, as the policeman Roy Ranson put it, 'an intelligent woman sentenced to a life as an upper-class bimbo'; not especially flattering to the other wives and girlfriends. It is also said that she was looked down upon as socially below the salt, although logically this should have applied to her sister as well, which it did not.[18]

Yet Veronica's own perceptions of her role at the Clermont could be very different from those cited on her behalf. 'I enjoyed the club, it was a waking-up time,' she later said. 'I knew he [Lucan] was a gambler. I therefore did a gambler's moll act with him. We posed as a happy holiday couple but we were in these situations to make money. Making money was the principal objective and we were a team.' In oblique reference to her apparent solitude, she also said: 'I sat away from my husband when he played so I might come and go without being obvious, so he'd never associate me with winning or losing.' In direct contradiction of the myth that Lucan abandoned her to loneliness, she said: 'I suppose I saw more of him than most wives did of their husbands, because I saw him in the daytime and at night.'[19]

Rightly or wrongly, this implies a collusion with Lucan, a sort of secret bond. So too do Veronica's criticisms of other people at the club:

> Most of the women... resented me because I had married one of the gamblers and they couldn't get their boyfriends to marry them. Not only had I married one of the gamblers but I had married the most attractive man in the Clermont... Most of the women subsequently wouldn't speak to me or went out of their way to be rude to me.

Enmity or rivalry between women is not uncommon. It is entirely possible that, intentionally or otherwise, some of the Clermont WAGs made Veronica feel out of place. Their glamour, too, may have been an issue. *En masse* they were like Bond girls. Veronica's youthful glow had begun to dim; photographs of her on holiday with the Howards show a thin-faced woman with narrow eyes, attractively cool-looking by today's standards but definitely underpowered by those of the time. Very much the peahen. One of the club members now describes her as 'a mousy, bitter little woman. Completely out of her depth in that ambiance. She hadn't got beauty or charm.' Easy to say that this is a frivolous and ungallant view. Not so easy to spend every evening like Jane Eyre in the midst of *Casino Royale*.

When, in 1966, Vittorio De Sica offered a film role out of nowhere to her husband, this would have seemed like further confirmation of his physical superiority. 'There goes that expensive gentleman,' said the mother of one of his gambling acquaintances, as he strolled casually out of the Eden Roc hotel. Veronica was later to say that people were always watching Lucan, speculating about him sexually; there is almost certainly some truth in this, because it is what people do. Nevertheless one has the sense that, Othello-like, she was hyper-alert to any hint that he might seek to stray, and that this was part of what made her so determined to stick to his side. In fact, as his old schoolfriend says, Lucan was as guiltless in this regard as Desdemona. 'He could have gone off with somebody else. He never showed any sign of it.'

Veronica claimed to have got along well with the male gamblers – 'it was the women who resented me, not the men' – and some of them did take a liking to her. 'She had a sort of quaint humour, which I thought was quite endearing,' said Michael Stoop, while Daniel Meinertzhagen, who displays none of the Clermont set's mythical kneejerk loathing for Veronica, recalls a drive with her in which she was very good company. 'It was when John was around that the trouble started.' That, indeed, was the crux of it. Despite her stated camaraderie with Lucan's friends, Veronica said: 'I know for a fact that some of the men wanted their girlfriends to sleep with John so that they could find out what Lucky was like in bed... They didn't have his background or his breeding and they were constantly trying to pull him down to their position. Naturally, that included sex... They tried to plant prostitutes on him and all sorts of things.'[20]

Whether or not this is how it was, and one strongly suspects that it was not that way, it all sits very well with the image of the Clermont as a hotbed of vice-ridden decadence. One can say that this world of Lucan's was awful, and that it was to Veronica's infinite credit that she did not fit, that she was 'a square peg in a round hole', as Nick Peto puts it. But that is not quite the truth, either.

One night at the Clermont, Veronica threw a glass of wine over another woman. In that milieu, it had the edifice-shattering momentum of a stolen kiss in E. M. Forster.

'I can't remember why it happened,' says Christina. Accounts differ: some say that it was an argument over what channel was showing on the television in the bar, some that it was during a row about sex discrimination. Whatever the reason, it did the unfor-givable thing of making private emotion into a public display. 'She threw a glass of wine in this girl's face, and called her a tart, I remember that. I think she thought she was eyeing John. You can imagine, everybody was talking about it.' It was a brief flash of fury, a sudden crack of a bar in the gilded cage. One can understand it, just as one can comprehend the compulsion to follow Lucan to the club every night. But this silly incident of the wine, which took place in 1972, was the sharp irruption of a slow, subterranean accretion of frustration. Not long afterwards came the separation of the Lucans, followed by the sequence of events that led to that other and much greater irruption, on 7 November 1974.

Up until 1972, the façade had been maintained. The evenings at the club had continued, as did the glamorous holidays: Venice, Rome, Monte Carlo (where the gamblers decamped in July, when the Clermont closed). Appearances were kept up: the invitation to this world read black tie and Balenciaga. But the marriage between these two unsuited, uncertain people, each utterly incapable of giving the other what they needed, grew steadily grimmer. So too did Lucan's gambling. His life became a straitjacket that grew ever tighter as he chafed against it. If only they had bitten the bullet and cut loose from each other! Instead they ground on together, walking into the Clermont like two white-faced automata: the stilted chat over the vodka martini, the stiff and joyless dinner, and then the illusory escape of the tables. The elegant, exigent club became the terrain on which the Lucans fought out the Strindbergian battle of their marriage. Beneath the formalities, tension tugged like a wire thread in the air between them, snaking its way up the golden staircase into the chemmy room. He was defying her by gambling; and, in his mind at least, she was defying him by watching, her baleful silence simultaneously urging him on and mocking his obsession.

The Lucan myth has it that the deterioration of the marriage was entirely his doing. Veronica herself later said: 'I had to be an obedient wife. If I did something he disapproved of, he would send me to my room to reflect on the errors of my ways.'[21] According to Roy Ranson she became alarmed by Lucan's habits, 'more aware of the perceptible shift in her husband's attitudes and behaviour'; meaning that he was growing ever more reactionary and immovable, as if the façade had become part of his very substance. And then – again according to Ranson – Lucan reverted to type in the most terrifying fashion. He began treating Veronica as if she were mad, and telling his friends and family that she was mad. It was 'a vicious and unrelenting campaign to brand her insane'. This accusation is at the heart of the myth, and has been accepted as truth for the past forty years.

Except that, once again, there is another side to the story.

The police knew that Veronica, upon whose word their case depended, had a history of instability. Their explanation was to blame her husband for making her that way. As one of the investigating officers now says: 'She was difficult. Some of the things she said...!

You couldn't be sorry for her or she'd eat you for breakfast. But she wasn't all bad. She was pushed into madness.' In other words, the fault had been Lucan's. It was the gentlemanly behaviour of the supreme non-gentleman.

Yet the idea that Lucan tried to send his wife mad is, when one thinks about it, quite ludicrous. It is pure *Grand Guignol.* Could anybody possibly believe such a thing, except of a man like the Lucan of myth? 'It must have been around the late 1960s when Lucan first decided that his wife had to go,' speculated Ranson, with an air of faux-sagacity. His reasoning, or best guess, is that Veronica's complaints against her husband's gambling had become unbearable, and that therefore she had to be stopped. At this point Lucan was not considering murder, merely stating that she was off her head. Murder came later.

It is attested, for instance by Stephen Raphael, that Veronica did complain about Lucan's gambling. She herself later referred to her understandable concern about provision for the children's future.[22] She also said: 'I should have been more extravagant. He wouldn't have had so much money to waste on gambling. I should have insisted on designer dresses;'[23] slightly baffling remarks given the couple's high-end lifestyle. Part of the problem, in fact, was that Lucan gambled in order to maintain it. His ambition, in so far as he had one, was to live like a lord.

Yet in her first interview after the murder, given in January 1975 to the *Daily Express*, to whom she was under contract, Veronica said something quite different:

> I never complained about him being out so late. After all that usually meant he was bringing home more for the family. On the good days there would be a trip to Cartier for me and a handsome present. It could amount to £4,000 or more. I still have the diamond bracelet he bought there for me... I have never known anyone so generous.[24]

So Ranson's theory, that Lucan was desperate for his wife to shut up and let him get on with his gambling, is only part-supported.

And what exactly was he achieving, anyway, by trying to send her mad? It was not as though he could *really* behave like Earl Ferrers, or like Mr Rochester, and keep her stashed away somewhere. A stay in an institution would be of limited length.

It could be said that Lucan's objective was to prove Veronica an unfit mother in a subsequent custody case. But he began expressing concerns about her condition in 1967, and the couple did not actually separate until the start of 1973. This was an extraordinarily long game to play, for a man who increasingly enjoyed the snap, crackle and pop of chemin-de-fer. It could also be said that he behaved out of straightforward sadism, that he was exacting revenge upon her for being the wrong sort of wife. But why, after nearly four years of average-to-miserable marriage, would this really rather arcane idea have occurred to a not especially imaginative man? Why not leave at once, rather than waiting six years?

The reason could, of course, have been something altogether simpler, although this seems never to have occurred to the myth-makers. Lucan was telling the truth, as he saw it. By 1967 Veronica was – in her husband's view – giving the strong appearance of needing treatment, and he tried to get it for her. Simple as that. Why was it so difficult for the police to consider even the possibility that Lucan was not, in fact, concocting stories about Veronica's mental state? That he was not taking her to psychiatric clinics for the fun of it: it wasn't much fun, after all? Because any suggestion that Lucan had done these things from genuine motives would have blown an almighty hole through the police version of events.

Veronica herself later stated that she had suffered post-natal depression, which first manifested itself after Frances was born in 1964 and recurred with her two subsequent babies. 'I felt less and less well with each child,' she said. 'These days I would have been given the right medication and got over it.'[25] This, according to the police, was the seed from which sprang Lucan's devilish plot to treat her as insane. Yet in a bizarre contradiction Ranson wrote that Lucan had at first been sympathetic to Veronica, but after the birth of George in 1967 he 'proved unable to cope' and told friends that she was behaving oddly: this may not have been perfect uxorious behaviour, but it does not equate to seeking to send her mad.

Her sister Christina wholeheartedly agrees that Veronica had a bad time after the births of her children. She also states, firmly and from intimate knowledge, that the difficulties began earlier. 'There had been psychological problems for a long time.' As James Fox wrote in the *Sunday Times Magazine*, Veronica 'was suffering from emotional disorders at the age of eight'. In other words, these were not invented by Lucan.

Only prejudice, prejudice against those terrible aristocrats, could engender belief in the story that Lucan wanted to do that. An alternative to the myth, put forward by people who were actually there at the time, and who have no reason to say this now except a frustrated desire to provide some balance, is that Lucan was not trying to make Veronica ill. He was trying to help her. His efforts were haphazard and incompetent; almost certainly, the treatment was not always of the right kind (although later a psychiatrist would state that Veronica's condition had been controlled by the prescription of lithium). Nevertheless there is evidence to suggest that, in the first instance, Lucan's behaviour proceeded from straightforward concern about his wife.

This is not to say that he was an exemplary husband, or that he was anything other than baffled by a complex situation. He did not display the kind of empathy that would be expected today. That was not his nature. He wanted the problem to go away, so that, as Christina says, 'the two of them could go on together'. He was as out of his depth as Veronica was said to be at the Clermont; he was Prince Charles again, albeit without the mistress, standing in rigid masculine bewilderment as his wife hurled herself against her own distress. And his refuge, gambling, was so much part of the problem that it required ever-deeper plunges to push away reality.

Lucan's sister Jane says frankly: 'He might have contributed to Veronica's illness, because of his lifestyle, which was pretty un-family.' At the same time, as a doctor, Jane believed that Veronica 'needed psychiatric care, and she got it. But I don't know if she had a good psychiatrist, or if John just found somebody who would dope her. I was aware that she was taking a lot of medication. So I don't know.' Meanwhile Kaitilin, who lunched with Lucan most Sundays, urged him to take the problem seriously. In the past she had been willing to get psychiatric help for her son. Now she recommended it for his wife. Later, when Kait explained some of this to the police, it was dismissed on the grounds of family bias. Kait, wrote Ranson, 'was almost as obsessed with her daughter-in-law's behaviour as was her son'.

Yet Christina, whose loyalties were inevitably conflicted, nevertheless is insistent upon the facts. In this she is supported by her husband, with whom she assumed eventual care of the Lucan children. She does not apportion blame within the original problem: only with how this was later portrayed. 'The situation was impossible,' she says, 'because Veronica *wasn't well.* It wasn't her fault. But that was why it started to fall apart.'

> And she had a very acerbic tongue, and when she wasn't well she would say some really quite cruel things. John had tremendous family back-up – Kaitilin, Sally and William [his younger sister and her husband, the Reverend William Gibbs]. They would all have helped Veronica too. But no one was going to be allowed in. That was the problem. She relied on me, quite a lot, but it was a sort of up and down thing. It was very sad. I mean, I probably knew her better than anybody in the world at that time, including her husband, and I knew she was desperately unwell.
>
> With each child that was born, the situation was getting worse... Veronica was getting absolutely desperate to have a son – and then we were away on holiday, and the call came through that she'd had a boy. And we were so happy, all of us, weren't we? We thought all her problems will be over now. She adored George. I mean he was absolutely her angel. But in herself she was much worse.

At first Lucan tried to deal with this, ineffectually. He did not behave like Ian Maxwell-Scott, who simply threw up his hands and lived away from home, saying that he could not tolerate his wife's behaviour. Lucan continued to defend Veronica, as he had done at the start of the marriage. 'There was a row with somebody at the club, who Veronica said had been rude to her. And he very much stood up for her.' Then, after George's birth, he took her to the Priory, the psychiatric nursing home in Roehampton now much favoured by celebrity addicts. 'That', says Christina, 'is what gave rise to the rumour that he was trying to have her put away, or something. But he was taking her to try and persuade her to have treatment.'

With regard to the damning allegations that Lucan sought to make his wife unstable, Christina says:

> Well, those would be her allegations, you see. Because the time she's referring to, trying to be forced, was when he took her to the Priory – and then when they got there she ran away, which I believe is perfectly normal practice if you are unwell. But that was turned into the fact that he was trying to incarcerate her.

'He says I'm mad,' Veronica would later tell her sister. 'He's made me like that because he's always trying to shut me up in places.' She reiterated this belief at her lunches with Zoe Howard. 'She kept telling me', says Zoe, 'that John wanted to put her in – not a lunatic asylum – but have her committed. She was slightly... She was quite clever. She could win over anybody. She was very clever at giving the right impression when needed. You'd feel sorry for this poor woman who's got this awful husband...' Despite some misgivings Zoe spoke in Veronica's favour at the 1973 custody hearing, although their closeness ended after Veronica threw an insult at Greville Howard.

It is said that Lucan's set did not hide their dislike of Veronica. Certainly that became true. However, as with any marriage where there are opposing camps, there is the crucial question of what had happened, in the first place, to provoke the taking of sides. 'The press put it that they just didn't like her,' says Christina. 'Nobody. But it's never been explained perhaps why they didn't. I mean she was always telling John that people had snubbed her and things, and he believed her. And then I think it must have come as quite a shock to him to realize that he'd been wrong.'

Veronica had never got along with Lucan's family. Now there were problems with his friends. Daniel Meinertzhagen says: 'She had an acid tongue.' Several examples of this are cited, which by definition cannot be verified; although Ranson admits that the Howards, for instance, were 'alienated' by Veronica. Incidents are also recalled by the Shand Kydds and by Lucan's old friend from Eton, who says: 'I think we were all as supportive as we could have been of Veronica, without being enthusiastic about doing it. Because of John, you know?' As for the idea that Lucan himself drove Veronica to a state of instability: 'No, that's not right. That needs to be said.'

Of course all this comes from the Lucan camp. It might there-fore be argued that these people are, even now, when it no longer makes any difference, trying to bolster him; this, after all, is the accusation that has been thrown at them for the past forty years. In fact commentators on the case have generally admitted that there were 'shocking outbursts in public', or that 'Lady Lucan was aggressive and unbalanced [with] a long history of psychiat-ric illness',[26] although the blame for this always somehow migrates to her husband. Meanwhile the recollections of Lucan's friends are supported by a complete outsider, the former nanny to the Maxwell-Scott children. She has detailed memories of Grants Hill in Uckfield, even down to the food (crayfish and raspberries) that was served at weekend parties attended by members of the Clermont set, including the Lucans. The nanny, who observed the situation between the couple, recalls that on several occasions 'Veronica had tantrums, big time'.

> Shocking for me, seeing people behave like that, but also trying not to notice because it wasn't my place to notice. I remember Susie [Maxwell-Scott] saying John is just pushed to the limit. There was

palpable friction between Veronica and John. It's like he almost looked forlorn, despairing, rather than aggressive and confrontational with her. Sort of – oh God. Embarrassed. I think embarrassed.

That, indeed, would be the reaction. Lucan would have been inhibited from confronting the situation; although that would not have been easy for anybody. Until this point his life had been a comfortable, one might say selfish business. He had absolutely no idea what to do when it proved impossible to recapture that golden pleasure in existence. The 3rd Earl of Lucan, whom his great-great-grandson is assumed to resemble, would have simply strode away from it all, as he did from his own much less problematical marriage; but not even an aristocrat could do that anymore. There was money to consider, the welfare of the children, the endless ramifications that normal people had to deal with. The freedom that had gone with unquestioned mastery was no longer Lucan's to command. What was left was a set of behaviours, a manner, a demeanour. He was imprisoned in the cage of class. Within the thoroughbred exterior was nothing that could deal with the reality of his marriage. He could not communicate directly with his wife, which meant that she could not with him. Anyway the thoroughbred exterior was what she liked. That does not mean that these people felt nothing: those who keep emotion locked away suffer just as much as those in whom it is on display. But for this couple, for what they may have regarded as the foreseeable future, the only possibility was to go on, spending evenings at the Clermont, spending money, dressing correctly, eating away at each other's strength and sanity.

When Lucan took Veronica to the Priory in 1967, and she refused to enter the clinic, the ensuing scene culminated in her agreeing to see a psychiatrist instead. 'I only did it', she later said, 'to show him that I would co-operate. He told me that it was the sign of a mentally ill person when they refused to have treatment.'[27] She was prescribed lithium, which helped. She was also given fluphenazine, an anti-psychotic drug that caused restless movement: Veronica's foot would tap relentlessly as she sat on the widows' bench (the rocking back and forth, which has also been ascribed to the drug, was a longstanding habit). These were terrifyingly powerful drugs to be taking. It was later said that they were 'partly' to blame for Veronica's paranoia and hallucinations. The suggestion, in other words, was that the fault (or some of it) lay with her husband's malevolent insistence upon treatment.[28]

Veronica's third pregnancy, with Camilla, was extremely diffi- cult.[29] After the birth in June 1970, she moved between psychiatrists. Among others she saw Dr Ann Dally, a controversial but free- thinking woman whose experience in obstetrics and gynaecology suggests she would have had a grasp on this situation.[30] Veronica left a holiday in Monte Carlo to visit Dr Dally, although later she implied that seeing these psychiatrists was a false move directed by Lucan. 'He was always sending me to doctors, then he would appear person- ally to pay the bill and ask them questions about me. He considered it his right as my husband to know. I fell into the trap of taking up some of my lonely life with doctors who would talk to me.'[31]

In 1971, when Veronica was again in a distraught state, Lucan took her to Greenways nursing home in Hampstead. According to her own account, she agreed to go under the influence of sleeping pills, administered by Lucan. When she arrived she 'felt she couldn't face it'.[32] As before, there was a scene; she ran away and took a bus home. The ex-police officer who now says of Veronica, 'Once you get into that mental health system, there's no escape', makes a serious point. The irony is that the myth is correct, because Lucan's attempts to treat Veronica made the situation so much worse; yet at the same time it is a falsification, because this was not what he intended. It is impossible not to sympathize: but for both of them.

Lucan now did as Ian Maxwell-Scott had done, and began spending nights away from home. He often stayed at the Eaton Row mews or the St James's Club. He also began confiding in friends about his marriage, and this was later interpreted as telling them that

Veronica was mad in order to undermine her. Certainly it did set in stone the alliances that were already being formed, which left Veronica isolated. 'The over-riding suspicion', it was later said, 'is that nobody, at least no male, ever tried to conduct a sensible conversation with her, and never tried to see beneath her anger and defensiveness... Her qualities were never weighed in that marginal socialite world of smart gambling where appearance counts a little too much and from which she was impatiently dismissed.'[33] There is truth in this, but it sets aside the fact that those of Lucan's set who were inclined to like her had, with time, found this difficult to do. Michael Stoop, who found Veronica to be 'clever, astute and subtle', went on to say that she was 'aggressive and unbalanced. It made her an extremely dangerous type of woman.' A man who worked at the Clermont states flatly: 'That wife of his was a ball-breaker. Whatever he did or didn't do, there was mitigation.'

'No long-term friendship could ever last,' says Christina, 'because she wasn't well. The whole thing was a nightmare, for everybody concerned.'

Lucan's own family despaired of the apparently insoluble situation. Veronica complained to them, as well as to Christina, that Lucan was physically violent and mentally cruel. She claimed that he had tried to strangle her and to throw her down the stairs. He countered that Veronica had hurled herself about the house to bring up bruises, then taunted him with the threat of arrest. The family members believed him, not her, for which they themselves would later suffer accusations: of taking the side of evil against innocence.

The police, naturally enough, took the view that he *was* violent during the marriage. Yet there is a contradiction within a story told by Roy Ranson. He gives credence to an allegation by Veronica that, when the couple went hunting, Lucan picked a fiery mount in the hope that it would throw her. Later, however, Ranson uses this story to an entirely different end. Lucan, he wrote, relayed Veronica's accusations about the horse to his friends, gleefully citing this as evidence of her paranoia. In other words, and despite the inherent paradox,

Ranson tries to have it both ways. Lucan wanted to injure Veronica physically, and damage her mentally, all with the same horse.

According to Ranson, this story about the horse was also one of the many rumours that rose within the Clermont like twists of smoke. It was whispered that Veronica did not merely make unreliable accusations against her husband, but that her own behaviour was bizarre and extreme. Such rumours, which grew stronger after the murder, persist even now and have become ever more lurid in the telling; they are absurd and utterly unbelievable.[34] But none of this mischief-making ever comes from people who actually knew the situation as it was. There is certainly no sense that it came from Lucan himself, although he could be blamed for starting the hare, as it were. It was the hysterical chit-chat of those on the fringes, the Clermont hangers-on who longed to contribute their snippet and who later spouted merrily to the press, who had a field day gossiping about poor old Lucky and his absolutely frightful wife. It is the kind of thing that happens in a club, a closed community: a grisly fact of life, and at least as damaging to Lucan as to Veronica.

The real source of the problem was John Aspinall. He positively loathed Veronica, being the sort of man who had no time for a woman who did not keep quiet and look gorgeous and let the men do their thing. He relished seeing her formally booted from the circle around which she had hovered like a spectre of doom. She was unlucky; a hex; she prevented Lucan from giving his full attention to gambling. As the stories about the marriage began to permeate the Clermont, Aspinall pranced about like his satanic majesty, fuelling the fires, making a florid show of loyalty towards his noble friend. 'Who knows into what red hell one's sightly soul will stray under the pressure of a long, dripping attrition of a woman who's always out to reduce you, to whom you are stuck and from whom you've had children,' he would later declaim.[35] Again it was Lucan who was damaged by this. Nobody could have been as bad as Aspinall made Veronica out to be; the conclusion, therefore, was that his defenders were the bad ones. The conflicted discretion of the rest became tainted by his shameless verbosity, just as the Clermont set, harmless in the main, was painted in his violent technicolour. There is the faint possibility that Aspinall foresaw this, and enjoyed the idea.

Certainly he and Lucan were close. Aspinall had fond feelings towards the man he called 'my fifth, sixth or seventh best friend'[36] (a typical tease), but they were also those of a cat that plays tenderly with a mouse. There may have been a kind of envy, for the young god who had strolled casually into the Clermont all set to make his pile. Soon Lucan would be wrapped tight in Aspinall's clutches; and there was an obscure sense, beyond the financial, in which Aspinall would relish this momentous fall. 'Yes, who needs a friend like Aspinall,' says Bill Shand Kydd; he was, as Harold Acton said of Violet Trefusis, 'the kind of friend who makes you long for a foe'.

But when Veronica Lucan snapped in 1972, and threw the wine into a woman's face in the bar of the Clermont, John Aspinall erected the barricades: we are all with Lucky, and the damnable wife can go to blazes. The end of the marriage, which had been resisted for so long, was now an inevitability.

In December 1972 Veronica sacked the nanny Lilian Jenkins, who had worked for the family throughout the whole period of the marriage breakdown, and was described as 'fiercely loyal to Lucan'. The dismissal, Lucan said, 'was at ten minutes' notice and against my wishes'.[37] There was a furious row. The Lucans then spent Christmas with his sister Sally and her family at their vicarage in Guilsborough, Northamptonshire. This, too, was a disaster. On Boxing Day Veronica returned to Lower Belgrave Street with the children. As 1973 began, Lord Lucan summoned his wife's GP, Christopher Powell-Brett, to confirm that she could be left. On 7 January he moved into the mews house at Eaton Row, and never returned.

House Blue

'I like a good detective story. But, you know, they begin in the wrong place! They begin with the murder. But the murder is the end. The story begins long before that – years before sometimes – with all the causes and events that bring certain people to a certain place at a certain time on a certain day. Zero hour.'

AGATHA CHRISTIE, *Towards Zero*, 1944

IT WAS IN 1973 that Lord Lucan's finances were irreparably weakened. The reason for this was not gambling in itself, although that had done its own damage. It was the attempt to gain custody of his three children, followed by gambling in an attempt to recoup the cost of the High Court case. When one has to win, one cannot; Dostoevsky's 'calm and calculating' head is set on fire by the lethal spark of necessity. Chasing a future makes it run away. All gamblers know this, but what one knows is not the same as what one does: that is how Lucan's life went wrong.

Although Lord Lucan is now a symbol of the gambler, embodying the very essence of its frantic follies, until his life reached its crisis point there was nothing particularly noteworthy about his gambling; not, that is to say, in the high-end world that he inhabited. There, he was just one of a kind. There were, as his wife put it, 'enormous swings of the pendulum', but that was normal. The swings were nothing like as extreme as those experienced by some of his friends. He did not, as David Stirling did in 1960, write an IOU to John Aspinall for £173,500. He did not lose as heavily as Daniel Meinertzhagen, and he certainly did not throw money around as maniacally as Ian Maxwell-Scott, who was by nature the gambler that Lucan is said to have been. Lucan did become that gambler: but by degrees, by a kind of chance.

Certainly his gambling worsened throughout the nine years of his marriage. He was selling things: books at Sotheby's, the three marble heads commissioned by the 2nd Earl, the Laleham property that had once been home to the Lucans' bailiffs. His living expenses with Veronica had been astronomical; as his sister says, 'he had to survive in that other world, the world of the highfalutin.' He was cash-poor. Nevertheless the situation could still have been salvage-able, for the very reason that it was still not one of absolute need.

That is not to say that becoming a 'professional gambler' had been anything other than folly. 'An intelligent person can do a very foolish thing,' says Stuart Wheeler. 'Perhaps not a very stupid thing, but a very foolish thing.' The choice, if it can be called that, had been born of two delusions: that it was possible to beat the odds, and that there was something earl-like about the gambler mentality. Winning with grace, losing with even more grace; these do require a noble stoicism. Non-gamblers would not see it that way, but there *is* a kind of gallantry about the way in which a gambler accepts fate. As Lord Lucan would have recognized, and with an intensity of fellow-feeling, one sees it in a Deptford betting shop just as in a Mayfair club. But in the club this gambling mentality permeates the man. It defines the man. To a Lucan, conscious of the ancestral centuries, this was a consoling retreat. As with Lord Hastings one hundred years earlier, it demanded nothing from him, although it took so much of what he had. It replaced the tricky business of making a life. And when life beyond the club became unbearable, it was hardly a choice at all to hole up within the silk and gilded bunker.

As much as anything, it supplied a routine. By the 1970s Lucan's days had acquired the rigid, repetitive quality that was again a form of refuge; 'if once the hair weren't accurately combed, the shoes properly laced, every object exactly placed, the same bus caught every morning, *The Times* always carried under the *left* arm, the entire structure would collapse. The deluge, in fact.'[1] Lucan was not a bus-traveller, but the principle was the same. Nick Peto says:

> I used to work in a commodities broking business at the top end of Piccadilly. John used to come virtually every day, swing round our office on his way to the Clermont. He always had his first drink, or two, of the day with us, at about half past eleven. I wouldn't say that was particularly unusual at that time, although he would have got up quite late, so it was early to be starting. It got him going in the morning. And he would leave us at about quarter past twelve and start gambling.

Then came lunch. An afternoon watching the racing, playing backgammon. Then back to Lower Belgrave Street, bath, change: and back to the clubs for dinner, more drinking, then the lethal move upstairs to chemin-de-fer until three, four or later. 'One morning,' says Pierrette Goletto, who was nanny to the Lucan children in 1974, 'I heard his friends walking past the house. He must have won – they were calling Lucky, Lucky, Lucky! It was six in the morning – they were coming back from the club and I was getting up.' The Portland, the St James's, Crockford's and the Ladbroke formed a tight circle of friendly satellites that could be landed upon at any chosen hour. But the sun around which they revolved was the Clermont.

As both he and the club slid past their prime, so they entered into a relationship that was something like a Faustian pact. Lucan offered his aristocratic bearing in exchange for a place of sanctuary. He was a diamond inside Aspinall's lovely jewel box: just by being there, sitting at the chemmy game with his languid *recherché* air, he ensured that the tone did not go flat. 'He was a presence at the table,' says Daniel Meinertzhagen. Lucan became a house player, a 'house blue', working for Aspinall. 'Not all the time, though, and only if it was a really big game. There were only a thousand members, so there wouldn't necessarily be enough players to make up a game. A house player would sit there and attract them. Aspinall would double John's hand to raise the stakes.' By the late 1960s several of the Clermont gamblers were playing for the house, having lost so much of their own money. Meinertzhagen himself was one, as were Charles Benson, Greville Howard and Nick Peto. 'I was a house player at two places,' says Peto. 'The Clermont and the White Elephant. We were all bust, really.' Of the stint at the White Elephant, where Lucan had celebrated the birth of his son with such delight, Peto later wrote:

> I had to play poker all night until the last people departed, which was normally about four o'clock in the morning. I was allowed to keep 25 per cent of my winnings, but if I lost, that would be put on the slate also. Of course in the morning I had to go off as normal to my job. Mancini [the proprietor] was a very tough cookie and I dread to think what would have happened if for any reason I had let him down.[2]

Aspinall's fist was wrapped in far softer materials, but nevertheless the house player was in an odd position: valuable yet beholden, like a butler. When the club was taken over by Playboy the system ended, being no longer necessary given the flood of new money and players. As a leaving present from Aspinall, a reward for services rendered, Lucan was handed an envelope containing his own bounced cheques.

Yet he was not actually broke. He had the trust money, the Belgravia house and the mews behind it, the residue of Laleham and Mayo, the heirlooms, the jewels, the silver. His money was not liquid, which meant overdrafts. He had certainly not 'made his pile' at gambling. The disappointment must have been crippling, if he allowed himself to think about it. But the knowledge did not stop him: he was unable to raise his head and see the world beyond, the one that would have shed its light upon folly.

How boring his life sounds. Wilfully so. There would have still been jokes, friends, excitements, the flame of alcohol; nevertheless it was a long way from the sane and healthy pleasures of powerboating, or standing in the winners' enclosure with his racehorse Le Merveilleux, or being young. But the alternative to the club ritual, which was life with his wife, had become impossible. Anyway Lucan had nothing now to spare for carefree pleasure. His energies, outside of gambling (which had a mechanistic aspect by this time), were grimly concentrated upon the penultimate battle of his marriage: getting his children away from his wife.

There are marriages that end decently. It does not have to be a descent into the inferno. But the nature of marriage, or partner-ship, makes it likely that it will be. To marry is to lay oneself bare to another person, to whom one is bound not by blood but by choice. There is little that the blood tie will not forgive, equally little that the marriage tie will; and when it comes to separation, the hardest thing of all to forgive is that one has made oneself vulnerable to this other, now alien person. The rage of Henry VIII against Anne Boleyn was that of a man who had exposed his truest self to a woman whom he now wanted not to exist. 'It amazes me now that for several months after she went I was v cut up about it, wanted her back, contemplated a *poem* on the subj if you don't fucking well mind,' wrote Kingsley Amis,[3] six years after his divorce from the novelist Elizabeth Jane Howard, with whom he had once been as adoringly besotted as a teenager. This has nothing to do with the person, everything to do with the mysterious destructiveness of the tie. 'Nobody can hurt you like a husband,' wrote Agatha Christie, whose own first marriage ended desperately. Of course marriage can do the opposite thing, enhance and strengthen two lives. But if the wrong natures collide, then the dance of lust and role play, which is how partnerships begin, will never mature into serenity. It can even turn dangerous. In a case of wife- or husband-murder, as Christie reiterated in her detective fiction, always look first to the spouse.

With the Lucans, strip away the veneer and it is clear that they could only bring out the worst in each other. Perhaps neither of them should have married at all, although in their different ways they both needed to do so. Even so, they might still have got away from each other intact, lived to fight another day, had there not been children in the marriage. Frances, George and Camilla were the spoils of war, the three aces in Veronica's hand. As long as she held them, the power was hers.

When a marriage ends, there are almost always two versions of its story: the wife's and the husband's. The battle of the marriage segues into a new power struggle, over whose version will acquire the illusion of truth. Each side acquires camp followers. In Lucan's case, he was supported, pretty much unreservedly, by everybody who saw him and his wife at close quarters. Yet Veronica's version of the marriage became the publicly accepted one. It is quite extraordinary, the extent to which the wife's part was taken by so many of the people at the edges of this story. After the events of November 1974 it was only right, of course, that Veronica should become an object of sympathy. But the way in which this permeated backwards, streaming through every aspect of the previous ten years, is striking. Facts were dismissed, ignored, or interpreted as being Lucan's own fault. As much as compassion for Veronica, in fact, what was really being evinced was visceral loathing for her husband.

Because a man of his kind is generally assumed to be the dominant partner, the weapons of the 'subjugated' woman are not easily perceived. They can be small, stealthy, deployed with a delicacy that is often beyond male understanding. Although the battle-lines were writ particularly boldly in the Lucan marriage, it is far from being the only one in which the wife has won the arguments in the public sphere. This is the prerogative of the apparently weaker party: the underdog, with whom the British instinctively sympathize. And because Lucan's supporters were, like him, assured and upper-class and incapable of expressing themselves with emotional intuitiveness, they too were dismissed. Even the Shand Kydds, who bore much of the brunt of the fallout from the marriage and took on the Lucan children; even kindly Kait Lucan, who was condemned for putting her son's interests in front of those of her daughter-in-law (a woman who ironically valued the title of countess as passionately as Kait had despised it).

At the 1975 inquest, Kait engaged the services of Michael Eastham QC to represent the interests of the Lucan family. In his first question to Veronica, Eastham said: 'You entertained feelings of hatred against your husband, didn't you?' Her representative vigorously objected. The coroner protested. Gallantry for the woman raised its head. Yet in conference Eastham argued:

> My instructions are as follows. By the beginning of 1973, the lady quite definitely hated her husband. I can prove that. Thereafter there were long litigations, heard *in camera*, which exacerbated the situation. The Earl only wanted to look after the children, and you will know that a large number of doctors expressed conflict.
>
> What I would like to have in evidence, was that there was a suggestion made of paranoia, and I would like to have in evidence that the situation deteriorated, as a result of the long and protracted proceedings. It could be made to sound a great deal worse than that.

The coroner deemed any such evidence inadmissible. 'Eastham was so frustrated,' says Christina Shand Kydd, 'because he just wasn't allowed to ask anything. Every time he tried to ask a question the coroner stopped him.'

'It was an absolute disgrace, the whole thing,' says Bill Shand Kydd.

In March 1973 Veronica employed a new nanny, Stefanja Sawicka, to whom she complained of the violence that Lucan had used during the marriage. 'Don't be surprised', she said, 'if he kills me one day.' She also employed a cleaner. On the first day, Veronica told her that she worked too slowly; the cleaner retorted that the house was appallingly dirty and walked out. Miss Sawicka, however, became friendly with Veronica. Although only briefly in residence at Lower Belgrave Street she was, later, of use to the police.

She was also a witness to Veronica's acute distress when an *ex parte* application at the High Court was granted for Lord Lucan to take temporary custody of the children. On the afternoon of 23 March, Miss

Sawicka was walking with George and Camilla in Green Park; Lucan approached, showed her the court order, and left with the children. At Frances's school he did the same thing. The headmistress and Miss Sawicka rang Veronica with the news, which was, in Roy Ranson's words, her 'worst fears come true'. She began screaming hysterically, running up and down the stairs of Lower Belgrave Street. In a panic the nanny summoned a doctor. Veronica also insisted that the police be called, but the 'sympathetic officers' could do nothing. The children had gone to Lucan's new home, a five-bedroom flat just eight minutes' walk away, at 72a Elizabeth Street. He had taken this large property (previously rented by a real James Bond actor, George Lazenby), extremely expensive at £70 a week, in order to accommodate them plus another nanny, Jordanka Kotlarova.

This action of Lucan's has been portrayed, unequivocally, as a kidnapping. Veronica, says Ranson, was 'given no chance to defend herself'; that, of course, is what *ex parte* means. It is a judgment given after only one side of an argument is heard, and pending a full hearing, for which Veronica's solicitors then applied. Later it would be said that Lucan's behaviour was 'lawless'.[4] It was the act of an emotional terrorist: Earl Ferrers again. It was the aristocrat, with his powerful sense of entitlement, of the family line that is his to own and bestow, treating the rights of a mother as legally negligible. According to myth, Lucan's view was that these rights still *were* negligible. No upstart wife was going to put her trumped-up cod-feminist ideas between an earl and his desires.

Yet a man who practised family law at the time, at the highest level, with no connection to the Lucan case, describes the *ex parte* process rather differently: without prejudice, as it were. The specific reason why Lucan was given temporary custody is unknown, although Veronica later said that two of her doctors provided evidence at the hearing.[5] The lawyer, however, provides a general analysis.

An *ex parte* is an emergency proceeding. It would have happened if a father was able to go to the court and persuade the court that there were serious grounds that the children be taken away from the mother and given to him. Pretty stringent evidence would be required. It would be most unusual, unless there was very, very strong evidence of serious problems, for very young children to have been removed from their mother and the family home.

On the night of Sandra Rivett's murder, Kait Lucan gave a resumé of her son's family situation to DS Graham Forsyth, the first officer to arrive at Lower Belgrave Street. As recounted at the inquest, her words were: 'He's separated. The children were made wards of court and Veronica was told to continue with medical treatment for her mental complaint.' Kait then explained the nature of this complaint. 'Manic depressive, not violent, except verbally. In the original court case it was thought she was a danger to the children.'[6] Later, Roy Ranson would write that Kait 'managed simultaneously to slur Veronica's name and totally distort the reality of the custody case'. The former lawyer offers a very different view. 'Lucan must have had evidence to convince the judge to make a highly unusual place of safety order. That's one of the technical terms used: place of safety.'

There was, however, the damning accusation that Lucan had staged a kidnap. Was that really what he had done? 'If he'd got a court order, then it wasn't a snatch. If he had a court order, handing the children to his care, then it's his job to collect the children.' The lawyer concedes: 'It could well have been that he acted before the wife was served with the order. If she *had* been served, she probably wouldn't have let the children go out with the nanny. And so therefore perhaps he was jumping the gun a bit... Waiting would have been the wiser thing to do. But we can allow for that.' It could be said, of course, that an *ex parte* application is an aggressive act in itself. There is no denying the shock and distress that it caused. Legally, however, it was not a kidnap.

The date for the full hearing was postponed until July. This gave Veronica time to prepare her own evidence. Towards the end of this period Lucan sent a letter to Marcia Brady Tucker, with whom he had stayed in America during the war. He wrote:

> We do have against us the natural inclination of most judges to award custody to the mother, but I have the best QC in the country working for me, and what is more important he is not a man with a reputation for being too brilliant on behalf of his client, right or wrong. The judges all respect him. The fact that the children have now been with me for the best part of three months – that they are all happy and contented – will also weigh very much with us. Also on my side I have the very strong evidence of my own family, George and Camilla's headmistresses and, of course, Veronica's psychiatric record going back to 1962 (before I met her).
>
> The best result for me would be to be given permanent care and control, with four weeks access for her. The worst result would be the return of the children to her with virtually no access for me. Both these extremes are unlikely, however.

The QC to whom Lucan referred was James Comyn. 'Oh, a very senior man,' says the former lawyer. 'You're talking somebody pretty serious. Somebody of that calibre wouldn't have had anything to do with a snatch.' Presumably Comyn took the view that, in the circumstances, Lucan had done better not to pre-warn Veronica by serving the order. He also must have believed that Lucan had a decent case; as did almost everybody who knew him, a certainty that has been portrayed as a further example of prejudice against Veronica.

Comyn was a Dubliner of extraordinary urbane charm, whose family, ironically in the light of Lucan's family history, had provided a safe house for Eamon de Valera during the Irish Civil War. Later he became a highly regarded judge. As a QC, he defended the Rolling Stone Brian Jones on drug charges and *Private Eye* against the libel action launched by Sir James Goldsmith. Both he and Michael Eastham would be described, with intense respect, as 'the last of the great all-round common law silks'. The dedication in James Comyn's book, *Comyn's Law Without Gravity*, reads 'To the man on the Clapham Omnibus who has stood so much'; he was regarded as a humane spokesman for the underdog who lacked a penetrating voice. It is interesting, therefore, that having taken Lord Lucan's case in the custody hearing, he later stated his belief that Lucan was innocent of murder.

As a result of the *ex parte* application the Lucan children were made wards of court, their interests represented by the Official Solicitor, Norman Turner. Like Comyn, he was a fair and intensely decent man; at the height of the ferocious disputes of the Heath administration, he had intervened to prevent three shop stewards being imprisoned for contempt by the Industrial Relations Court. 'I am concerned', he stated with quiet firmness, 'with the liberty of the individual.' He was obliged to interview Lucan's daughter, Frances, before the High Court hearing. What she said to him, which cannot be recorded, was relayed back to Veronica by her own solicitor.

Christina Shand Kydd, who was called by Mr Turner to give evidence at the hearing, says: 'The Official Solicitor was very good. And he said beforehand: of course, Mr Justice Rees is renowned for being a woman's judge. And I know that John was worried about that. His counsel had said we haven't got a good judge for us.'

Exactly one hundred years before the Lucan family case, the 1873 Custody of Infants Act had established a presumption of maternal care for children up to the age of fourteen. In its original form, passed in 1839, the act had been more limited: the presumption had applied only to children under seven, and it had most certainly not applied to an adulterous mother, or one named as guilty in a criminal conversation action, as the 2nd Countess of Lucan had been. Nevertheless this act, known as the tender years doctrine, 'once and for all stripped traditional unlimited patriarchal authority from the father'.[7]

In 1925 the divorce court was instructed by law to make the welfare of the children its priority. The tender years doctrine was replaced by the 'best interests of the child' rule; yet in practice this has made little difference to the presumption that the mother should have custody. In the past, common sense did suggest that a woman, whose chief 'job' was childcare, was better placed to provide it. Clearly this situation has changed over time, for the simple reason that there are now so many working mothers. The primary custody presumption has not changed.

As early as 1974, a pressure group called Families Need Fathers was arguing that paternal rights were being overlooked by the family courts. In 2003, Fathers4Justice began to put the issue more forcefully: they could have had a field day with the Lucan case. Governments have recognized some of the organization's concerns. Yet despite equality legislation it is still the case, most usually, that a father must prove a mother unfit before he is given primary custody. A mother can gain custody without having to prove anything against the man.

The Lucan case was different, in that its terms had already been set by the *ex parte*. Because Veronica had to rebut the decision that the father should have custody, she did have to prove his unfitness. 'The once meek Countess', wrote Ranson, admiringly, 'was prepared to fight like a tigress for her children.'

The lawyer, who worked on similar cases at the time of the Lucan hearing, says:

> So I'm putting myself in the position of acting for her. I would look for everything that I could fight with. What would I fight with? I would say that this [the *ex parte*] was done behind my back. Yes, I had a temporary problem. Yes, I was ill. Mental flu, whatever.
>
> And why was I in that position? *Because of him.* He had to leave the house because I couldn't cope with him. He was violent, and did these unpleasant things to me. I would be dredging all that up. Now this still goes on, and it depends entirely on the parties themselves, whether they wish to go for the jugular. In every part.
>
> It is very easy to do. If you wish to make something out of it, you can, and then the dirt sticks. The blood flows. Now his *ex parte* application – the judge only heard one story, but it must have been

really, really damaging. So if I was advising her I'd say yes, you had a problem, but you're better now, and you're better because he's gone. And then I would say: he has an unsettled way of life, some suspect friends who will conspire with him, et cetera...

This, indeed, is very much what happened in court. Lucan's character was attacked in every which way. His gambling lifestyle was a legitimate target, but then the blows went lower: there were allegations not just of violence, but of deviancy, of *le vice anglais*, of Lucan demanding that Veronica wear a rubber exercise suit in bed. 'I don't know of any proper corroboration of the things she said about John,' says his sister Jane. The claims leaked out, and were referred to in Muriel Spark's novel about the Lucan affair, which is entirely on Veronica's side.[8] By definition, of course, such allegations are impossible to prove. What goes on in marital bedrooms is a mystery. In a 1981 interview, Veronica said that after Lucan moved out of Lower Belgrave Street 'sometimes at night he would phone for me and I would visit him and then return home';[9] this lordly demand, and her apparent acquiescence in it, throws yet more murk into the mix. Later she herself would say that 'no respectable man would have me because of the embarrassing things about our sex life that came to light when my husband wanted custody.'[10] The passive construction of that sentence throws the blame, as ever, on to Lucan. 'He thought his wife would observe secrecy in the matter of his sexual sadism, but she didn't,' wrote Spark. 'But as he was trying to make her out to be mad, obviously she had a moral right to reveal his mental condition.' Which is one way of saying that the anti-Veronica rumours floating around the Clermont club were being repaid with interest.

Whether truly represented or not, Lucan's sexual predilections would have counted for little had they not been underscored by the other accusations. For him, however, the agony would have been intense: worsened by his innate privacy and pride. It was the criminal conversation action again, with its ferocious exposure of 'guilty intercourse'. *The Times* was not present to record proceedings, but Lucan must have feared that they would become known anyway; it is possible that this is what prevented him from starting divorce proceedings. Otherwise that would have been the logical next step. In 1969 a reform act had brought in the concept of 'intolerable behaviour': given Veronica's later allegations this should have been a gift to her, had she actually wanted a divorce (later she would say: 'I was always negotiating for the marriage to be mended').[11] The 1973 Matrimonial Causes Act introduced the concept of 'irretrievable breakdown', intended to make divorce easier and less ugly. 'It should have made it better for Lucan,' says the lawyer. 'But things don't change overnight, and there was still a mentality that you could spill some dirt to frighten somebody.'

Alongside the solicitor, Veronica had a psychiatrist to speak against the *ex parte*. In April 1973 she had stayed at the Priory, this time of her own volition, in order that a doctor from the clinic could prepare a report for the court. 'I decided if Lord Lucan was going to try to prove me mad, I would prove that I wasn't.'[12] Dr John Flood testified that she was not schizophrenic and therefore did not need to take fluphenazine. With lithium, her condition could be fully controlled: cured, in fact. Therefore, concluded Dr Flood, Veronica was a fit parent. This judgment, made in good faith, is nonetheless regarded as a deeply casual one by the Shand Kydds, who later assumed responsibility for the Lucan children. 'I just simply do not know how the psychiatrist could have said that,' says Christina. 'That she would be fine, basically. None of us could believe that he had said that.'

In a letter written to Michael Stoop in the early hours of 8 November 1974, Lucan wrote that 'a crooked solicitor and a rotten psychiatrist destroyed me between them'. This, of course, was his own interpretation. His bitterness was increased by the fact that the expense of their work would be his expense. He was obliged to pay for the privilege of having his own life destroyed. Christina Shand Kydd, who spoke for Veronica at the hearing, nevertheless expressed powerful reservations that were deeply resented by her sister:

> What I said wasn't *not* favourable. I was trying to be as favourable to her as I could, but I was in a terrible situation. My evidence, which was really quite strong, was basically no, she couldn't look after the children, until she had some medical help. And after medical help, I was sure she would be fine. I was trying to be kind, but at the same time get through to the judge that this was not a good idea. And my mother said the same thing. With help, yes. Without help, no. And we were just completely ignored. It was a farce, really.

Zoe Howard was a final witness for Veronica:

> Even I didn't think she'd win it! But in my brain, at the time, I thought the children need their mother. However she is feeling, whatever. I just thought they were much better with their mother, who's at home, rather than with John, who's gambling. So I was happy to do it. I wanted to help, I was fond of Veronica then. I was twenty-two, I didn't have children, but you think of the mother as looking after them. And then at the same time I never thought she'd win, because of her... whatever she had.
>
> I saw John in Annabel's, a few weeks later, and I was quite nervous. But he said hello – we didn't say very much. But he did smile, he did say hello.

Against this, on Lucan's side, were affidavits from Kait and other family members; testimony from friends, from Lilian Jenkins, from the children's headmistresses; and tape recordings made by Lucan of conversations with his wife. Although Christina and her mother were ostensibly pro-Veronica, what they said was actually very guarded. Given that Lucan was backed by the evidence that had gained him the highly unusual *ex parte* application, his was, logically, a winning case.

Nevertheless, on 20 July 1973, Lucan was advised to concede. The hearing had already lasted nine days, and had cost him upwards of £20,000. Veronica was given custody, with the proviso that a nanny must be in residence. Lucan was given access on every other weekend. This was better than the worst scenario he had outlined to Mrs Tucker, although not much.

Lucan was a good loser, he could lose ten grand at chemmy and remain cool and unmoved, but when the custody case was over he sat stricken on a bench outside the courtroom with his head in his hands. This was not what happened to somebody like him. 'His expression changed completely,' Lilian Jenkins would later say. 'He didn't smile and looked older. His faith in the law was quite shaken.'[13] From this time on, the façade would start visibly to crack: Veronica had inserted her dainty stiletto behind its shield. On the great battlefield of the Lucan marriage, she had won the day. She had taken his home, his money, his reputation, his self-respect and his children. As an act of revenge by an abandoned wife, it was magnificently complete. She could not have done better had she had a top PR firm and the whole of Twitter at her disposal. 'He told people', she later said, 'that no matter what you did as a husband it was always against you. He had to trot out the usual lines.'[14]

If he were honest he would have had to admit, not without a certain wry admiration, that she had played her hand better than he. She had commanded the sympathy of the court with her female vulnerability. He was guilty, through and through, of anything that she cared to name.

'The trouble was,' says Christina simply, 'his looks were always against him.' It was the aristocracy, at it again, still believing that they had the right to whatever they chose to take.

The judge, Sir Stanley Rees, was said to have taken a strong dislike to him. In Rees's 2001 obituary, it was said that he had found Lucan 'arrogant and untruthful and was less than pleased to discover that the earl had recently flouted the law by snatching the children from his wife'. This perverse interpretation reads very much like prejudice: the terrible imponderable in a courtroom.

As Lucan emerged into the sunlight on the Strand, probably headed for the nearest triple vodka martini, Veronica returned to the family house. Christina says:

> The children were just literally, that afternoon, removed from their father's flat – their belongings all sort of shoved in paper bags – and just pushed into Lower Belgrave Street, goodbye, and the door slammed. And it wasn't Veronica's fault – that's what I try and say all the time. She was let down, wasn't she, by the psychiatrist at the Priory and by the judge, really. None of them looked further than the end of their noses, really. And none of them, in my opinion, thought about the children.
>
> Everybody was distraught that the children had been taken back like that, without proper supervision. She loved the children. She just couldn't cope. She was taking lots and lots of pills – she used to spend a great deal of time in bed [a statement backed by Lilian Jenkins, who recalled that Veronica 'practically *lived* in her bedroom, in a sort of twilight world, with the blinds drawn all day'[15]].

Within all the violent verbal bloodletting there was, of course, a very real issue: Lucan's gambling. Had he won the custody case, and acquired his family without what he perceived to be its disruptive element, it is entirely possible that he would have gambled less. He would have become happy, and happy people are not addicts. He must have known that his lifestyle would play badly in court. Yet he clearly believed that his evidence against Veronica would outweigh it. As Veronica herself later put it: 'He had gone around telling everyone that he was going to win and that the courts couldn't fail to see his argument.'[16] Again, however, one might say that he had already won the children once, and therefore could reasonably assume that he would win them again. 'You wouldn't think that anyone who was a gambler would get custody of three children, would you, really?' says his old schoolfriend. 'But he did, at that first hearing.'

The loss of the children was a blow that Lucan could barely withstand. His love for them is well-nigh undisputed. Veronica told the inquest that his attitude towards them was 'very affectionate'. Only Roy Ranson says: 'I believe that, rather than the much quoted love of his children, it is his lack of money, all of it lost through uncontrollable gambling, that provides the key to this case.' Otherwise it is recognized that he was always a kindly, easygoing, generous father, far more so than was usual at the time within his class, and that he subsequently became overwhelmed with the need to have the children in his care.

'We hear now about fathers who kill their children because they can't see them,' says Pierrette Goletto, the French girl who spent several months as nanny at Lower Belgrave Street in 1974. 'And this is forty years ago – the rights of a father were completely ignored. But he adored his children.'

'He was always very interested in the fact that his children get a good education,' says Jane, 'and not fritter themselves away': as he had done. 'He always said they were absolutely perfect,' says his old schoolfriend. 'Perfect, the three of them.' The Maxwell–Scott nanny describes weekend parties at Grants Hill House, at which a collection of children would be deposited in the nursery:

> The parents would come in, and they'd often be drunk, and they would say oh, it's the monkeys' tea party. They'd sort of poke fun at them. Lord Lucan never did. He'd come in to the nursery – normally when they came in they'd say, this is Johnny and he's allergic to whatever, and we'll see you on Sunday night. Dumped! But Lord Lucan used to come in and out, in and out.
>
> He talked to me as if I was a person. He played the piano, and so do I, and I can remember exactly, we played a duet and Frances sang it in German. He used to give me a fiver – a huge amount of money – he was the only one who did that. He would be very loving to the children. It was noticeable, he stood out because he was very paternal.
>
> I suppose afterwards he felt he had totally lost them, and he couldn't live with that.

At the inquest into Sandra Rivett's murder, Bill Shand Kydd was asked about Lucan's relationship with his children. 'He was very fond of them,' he replied. 'He was very worried about them. He considered they were not being properly looked after.' Veronica's solicitor objected to this, and the objection was upheld. But Bill was in a position to know Lucan's feelings. The children often spent weekends with their father at Horton Hall, the Shand Kydd home. Christina says:

> We bought a completely new set of clothes for all of them, that they
> just went into when they got to us. John would play endless games
> with them, and with our children, on the lawn and things, and they
> had really lovely happy times. And then you had the agony – and
> it must have been even worse for him – of taking them back on the
> Sunday night.

Lucan also spent access weekends with his younger sister, Sally, to whom he remained very close, or at homes belonging to friends such as the Earl of Suffolk and Berkshire, who lived at Charlton Park in Wiltshire. 'And then I think Veronica would be terribly unhappy,' says Christina, 'because the children weren't there. Because although she liked being alone, she was terribly lonely, I think. It was hopeless.' 'When she got control of them,' says Bill, 'there was nothing he could do.'

It is said that Lord Lucan was unable to accept this defeat, but that is not quite accurate. Defeat is precisely what a gambler *can* accept. What they object to is the skewing of the odds. A bent game. That is what he believed the custody case to have been. It is impossible, in those circumstances, to bring the game back to a fair footing. All that can happen is more of the same, low tactics, a fight to the death. The myth is quite right when it says that Lucan spent the next fifteen months engaged in dubious activities, designed to have the court order overturned. What it does not say is why he felt compelled to do these things. It also says that Lucan spent this period gambling with a terrifying abandon and borrowing money from all sides. Again, it does not say that the court case had blown a socking great hole in his already precarious finances, which he spent the rest of his known life trying to fill.

'He would have needed a huge amount of money,' says Christina, 'because remember he had to pay her costs as well. And he just didn't have it. He wanted to appeal, but his counsel said it will cost you thousands, and you're unlikely to win. What with the evidence that was given by [Dr] Flood and Veronica's picture of him... She painted quite a picture.'

Nevertheless Lucan, tormented by thoughts of what might be going on at his house, became immersed in a campaign to have the judgment reversed. He ploughed on and on, rather as the 3rd Earl had done when he believed himself wronged. The question is whether his methods were simply attempts to acquire genuine evidence that his wife was an unfit parent; or whether, as the myth suggests, Lucan was escalating his former behaviour in the renewed hope of driving Veronica into madness, or even suicide.[17]

For instance: Lucan often used a pocket cassette recorder to tape conversations when he phoned or visited Veronica. He had begun doing this before the custody case, in fact, and some of the tapes formed part of the evidence at the hearing. So James Comyn, although he may have had misgivings, had obviously been prepared to use them; and Michael Eastham hinted that he might do the same thing at the inquest (the coroner forestalled any such action).[18]

More usually, however, Lucan's willingness to tape his wife has been regarded not as an act of desperation, but of warped terrorism. The police, who found seventy hours of recorded material at the Elizabeth Street flat, certainly portrayed it that way. Furthermore, according to Roy Ranson, Lucan was fixing the game when he taped Veronica; he would needle her into a state of rage, then switch on the machine and record what sounded like an unstable woman. Veronica herself endorsed this, saying: 'He [Lucan] would say something so outrageous, in a holier-than-thou voice, that I'd fly into a fury. My language on occasions was more Billingsgate than Belgravia.'[19]

Yet Ranson's inspector, David Gerring, would later offer a rather different view, stating that the tapes were 'pathetic rather than revealing'. Gerring described a lot of 'Hello – how are you – what have you been doing', interspersed with long pauses. 'The impression I gathered was that Lucan was himself disturbed,' he concluded, although no reason is given for this assertion. Another account of the conversations, which came from a newspaper, had Lucan murmuring 'yes, dear, yes, dear' throughout. It described Veronica 'firing off a barrage of criticism against her husband'; at one point she 'refers to him disdainfully as "poor old Blucey", a pet name [possibly a reference to his 'house blue' status at the Clermont]'.[20]

At the start of 1974 Lucan employed Devlin and Co., a firm of private detectives based in Baker Street, to watch the Lower Belgrave Street house. Some of their findings were unsensational in the extreme: at 3.20 Veronica walked down the street; at 3.25 she walked up it; and so on. Devlin's revved into action, however, when a Mrs Elizabeth Murphy took on the job of nanny. At the end of February a report was sent to Lucan, detailing Mrs Murphy's movements on a particular Saturday morning, after she and the children had been followed to a newsagent's shop in Ebury Street. 'A few moments later they left those premises and were followed to the Irish Club, 82 Lyall St, London SW1, where they arrived at 12.10pm. Thereafter Mr Cranstoun [the tec] observed Mrs Murphy and the three children sitting at the bar drinking from glasses.'

The hapless Mrs Murphy was an alcoholic, who had been twice sacked from former positions for heavy drinking and encouraging her charges to drink. She was a kind woman, but it would have been a strange father who was comforted by the thought of her acting as nanny to his children. Lucan replied to Devlin: 'Thank you for your most useful report. I would like if possible the same arrangement for next Saturday and Sunday. Remember that my wife is extremely suspicious (the psychiatrists agree on a form of paranoia) so that if she was to go out with the three children and your man followed them he would have to be very careful.'

Lucan made a complaint to the Official Solicitor, and Mrs Murphy was sacked. She was then hospitalized with a cancer that was soon to kill her. 'May I say "thank you sincerely" for visiting me in hospital,' she wrote to Lucan, 'and your gift of lovely grapes, it was most considerate of you. I did not see Lady Lucan, perhaps she was tied up with household affairs...'

Again Roy Ranson took the view that Lucan was manipulating the situation to incriminate his wife. Mrs Murphy died, wrote Ranson, 'never knowing that the unhappiness of her later days had been directly caused by the Lord she had thanked so profusely'. In other words, by following the nanny who was having a midday drinking spree in the Irish Club with his children, and reporting her flagrant unsuitability to the authorities, Lucan had acted disgracefully. By visiting her in hospital, he was acting hypocritically. 'The level to which Lucan now sank in his battle against Veronica', spat Ranson, 'was demonstrated by his subsequent behaviour towards the unfortunate Mrs Murphy.'

Devlin's were expensive, as much as £400 a week on some occasions. Therefore Lucan did some of their work himself. As he had in fact done ever since the custody judgment, he would park his dark-blue Mercedes on Lower Belgrave Street and watch the house through his sunglasses. He also sometimes watched his children when they went out to play in the nearby squares and parks. 'Quite often John was there in his car,' says Pierrette Goletto, 'and he was looking at us. I don't think the children saw him. It was a very sad situation.'

'I think', Veronica would later say, 'he walked past the house to see the children or maybe just to walk past the house where we lived. I think that is a strong indication we were both hoping to get back together again.'[21] It was a view that she would reiterate after the murder: that the marriage had not in fact been over. The implication is that, despite having accused her husband of things that no man could forgive, she still in some way longed to have him back; and perhaps found it unforgivable that he did not want to return.

In December 1973 Lucan wrote to his lawyers:

Today was Camilla's Nativity Play and Frances's Carol service. Veronica informed me of neither, but other parents had told me. I arrived at 11.10 for the play and, not seeing Veronica, I sat through it. At the end of the performance Camilla came down from the stage to see me. If I hadn't been present she would have been one out of just two or three children who didn't have a parent present. Camilla's new nanny [Christabel Martin] came up to me after a short time and took her home. In the afternoon I went to Frances's Carol Service. V arrived at 2.15pm, stood next to me and started to tell me that I was in breach of the court order. I told her to be quiet. At the end of the Service I left without saying Hullo to Frances.

Christabel Martin was just one of the procession of nannies who marched in and out of Lower Belgrave Street between the end of the custody case, on 20 July, and the arrival of Sandra Rivett thirteen months later. One, Hazel Drobbins, stuck it out for four days. Two Spanish girls lasted a little longer. Pierrette Goletto stayed for several months in 1974, followed very briefly by Nadia Broome; then by Sandra. Lucan wrote in the letter to his lawyers:

I told my wife on Friday that I was not prepared to pay £35 a week for the new nanny. She said that it was impossible to get anyone for less [in fact Sandra was paid £25]. She accused me of trying to 'sabotage' her. In ordinary circumstances, £15–20 is the going rate. I recognize that the circumstances are not normal, and that I must pay more. But there are limits. Am I obliged to bribe someone to live at 46 Lower Belgrave Street so that my wife may comply with the court order?

The answer to this, apparently, was 'yes'. The Knightsbridge Nannies agency issued a writ for unpaid fees in April 1974. According to the police, Lucan was deliberately dilatory in his payments; he wanted a constant turnover of nannies to make it look as though Veronica was *not* complying with the court order.[22] Ranson also threw in the notion (partly contradicting the assertion about the non-payments) that the nannies left because they were uneasy about being 'spied on' by Lucan. Meanwhile Lucan himself suggested that some of them had found Veronica a tricky employer. 'She got through a lot, did she?' says the former lawyer. 'I mean, the girls must have got the money, or the agency wouldn't have provided them.' Pierrette Goletto's recollection is that the woman who ran the agency was, in fact, a friend of Veronica's. This was confirmed by Veronica herself at the inquest.

The unsatisfactory quality of some of the nannies – 'Some of them were nice, and some were absolutely appalling,' says Christina – may have been a factor in Lucan's reluctance to pay for them. Who would rush to spend money on a girl who walked out after four days? Although in the letter to his lawyers Lucan accepted that he had to keep forking out, he would have been heartily sick of doing so. As well as the nannies he was giving Veronica £40 a week for living expenses, and running her establishment on top of his own. Payments were, as she said at the inquest, 'erratic', although the money came 'in the end'. Pierrette Goletto recalls that when Lucan came to the house 'he was nagging Veronica – telling her he was stopping the money, and things like this. All the food we were having came from Harrods, and he stopped it.' Pierrette herself strode round to Elizabeth Street and asked Lucan to reinstate the Harrods account, which he did.

Part of the problem, of course, was his pitifully feeble cashflow. But there probably was, too, a desire to exact a petty revenge. At the end of 1973 Lucan received a letter from Veronica's milkman: 'Your wife Lady Lucan asked me to send her account to you, but the amount of £57.62 has not been forthcoming. As we have sent several accounts, we have been forced to stop supplying. However Lady Lucan assures me on the telephone that you will pay this account directly you receive this bill.' The payment to the milkman was one of the last cheques that Lucan ever wrote.

*

In October 1985, a thirty-seven-year-old man named Nicholas Boyce was tried at the Old Bailey for the murder of his wife. He had headbutted and strangled her at their London home while his children were asleep, cut up the body and distributed its parts in skips and dustbins. Boyce, a good-looking man with a degree in economics, who at the time worked as a cleaner, had given himself up to the police. He admitted the killing and said that the removal of the body, unspeakable as it was, had been done to protect his children. He pleaded extreme provocation.

'It is easy', said counsel for the prosecution, 'to make allegations about her in court – she is not here to defend them.' The defence replied: 'You are examining a non-stop form of humiliation and degradation which drained every bit of respect from a grown man.' Boyce, his counsel claimed, had suffered months of mental torture, accusations of sexual deviancy, threats that his wife would leave home with his two young children and deny him access. 'If you divorce me,' she was reported to have said, 'I'll make sure I get custody of the children.' She had forced him to take the cleaning job. He was, he claimed, terrified of her. 'She screamed abuse and accusations – could it not have worn down any person? He finally broke in circumstances in which an ordinary man may also have done.'

Boyce was convicted of manslaughter. Sentencing him to six years, the judge said: 'Before these dreadful events you were hard-working, of good character, devoted to your children and a good father. You were simply unable to get on with your wife.'

Nicholas Boyce's wife was Christabel Martin, who worked as nanny to the Lucan children following the custody case. Originally employed as a temporary, she returned to the job after the dismissal of Mrs Murphy. She volunteered to do so again after the murder of Sandra Rivett. There was even a later, rather wild suggestion that she had done occasional shifts on Sandra's days off.[23] Like most of the nannies she was very young, just twenty-one in 1974, and she grew close to Veronica. It was Christabel who told Roy Ranson that Lucan had been trying to force his wife into a state of mental breakdown. She told him other things: that the delayed payments to the Knightsbridge Nannies agency had been a deliberate tactic; and that Veronica had warned her not to discuss the household with Lucan because he would distort information for his own ends. It was Christabel who said that Veronica was nervous because Lucan still had a key to the house;[24] that Veronica lived in fear of him.

In rebuttal of Lucan's contention that some of the nannies had found Veronica difficult, Ranson wrote that they 'usually found her to be a sympathetic and friendly employer. The nannies discovered that it was Lucan whom they needed to avoid [this despite the fact that those who stayed only a few days would scarcely have met him].' It is quite true that both Christabel and Stefanja Sawicka spoke out strongly for Veronica. They were in her confidence. So too, it would later be said, was Sandra Rivett. Of course the poor woman could not confirm or deny this. Sandra only worked at the house for ten weeks before her death; afterwards a suitcase was found in her bedroom still partly unpacked; but Veronica subsequently portrayed a friendship of some depth between them:

> She was very sensitive to my situation. She would call me on her day off if she went anywhere. She used to say I was vulnerable. She did not like my husband. She saw him far more than I did because she used to hand over the children when he came for them at access. Often I didn't want to face him... She told me once that he frightened her. I suppose that sounds melodramatic in hindsight, all these years later. But that was what she said. He called round one day and she dealt with him and afterwards she came into the kitchen and said that she found him frightening. He could be intimidating with that great height and bearing. I knew what she meant.[25]

Yet Pierrette Goletto, nanny to the Lucan children throughout part of 1974, presents a very different view. Her sympathies, firstly of course with the children, in the matter of the marriage were straightforwardly with the husband. A sunny-natured and confident

Frenchwoman, she cuts through the image of Lucan as glowering monster and presents instead a friendly, faintly bewildered man, whose oddities of behaviour were rendered comprehensible by his situation. 'I liked to talk to him. He loved the south of France, it was nice to talk to him about it. I liked John. He was there for his children.' After the murder Pierrette was interviewed by the police, although she had left Britain by that time. 'They asked me: why did I go away? Did I know this was going to happen? Well, I knew that the situation between John and Veronica was getting worse, it was obvious.'

Pierrette, who now runs a language school near Nice, recalls visiting Chancery Lane to be interviewed by a lawyer for the job as nanny. 'Perhaps it was because I came from France,' she says. 'But I was told later that John wanted to be sure that the person was reliable.' This would appear to contradict the police assertion that he wanted the nannies to keep walking out.

Pierrette has extremely precise memories of 46 Lower Belgrave Street, its geography and its inhabitants. She describes an odd situation: bleak, stark, the life of the house concentrated in the nursery and in the basement kitchen, where she taught the children to cook.

We had such fun, the children and me. But of course it was a strange atmosphere! It was not a normal family home. OK, it was in the best part of England, it was a beautiful house. I was given a car, a DAF, and driving through London – taking the children to the park, the school, everywhere. Veronica was taking medication. I was really sorry for her. But for the children, and for me, it was hard work.

Pierrette also confirms the assertion by the former nanny, Lilian Jenkins, that Veronica spent a good deal of time in her bedroom.

Among the allegations by Christabel Martin was that Lucan rang the house repeatedly. The police later referred to frequent threatening anonymous calls, made to a number that only he knew (which would also mean that he wanted Veronica to know who was ringing her). Again, however, Pierrette contextualizes them as the kind of stupid thing that warring couples do.

There was ringing often, but Veronica was ringing [him] often. It was both ways.[26] She wanted him to come back – not to go to casinos, not to spend money, and not to be with some of his friends. Because she was always saying that his friends didn't like her. She was always telling me that she hated John, because he had left her and she did everything for him. And then one day she cried and she said to me, she adored him from the first day.

It was obvious to Pierrette that Lucan was sitting in his car, observing the house and his children. 'They said he was following... He wasn't following them, he was watching them.' Equally obvious was the presence of a private detective. 'He was parking just opposite, in the same place always. To me, it didn't shock me.' On one occasion a man visited, purporting to be a friend of the Lucans, and asked questions. 'He wanted to know what was happening with the children. Asked if I was coping OK.'

Like the other nannies, Pierrette had been told by Veronica that Lucan was violent, although she herself was perfectly comfortable with him (as evidenced by her willingness to confront him about the Harrods account: 'I went round to his flat, I wasn't frightened. No way.'). With regard to the Lucans, her own recollections are of:

Word fights. Saying nasty things together. Screaming, arguments, yelling at each other. He would come to the house – and sometimes I would get the children and Veronica would say to me not now, I want to talk to my husband. So she'd send me upstairs to the nursery, and I obey, I stay there with the children – and I knew it was going to be a fight.

But I never saw her with any bruises – and I saw her every day. Come on, John was six feet tall, she was a tiny little thing – you could have put her on the end of your finger like a puppet. She was telling me he was violent, to be careful with the children, but I didn't see any marks. He never showed me that aspect of being violent.

Given that Lucan was named as a killer, it seems only logical to see his life through the prism of that judgment, and believe that he had behaved appallingly beforehand. After the murder, Veronica said: 'My husband was a violent man and he had tried to kill me before.'[27] John Aspinall, in his usual indiscreet way, claimed that Lucan had given Veronica a few knocks (the subtext being: only what she deserved), and another friend says, with some reluctance, that 'she might have egged him on – you don't mean to hit badly, but...' Utterly untenable though this is, it does happen. Friends were said, after the inquest, to have 'almost ashamedly recalled incidents that had caused him to shake with rage',[28] although neither the names of the friends nor the nature of the incidents are known.

The most damaging thing that a man can do to a woman is inflict violence upon her. But the most damaging thing that a woman can do to a man is accuse him of violence. Lucan's sister Jane, who saw him several times in the fifteen months between the custody case and the murder, refers to the 'violent outlook' that was developing in him at that time, the product of frustration and despair. There is nothing starry-eyed about Jane's sad, conflicted vision of her brother. She does not flinch from describing him with honesty. Nevertheless she has extreme difficulty in imagining him inflicting actual physical harm. 'He had a very soft side. Underneath this rather fierce exterior.'

'He was a sweet man,' says Christina Shand Kydd. 'Had a sweet side that he, being a typical Englishman, would not show willingly, if you know what I mean.' 'He was always charming,' says Nick Peto, who knew Lucan well. 'I find that hard to believe. I can't imagine him doing anything violent.' 'I never saw him angry, in any way,' says his old schoolfriend, 'except on a golf course, when he hit the ball into a tree, and it sort of perched up there, and we had to dislodge it. He was so angry. He said, that's a bad shot. But I never *really* saw him angry at all.'

There was, of course, the façade, beneath which lay who knew quite what? But what was said later, that Lucan evinced all the arrogant aggression of his forebears (two of them, to be precise: Sir Richard Bingham and the 3rd Earl), is wisdom after the fact. 'In the years since the murder I have learnt of the other side of Lucan,' wrote Ranson, who was prepared to say absolutely anything in support of the police case, 'the less patient, the less even-tempered, the more violent man that he was becoming.' Patience and even temper were indeed scarce by this time, at least towards his wife. Yet so too was the actual evidence of violence. This is not to deny that it happened, only to say that there is no proper corroboration. The melodramatic story of the horse, chosen to throw Veronica when she went hunting, was contradicted by Ranson himself. It was also said that Lucan attacked his doberman pinscher, Otto, in a fit of rage. 'He doted on that dog, on all his dogs,' says Jane, who in fact cited Otto as evidence of her brother's softness. An officer who worked on the case now says that Lucan used an electric probe on the dog, an allegation that can only have come from the usual sources. Lucan's schoolfriend sternly refutes it. 'No, he never treated that dog badly.'

So perhaps the only thing he treated violently was his wife; although against this is the argument put forward by Pierrette Goletto. Veronica's fragility was such that a man, particularly one at least a foot taller than she and more than twice her weight, could have taken her out with a single blow.

Like other people in this affair, Pierrette saw the literal weakness of Veronica, but sensed that it was Lucan who was truly the weaker of the two. Beneath the *Doll's House* role play – the big man, the supplicant wife – something very different was going on, more like a fight between a maddened bull and a nimble matador. Pierrette says:

> He didn't have a leg to stand on. And don't forget, she can play that
> she was the poor woman, the martyr. She was quite good at it.

And then there is this. In the course of a long interview given in 1981, Veronica herself said of Lucan: 'He was not a violent man. He could be studiedly cruel, but not spontaneously.'[29]

The Clermont, where Dominick Elwes was telling Lucan 'to brace up and be a man' and members were openly whispering about his problems, was now a refuge more from habit than anything else. All Lucan's habits were a refuge: the lamb chops, the Stuyvesants, the alcohol, the gambling. The gilded gleam of the club, once so alluring, now had a brittle aspect. One needs a kind of toughness to live one's life in the social arena. People want lightness, laughs, the shallow sparkling spray of flirtation and faint malice; introspection is for home; to bring it out for the evening is crashing bad form. But Lucan did not really have a home. So he sat on at the Clermont, drinking and gambling ever more doggedly, his dry humour submerged in a mudslide of misery. He acquired a girlfriend, Andrina Colquhoun, an extremely pretty debutante nearly twenty years his junior, but the relationship was casual and almost certainly platonic. He was still handsome, still immaculate, what with the club arranging his laundry, but he now looked different: the shallow sculpture of his face was softened and puffy. He was no longer the beau ideal of Vittorio De Sica's dreams, more a recumbent Rowlandson, an eighteenth-century earl prematurely aged by the mysterious harshness of easy living; and by anxiety.

'People became listening receptacles,' says Daniel Meinertz-hagen, who still lunched with Lucan most days. 'He was obsessive about the children and Veronica. It was horrible for him. I remember going round to his flat and seeing all the children's Christmas presents laid out on the bed. Very sad. But he became', he adds apologetically, 'a bit of a bore.'

The then girlfriend of one of his set says:

> We had dinner with Lucan actually quite a lot, and he talked *obsessively* about his children, and the custody, and the case, and the wife. Absolutely obsessive. Slightly to the point where I said, gosh, do we really have to have dinner with Lucky Lucan again?
>
> He obviously thought he would have been a more suitable parent. He was saying it to the table, general topic of conversation.

Everyone was totally sympathetic, and rightly so. It was only me thinking oh crikey, have we got to hear this again. Probably unfair of me. But I thought it was a bit of a gramophone record going round and round and round... Looking back now it was absolutely horrid for him. Horrid. Having a wife whom he didn't trust with his children.

After dinner came the tables, and yet again the necessary delusion that here was where money could be made, where it could all come right. The court case; the bills for Veronica's legal team; Veronica's food account at Harrods, which was stopped and reopened, stopped and reopened; the nannies; the milkman; the £70 every week for his own flat: it all careered around his head as he held his chemmy cards and prayed to God that they totalled nine. He began throwing dice: a fool's game if ever there was one. When the police went round to Elizabeth Street, they found a heap of unopened bills. 'Always a good sign,' says the former officer, 'if you don't open the mail.'

His bank managers were writing to him with the ghastly courtesy of barely concealed contempt. He had four accounts, with Lloyd's, the National Westminster, the Midland and Coutts, which he juggled as if their contents were on fire. 'I was very pleased', wrote his manager at Lloyd's in Pall Mall, not long after the custody hearing, 'when you paid in £6,000 the other day to restore the position on your Current Account. You can imagine my disappointment when cheques totalling no less than £3,500 were presented to me for payment yesterday in the absence of funds, particularly as the cheques were all in favour of Cash or Clubs and have, I surmise, all gone in one particular direction...' Three months later the manager was writing again. 'You will know from my recent letters how disappointed I am that you have not been in touch before this to let me know what arrangements are being made to adjust your overdraft here which stands at £4,238.94 as I write. I must confess that I find it difficult to understand why you have not corresponded with me.' At the same time Coutts, who managed the family trusts, refused a

£20,000 overdraft. A bank statement with them, dated 16 November 1973, shows a balance of £10,417.56 reduced to £569.86 by 3 December. Withdrawals to 'Cash' are made on a near-daily basis: £12,000 on one day alone, 21 November. Lucan began raising money on the promise of selling the family silver, some of which had already gone to Christie's.

He also began borrowing. His mother lent £4,000. Selim Zilkha, chairman of Mothercare and a business associate of James Goldsmith, lent £3,000, as did Stephen Raphael. 'He borrowed from Sally and I,' says his sister Jane. 'It was sort of up and down. One time, John was a little bit, without any shame, he was going to ask the Brady Tuckers to see if he could get some money. Certainly the last time they wouldn't give him any money – they may have done before, I don't know. Just because he was, you know, going under financially, rapidly.'

In fact Lucan had, on this last occasion, asked Mrs Tucker for £125,000 (not £250,000, as was claimed by Veronica;[30] but still an unbelievable request). She turned him down. Instead of giving up he visited Mrs Tucker's son, the Reverend Luther, in Munich. In November 1973 he wrote:

> Although I have made my proposals in the bluntest possible way, as being a straight purchase of the children by you, on my behalf, the offer would naturally have to be dressed up in order to give Veronica the maximum amount of face saving. It may seem incredible to you that she would entertain such a monstrous proposal, or that it should be necessary to go to such extreme lengths when a solution should be available in the courts. But I am reasonably confident that the offer would be considered by her. I regret having to involve you and your family in my domestic problems, but I did everything I possibly could in court and although we did not have judgment given against us (we conceded after two weeks' ruinous court action) we ran into a brick wall in the shape of the current shrink.
>
> If I could have afforded to battle on there would have been an

appeal. But even if we were still successful there would be nothing to prevent Veronica from going back once a year to ask for their return. The financial solution would have the advantage of Lady Lucan herself applying to the courts to return the children to me. In a way, this would be more binding on her than a court order based on a relapse – alleged to have been temporary – in her mental health.[31]

Luther Tucker's reply, clearly that of a friend but nonetheless filled with the polite alarm of somebody seeking to dodge a street chugger, asked if no other course could be taken but to buy back the children. 'Only more court action,' Lucan replied. 'All the alternatives would involve legal struggles with a hostile and obstructive Lady Lucan.' His loan application, as was becoming the norm, was turned down. The fact that he could couch his letter to the Reverend Tucker in such apparently rational and controlled terms, while asking for something so fantastic, says more than if he had openly begged. It implies a disconnection from reality: never something that Lucan had much liked.

'I saw him from time to time,' says Jane.

He would always come and see us over here [in New York], and we stayed with him in Elizabeth Street as a family. I think we did some outings with Veronica and the children, in order that the cousins would see each other. I was aware at that time that John was taping the phone calls, and he was also quite edgy. He was just so obsessed by the whole – obviously – because it was wrecking his life.

And he couldn't see how he was going to manage. That was another cause for his tremendous anxiety. Certainly the children were the root of it. But then the practical part of living, and needing cash...

With Jane, a family member, the façade was altogether dropped. That was not possible at the Clermont, where panic fossilized into a slow, slurred rigidity. 'He was bombed,' says the man who then worked at the club. 'From eleven in the morning until four at night.

Now you tell me if he was in his right mind.' But with his friend from Eton a different kind of behaviour took over: not so much a dropping of the mask, more an outbreath of relaxation, a simple reversion to an earlier, happy self, as one can do with old friends, no matter what else is going on.

> The last time I saw him, I would think, was four or five months before the event. We had dinner together, it was in Hill Street, some gambling club [the Ladbroke] where the food was very good and didn't cost anything. For obvious reasons. I didn't think he'd changed at all. I really enjoyed that particular evening, at the time, and in retrospect. He was always the same, poking fun at himself, and people like me! Yes. It's very, very sad.

> Anyway we had dinner, and I do remember one thing. Him talking about the custody of the children, all this complete shambles of the doctor [Flood]... we went through all that. And then he said, the problem about Veronica is that she is part perfectly wonderful person, but part evil. I remember him saying evil. And he said: from her interests, and from the children's interests, she's better off the hill. It's what you say about a stag, you know, when they're killed you take them off the hill. He did say that.

> But he didn't say it in any way like he was going to do anything about it.

One wonders what, if anything, Lord Lucan thought about his life, in the weeks leading up to the night of 7 November 1974. A once-unimaginable life can become all that there is, quite easily. Sometimes it happens by such stealthy degrees that a person can never tell how golden youth has dulled into hopelessness. In Lucan's case it happened more dramatically, and it need not have happened. By his own semi-volition he brought himself to a position where, at nearly forty, he was without a family, a family home, any money that he could lay his hands on, any reasonable future. He might have escaped the consequences of his choices, which were scarcely choices at all, but instead they gathered together like furies to overrun the life he should have had. His nature led him to inhabit his aristocratic heritage in a way that was beautiful, in his eyes, but illusory; it brought great pleasure, but it was a mirage, like the lucent glory of the Clermont club. Now it was 1974, and reality lay inside every unopened bill. Lucan himself, as a gambler, might have said that it was fate that had brought him to this endgame. Still, as Charles Ryder said of Lord Sebastian Flyte, who lived out his days in a Moroccan monastery as the shambolic local lush: 'It's not what one would have foretold.'

'I think about it quite a lot, and I just think, well, hell of a waste,' says Lucan's schoolfriend. 'But he was a survivor, we thought, you know?'

On 26 August 1974, Sandra Rivett took up her position as nanny at 46 Lower Belgrave Street. She was a good-natured and kindly woman, and in the short time that she spent with them the Lucan children formed an affectionate relationship with her. She brought a cat, Tara, to join the one belonging to Frances. She also brought a kind of normality, a warm presence that filled up the formal, almost museum-like rooms of the house.

Lucan approved of Sandra ('she was a good kid,' he told Susan Maxwell-Scott), and expressed his pleasure with her to the Official Solicitor. But according to the police he was inwardly distraught at her arrival. Through what Ranson called his 'intelligence network', he learned that Sandra and Veronica were friends. 'She was very sweet,' says Christina Shand Kydd. 'The children were definitely very fond of her. Veronica liked her.' Veronica was certainly happier and this, wrote Ranson, 'marked a turning-point in Lucan's attitude'. Here was a nanny who would stick, who could not be used as a connivance against his wife. If the police reasoning is correct, Sandra was Lucan's nemesis as well as his victim, as she had unwittingly destroyed his dream of overturning the custody judgment.

The police contention, therefore, was that in September 1974 Lucan gave up on this hope, and made other plans as to how he might reclaim his children. His demeanour reverted to its old dry good humour. He was feeling fine because he was plotting domestic murder.

In fact, throughout the last few weeks of his known life Lucan seemed in some ways unchanged, and in others quite different; as though the façade had half-detached itself and was swinging back and forth on its hinges. He continued to see his friends, including Miss Colquhoun, and to visit the Clermont. On 29 October John Wilbraham, who had acted as best man at his wedding, stayed at Elizabeth Street and found Lucan in cheerful mood. On Sunday 3 November he had dinner with his mother, then studying for her Russian 'A' Level, and asked her to lend him a book called *The Intelligent Woman's Guide to Socialism*. Before this he had spent his access weekend at the home of his sister Sally. Earlier that year, in July, they had taken their children for a happy family holiday in Estoril.

'During the last weekend we spent with Daddy,' Frances would later say in her statement to the police, 'Camilla told Daddy that Sandra had boyfriends and went out with them. Daddy asked when Sandra went out with her boyfriends, and Camilla said Sandra went out with her boyfriends on her day off. Then Daddy asked me when Sandra had her days off. I said her day off was Thursday.'

Lucan returned the children to Veronica for the last time.

This calm, collected behaviour all concurs with the police theory. Yet other things do not. Instead they suggest a continuation of the agitation described by Lucan's sister Jane. On 24 October, for instance, Lucan had a meeting with James Comyn to discuss the weary subject of revisiting the courts. Earlier that month he had gone to Paris and asked James Goldsmith for a £10,000 loan with which to 'buy back' the children. 'He told Jimmy', wrote Annabel Goldsmith, 'that Veronica was using the children to "torture" him.'[32] It is hard to see how this sum could be deemed adequate, except as some sort of down payment; anyway Goldsmith, who disliked lending money, turned him down. Instead he offered a sum as a gift, which was refused, although Lucan did accept a guarantee of £5,000 for an overdraft at the Midland.

In September, another friend agreed to guarantee a more dangerous loan: £3,000 for six months from Charles Genese, money-lender to the upper classes, who charged interest at 48 per cent. Genese was a familiar figure to types like Lucan: 'They'd stop him on the street,' says the former police officer, 'ask him for a loan when they wanted a night's gambling money.' In fact Lucan went to Genese's offices, where he asked to borrow £5,000, which was deemed too large a loan. According to Genese's evidence at the inquest:

> [He] was reasonably open in that he told us that maintenance, school fees, bank overdrafts, rates and household expenses were on a par if not more than his income. He was living at what I knew to be a rather high standard. He told us that he had put some silver up for sale by auction and from the proceeds later in the year would be able to pay off what he had borrowed.

Lucan paid Genese £120, the first instalment on the interest, two days in advance of its due date.

On 13 September, Lucan visited the Trustees Office at Coutts bank and asked for capital to be released for the payment of school fees (although his son's education was covered by a trust). This required approval from the Official Solicitor. Lucan took fright, fearing that the request might damage any chance of reversing the custody decision. He then arranged with Christie's that the collection of family silver should be sold on 27 November. On or around 23 October, he had dinner with Michael Stoop at the Portland bridge club and asked if he might borrow a car. Stoop later told the inquest:

> I had a Mercedes, and I suggested that he might borrow that. I thought he'd prefer the Mercedes. My Ford is a pretty dirty old banger. But I imagined through natural good manners he didn't want to deprive me of my better car. He wanted the Ford specifically

for that evening. I didn't ask any reason and he didn't offer any. I was going home to change for dinner. I left the keys to the Ford in the car and said that he could collect it when he wished.

Lucan's own Mercedes, for which he was paying £85 a week, was found outside his flat with a cold engine on the night of the murder. In January 1975 it became the trigger for the declaration of Lucan's bankruptcy, when a hire purchase company and repair firm claimed a total of £1,552, stating that 'with intent to defeat or delay his creditors he departed out of England on or about 8th Nov 1974'. At the time that the Ford Corsair was loaned, the most likely reason seemed to be that Lucan wanted to carry out his surveillance of 46 Lower Belgrave Street in an unknown, nondescript, seven-year-old car. Stoop's evidence suggested that Lucan needed the Corsair for one particular evening, so it is possible that his Mercedes was temporarily faulty; although he did not return Stoop's car thereafter. Then there is the explanation put forward by the police, that the Corsair was to be used to transport Veronica's body.

In October at the Clermont, Lucan lost £10,000 in one night at dice. This was the gambling of somebody positively hastening towards the end. Lucan arranged to pay back the debt in instalments of £200 a month: thus the list of financial commitments stretched out a little further.

He did not stop visiting the club, but his credit was threatened. The nonchalant earl who had once commanded the Clermont, bestowing his presence as one who could get away with murder in there, was now a supplicant. Aspinall might have helped him out, but Aspinall was gone, and without his ambivalent protection the veil of illusion was removed. Lucan was just a mug gambler. He was a better-dressed version of the shambolic North Londoners who shovelled their lot on the last race at Harringay dogs. He was Lord Hastings, told by the bookmakers: 'Now mind, I'm to be *paid* this.' Like Hastings, he had begun to stagger under the repeated blows of his losses. The formerly ice-cool gambler was said to sweat when he played. Charles Benson later recalled an evening, about a week before the murder, when he himself was playing in a backgammon tournament. Lucan 'started slumping over our board and making silly comments and actually touching some of the pieces, which is absolutely not done'. Almost anybody else, said Benson, 'would have been slung out. It was undignified and very sad...'

In those surroundings, it was a transgression akin to chucking a glass of wine in somebody's face. What had caused it was the fact that Lucan had chucked the wine, and rather more than one glass of it, down his own throat: his intake was steady and remorseless. It was now illegal to drink at the tables, but in every other way Lucan needed booze to keep going. 'He *was* drinking more heavily,' says Christina Shand Kydd. 'He was so worried about the children. Well, everybody was.' Drinking in that way has an odd effect: although occasionally it slops over, as in the incident described by Benson, the body becomes so accustomed that much of the time the effects are contained. One appears as normal. Stuart Wheeler recalls that 'two days before he disappeared I was playing backgammon and Lucan was sitting behind me, and occasionally in an amused way giving me a bit of advice. And I had not the slightest inkling of what was to come.'

Unable now to depend upon credit at the Clermont, Lucan spent the last week or so gambling at the Ladbroke Club, whose proprietor Cyril Stein was engaged in a steely rivalry with Victor Lownes. Let it all go, seemed to be the fatalistic idea. When the details of bankruptcy were disclosed, 'Ladup', or the Ladbroke Club, was found to be Lucan's chief single creditor: five dishonoured cheques totalled a debt of £11,800.

He also owed £3,000 to Charles Genese; £3,608 to Coutts; £1,124 to the Midland; £5,091 to Lloyd's; £5,400 to the National Westminster, a debt that was cancelled by the cashing of Lucan's life insurance policy; £1,890 to the Inland Revenue; £1,037 to his landlords at Elizabeth Street, who repossessed the flat in December 1974; £2,257 to utilities companies; £227 to military tailors Cooling,

Lawrence and Wells for the storage of his coronet and ermine robes, a claim that was withdrawn; and £183 for a flight to Munich, presumably to visit the Reverend Luther. There was also £66.57 to Harrods for cigars and wine; £163 to Boss and Co. for repairs to two guns; £9 to Cartier for a crocodile watch strap: these last show that Lucan was still, *malgré tout*, seeking nothing but the best. In for a penny, and all that. There was also a collection of private loans, amounting to £13,000.

Together with the money owed to the Clermont, and the residue of what was still to be paid on the custody case, the entire debt was some £65,000. Much of it had been run up in the last two months before the murder. Lucan's position, in a way, was that of anybody who has ever descended into a vortex of debt. In other ways the situation was different. It was essentially self-inflicted. And Lucan was worth twice what he owed, although the costs of settling the bankruptcy eventually pushed the debt to around £90,000. A sum of £118,000 was finally taken from the estate. Furniture and jewels remained: 'I don't want to unnecessarily remove anything from Lower Belgrave Street immediately,' said Dennis Gilson, the accountant who was appointed trustee in bankruptcy in August 1975. 'I just want to discover what I can take to sell.' Veronica was told that she could pick what she wanted to keep, 'the wife's share', and the rest would be sold. This included personal items such as Lucan's coronet and robes; his Cartier watch inscribed 'Lucky, God bless him'; gold cufflinks engraved with the letter 'B', for Bingham; and gambling chips embossed with a coronet.

Most of Lucan's assets, it is true, were not disposable. The Lower Belgrave Street house had been deemed Veronica's place of family residence. Anyway the house was owned in trust. So too was the Eaton Row mews. There was, however, some money in overseas bank accounts in Switzerland and Bulawayo, and gold items found stored at Lloyd's. 'He'd get a couple of grand, and squirrel it away,' as Bill Shand Kydd puts it. His sister Jane recalls a particular visit to America:

He came over here then went to Las Vegas, and made a lot of money and shipped it home. Which seemed to be a sensible move. Whether he had any savings, or thought about the future – I don't know. I would imagine less so than most normal people, who set aside something for a rainy day. If you're a gambler by nature, you almost don't have that in you.

That, too, is perfectly true. Nevertheless some thousands had been set aside, although the larger part of this, an estimated £14,000 in the Bulawayo account, was frozen owing to the sanctions then in place against Rhodesia. The money in Switzerland was considerably less, thought to be no more than £4,000. There was also said to be an account in the Bahamas, although this is unconfirmed. 'His affairs were in a dreadful jumble,' said Gilson. When the Lucan estate was finally proved, after the High Court declaration of death in 1999, it totalled just £14,709: left to his wife.

In the autumn of 1974, however, there was the imminent sale of the silver, expected to realize some £35,000. Lucan had been proferring that sale, left, right and centre, to all his banks and creditors, rather as a poor soul pawns and redeems the same piece of family gold; but, again, the situation was not the same. Lucan had the safety net of the privileged. The gaping financial holes could have been repaired, the custody judgment calmly revisited, if he had changed his life into a sensible one. He was only thirty-nine. He might still have got straight, if he had found the will to do it; or found the humility to discuss his problems openly, rather than hedging and boozing, trying and failing not to be a bore. But he could not. Only the pasteboard life of an earl remained.

On Wednesday 6 November, a dry, cool and sunny day, Lucan did something unexpected: he had a piano lesson. He had played Bach on the piano at Lower Belgrave Street, which stood in the basement breakfast room and the next day would be splashed with Sandra Rivett's blood. Caroline Hill, who taught him, had also been giving lessons to Frances. Veronica had now decided that her daughter should no longer attend and Lucan, not wanting to lose the slot, had gone in her place. 'My goodness,' Caroline Hill later said, 'how he loved those children! He talked about them constantly.'

In the afternoon he went to the Heywood Hill bookshop in Curzon Street, as he did regularly. There he ordered two detective novels (significance has sometimes been read into this taste for crime fiction, which if true implies murderous tendencies in a very large number of people), and bought a book about Greek shipping millionaires.

He visited his uncle, John Bevan, had a drink and seemed his usual self. Accounts differ, even between Roy Ranson and his deputy David Gerring, as to where Lucan spent the rest of the evening. Ranson says that Lucan dined at the Ladbroke Club. Gerring, whose version is the more likely one, says that he attended a large supper party at Selim Zilkha's house in Portland Place, where the 4th Earl of Lucan had had his London home. John Aspinall and Charles Benson were also present. At the party Lucan offered to deliver a parcel for one of the other guests, saying that he would do so on Friday or Saturday of that week. Was this an attempt to establish that life, for him, would be going on as normal? Both accounts of the evening say that Lucan's friends found him in good form.

After dinner he went to the Clermont, then downstairs to Annabel's, where he met Andrina Colquhoun and arranged to see her the following day. 'He was in normal spirits,' she later said. 'His behaviour didn't suggest he was unduly worried or depressed. Like everybody else he was a bit down – things like inflation, money, the government – but nothing unusual.'[33] Earlier, in the House of Commons, the MP who would soon become Leader of the Opposition, Margaret Thatcher, had moved an amendment to the debate on the Queen's Speech, stating that it 'in no way measures up to the peril facing the country'.

The newspapers on 7 November were filled with speculation as to what would be in the next week's Budget, the third in eight months. The following day would be very different: full of rushed reports of the bomb that was thrown, at 10.17pm, into a pub opposite the Woolwich Barracks, killing two people and injuring twenty-six. Although the *Evening Standard* would cover the Belgravia murder, it was not until Saturday that the national newspapers, for the first time, made Lucan their story.

On the Thursday, a dull and drizzly day, Lucan rose before his usual time and rang his lawyers. He also rang Frances's headmistress. Frances had previously told friends that Veronica did not bother to take her to school on Sandra's day off; Lucan asked if Frances had come in that day, but the headmistress did not know. Later she rang him back to say that Frances was not in fact at school. The call went unanswered.[34] 'On that day I didn't go to school,' Frances would say in her police statement, 'because the bus didn't come for me, so Mummy said I need not go.'

At 10.30am Lucan was telephoned by Andrina, who asked about their plans that night. He was a little vague, but suggested a possible meeting at the Clermont. He did not appear at the club for lunch. At about 3pm Andrina went there to look for him. She then rang the Elizabeth Street flat, where there was no reply. At 4.30, after her working day as a photographer, she drove past the flat, where there was no Mercedes outside. She then left for the country. That, effectively, was the end of her contact with Lucan.

Before this, at around 4pm, as the London sky was beginning to shadow, Lucan had been in Lower Belgrave Street. He had in the past visited the chemist at the end of the road and asked the pharmacist about different pills, presumably those prescribed for his wife. On the 7th he took in a capsule that was identified as a Limbutral 5, an anti-depressant. Possibly he also passed his house, as was his habit. It would have presented its familiar, reserved face: standing among its aristocratic kind, tall and seemly, its façade impregnable. And Lucan was doing the familiar things: the daily promenades from Elizabeth Street to Lower Belgrave Street, from Belgravia to Mayfair; the close circling of the brick and stucco house where Veronica sat, near-motionless, in her stately lair.

At about 4.45pm Lucan rang a friend, a literary agent named Michael Hicks-Beach, whom he invited to come to his flat that evening at 6.30. Lucan had written an article about gambling for a student magazine: again, unexpected. He wanted Hicks-Beach to look it over with a professional eye. The men had a couple of drinks together, chatted convivially about the piece, then Lucan drove his friend home to Oakley Gardens in Chelsea.

Presumably Lucan had used the Mercedes to go to Lower Belgrave Street that afternoon, else it would have been seen by Andrina. According to Hicks-Beach, however, Lucan gave him a lift in a different car: in other words, the Ford Corsair. He had also changed his clothes. The chemist described him wearing a blue suit. When he saw Hicks-Beach, he was dressed in flannels and a sweater.

Lucan dropped his friend home at about 8pm, just as Hicks-Beach's wife was watching the end of *Top of the Pops*. At Lower Belgrave Street, Lucan's daughter Frances had seen the same programme on the television in the third-floor nursery. After her bath she had spent part of the evening there, playing a game on her own.

Earlier, at about 5.15, the time when his children were having tea with Sandra Rivett and their mother, Greville Howard had rung Lucan and invited him to the theatre that night. Howard was living in the Eaton Row mews, having split amicably from Zoe two years earlier. Lucan replied: 'That's very kind of you, but I don't think I will.' Instead he invited Howard and his party of three for dinner at the Clermont at 11pm, after the show. Lucan rang and made the booking. The Clermont recorded Lucan's request as a table for four people, yet the party was for five. An unintentional betrayal of the fact that his evening held other plans? When Howard and his friends arrived at the club, they asked for a fifth chair, which remained empty.

While Frances watched *Top of the Pops* in the nursery, on the second floor below Veronica was also watching television: *The Six Million Dollar Man*, then *Mastermind*. With her on the marital bed were her two younger children, George and Camilla, and their nanny

Sandra Rivett, who had changed her night off. That evening Sandra had received a phone call from her boyfriend, and had spoken to her mother. A woollen blanket was spread on the bed. Veronica was propped up with three pillows, her cigarettes to hand. The women had the air of being curled up for the night, although they were dressed in their day clothes.

According to Billy Edgson, the linkman at the Clermont, Lucan appeared outside the club that night at about 8.45pm; he was driving the Mercedes and pulled up by the door. He asked if 'anyone was in'. The regular gamblers would almost certainly have been gathering, but Lucan drove away again.

At Lower Belgrave Street, Frances had joined the others in her mother's bedroom at around 8.05, then returned to the nursery at 8.30 after the ending of *The Six Million Dollar Man*. A few minutes later Sandra put the two younger children to bed. Frances, who had returned briefly to her game, heard her do so.

What happened next is unclear. The one certain thing is that at some point before 9pm, Sandra went downstairs, to where a man was waiting.

PART III

The Investigation

'Was it possible, even remotely possible, that the
man's statement was true? Was this that thousandth
case where circumstantial evidence, complete in every
particular, was merely a series of accidents, completely
unrelated and lying colossally in consequence?
But then, the thinness of the man's story – that
fundamental improbability!'

JOSEPHINE TEY, *The Man in the Queue*, 1929

Murder

'Blunt head injuries inflicted by a named person. Murder.'

FROM THE DEATH CERTIFICATE OF
SANDRA ELEANOR RIVETT, REGISTERED IN JUNE 1975
BY THE CITY OF WESTMINSTER REGISTRAR

POSSIBLY THE GREATEST pleasure of reading detective fiction is the illusion it gives that there is such a thing as omniscience. Hercule Poirot, who applies order and method and finds that no problem can resist them; Lord Peter Wimsey, with his 'now we know how, we know who'; Sherlock Holmes, who realizes that the absence of incident, the dog that does not bark, is as important a clue as its presence. Not for them the ambiguity, the obfuscation, the lies that cannot be penetrated. Nothing remains unknown. Truth has its own natural force, and must come to light if a brain is able to perceive it.

The surest means to find the truth is identified by Miss Marple. 'So you see that if you disregard the smoke and come to the fire you know where you are. You just come down to the actual facts of what happened.'

Although in detective fiction this is always possible, Miss Marple's creator, Agatha Christie, knew perfectly well that it was not so easy, in real life, to perceive *what really happened*. Smoke thickens around facts until it is impossible to see them glinting in the darkness. Christie was almost tormented by fascination with the cases of two unsolved domestic murders: the death of Charles Bravo in 1876 from antimony, and the Croydon poisonings of 1929–30, in which three members of the same family were killed with arsenic. Christie wrote of the Croydon case 'that if I die and go to heaven, or the other place, and it so happens that the Public Prosecutor of that time is also there, I shall beg him to reveal the secret to me'.[1] She herself tried very hard, but could not quite trace the thread of truth. How she must have longed to inhabit the idealized minds of her two detectives, and enable that cerebral *deus ex machina*!

Not long before her death she had made the sudden, questing remark: 'I wonder what *has* happened to Lord Lucan?' Had she lived longer, her interest would doubtless have deepened. Like the Bravo and Croydon cases, this was her sort of crime. It was about the mystery behind the façade. It was about motive, character, conceal-ment: the human dynamic, writ large by murder.

It was also a case whose simplicity was deceptive. Classic domestic killing gone wrong? It certainly looked that way, but if Agatha Christie had written the story she would have argued that what seemed to have happened on 7–8 November could *not* have happened. Too many facts did not fit the official solution. Too much remained extraneous. If a fact does not fit a theory, then it is the theory that must be discarded, not the fact. Otherwise the solu-tion is unsatisfactory. 'Each of these unrelated facts must fit into its appointed place,' says Hercule Poirot. 'There must be no loose ends.' That is the tenet of fictional detectives, and it takes them to truth.

Again, of course, real life is different. Perhaps the unexplained is merely part of the story. The Lucan myth, certainly, is happy to bear the weight of inconsistencies within it.

Yet the myth is not the truth. The truth of the Lucan case lies somewhere within a knot of contradictions, a list of unanswered questions. Just as there is an opposing version of so much that hap-pened in the Lucan marriage, so there is of almost every event that took place on the night of 7–8 November. The story of the murder was also the story of the marriage; more so than in any other case of domestic killing. And because, despite the certainty of the myth, uncertainty still abounds, so too do alternative theories: the meta-fictions imposed upon what is unknown, but nevertheless was what really happened.

To the police, what happened is known, and no smoke lingers to occlude it. The murder of Sandra Rivett and the attack on Veronica Lucan were deemed to be solved within an hour or so of their occurrence. Two uniformed officers, Police Constable Beddick and Police Sergeant Baker, entered 46 Lower Belgrave Street just after ten o'clock on the night of 7 November, followed a little later by the first CID officer. From that moment the case was over; all that remained was to find Lord Lucan. Every complexity was trodden into oblivion by the simple force of the police belief in his guilt. What they found inside the house would convince them that evil had been present, and in Lucan's guise.

The two officers had been patrolling Belgravia in a police van when, at 10pm, they received a call reporting an incident in the Plumbers Arms pub. A woman, subsequently identified as the Countess of Lucan, had entered the bar some ten minutes earlier. She was wearing a pinafore dress and jumper, and according to a later police account was barefoot. She was, as the head barman told the inquest, 'head to toe in blood'. There were eight people in the pub, a small, square, intimate place with three tiny bars. In those days of regulated hours it was approaching closing time; when the door opened, those inside would probably have thought that it was somebody trying to get in a couple of last drinks. Instead what stood before them was a tiny creature with a soaked and defiled appearance, her head full of clotting blood, her white forehead striped dark red. The barman, Arthur Whitehouse, said:

> I caught her before she fell on the floor. I laid her on a bench. She was quite all right for a few minutes and then a state of shock took over. I covered her over, she then started shouting 'Help me, help me, I've just escaped from being murdered', and shouting 'My children, my children, he's murdered my nanny'. But no name was mentioned.

Mr Whitehouse rang for an ambulance, which did not come for some twenty minutes. He also rang the police. PC Stanley Chapman arrived at the pub and went with Veronica to St George's Hospital, Hyde Park Corner, where she remained for six days. At the inquest, Dr Hugh Scott, the Chief Casualty Officer at the hospital, reported that she had been 'very distressed' on admission. She had protested when staff cut away her jumper, saying that it was her 'very best'. The doctor found evidence of about seven lacerations to her head, for which sixty stitches were inserted into her face and scalp. There were also lacerations at the back of her throat, more painful than the other injuries, and probably caused 'by fingers being thrust forcefully into the mouth'. Her neck had been wrenched, although there were no marks on it. In reply to two further questions at the inquest, Dr Scott confirmed that Veronica's injuries would be difficult to explain as a fall; and that it was 'possible, but very unlikely' that they were self-inflicted.

When Beddick and Baker received the call to go to Lower Belgrave Street, they found the front door closed. The house was dark. It looked just as it always did, like all the other houses on the street. From 10.05 it began to look different: the policemen kicked down the door. It had a chain and four locks, one of which had been engaged. The chain was put up at night, except on Sandra's days off. Veronica had expressed the fear that her husband could enter the house at any time, so this was a natural precaution; but, as she told the inquest, on the 7th she had forgotten to do this.[2] In the hall the light bulb was burned out. Later Veronica would say that she practised economy by not replacing bulbs, 'to fend off any suggestion of household extravagance from my estranged husband',[3] although she also said that both she and Sandra were too short to replace them easily. Baker sent Beddick for a strong torch. He himself moved towards the basement. At the top of the stairs leading down to it was a piece of lead piping.

Detective-Sergeant Graham Forsyth was the first CID officer to arrive, at 10.20. 'I was going a bit potty,' he says, 'because there was no bloody light. But I knew that skulduggery was afoot. There was blood all over the shop. When I saw the girl, I thought: oh Christ, they've beheaded her.'

Sandra Rivett was doubled over, bundled with her head and feet outermost into a mailsack. She lay at the bottom of the basement stairs, in the open space between the kitchen at the front of the house and the breakfast room beyond. There was a great pool of her B group blood in the area behind the body, and another at the bottom of the stairs, where lay some crockery. Her blood had also splashed across the breakfast room to the left of the stairs: onto a rosebowl, the children's encyclopaedia that lay on the piano, the pictures and portraits. To the right there was more B group blood, against the stair wall and trickling down to the skirting board. This 'directional splashing', as it was described at the inquest, was said to have come from a wound that was already bleeding. The ceiling was sprayed, again from repeated strikes. DS Forsyth told the inquest that he had seen 'what appeared to be footmarks in the blood, which led to a room containing a centrally-heated boiler [behind the staircase]'. There was also blood from a fabric impression halfway up the staircase, thought to have been smeared on the wall by the assailant.

The divisional surgeon for the Metropolitan Police, Dr Michael Smith, arrived at 10.45pm. He would later tell the inquest: 'On the floor I saw a large canvas bag, which appeared to contain a human body. I also noticed bloodstains on the floor. I didn't disturb the bag in any way. I was satisfied that the body was dead, and that the death was not due to natural causes.'

Sandra was wearing a flowered smock over her dress. Her black shoes, described as 'sensible working shoes' by Roy Ranson, although in fact patent courts with a neat heel, were placed beside her. The mailsack, of American origin, was pulled loosely together by a cord with the top folded over. Sandra's left arm, on which she wore a little gold watch that was later given to her son, had fallen out.

Her injuries were terrible: 'a fearful amount of violence', as was said at the inquest into the death of Marie Riel, found in the basement of her nearby Park Lane home one hundred years earlier. The pathologist Keith Simpson, who performed the autopsy on Sandra Rivett, described 'six splits from heavy blunt injury to the scalp'. There were also 'three areas of heavy bruising'. The first of these was the face, and Simpson detailed the injuries thus: 'One lay over the right eye, one and a half inches; the second lay on the right corner of the mouth, three-quarters of an inch, close to the end of the upper lip; and the third lay over the eyebrow.' The second area of bruising was 'on the top of both shoulders, without splitting the skin'. The third area was on the front of the right upper arm: 'a series of four in-line bruises, as if fingers had been gripping the arm heavily'. There was also some superficial bruising on the back of the right hand, 'likely to result if the hand were placed between the blunt instrument and the body. These were protective injuries.' Lastly were some minor injuries to the face, the 'left eye and mouth'. These were not caused by a weapon, but by a fist or hand slap.

The heavier injuries were described as:

> Four splits in the scalp on the right side of the head, above the right ear. Two lay in front of the other two, towards the right eyebrow in the hair margin. In no case did I find the scalp fractured beneath these splits. On the back of the head there lay the fifth and sixth splits in the scalp. These lay above the nape of the neck, two and a half inches apart.

Simpson's report continued:

> There was a great deal of blood, mainly from the nose and mouth into the air passages and the skull. This was not fractured, but there was a good deal of surface bruising to the brain, and these injuries must have caused the unconsciousness. It was these injuries, together with the bruising of the brain, that had caused death.
>
> I attribute death to blunt head injuries, inhalation of blood, and it was this that had made it clear that no further gain of consciousness had followed.

The police later stated that a light bulb, belonging to the socket at the bottom of the stairs, had been removed and placed on a chair. During the inquest into Sandra's death, a newspaper quoted Sergeant Baker as saying that, when he returned to the basement, he 'found a light switch' and 'switched the light on';[4] this may have referred to a different bulb, or have been reported in error. Certainly when the police first entered the basement the only light was a small red glow from a kettle in the kitchen, and the dusky stream that came in, through the slightly open slats of the blind above the sink, from the street lamp directly opposite the house. The outer door, at the bottom of the steps leading from the basement up to the pavement, was locked. The back door at the rear of the basement was unlocked. It led to a small garden, which contained some carved stone heads and was surrounded by a high wall. Sandra's blood was later found on some of the ivy leaves in the garden.

It was one o'clock in the morning of 8 November when Detective Chief Superintendent Roy Ranson first arrived at 46 Lower Belgrave Street. He had been telephoned at midnight at his house in Kent by David Gerring, the detective chief-inspector who was head of CID at Gerald Road. This charmingly homely police station, now no longer in use, stood in the middle of Belgravia; a white house like all the rest, except for the blue lamp that hung outside in place of the usual black carriage-lights. Inside the station were copies of Debrett's, Burke's Peerage and the Almanack de Gotha. Close by was the Duke of Wellington pub, 'the Boots', where the police spent much of their time ('they loved us, we loved them,' says Graham Forsyth) and would soon be drinking regularly with a mass of journalists. Some of the favoured press members would gain an *entrée* to Ranson and Gerring's inner sanctum, complete with bottle of whisky. 'We used the press, they used us. Two-way traffic. The media can be very useful.' Over the weeks that followed, as Lucan's disappearance became a running story in the newspapers, 'Roy and Dave took opposing views,' says Forsyth. 'One said he's dead, the other said he's alive. That was deliberate. To keep the story alive.' In June 1975, when Lucan was reported as having been seen in Cherbourg, the entire story was a police construct. 'What we needed was a sighting. We'd ring them all up and say: this is on. So the world and his wife go to France...'

When Ranson arrived at the house, Graham Forsyth had already gone in preliminary search of Lucan. 'My interest was: where is this jerk? He's giving me a headache.' Forsyth broke in to the Eaton Row mews through the upstairs window, and found some of the lights switched on. He also visited Elizabeth Street, where two constables would subsequently be stationed. The flat was sparsely furnished, unlived-in: it contained a piano, Lucan's ermine robes, alcohol and a large number of unopened bills. Laid out on the bed were a suit, shirt and tie, some loose change, a wallet, and the keys to the Mercedes. Lucan's passport was also in the flat.

At Lower Belgrave Street, Veronica's bedroom had been examined: the light beside her bed was the only one left burning in the house. A blood-stained towel was found spread on a pillow. Upstairs, the uniformed officers had found George and Camilla asleep and Frances standing beside her bed. A television was playing loudly in the nursery.

At about 11pm, Kait Lucan arrived at the house. ('Out of the blue appears Mummy,' says Forsyth.) A little earlier Lucan had telephoned Kait's flat in St John's Wood, where she had care of the old family nanny Flora Coles, and asked her to collect the children. Forsyth made notes of Kait's account of this conversation, some of which would later be disputed at the inquest. One phrase remained constant, however. Lucan had said to his mother: 'There has been a terrible catastrophe at number 46.' 'I loved that word!' says Forsyth. 'Catastrophe.'

Kait then returned to her flat with the children, accompanied by PC Beddick. 'I said, stick with her and see if he rings.' Lucan did indeed ring his mother again. Kait relayed their conversation to the inquest:

He said, have you got the children? I said yes, they're here in bed, and to the best of my knowledge and belief they're asleep. He said, that's all right, then. I said, what do you intend to do? I got nowhere. I also said, the police are here. Do you want to speak to them? He hesitated and then said no, I don't think I'll speak to them now. Tell them I'll phone them in the morning, and I'll phone you too. Then he rang off.

David Gerring later wrote that Beddick should have 'snatched the phone' away from Kait. He implied that the PC was frozen into immobility by a kind of deference. 'You had to genuflect to her,' says Graham Forsyth. Already, in the first hours of the investigation, it was clear that this case would be defined by class: by a sense of the invisible barriers that were erected around Lucan and his world, and by the police hackles that were raised in reaction.

As Ranson arrived at Lower Belgrave Street, Gerring returned to Gerald Road, where dedicated phone lines were being installed for the investigation. The news agencies, which monitored police radio frequencies, were by now aware that something wildly out of the ordinary was going on. Soon the press would begin to gather in the drizzle outside the house. On 9 November the national newspapers, whose first stories were of approximate but general accuracy, also carried this statement from Scotland Yard: 'We are treating this case as one of murder and attempted murder and we feel that Lord Lucan should be told of the details as soon as possible. We are anxious to interview him.'

At around 2am, Ranson and Gerring went for the first time to see Veronica in hospital. She was a pitiable sight, tiny and frail, her head black with stitches. Ranson asked: 'Does that hurt very much?' She nodded. She asked if the children were all right. Then she said: 'Have you found him?' Asked if she had any idea where Lucan might be, her reply was characteristically dry: 'Your guess is as good as mine.'[5]

The first interview was informal and necessarily brief. 'It was obvious she'd taken a sedative because of her injuries,' Gerring would later tell the inquest. 'She looked as if she'd taken drugs.' On the evening of 8 November, at about 6pm, the two policemen returned to the hospital, where Veronica made a verbal statement. 'Her understanding was extremely good. I left Sergeant Forsyth to take the written statement. The written statement was remarkably close to the verbal statement.'

Quite understandably, the police felt a great and instant sympathy for Veronica, and this never wavered. Graham Forsyth, who would soon become her *de facto* bodyguard, and was described as 'the only one who could handle her',[6] felt not just compassion but respect for her spirit. 'I've got admiration for people who take kicks and stand up for themselves. Some people might lay down and die – but she didn't.' Her statement to him was twenty pages of longhand, nine sheets of typed foolscap. She was, wrote Gerring, 'a highly convincing witness'. According to Ranson, she 'never varied from the essential facts of her account of that night – to my mind a clear indication that she had told the plain, unvarnished truth'.

What Veronica told the police, and later the inquest, was as follows.

Until 8.30pm on the evening of 7 November, she had been watching television in her bedroom with the children and with Sandra Rivett. At about 8.55pm Sandra, who had gone upstairs to the third floor and had put the two younger children to bed, came down and asked Veronica if she would like some tea. 'I had the habit of getting myself a cup of tea at that time, I had been doing this since our separation, but it wasn't a very usual thing for her to put her head round the door.'

As Sandra went downstairs, Veronica remained on the bed with her daughter Frances, and began to watch the nine o'clock news on BBC1. Although Sandra was later found close to some smashed crockery, Veronica said that she did not recall her taking any cups downstairs. 'She may have had them in her own room.'

At about 9.15, having heard nothing amiss, Veronica began to wonder about the tea. She went down to the ground floor and looked towards the basement. There was no light on. At the inquest she was asked whether one could use a two-way switch, at both the top and bottom of the staircase, to turn on the basement light: 'I believe you can, it may be possible.' Veronica did not try the light switch, as it seemed obvious that Sandra could not be making tea in the dark. She did, however, call her name.

As she did so she heard a noise. 'Just a noise of somebody, or something, in the downstairs cloakroom.' The cloakroom was situated at the rear of the ground floor. In front of it was an ante-room, or half-landing, with a low ceiling of six feet six inches. Four steps led from it to the head of the basement staircase, where Veronica was standing, with the door to the basement secured back against the wall 'I walked towards the sound, or at any rate moved towards it,' she said. 'Somebody rushed out and hit me on the head.'

She recalled 'about four' blows. The assailant did not speak, although after a moment Veronica screamed. 'The person said: shut up.' The voice was instantly recognizable. 'It was my husband.'

Lucan then 'thrust three gloved fingers down my throat and we started to fight'. He also attempted to strangle her and to gouge out her eyes. The pair grappled on the floor of the ante-room, where Lucan continued trying to throttle her. 'We fell into the basement doorway and on to the stairs,' she said. A metal support on the balustrade was dislodged. According to the police, Veronica bit her husband. At the inquest, in reply to a question from her counsel, she explained how she had finally brought the assault to an end. She managed to sit up between Lucan's legs and grab his testicles. 'He desisted, yes.'

There was a suggestion that her counsel, in asking this question, was seeking to clarify how Veronica had survived injuries similar to those that had killed Sandra Rivett (who was described as having a 'particularly thin skull'). Veronica's own explanation was: 'Good breeding.'

As the attack ended, Veronica asked if she could have some water, and Lucan escorted her to the cloakroom, in darkness, where she drank: only hot water was available. They returned to the ante-room staircase. At the inquest Veronica was not asked about any conversation that took place at this point: as Lucan's wife she was unable to give evidence about the murder of Sandra Rivett, only about the assault upon herself, and this set stringent limits upon the questioning. To the police, however, she did offer more information. As soon as she was able, Veronica asked where Sandra was. At first Lucan said that she had gone out. Then, in Ranson's words: 'Standing on the staircase Lucan confessed to his wife that he had killed the nanny.' He also told her that he had done this in error, and that she, Veronica, had been his intended victim. Later it would be said that the inquest had been favourable to Lucan, as well as to Veronica, in keeping this evidence from the jury.

In Veronica's account, no timing was given for how long the couple spent in the ante-room, but at some point Lucan agreed that they should go to the bedroom and inspect Veronica's injuries. They went up to the second floor, Veronica leading the way; perhaps a little surprisingly. In the bedroom they found Frances still watching television. She was sent upstairs, according to her own statement by her mother, and the set was switched off. To the police, Veronica said that she ran into the *en suite* bathroom so that Frances should not see her. To the inquest she gave a slightly different sequence of events. 'We went together into the bedroom, before I lay on the bed, and together we looked at my injuries. After we had done that, I think I said I didn't feel very well, and he laid a towel on the bed, and I got on it.' According to Ranson, Veronica suggested to Lucan that he stay and look after her for a few days until her bruises had gone; this, presumably, was intended as a ruse to lure him into the belief that she would not give him away. At the inquest, again, nothing was asked about any conversation between the couple. Instead Veronica told the coroner: 'Very vaguely I understood that he was going to get a cloth to clean up my face.' Lucan went into the bathroom. 'I heard the taps running and I jumped to my feet and ran out of the room and down the stairs.'

According to the barman at the Plumbers Arms, it was 9.50pm when Veronica entered the pub. This, by her account, was some half an hour after Lucan's assault on her had begun.

'You have no doubt that it was he?' asked the coroner at the inquest. She said: 'No doubt at all.'

Veronica then described her husband's clothes. 'He was wearing a sweater of sorts, no tie and grey flannel trousers. That's the best I can do.' The trousers would appear to have corresponded with fibres found at various sites in the house, and possibly with the fabric impression on the stair wall, although obviously no test was possible. Veronica also said that Lucan had worn gloves during the attack, which were removed at some unspecified point.

At the end of her evidence, the coroner asked if Veronica had seen anybody else during the course of the struggle.

'Did anybody brush past you? Did you hear sounds?'

'I saw nobody else.'

'Nor at any time during the evening?'

'Nor at any time during the evening.'

'I am going to ask my officer to reiterate your evidence. Is there anything you wish to alter?'

'No, there is nothing.'

Lucan's own account, which emerged at the inquest through the testimony of others, was entirely different from that of his wife. It was a proclamation of innocence. His word against hers: as always. It is beyond doubt, however, that he was at Lower Belgrave Street that night, as he was seen by his ten-year-old daughter Frances.

Veronica's account was, as Roy Ranson put it, 'broadly confirmed' by the forensic evidence at 46 Lower Belgrave Street. The area at the head of the basement stairs was sloshed and sprayed with her A group blood. The carpet of the four ante-room steps was stained with blood. On the wall to the left of the ante-room was a radiating pattern of blood, said at the inquest to have been caused by strikes on an already open wound. The blood had flicked off sideways, as had a piece of Veronica's hair. Repeated strikes had also created a necklace pattern on the ante-room ceiling and its lampshade, and on the cloakroom door behind. This blood was said to have been 'trajected backwards'. There was extensive bleeding found on the wall near the top of the staircase, and some on the basement door, as well as some hair. There was also a small amount of blood on the wall beside the third step down. Inside the cloakroom, more hair was in the basin, as well as a mixture of A and B group blood. The hair also tested positive for both A and B groups, A being dominant.

There was a further mixture of A and B group blood in the basement. A small drop of A group blood was found on the kitchen floor, alongside a drop from B group. On the sack containing Sandra's body, from which six blood samples were taken, two were found to contain a combination of A and B group. In all, six instances of non-B group blood were found in the basement at Lower Belgrave Street, including a droplet of A group on a work surface at the front of the kitchen. There was also a mix of blood on Veronica's clothes. It was mostly A: heavy bleeding on the neck and sleeves of her jumper, heavy on the right shoulder of her pinafore dress, light on her tights. More A group was found on her skirt. At the back of the skirt was some B group blood, and an AB mixture. There was B group on her shoes.

At the inquest Dr Margaret Pereira, senior scientific officer in Biology Division at Scotland Yard and described by Ranson as 'first rate', stated: 'In my opinion, Lady Lucan was battered on the stairs by an attacker standing in the ante-room.' Michael Eastham, for the Lucan family, asked the doctor about the anomaly of the blood on Veronica's shoes. How, he said, could this have happened? Dr Pereira thought that Veronica might have gone into the basement, something that she herself strenuously denied. 'That', said the doctor, 'is a likely explanation for the Group B blood on her shoes.' Straightaway the coroner intervened. He asked if an alternative possibility was that the blood had come from her struggle with the attacker. 'Yes, if Lord Lucan had been covered in Sandra Rivett's blood.'

Michael Eastham then asked which was the more likely explanation of the two.

'It's a difficult question. Perhaps if I could have the shoes...'

Dr Pereira examined them. Then she said: 'No, I can't tell. The blood staining could have come from either source.' Roy Ranson's own explanation for the incidence of B group blood on Veronica's shoes and clothes was that 'Lucan's clothing would undoubtedly by that stage have been soaked in the dead nanny's blood'.

The doctor was also asked by Eastham about the A group blood found on the mailsack. For this she had no easy explanation, other than that the sack had brushed against the wall at the top of the stairs when it was carried from the basement. (Dr Pereira did not examine the sack *in situ*, but at Scotland Yard on the morning of the 8th.)

Surely, said Eastham, the blood would have dried by the time the sack was removed? The reply was that 'blood is still capable of making smears if it is clotted or not. It's difficult to say how long blood remains wet. It could take a few minutes or a few hours to dry.'

A press photographer would later say that the mailsack had been wrapped in polythene sheeting when it was taken from the house. If it was covered *after* it was brought up to the ground floor, then Dr Pereira's theory becomes a possibility. Roy Ranson's own account, which does not mention the polythene, describes the sack as having been hard to manoeuvre up the stairs; contact with the stair wall, went the implication, was almost impossible to avoid.

The presence of blood was fact. The deductions from its presence should therefore lead to truth. The women who were attacked had two different blood groups, and the significance lies in the presence of those groups where they should not have been. Why was blood group A found in the basement and on the mailsack? Why was blood group B found on Veronica's clothes? Did the presence of A and B groups in various sites imply a mixture of blood from the two women, or from a third party whose blood group was AB?

The simplest inference from the blood evidence is that Veronica

Lucan went into the basement at Lower Belgrave Street. This was the explanation put forward by Dr Pereira, before the coroner suggested a different one. Roy Ranson wrote that Veronica had stated, 'from the very first moment of the inquiry, that she had never set foot in the basement'. He also said what was demonstrably untrue, that forensics confirmed 'every word that she had said'. It is of course very possible that group B blood was smeared on her skirt by her assailant, although it seems less likely that it would have transferred to her shoes, particularly to the sole of her left shoe.[7] As for the group A blood in the basement: if this did come from Veronica, either she entered the basement *after* her own wounds were inflicted, or the attack upon her began in the basement, then moved to the top of the stairs.

The mixture of A and B blood in the cloakroom basin, on the sack and on the weapon opens up the faint possibility that the attacker belonged to AB group (Lucan's own blood group is not known). Both women put up a fight and could have drawn blood. According to Dr Pereira, however, the AB was more likely a mixture of the two blood types. Nor would an AB group attacker explain the separate incidences of A and B in places where it should not, logically, have been found.

The police became uncomfortably aware of this. Hence Ranson's description of the considerable difficulties in removing the mailsack from the basement (which the official theory requires Lucan to have planned to do alone). Accidental contact is, indeed, the explanation for all the anomalies in the blood analysis. 'There was blood all over the shop,' says Forsyth. 'So you got transference.' The blood, wrote Gerring, was transferred either by a 'blood–spattered Lucan' or by the police themselves. 'Come on, you've got blood splashed and sprayed everywhere,' he later said. 'You've got forty or fifty policemen and photographers and forensics walking around. Of course you'll get blood transferred. It would be a miracle if you didn't.'[8]

With regard to the presence of A group blood in the basement, which Dr Pereira told the inquest she could not explain, Ranson wrote: 'The answer, I am convinced, lies in the many movements of officers, dogs, scientists, fingerprint experts and undertakers.' There was also the fact that drops of B group blood were found on ivy leaves in the garden, and that footprints led from Sandra's body to the back of the basement. Blood on the floors, Dr Pereira told the inquest, could have been transferred by 'anyone with big feet, such as a police officer', a remark that met with some hilarity (and did not explain why footmarks were seen by DS Forsyth, before the police descended *en masse*). It was also suggested, with perfect seriousness, that the two cats in the house might have caused the transference.

In other words, and in order to explain away facts that did not fit the official theory, those in charge of the investigation were obliged to admit that 46 Lower Belgrave Street had become a contaminated crime scene. It was seething with policemen, a free-for-all, with every PC then on duty in central London going round to take a look. More than fifty sets of police fingerprints had to be eliminated.

At Elizabeth Street, where Lucan's belongings were cleared, a similar chaos ensued. Later it would be claimed that some unidentified officers had used the flat for parties: 'In the days after the Earl vanished, detectives used the flat like a private club, inviting colleagues from all over London to drink his booze, paw his possessions and even ride his exercise bike. And when forensic teams finally dusted the flat in Belgravia, Central London, they found so many fingerprints they could not identify the earl's.'[9] Although a fingerprint was found inside the Ford Corsair similar to one in the flat, no certain match with Lucan's fingerprints was ever possible, as they were never identified beyond doubt. At the inquest it was stated that the only prints found in the basement were those of the police, the victim, and the children. (Veronica, whose prints would surely have naturally been there, was not mentioned.) Nor was Elizabeth Street ever checked for a match with the grey-blue woollen fibres found at the murder scene. Dr Pereira reported seven on the towel in the cloakroom, four on a towel in Veronica's bedroom, and a quantity on the piping. There were also some fingerprints on the piping, impossible to lift because of the stretched tape bandaging around it. Lucan was said to have worn gloves, but prints could have been made at another time. The piping was described as nine inches long, weighing some two and a half pounds, and 'grossly distorted'.

Although an obvious weapon, the piping presented two problems. When it was first seen by Sergeant Baker at the top of the basement stairs, he described it as looking like 'a doll's leg'. It was, he told the inquest, 'turning red'. This oddity has been explained in a couple of ways. It could have been a trick of the light. Or it could have been, as Ranson would later suggest,[10] that Lucan had washed the piping in the cloakroom before leaving the house, removing the surface redness, and that the blood beneath the bandages was seeping through.

The likelihood that Lucan stopped to do this is, of course, remote to non-existent. Far more probable is that Sergeant Baker was simply mistaken in his impression. However, the possibility that the piping was rinsed at some point would help to explain the other anomaly: that none of Sandra's hair was found on it. At the inquest, the pathologist Keith Simpson said that the piping was 'highly likely' to have been the murder weapon, as it was consistent with 'some of Sandra Rivett's injuries'. Dr Pereira found on it a mixture of A and B group blood, with a preponderance of A. She also found several of Veronica's hairs; but Sandra's hairs should also have been found on the piping.

A subsequent analysis of the piping could never take place, however, for the simple reason that it disappeared. 'It has not been stored as it should have been,' it was later said, 'and the lead pipe is missing.'[11]

In 2004 Scotland Yard made a public announcement that it was re-examining the case. 'The investigation into the murder of Sandra Rivett and the disappearance of Lord Lucan remains open. As with any unsolved murder, the investigation is subject to review to examine evidence and any possible new lines of inquiry. We are now able to use modern techniques, including the use of DNA, in reviewing our cases.' This all sounded very good, very scientific. It made no mention of the fact that, without a murder weapon, it was clearly doomed to founder. The use of DNA evidence is now, of course, a scientific means to establish the 'what really happened' that in crime fiction emerges from the omniscient brain of the detective. At the time of the Lucan case this was still another ten years in the future: all that could be done was establish blood types, fingerprints, hairs, fibres, what now seems like the Heath Robinson mechanics of forensics.

Nevertheless, and even by those more basic standards, the Lucan inquiry was as shambolic as the Charge of the Light Brigade. Evidence was destroyed, literally walked all over, and, when it presented difficulties, brushed aside. 'It's no good going on bits and pieces,' David Gerring would later assert, in typical Gene Hunt style. 'As a policeman, you have to go on the whole thing.'[12] 'We knew who did it,' says Graham Forsyth.

'The police never looked for anybody else,' says Christina Shand Kydd. 'They made up their minds, that minute, that he had done it. Straightaway. And there was no question of ever looking at any other evidence – they weren't interested. Whatever you said to them, about anything else, was just completely bypassed.'

'I wasn't very impressed with the blood analysis at the inquest,' says Bill Shand Kydd. 'There were things that needed investigating.' 'That's what you kept on saying,' says Christina. 'And they didn't like us, for that reason.'

'The blood evidence is so ambiguous,' says Lucan's sister Jane. 'I think the police did deserve a lot of blame, for not doing it better. Are they very defensive?'

At 9.50pm on 7 November, as Veronica Lucan was entering the Plumbers Arms, Lord Lucan was still in his former home at Lower Belgrave Street. The couple were separated by just one hundred footsteps. Some of what Lucan did in the next three and a half hours is known. His daughter Frances said in her statement:

After Mummy told me to go upstairs I got straight up and went upstairs to my bedroom, which is on the top floor of the house. I got into bed and read my book. I didn't hear anything from downstairs. After a little while, I don't know how long, because I don't have a clock in my room, I heard Daddy calling for Mummy. He was calling Veronica, where are you?

I got up and went to the banisters and looked down and saw Daddy coming out of the nursery on the floor below me. He then went into the bathroom on the same floor as the nursery. He came straight out and then he went downstairs. That was the last I saw of him. He never came up to the top floor of the house that night, either to look for Mummy or to say goodnight to me.

Lucan then left the house. He secured one of the locks on the front door. What happened next is less certain, but it is overwhelmingly likely that he went directly to 51 Chester Square, five minutes' walk away (almost certainly, of course, he was driving). This would have taken him along Lower Belgrave Street, towards the Plumbers Arms, then down a right-hand turn just before the pub. Roy Ranson actually suggests that Lucan may have headed towards the pub, almost as if he intended to enter. The Chester Square house was owned by the rich Swedish gastronome, Charles Florman. He and his wife Madeleine were acquaintances of Lucan; great hosts, whose dinner parties were attended by a variety of people including both the King of Sweden and Tony Curtis, although on the night of 7 November the house presented a darkened face. Lucan rang the doorbell. Mrs Florman, alone and in bed, was too nervous to answer. About a week later she would tell Dominick Elwes about some mysterious brown marks on the doorstep. She did not report these to the police, although Elwes did. The marks were later reported to be smudges of B group blood. Despite house-to-house enquiries, they had not been noticed by the police.

Some time after 10pm Mrs Florman received a phone call. A man said 'Madeleine? I know you...', followed by a disorientated muddle of words. She believed the voice to be that of Lord Lucan, which it almost certainly was. Their daughters attended the same school, and the obvious inference is that, as she was the nearest person to 46 Lower Belgrave Street, he wanted her to arrange some sort of check on the children. As he began to speak, he probably realized that this was not a good idea.

He then rang his mother and, in her words to the inquest, asked her to 'get the children out as soon as possible'. Reports as to the time of this call are confused. Kait's own accounts varied. She had been out that evening at a meeting of the Marylebone Labour Party Association, and told the inquest that the phone was ringing when she entered her flat. 'It surprised me by its lateness. It was between 10 and 10.30pm. I don't pretend to exactitude.' At the inquest, Graham Forsyth stated that Kait told him, when she arrived at Lower Belgrave Street, that Lucan had rung at about 10.45. Given that Kait reached the house around 11pm, this was quick going from North London if she had only just spoken to her son.

The next fact is Lucan's arrival at the Maxwell-Scott home in Uckfield, Sussex: some fifty miles from London. The drive would normally take at least an hour and a half. At night, and in an era of far less traffic, a fast driver like Lucan might just do it in an hour. Susan Maxwell-Scott told the inquest that he 'called in at 11.30'. If that is so, then Kait is correct in saying that Lucan telephoned between 10 and 10.30 (the assumption, surely correct, is that he rang her *after* Mrs Florman). There is, however, no knowing the exact time he reached Uckfield.

What is entirely unknown is where Lucan made the calls to Mrs Florman and to Kait. The police checked phone boxes in the Belgravia area for blood, despite the fact that neither woman reported any pips before Lucan spoke, meaning that he used a private phone. It is theoretically possible that the calls were made on the road, some-where between central London and Sussex, but no obvious location presents itself. Instead it is suggested, and seems to be generally believed, that one of Lucan's friends took him in for the brief span of time between the murder and the drive to Uckfield. The person most likely to have done this was John Aspinall: he lived at 1 Lyall Street, just three minutes' walk from Elizabeth Street.[13] Nobody actually knows if Aspinall was at home that night, yet the myth has grown that Lucan used his phone, perhaps to make more calls than the two that are known about, perhaps also to receive help and advice. It is even suggested that Aspinall lent Lucan some clothes. Yet Susan Maxwell-Scott recalled Lucan as wearing a shirt, grey trousers and sleeveless pullover. This is the same description given by Veronica; and indeed by Michael Hicks-Beach, with whom Lucan had a friendly drink earlier that evening, in the world before it caved in.

Geographically, the logical place for Lucan to have made the phone calls is from his own flat. From Lower Belgrave Street to Elizabeth Street is a distance of some eight minutes on foot, if one takes the quickest route, which is to cut through Chester Square. Quicker still, of course, by car. Lucan could have passed the Florman house and decided, on impulse, to try the door. This certainly makes sense. It may not have made sense to go to Elizabeth Street, where the police might turn up at any moment; but nor, by that reckoning, should Lucan have been ringing a doorbell just a couple of minutes from the Plumbers Arms.

Ranson says that Lucan 'does not appear to have returned to his own flat'. No blood was found in it (the flat was not, of course, evidentially preserved). Nor was there any blood at Eaton Row, where the calls might also have been made. But the question of the blood, exceedingly vexed with regard to the crime scene, remains so with regard to Lucan himself.

Just how bloody would a man be, after perpetrating two assaults of the kind that Lucan is said to have committed? The eminent pathologist Keith Simpson, whose evidence at the inquest was detailed, dispassionate, and less susceptible to suggestion than Dr Pereira's, met the Shand Kydds some time after the event. He told them, as Christina puts it: 'Whoever did it would have been smothered. That amount of blows on the head, the blood would have been coming out like a huge fountain.' Even more to the point, the terrible business of forcing a body into a sack would have been extraordinarily bloody. And the basement at Lower Belgrave Street was a horror scene. 'The blood was all still there a few days later,' says Christina, who was obliged to visit the house. 'Lots of it.'

Therefore Lucan, by rights, should have been drenched. Indeed the police case stated that he must have been, in order to explain the presence on Veronica of Sandra's blood: it was there because Lucan put it there. In Ranson's word, he was 'soaked'. Yet the only blood reported in Veronica's bedroom was on the towel where she had lain. 'No blood in the bedroom is ridiculous,' says Christina. In fact Veronica's shoes should also have left marks, although David Gerring describes her entering the Plumbers Arms 'barefoot', so these may have been discarded after the attack. Nor was any blood reported in the third-floor nursery and bathroom, which Lucan entered before leaving the house. In response to this, Graham Forsyth now says that 'it doesn't necessarily happen that you're covered in blood' after these types of attack. But one can't have it both ways. If Lucan was not smothered, the question arises once more as to why Sandra's blood was on Veronica's clothes.

Blood was found in the Ford Corsair, although not vast quantities: when the car was seen in Newhaven on the morning of 8 November, witnesses described its interior as 'dirty'. Some group B blood was found on the inside of the passenger window. On the floor of the passenger side was hair matching Veronica's. There was group A blood on the dashboard, and an AB mixture on the armrest of the passenger door. A mix of groups was found on both the front seats.

Group B blood was found, belatedly but presumably accurately, on Mrs Florman's doorstep; this is odd given the absence of blood either in, or leading to, the bedroom. Nor was any found in Susan Maxwell-Scott's drawing room, although the envelope to one of the letters that Lucan wrote at the house was smudged with unidentified blood, possibly from a cuff.

There was, too, Susan's evidence regarding Lucan's clothes. She told the inquest that she had noticed a damp patch at the side of his right hip, as if something had been sponged away. She could not be questioned as to the nature of this something, but subsequently testified that Lucan had entered the basement after the murder and 'slipped in a pool of blood'. The fact that Susan, who was entirely pro-Lucan, freely hinted at this stain gives her evidence an appearance of openness; which may have been her intention. She was also making clear that Lucan, even if innocent, would naturally have come into contact with blood. This was perfectly true. After all, if Veronica could be marked by her husband, then the same argument applied the other way. It was also true that if Lucan had been minimally bloodied from entering the basement, he could have transferred Group B smears to his wife's dress; that is not the police's contention, however, nor would it easily explain the blood on her shoes.

What is as near as possible to certainty is that the amount of blood generated by the attacks, and the handling of Sandra's body, would have been immeasurably greater than one splash across the hip. David Gerring, who disliked Susan, mistrusted her legal training and suspected, along with his superior Ranson, that she had a massive crush on Lucan, charged her with lying about this. He questioned her as to the state of Lucan's clothing, saying that it must have been covered in blood, and would she admit as much? She did not, and had the evidence of her completely bloodless house (which could of course have been cleaned) to support her.

Against this, however, was the statement made by Frances, which contained a crucial and intriguing remark. Describing the sudden appearance of her parents in the bedroom, she said:

> As far as I can remember Daddy was wearing dark trousers *and an overcoat*, which was full length and was fawn-coloured with brown check. I was sitting on the bed as they came in the door and I couldn't see them very well. There were two lights on above Mummy's bed and one other side light on... I couldn't see if Daddy's clothes had any blood on them.

The overcoat referred to by Frances is rarely mentioned in accounts of the case. Gerring does allude to it, but in a confused way. He suggests, according to convenience, that Lucan was wearing it as a protective garment when he committed the attacks, and that he used it to hide his bloody clothing afterwards. Ranson, who dismissed Frances's statement as much as possible, does not refer to it at all. On the contrary: he wrote, quite specifically, that there was 'no indication that Lucan had anything other than light, casual clothes'. This sentence, which glides easily over the contention that these clothes were covered in blood, must have come from Veronica's description. She did not mention a coat. Yet the coat could support her in an important way: it allows the possibility that the clothes beneath it were blood-boltered, and that he did therefore contaminate her with Sandra's blood (although her shoes remain a difficulty). Did Lucan put on the coat before going upstairs, against the fear of seeing his children: because he was smothered in blood, or because he was bloodied to a lesser degree by innocent transference? Or was he simply wearing the coat anyway, because he had recently entered 46 Lower Belgrave Street from the outside?

Lucan arrived at Grants Hill House in Uckfield, at a time unknown. What happened there is also, mostly, unknown. Susan Maxwell-Scott gave evidence to the inquest, but much of it is clearly uncorroborated.

Her manner was cool and confident as she described to the court how Lucan had called up at her bedroom window and asked if her husband, Ian, was at home. Ordinarily this would not be the case, as Ian spent his weeks in London, but Susan explained this by saying that Ian had told Lucan he would be at Uckfield that particular evening. After she had let Lucan into the house, she gave him 'a good measure of Scotch', and listened to his story.

This, then, was the version of the events of 7 November that would form Lucan's defence at the inquest. It had earlier, and in far less detail, been told to his mother.

According to Susan, Lucan began by saying that 'he had been through a most nightmarish experience', which was 'so incredible he didn't think anyone would believe him'. She described him as being in a state of shock, 'but controlled shock'. He had, said Susan, 'been walking past Veronica's house on his way home to change for dinner'.

At this point, the coroner interrupted. 'The word "walking"', he said, 'is very important.' The reference was to the fact that Lucan, on foot, would have had a far better view of 46 Lower Belgrave Street than from his car. This was fundamental to his defence.

'Well, I am almost certain,' Susan replied. 'He could have said he was passing, and I assumed he was walking. I don't know what my police statement said but that is more likely to be correct.'

'The statement says walking.'

Ah, well, that would be correct then. He said he saw through the blinds of the basement what looked like a man attacking his wife. He had been saying to me that it was all an unbelievable coincidence and I knew, because he had told me on the previous occasion, that he was in the habit of walking past the house [to check on the children]. He said he let himself in through the front door, to which he had a key, and ran down to the basement. As he entered he slipped in a pool of blood as he got down to the bottom of the stairs. He wasn't, of course, telling it like a story. It came out in bits and this is my best attempt at a narrative.

The man he had seen attacking his wife ran off. Whether this was on hearing Lord Lucan running down the stairs, probably calling out, or whether it was on seeing Lord Lucan coming into the room, I don't know, but the man made off. Lord Lucan, perhaps unfortunately, rather than chasing the man, went straight to his wife. He said the man made off. In my imagination it was probably out of the back door. He went to his wife who was covered in blood and very hysterical.

Susan was asked for further details as to what Veronica had said, to which she replied that: 'She cried out to him that someone had killed the nanny. And then, almost in the same breath, she accused

Lord Lucan of having hired the man to kill her, not Sandra. This, Lord Lucan told me, was something she frequently accused him of, having a contract to kill. He claimed she got the idea from an American TV movie.'

After this, Lucan calmed Veronica and took her upstairs. 'His intention was to get some wet towels to mop up the blood and see how severe her injuries were. Then he was going to telephone for a doctor and for the police. But while he was in the bathroom Lady Lucan left the house. He told me he heard the front door slam and Lady Lucan out in the street screaming "Murder! Murder!"' This sounds like dramatic licence, although Lucan may have caught the tail-end of Veronica's exit. Ranson says that he called her name as she fled. That is not how Frances reported it: she heard her father say 'Veronica, where are you?', then go up to the third floor (the apparent implication being that he was looking for his wife). He may also have switched on the television in the bedroom, so that the children would not hear anything that might later happen downstairs.

The questioning moved to Susan's judgment as to Lucan's state of mind.

My words are that he obviously panicked. He put it another way. He said he felt there he was with all that blood, with the body, a murderer who had got away and with a wife who would almost certainly try to implicate him. He said he was sure she would try to implicate him. After all, she had already accused him of hiring this man. He told me he reckoned no one would believe his story. I did my best to convince him that people would believe him. It was quite incredible that he should have had anything to do with it.

During their talk, Susan suggested to Lucan that Sandra Rivett might, in fact, have been the intended victim of the crime. 'But Lord Lucan said it wouldn't be anyone wanting to kill her. He said she was a good kid or a good girl. He told me he'd spoken to the Official Solicitor and said the children had got a nice girl for a nanny, at last. He was very pleased with her.'

Under hostile cross-examination from Brian Watling, representing the police, Susan was asked about her training as a barrister; this was to suggest that she was sharp enough to put over a story. Watling then said:

'Is it right that Lord Lucan at no time described to you this man he had "seen" attacking his wife?'

'Not entirely right. Lord Lucan did not see him clearly enough to describe him.'

'Did he describe him at all?'

'Yes, he said he was large.'

Watling asked if Lucan had seen the mailsack, to which Susan replied that he had.

'Did he examine it?'

'No.'

'But when Lord Lucan left that house he knew that the nanny had been killed?'

'Veronica had told him that the nanny had been killed. She told him that the man had killed the nanny and had attacked her. He saw the man attacking his wife, anyway.'

To the coroner, Susan said:

'I think Lady Lucan indicated to him the nanny in the sack. He described to me the basement area as being horrific, covered in blood and he assumed she was in the sack. I assumed he was squeamish and did not want to look too closely.' By this account, the group A blood on the sack did not come from Lucan.

The questioning as to whether Lucan had been 'walking' past the house, and thus able to see through the window, would be examined again when Kait Lucan gave evidence. It was implied, very strongly, that both Kait and Susan were using the word 'walking' in full knowledge of its helpfulness to Lucan.

Graham Forsyth, who met Kait when she arrived at Lower Belgrave Street, had made notes of their conversation, in which she related what had been said on the phone by Lord Lucan. DS Forsyth reported her words to the inquest: 'He said he was driving past the house, and he saw a fight going on in the basement between a man and Veronica. He went in and joined them.'

This word, 'driving', was obviously very damaging.

When Kait herself testified at the inquest, she agreed that DS Forsyth's report of the conversation was 'substantially correct'. But 'her impression' was that Lucan had said he was passing, not driving past. He had, she said, 'interrupted a fight in the basement'. How, she was asked, had he seen this fight?

'He told me he was passing. This didn't indicate whether he paused and peered in or whether it was so obvious on passing. I know he frequently did go past the house and look at it. It was very near his own flat.' She also said that he had been muttering incoherently during the conversation. He was 'in a state of immense shock. As if he'd been knocked for six.' He said: 'Oh mother, there was something terrible in the basement. I couldn't bring myself to look.'

Brian Watling's cross-examination was, again, highly aggressive. Did Kait know, he asked, that one could be prosecuted for giving a false statement to the police? Yes, she replied calmly, she knew it.

Watling then questioned her about the discrepancies between her police statement and the evidence that she was now giving. Firstly, she had told the police that Lucan had rung her at 10.45pm, whereas she now thought the call had come earlier. Watling's idea, a slightly twisted one, was that Kait was suggesting that Lucan had had no time to invent a defence before ringing her, and therefore must have spoken the truth. (Against this, Ranson later wrote that 'within a few minutes of the killing, Lucan had come up with an account that sought to explain away some of the most damning evidence against him'.)

Kait replied: 'I'm sure the statement must be correct, because that is what I said at the time. But I'm still under the impression that the hour mentioned was unduly late.'

'Did you also say in your statement that you "had the impression there was a third party present at number 46 during the attack" but that you "couldn't be exact about this"?'

'Yes, that's right.'

'Yet you've just told the court that your son "interrupted a fight between Veronica and another man".'

'Yes. And when I was asked by the police to repeat the conversation in which he said he had interrupted a fight, I quite unaccountably failed to mention this.'

'You see, you didn't say anything in your statement about your son interrupting a fight. You're just saying that now. At the time you merely said that you "had the impression that someone else was present".'

'Look, the words "I interrupted a fight" were his words, and I imagine that, when I made the statement, the impression that there was a third person present was an obvious deduction from the statement that he had interrupted a fight.'

'Yes, but why didn't you tell the police that he had interrupted a fight so that it could go in your statement – no deductions, just plain statement?'

'It *is* a plain statement, and this is a plain statement. The upshot of the two is the same.'

'That is a matter for the jury to decide. The point is that you didn't use in your statement the words which you now tell the jury your son used.' Watling concluded: 'I need go no further. The jury have seen this woman for themselves.' Eastham objected to this astonishing rudeness; staggeringly at odds with the deferential treatment shown to Veronica. In its small, biting way the remark showed, not just the prejudice that now flourished against Lucan and his supporters, but the nose-thumbing liberation with which it was flaunted.

Kait came over badly. Her clipped, steely self-control was inimical to the court. But she was simply not the kind of person to show distress and disorder; she was the kind who, like the queen in the days after the death of Diana, Princess of Wales, maintains a mask at all costs: showing one's feelings was not what one did. It was an attitude that the times no longer admired. The fact that Kait would have been dying inside was not intuited. She would not have wanted it to be; but her determined resilience did her a disservice, and her son an even greater one. Nor did Susan Maxwell-Scott convey at all the impression that she sought to do, with her nerveless, smiling delivery, her faintly disdainful repetition of the word 'hysterical' to describe Veronica's behaviour. These, it seemed, were cold people.

By implication, they were also liars, so blind to everybody outside their own class that they were prepared to take the side of a demonic aristocrat against two grotesquely assaulted women. The story related by Kait and Susan, that Lucan had 'interrupted' a fight in the basement, was damaged by the police testimony. Equally powerfully, however, it was discredited by antagonism in the court.

It was not, anyway, a very good story. Graham Forsyth told the inquest what was indeed the truth, that from a car it was utterly impossible to see into the basement of 46 Lower Belgrave Street. Roy Ranson later confirmed this. However David Gerring, the final inquest witness, stated that even if a person was walking past the house, it would not be possible to see the site of the attack. He had done experiments with another officer. All that could be glimpsed, if one crouched down outside the window, was a pair of feet. With no light in the basement, one could not even see that. Actually the picture conjured of a coal-hole under the stairs was not entirely accurate. 'It was never that dark in the basement,' says the former nanny Pierrette Goletto. 'There was a street lamp right outside': as indeed there is, directly opposite number 46. The newspaper account of Sergeant Baker's evidence, in which he was reported to have 'found a light switch' in the basement, was probably mistaken; but it does raise the very faint possibility that there was another working light source.

It is not easy to see into the basement at Lower Belgrave Street, because it is not set back very far from the pavement. It is almost flush with the street. Nevertheless one can see a little more than was implied: the sink at the window, some of the room behind, the bottom of the staircase. Veronica herself later said: 'The police said this was not possible, but actually if the blinds weren't drawn properly you could see in.'[14] That is why the small quantity of group A blood found in the basement was significant. It rendered just conceivable the notion that an attack had been launched there upon Veronica, and had continued as she ran up to the ground floor. Hence the absolute insistence by the police that Veronica had never been in the basement that night. This was necessary, to discredit Lucan. 'There was no sign of a fight in the basement,' David Gerring told the inquest: he meant that Lucan's story was a lie, although he himself was eliding the facts. There was a great deal of evidence of a fight in the basement, albeit very little to say that this fight had been with Veronica.

If Lucan had indeed 'interrupted' a fight, then, as Kait said, the obvious deduction was that a third party had been present. Gerring was questioned about this by Brian Watling. There was, he said, no sign of forced entry at Lower Belgrave Street, and no evidence that anybody had a key except the Lucans.

'And have you been able to trace any third person who might have been in the house that night?'

'None whatsoever, sir.'

'Have you made very extensive efforts to do so?'

'Very extensive, including inquiries in the area and forensic work across the whole of Belgravia.'

Watling concluded with an insidious lawyerly thrust. 'How long', he asked, 'have you been a police officer, Mr Gerring?'

'Over twenty years, sir.'

And who could argue with that, except the lunatical upper classes? Later Roy Ranson would return to the story proffered by Lord Lucan. There was, Ranson said, no forensic evidence to suggest the presence of another person at 46 Lower Belgrave Street. Nobody in Belgravia had seen 'this large and blood-stained man' (they didn't see Lucan either, but that was by the by). There was nothing to say how the man had entered or left the house; he could not have exited by the front door (in fact there is no reason why he could not have done just that), nor through the garden (it was true that the wall is high; nevertheless there was the evidence of the blood found on leaves, and the inexplicably unlocked back door).

But the clincher was that Veronica 'saw no other person in the house except her husband'. That was what she had said, and therefore, for Ranson, the matter was at an end.

Lucan could not deny having been at the house, because his daughter had seen him. But if he had given another, innocent reason for entering the property, there was a chance that he would have been believed. It would simply have been his word against Veronica's. As it was, his word was wholly compromised. His defenders, including Michael Eastham, were stuck with a story of the grossest implausibility. Once again, Lord Lucan had brought his fate upon himself.

At about 12.15am Lucan asked Susan Maxwell-Scott if he might ring his mother. She offered to leave the drawing-room, but he said there was no need. During this second call he sounded less *bouleversé*; 'more on all fours', as Kait told the inquest in the alien, upper-class idiom of all Lucan's supporters. ('If they sometimes sounded like characters from a play by Coward,' it was said, 'that was because the playwright had modelled his dialogue on theirs.'[15]) Later Kait would speak of her lasting regret that she did not force him to speak to the policeman in her flat. It is a mystery, incidentally, why no attempt was made to trace the call.

Susan's recollection of the conversation was essentially the same as Kait's, although she remembered Lucan saying: 'Has Veronica turned up?' He then tried to ring Bill Shand Kydd, as Kait had done earlier without success ('I was told that he was not available,' she said to the inquest. 'This was a mistake'). Again Bill did not hear the telephone.[16] It is possible that Lucan made other calls, but this is unknown. 'After that', said Susan, 'he asked if he could borrow some notepaper.'

Lucan wrote at least two letters, probably seated at the beautiful Georgian table in the Maxwell-Scott drawing-room, with its ink-wells and letter rack; the sort of table he had used all his life. Both letters were to Bill Shand Kydd. They were received on Saturday 9 November, postmarked Uckfield.

The first letter was written on two pages in Lucan's slanting, public-schoolboy hand. It reiterated the story told to both Susan and his mother.

7th Nov 1974 [sic: the letter was written in the early hours of the 8th]

Dear Bill,

The most ghastly circumstances arose this evening, which I briefly described to my mother. When I interrupted the fight at Lower Belgrave St. and the man left Veronica accused me of having hired him. I took her upstairs and sent Frances up to bed and tried to clean her up. She lay doggo for a bit, and while I was in the bathroom left the house. The circumstantial evidence against me is strong in that V. will say it was all my doing. I also will lie doggo for a bit but I am only concerned about the children. If you can manage it I want them to live with you – Coutts (Trustees) St. Martin's Lane (Mr Wall) will handle school fees. V. has demonstrated her hatred for me in the past and would do anything to see me accused. For George & Frances to go through life knowing their father had stood in the dock for attempted murder will be too much. When they are old enough to understand, explain to them the dream of paranoia, and look after them.

Yours ever, John

At the inquest, Bill was questioned about the contents of this letter. Proceeding cautiously, Michael Eastham began: 'Bearing in mind the coroner's ruling concerning what is admissible evidence, I must ask you to answer just yes or no. Do you understand?'

The reply was a nod.

'"Veronica has demonstrated her hatred for me in the past..." Do you understand what he means by this?'

'Yes.'

'"And would do anything to see me accused..." Do you understand what he means by this?'

'Yes.'

'Could you give evidence about it?'

'Yes.'

'Could you, if asked, give evidence about the paranoia?'

'Yes.'

That was the end of the questioning. Now, in reference to the letter, Bill says: 'Of course I know what he meant. He meant Veronica's paranoia.'

The second letter, written on two sides of a single sheet, read:

<u>Financial matters</u>

There is a sale coming up at Christies Nov 27th which will satisfy bank overdrafts. Please agree reserves with Tom Craig.

Proceeds to go to:-

Lloyds, 6 Pall Mall,
Coutts, 59 Strand,
Nat West, Bloomsbury Branch,

who also hold an
Eq. & Law Life Policy
(P.T.O.)

The other creditors can get lost for the time being.

Lucky

It is clear, from Lucan's words to his mother – 'Ring Bill Shand Kydd' – that Bill was the person he most wanted to speak to that night. He had first tried Mrs Florman, because she lived so near to his children. But the obvious inference is that, before speaking to Kait, he had tried to ring the Shand Kydds' London home, in Cambridge Square just north of Hyde Park. What has never been said before is that at some point after the events at Lower Belgrave Street, Lucan actually drove to the Shand Kydd flat.

'That's what we were told, yes,' says Lucan's old friend from

Eton. 'He went there, couldn't get a response, so he went to the Maxwell-Scott house.'

This information was part of what Susan Maxwell-Scott withheld, and for some time. How much more she did not say is unclear. Certainly she did not offer the police the news that Lucan had been in her house on the night of 7–8 November. 'I had no reason to,' she said. It was only when Bill Shand Kydd went straight to the police with Lucan's letters on the morning of Saturday 9th, and explained to them the significance of the Uckfield postmark, that Susan was obliged to make a statement.

'She would have been lovely to Lucan,' says her former nanny. 'She would have been fond of him. If she was sober she would have been calm – she would have had a sound mind – and she would never have spoken to anybody. She would have known how to evade all questions, with her legal background, she would have known how to avoid questioning.'

Cambridge Square is separated from Belgravia only by a drive up Park Lane; nevertheless the diversion would have delayed Lucan's journey to Uckfield, taking the arrival time closer to 12.15am, when he rang his mother. Possibly Susan said that he had turned up at 11.30pm to imply that Lucan had driven to her directly. However, his alleged stopover *chez* Aspinall is highly unlikely; there really wasn't time. It was later claimed that 'the person who provided Lucan with a telephone for his first and second calls was saying nothing'.[17] The belief in this secret visit died hard. Yet it is well-nigh impossible that Lucan did any such thing. The probability remains that Lucan made the phone calls from his own flat, soon after 10pm. He would have done it as quickly as possible. Then he drove away from Belgravia for good.

It is interesting to note that Stephen Raphael, an old and trusted friend, lived very close to the Shand Kydds, in Southwick Place. But again, the idea that he might have visited Raphael makes little sense. If Lucan had managed to see his friend, or indeed any of his other close circle, why bother to visit the Maxwell-Scotts? He needed a place where he could hole up for a while, use a phone, take stock. He did not need two such places. 'I suppose he wanted to think, talk it through,' says Christina. By then it may have occurred to him that going to Susan, the only friend who would definitely be in the country, put him at a safer distance from the murder scene. Nevertheless it was Bill whom he had wanted.

'It was very, very unfortunate', says Christina, 'that John didn't get hold of us that night. It would have made all the difference, because Bill would never have let him go.' Eventually Kait did manage to reach Christina on the phone. 'I got the call, from his mother – and she said the nanny has been murdered. It never ever crossed my mind that John... I thought something else. I mean, I was absolutely astonished when it came over the news or something, the next day, that they were looking for John. Because Kaitilin didn't say...'

According to her evidence at the inquest, Susan Maxwell-Scott did her best to stop Lucan leaving her house. 'I tried to persuade him to stay the night. I suggested it was a good idea to stay and then telephone the police in the morning. But after slightly agreeing he said no. He said he must – and he stressed the word must – get back and clear things up. When he said "get back" he did not mention London.'

The coroner then said: 'Did he ask you if you had any sleeping pills?'

'Yes he did. He said he was sure he would have difficulty sleeping and he asked if I'd got any tablets. I said I hadn't. The best I could find was some Valium. There were only four pills left at the bottom. It wasn't a strong dose. But he took them with some water and then said he had to be getting back.'

'What time did he leave?'

'To the best of my recollection, about 1.15am.'

'What happened then?'

'I went to bed.'

'And have you seen him since?'

'No.'

'Has your husband?'

'No.'

Just as the time of Lucan's arrival at Grants Hill House is uncorroborated, so too is the time that he left (in what Susan described as
'a dark saloon'). It might never have been known that he was there
at all, except that the two letters to Bill Shand Kydd were posted in
Uckfield, with stamps provided by Susan.

Lucan also wrote two letters to Michael Stoop. These were sent
to Stoop's club, the St James's, and received on Monday 11 November. They were unstamped, which would have caused a day's delay.
Lucan had used a Lion Brand writing pad identical to one found in
the Corsair. Only one of the letters was produced by Stoop to the
police. It was written on the pad's blotting sheet, and the envelope
was missing. It read:

> My dear Michael,
>
> I have had a traumatic night of unbelievable coincidence. However
> I won't bore you with anything or involve you except to say that
> when you come across my children, which I hope you will, please
> tell them that you knew me and that all I cared about was them. The
> fact that a crooked solicitor and a rotten psychiatrist destroyed me
> between them will be of no importance to the children. I gave Bill
> Shand Kydd an account of what actually happened but judging by
> my last effort in court no one, let alone a 67 year old judge, would
> believe – and I no longer care except that my children should be
> protected.
>
> Yours ever,
> John

Stoop picked up his letters at the St James's Club on the afternoon of the 11th. He then rang Gerald Road police station, and
by his account was asked by the duty officer to bring in the letter
when he was passing. This was contested at the inquest. In cross-
examination Brian Watling said: 'Is it right that it was you who said

you couldn't take it round, because you had an important meeting to attend?' Stoop replied: 'I don't think so.' In fact it would be 3am that morning when he took the letter to the station.

Previously, Michael Eastham had questioned Stoop about the missing envelope, first asking if it was handwritten.

'I don't really recall. I had several letters at the same time and threw away the envelopes.'

'If you had looked at the envelope and recognized Lord Lucan's handwriting, would you have appreciated that it was rather important to keep the envelope?'

'I was really rather keen to read the letter.'

Returning to the key question, Eastham asked: 'Are you sure you didn't look at the postmark? It was rather important to establish where he was.'

'I'm afraid I don't know.'

'And if you told the police the same minute the envelope would still be there in the wastepaper basket, wouldn't it?'

'I suppose so, yes.'

'As far as you are aware, nobody emptied the wastepaper basket in those five minutes?'

'No.'

In other words, the police should have hotfooted it to the St James's Club; it is a downright mystery why they did not. If Stoop could be accused of dilatoriness, so too could they. By the time Stoop took the letter in to Gerald Road, the rubbish at the club had been disposed of (if indeed the envelope had ever gone into the wastepaper basket).

Eastham then questioned Stoop about the contents of the letter. Again he emphasized that replies should only be in the form of 'yes' or 'no'. He asked whether the 'crooked solicitor' and 'rotten psychiatrist' referred to court proceedings about Lucan's children, and was answered that they did. The same question was put about the reference to the 'last effort in court', and the same reply given.

'"And I no longer care except that my children are protected"...
Did you understand that?'

To this Stoop said: 'I can't answer that with a simple yes or no.'

'I know you can't, but I am in a difficulty. May I put it this way:
if I asked you against what or against whom the children had to be
protected, could you answer that?'

True to form, the coroner instantly intervened, saying: 'I warned
you about this line of questioning. If you have any questions, please
restrict them to the direct evidence.'

Eastham, unable to ask anything further to the point, said that
he had no further questions.

It was not until 2004 that James Fox, who had written the article
about Lucan for the *Sunday Times Magazine* published the week
before the inquest, revealed that a second letter had been written to
Stoop and withheld from the police.

'Stoop showed it to me', Fox later wrote, 'when I interviewed him
in early 1975 in his London flat. My scribbled notes record: "small-
ish paper... no envelope... keys in glove compartment... in Norman
Street (or Newham St)... Please forget you ever lent it to me... burn
envelope".' From this Fox inferred firstly that Lucan himself had
driven to Newhaven. 'His mistake about the proper name of Norman
Road sounds like his own.' It seemed clear that Lucan was anxious
for Stoop to recover his car; and even more anxious that nobody
should see the postmark on the envelope. In 2004 Fox rang Stoop,
then aged eighty-two, and reminded him of the letter. '"I think I did
show it to you, rather foolishly," he said. He told me that he hadn't
noticed the envelope, hadn't even looked at it. Nor had he done
what Lucan asked – burn it. "I just chucked the thing in the wastepaper basket as far as I remember." And the postmark? "I didn't
look, no." I told him I had decided to write about it. "I just wish you
wouldn't," he said.'[18]

The second, natural inference made by James Fox was that Lucan,
with his insistence on the destruction of the envelope, 'was not
about to walk into the sea the morning he left the car in Newhaven.

He had a plan.' Unless, of course, Lucan had believed that Stoop could retrieve the car before the police did; and that nobody would ever know he had driven to Newhaven. Clearly he did not mind it being known that he had visited Uckfield. By asking Susan to post the letters to Bill Shand Kydd, he was supplying a definitive clue to the fact that he had been there. This could have been intended as a decoy; although a far better one, if Lucan had been plotting in this way, would have been a postmark that did not point to any of his friends. Alternatively it could have been that Lucan knew he was driving on, to the sea, and that it was better to leave the letters with somebody whom he could trust, rather than sending them from somewhere closer to his final destination, where he hoped to be left undisturbed.

Previously, Fox's own view had concurred with this. 'My certainty that Lucan drove the car to Newhaven persuades me to this day that he died near the port and in the sea, and that his body was consumed within forty-eight hours by crabs.'[19]

Stuart Wheeler says:

> Certainly I know what Michael Stoop thought, which is that Lucan got on to a steamer and jumped off, and the reason the body hasn't been found is that it was cut up by the propellers. I knew Michael quite well. He used to come and stay with me occasionally. And he was absolutely convinced that Lucan was dead. Now whether he had some very good reason for that, I don't know. As far as I know he never revealed the contents of that letter [the one shown to Fox; or even, just conceivably, a third]. But he was certain that he was dead.

The car was found in Norman Road at 2.40pm on Sunday 10 November, the day before Stoop received Lucan's letters. Somewhat typically of this investigation, discovery of the Corsair was delayed by the fact that the bulletin had put out the wrong registration number. Stoop had told the police about its loan the previous day. It was found by Sergeant David de Lima, then on patrol duty in Newhaven. Ranson and Gerring drove straight to the quiet street, a homogeneous line of respectable red-brick terraced houses, set some half a mile back from the sea. There, in a large space between a Mini van and a Morris, was the Corsair, a plain-looking English car with its roof-rack and alligator-head bonnet, as ordinary as a Lion Brand writing pad or an evening spent watching *The Six Million Dollar Man*.

The police would state that the Corsair had been parked at some unknown point between 5am and 8am on 8 November. Ranson and Gerring's accounts differ slightly: Ranson described two witnesses, one of whom saw an empty space at 5am, another who saw the car at 8am. Gerring, perhaps seeking greater verisimilitude, wrote of a single witness. 'I found this chap who lived over the road from where the car was parked, and he had some eye trouble. His doctor had advised him to focus on something when he had a spare moment.' At 5am the man had 'focussed on an empty space over the road'. At 8am he looked out of the window, and 'the Corsair was there'. The convenience of this is remarkable, although there is no reason to doubt that the car was, indeed, left in Norman Road that morning. A couple who lived opposite, and who had presumably thought it an abandoned vehicle, had looked inside. They saw a tax disc on the floor and a 'dirty' interior.

If the witnesses were accurate in their timings, and Susan Maxwell-Scott in hers, the question arises of what Lucan did in the four hours or more between leaving Uckfield and arriving in Newhaven. If he himself drove the car there, then the simplest explanation is that he slept for a while somewhere on the road, under the influence of Susan's valium; clearly other explanations are possible. The distance between Grants Hill House and Norman Road is just seventeen miles. It is a strange journey: along roads that are wide and calm, but not soothing. A sort of world's end journey. Massive hills rear up ahead, great strong cliffs to the left. Newhaven itself is a grand and shabby muddle, the sense of the sea very powerful. There is a smell of salt, and the sound of gulls scratches the air. Like all ports, it is discomfiting: but also ordinary, dull, grey. A very great distance from the glittering Clermont, or from the ancestral consolations of the churchyard at Laleham.

Practically speaking, the car was not parked conveniently for somebody looking to escape or end their life in the water; one would have to walk through the town to reach it. What was the significance of where it was left? The only certainty is that it is an enigma, like so much in this case. If the position of the car was a blind, then it was not a particularly good one, because its half-mile distance from the sea aroused instant suspicion. Furthermore, if a Machiavellian plotter had suggested using the Corsair as a decoy, then they should also have had the wit to clean the blood that was inside it; although that, of course, may not have been a priority.

Or was the position of the car not significant at all? Was it simpler than that: a person driving in the dark, somewhat drunk and disorientated, through a town that is cut in half by the river Ouse and not the easiest place to negotiate, had turned off a main road into the first residential street where the car would be kept safe for its owner.

Before towing the Corsair to the Forensic Science Laboratory in Lambeth, the police broke into it (if Lucan had indeed left keys in the glove compartment, it seems odd that it was found locked). In the boot were two bottles of vodka. There was also, it would later be reported, a length of piping. At the inquest, a doctor from the Metropolitan Police laboratory described this piping as almost twice the size of the piece found at Lower Belgrave Street, being sixteen inches long and some four pounds in weight. Both lengths were corroded, perhaps part of an old plumbing system, and both bore traces of blue paint from a hacksaw blade. 'They may have been cut from the same length,' said the doctor. 'But it is highly unlikely that the bit found at number 46 was ever joined on to the bit found in the car.'

This second length of piping was an apparently conclusive find. It was not exactly necessary to the police case, although, as was later said, 'without the twin bludgeon, none of the evidence would have been enough in itself to contradict [Lucan's] story'.[20] The police had their man, and now they had an incontrovertible piece of proof.

Nevertheless there is something strange about it. Why would Lucan have cut *two* weapons with his hacksaw, and why then use the smaller of the two, given that the heavier pipe would have done the job far more efficiently?

A subsidiary question is where he prepared these weapons. Not Belgravia, one imagines. Graham Forsyth was sent to find the possible source of the piping, a task that included a profitless search of the vicarage at Guilsborough, home to Lucan's sister Sally. The Lucan children had gone to stay at the house on 9 November, and Frances and George had been quickly enrolled at the village school.

'It was Sally', says Lucan's other sister Jane, 'who called me to tell me what had happened. She was adamant that John hadn't done it. I couldn't imagine he had done it either. Such a bloody thing. We obviously talked for many, many hours, days, months, about it.'

On 13 November, another High Court hearing took place about the children, who remained wards of court. Custody for Veronica was opposed, this time by the representatives of Lord Lucan. As she put it: 'Some of the family plotted to get custody of my children while I was in hospital.'[21] The Shand Kydds, to whom Lucan had expressed in his letter the desire that they should have care of the children, attended court. Veronica, who had left hospital to go to the High Court, arrived in a police car as the hearing ended; her escort was heard to shout 'Don't get out' (the implication being that she would want to avoid her sister). Again the case was considered by Mr Justice Rees, and one wonders what he thought about his decision to hand the Lucan children to their mother sixteen months earlier; perhaps he felt still more justified.

No conclusion was reached on 13 November. The Official Solicitor, Norman Turner, stated: 'I cannot say one word.' The Reverend Gibbs, later a vociferous defender of Lucan – 'This is not British justice,' he said after the inquest – told the press that he did not know when, or if, the children would be leaving his care. 'I found him a most uncharitable man,' says Graham Forsyth, whose loyalties were very much in the opposite camp.

21. Sandra Rivett.

22. 46 Lower Belgrave Street on 8 November 1974, the day after the murder of Sandra Rivett.

23. The Plumbers Arms, at the end of Lower Belgrave Street.

24. Grants Hill House, the home of Ian and Susan Maxwell-Scott, visited by Lucan on the night of the murder.

25. Susan Maxwell-Scott at the inquest into the death of Sandra Rivett, June 1975.

26. The Ford Corsair borrowed by Lucan, found parked in Norman Road, Newhaven, on 10 November 1974.

27. The police hunt for Lord Lucan on cliffs near Newhaven.

28. Detective Chief-Superintendent Roy Ranson, who headed the inquiry, and Detective Chief-Inspector David Gerring (right).

29. Lady Lucan returning to the house at Lower Belgrave Street after the murder. Her unofficial bodyguard, Detective-Sergeant Graham Forsyth, is to her left.

Daily Mirror

LADY LUCAN FACES THE WORLD

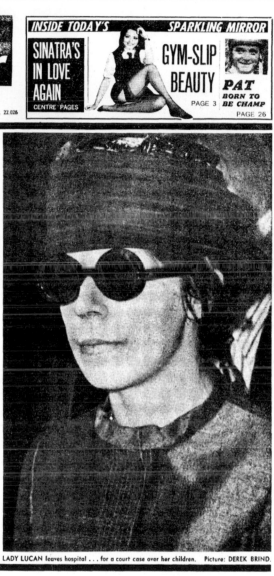

A hat covers the scars. Dark glasses hide the anguish. This was Lady Lucan yesterday, facing the world for the first time since her brutal attack. Her husband is now wanted for the murder of their nanny.

FULL STORY—PAGE FIVE

LADY LUCAN leaves hospital . . . for a court case over her children.   Picture: DEREK BRIND.

30. The front page of the *Daily Mirror*, 14 November 1974.

31. Kaitilin Lucan is driven to the inquest, 17 June 1975.

32. Roger Rivett, Sandra's estranged husband, arriving at the inquest.

33. Lady Lucan with her children George and Frances, 22 November 1974.

34. Lord Lucan in a West End club, 30 April 1973.

35. 46 Lower Belgrave Street today.

36. 'Jungly' Barry Halpin (centre, with guitar) in Goa. The folk singer was one of the many men who has been mistakenly identified as Lord Lucan.

Later that day Veronica was interviewed by Ranson at Lower Belgrave Street, where her telephone was monitored and an armed policeman installed.[22] It can hardly have been easy to return to that house. The day before the inquest in June 1975, by which time Veronica had already publicly expressed the belief that her husband was dead, she told a newspaper: 'I still get frightened, especially at night when I am at home, that my attacker will come back and try again to kill me.'[23]

On 15 November, Mr Justice Rees awarded custody of the children to Veronica. Four days later she was reunited with George and Frances. Camilla, who was ill, remained with her aunt. The 20 November headline in the *Daily Express* read: 'Fast Line to Joy', above a photograph of Veronica in a railway carriage, opposite a very relaxed-looking DS Forsyth, who had a foot up on the seat. Veronica was described as bearing 'slight facial scars', and was pictured with her hair uncovered, freed from the specially tailored hat that had previously covered her wounds. The pair were travelling to a safe house in Devon, where the two children would join them; Frances was interviewed there by a female officer. Although the booking had been made in the name of 'Mrs Jones', the press crowded on to the train. 'You couldn't cry about it,' says Forsyth. 'We gave them a photo, then jumped off and ended up at the local Chief Constable's office. She was very game. She said, he stays with me.' It was later said that Forsyth was 'almost [Veronica's] only companion for several months, until it was felt that the danger had passed'.[24] Great emphasis was always placed on Veronica's isolation. When she returned home from the three-week stay in Devon, however, Christabel Martin was again employed as her nanny, and also in attendance was a stridently eccentric girl named Mary-Geraldine O'Donnell, a semi-professional 'minder' to upper-class women. Miss O'Donnell claimed to have been supporting Veronica for more than a year before the murder, although Veronica herself later asserted that 'Sandra was my only friend'.[25] After the event, Miss O'Donnell acted as a (possibly self-appointed) spokeswoman and appeared on television dealing with the press. On 21 November she gave an interview to the *Daily Mirror*, stating that Veronica had been 'hoping to patch up her marriage'.[26]

One wonders sometimes why this did not happen. Why Lucan did not simply bite the bullet and move back into 46 Lower Belgrave Street; not to 'patch up' the marriage, but to save money, and above all to ease his mind about the children. It was a big house: six storeys. He could have led a separate life from his wife. Could he not have borne to do it?

'I doubt it very much,' says his sister. 'Because I think there was a hatred there, and an anger.'

As Veronica was reunited with her children, so Ranson and Gerring were in Newhaven, in grim pursuit of their quarry. On 10 November, the day that the car was discovered, they visited guesthouses and hotels. Forty officers, who had been engaged upon house-to-house inquiries in London, were diverted to the port and joined by local police. On the 11th David Gerring went to the ferry terminal, trying to discover if Lucan had obtained a forty-eight hour passport: at the time, an easy thing to do. Around one thousand boats and fishing trawlers, moored on the unlovely mudflats beside the pier, were searched. So too was every ferry to Cherbourg and Saint-Malo (where Lucan would later be 'sighted'), and those to the nearest destination of Dieppe. It was confirmed that security checks were lax; that Lucan could already have crossed the Channel, or flung himself into it.

Might he have taken a boat from the marina? None was reported missing. Did he know Newhaven? He had almost certainly sailed from there in the past. Did he have a boat of his own? Some people said that he did, some that he did not. But it was also said that shipping movements were recorded at Newhaven, that the pier was manned constantly. Forty frogmen searched the area near the mouth of the Ouse, explored a deep depression known as The Hole. But no body was discovered.

'It was damn cold on the night he vanished,' Ranson said to the press. 'How can a man get far in the middle of the night, in the pouring rain and the wind, without an overcoat? [sic]' It is usually stated that the weather was terrible on the night of 7–8 November, although in fact the weather report in *The Times* described the south-east as 'mostly dull, occasional rain or drizzle', and the English Channel as relatively calm: 'sea slight', then 'moderate'. Assuming reasonable accuracy, the weather therefore offered no clue to where Lucan might be.

Might he have jumped from nearby Beachy Head, the terrifying white cliffs favoured by suicides? Again, no body was washed up. Might he have crawled with a spare bottle of vodka into the vast undergrowth of the South Downs, found a pothole, died from exposure, shot himself? His guns were kept at Lower Belgrave Street, but did he have another? Might he have holed up in a nearby Napoleonic fort? The search became imponderable, overwhelming: an attempt was made to investigate the Downs in a five-mile radius from Newhaven, but this was estimated to require 1,000 policemen working for an entire month. Photographs from the time show uniformed officers scything their way through shoulder-high tangles of gorse. The army offered one hundred men for three days. Later, Wing-Commander Kenneth Wallis took an autogyro over the area, a machine like a flying bicycle fitted with a camera that took X-ray photographs. In its excitable futility the search was reminiscent of the one for that other disappeared person, Agatha Christie, whose car was found abandoned on the similarly impenetrable North Downs in 1926. Oddly, her whereabouts had also been conveyed in a letter sent before she vanished; whose envelope, again, was thrown away.[27] She, it quite soon transpired, was not on the Downs at all. After a few days it began to be said that the same must be true of Lord Lucan. 'The earl's car "a false lead",' wrote the *Daily Express* on 16 November. 'Detectives hunting Lord Lucan are now considering a theory that the car he drove on the night of the murder was abandoned as a deliberate false trail.'

Four days earlier, a warrant for Lord Lucan's arrest had been granted by Bow Street Magistrates' Court. Bets were laid at Gerald Road as to when he would ring the station, or stride in with a crack solicitor at his side; but by the 12th it had become apparent that this was not going to happen. Now the police had the authority to search the homes of his friends. The investigation would turn to that entity so dominant within the myth of this case: the Lucan circle.

The Circle

'It was up to him to show the old boy that he for one was not given over to any unworthy prejudice; after all, nobody could help being an aristocrat, could they?'

KINGSLEY AMIS, *Take a Girl like You*, 1960

'But he gained a queer sort of momentary self-respect in his nothingness, a sense that choosing to be nothing... was the last saving grace of a gentleman; his last freedom, almost.'

JOHN FOWLES, *The French Lieutenant's Woman*, 1967

ACCORDING TO THE Lucan myth, Sandra Rivett has become a double victim in the forty years since her death. She was murdered, and now she is forgotten; while her murderer is remembered. Yet the irony is that Sandra is also overlooked within the myth itself, portrayed only as a symbol of aristocratic contempt for the innocent lower orders. After the inquest, the press raged on Sandra's behalf. 'Note the name again: SANDRA ELEANOR RIVETT. Hardly surprising if it does not ring an immediate bell,' wrote the *Sunday Mirror*. 'But everyone knows the name of Lord Lucan.' Indeed they do; and not least because of the press.

At the inquest, which opened on Monday 16 June 1975, the tiny oak-panelled coroner's court in Horseferry Road divided clearly into factions, and what most mesmerized the reporters was the wall of ice, invisible yet palpable, between Lucan's supporters and his wife. It was an extraordinary piece of theatre. Veronica arrived every day in a police car with DS Forsyth, lunched with him at the police canteen, and sat separately. She wore the same outfit every day, a black coat and white turban. With her pallor, her eyes from which all expression seemed to have been exhausted, she looked like a carefully dressed-up Little Match Girl. She was, wrote the *Daily Mail*, 'barely acknowledged by her mother-in-law, by friends who had once holidayed with her, even by her own sister'. One is reminded of Diana, Princess of Wales, seated sorrowfully in front of the Taj Mahal. Directly in front sat Christina Shand Kydd, a sun-tanned and glamorous figure in deep-blue velvet. Veronica was described as having the spectacular ruby clasp of her sister's pearls jammed right in her eyeline, as if in mockery of her own relative penury (although five months earlier, when the *Daily Express* had interviewed Veronica, she herself was described as wearing a 'neck-lace with a huge diamond and blue sapphire pendant').[1] Christina variously sat with her husband Bill, with Kait Lucan, with Sally Gibbs and with Sally's vicar husband William. Susan Maxwell-Scott, in a large pink hat, sat with her husband Ian, who carried a straw trilby. They all lunched together at the Barley Mow pub over the road, which on the second day of the inquest ran clean out of beer. Out on Horseferry Road a woman shook a tin for a society support-ing battered wives. Her placard read: 'It affects us all, rich and poor.'

Meanwhile inside, at the back of the court, sat two players in a very different drama: the quietly respectable figures of Sandra's father and his sister Vera.

'My daughter's name has hardly been mentioned,' said Mr Hensby. 'Yet she is the reason why we are all here.'[2]

This was unanswerable. The storming battlefield of the Lucan marriage, in whose crossfire Sandra had apparently been caught, had overwhelmed the death of this one young woman, and the grief of her father Albert and mother Eunice. 'What those parents must have gone through,' says Lucan's old schoolfriend. Sandra's son, Stephen, who like Lady Frances Bingham was ten years old at the time of the murder, would later recall the night in 1974 when two police officers arrived at the Hensbys' caravan in Basingstoke. Stephen, born out of wedlock, had been formally adopted by his grandparents at fourteen months; he believed that Sandra was his sister. This kind of benevolent lie was usual fifty years ago. Social attitudes in the 1960s were liberal only within a very small but vociferous group of people. Now Stephen was told that his sister had died. Two years later he learned from a book that Sandra had in fact been his mother, and that she had been murdered.

Sandra had two sons. She was eighteen when she gave birth to Stephen, naming 'John Andrews', a builder, as his father. Three years later, after an affair with a local estate agent, she had her second baby, Gary, who was adopted by a couple in Hampshire. A letter to them read:

> I'm pleased to tell you that we have a baby son for you. He was born on February 4th and weighs 7lb 8oz. His mother is a single girl aged 21. She was educated at secondary modern school and has recently been employed at a wholesale chemist. She already has one little boy who at the moment is being cared for by her parents, and she feels that she can't possibly bring the baby up properly herself.
>
> The baby's father is a man she has known for quite a long time but he is married to someone else. Unfortunately, while his wife had a period in hospital, she [Sandra] visited his home on a number of occasions to help in the house. Intercourse occurred and she became pregnant... She did not want to break his marriage so came away from the area.

Gary, whose name was changed by his adoptive parents to Neil, was born while Sandra was staying with her sister Teresa in Portsmouth. 'Sandra was lovely with kids,' said Teresa, 'but I just don't think she was cut out to have them herself. There was nothing we could say. It was her business.'[3] Four months later, in June 1967, Sandra married Roger Rivett, at twenty-two a year her senior.

There was a great gulf between the lives of the Rivetts and the Lucans. The wording of their marriage certificates says this very simply. The description of the couple who married at the church of Holy Trinity, Brompton, read:

Richard John Bingham, gentleman, 49 Egerton Gardens, father
peer of the realm
Veronica, company director, 34 Wilton Crescent, father army
officer[4]

The description of the Rivetts, who married in the registry office
at Croydon, was:

Roger Rivett, able seaman, 6 Stoats Nest Village, Coulsdon, father
a gardener
Sandra, domestic aged persons' home, 49 Nunehams Rd,
Caterham, father a porter.

Fifty years ago, the two worlds presented in those few lines
would have been as remote from each other as the earth and moon.
Less so today; for all that the prejudice against privilege is more
powerful than ever, the gap has narrowed immeasurably: not just
because of the forces of meritocracy, egalitarianism, demystifica-
tion, but for subtler reasons connected to the growth of a new class,
just emerging at the time of the Lucan marriage in late 1963: the
class of the rich and famous. Today, the sort of person who might
live in Egerton Gardens is more likely to be a Premier League footballer than a young aristocrat; and the world is now acutely familiar
with the doings of a footballer, his evenings spent at restaurants in
Knightsbridge or Mayfair, his shopping trips down Bond Street, his
patronizing of Asprey's or Burberry, his wife's longed-for custom
at Dior or Ferragamo, his racehorses, his majestic holidays; the
accoutrements of lives that once belonged only to the unknowable
upper classes. Few people today can afford these things, but they
know all about them through the new kind of person who can. The
class of the rich and famous has brought privilege illusorily closer.
PR has done its work. The world of the Lucans, with its yachting
trips, its interior decorators, its designer clothes and tailoring,
its jewellery, is no longer remote as it would once have been;
we know too much about Roman Abramovich, the Beckhams, the

Oscar red carpet, to be bedazzled by it. Only the title, the earldom remains; meaningless, yet somehow impregnable; and hated on that account.

To Sandra Rivett, 46 Lower Belgrave Street must have seemed a fabulous refuge. Her life, up to that point, had been restless. Born in September 1945, she attended school at Caterham, Surrey, close to her family home, then took a variety of jobs. She became an apprentice hairdresser; a secretary in Croydon; a nanny for a doctor. In 1963, in an odd echo of Veronica's own medical history, she entered a mental hospital as a voluntary patient. Again like Veronica, she had suffered badly over an unhappy love affair. It was at the hospital that she met the father of her first son. He did not want to marry her. She prepared to give up the baby, but her kindly parents took him into their home. Sandra continued to earn her living, although this was disrupted by her second pregnancy.

Soon after her marriage, Roger Rivett was sent abroad for eleven months with the navy. After about six months Sandra's letters grew infrequent, and the couple effectively became estranged; but in 1969 Roger bought himself out of the service and began working close to home. Sandra took a job as a cleaner at the Reedham Orphanage in Purley. In 1971 the Rivetts took a furnished flat in Kenley, near Croydon, at a cost of £9.25 a week. Nevertheless the marriage was clearly not made to last. In 1973 Roger again went abroad, working for Esso on a tanker. When he returned in April 1974, he moved almost immediately into his parents' home in Coulsdon.

By now Sandra, who had kept on the Kenley flat, was on the books of a domestic agency in Belgravia and working for an elderly couple. A friend from the Reedham job, Rosemary Jordan, saw a lot of her at this time; they went dancing together, and Sandra confided in Rosemary about her love life. She told her about the new job as nanny to the Lucan children. The police said that the Belgravia agency found her the post, which she took up on 28 August 1974 for a wage of £25 a week, although at the inquest Veronica seemed to suggest that Sandra had come through Knightsbridge Nannies.

'Sandra was a lonely girl,' she would later say. 'Her husband had left her and she seemed to have little to do with her parents who lived outside London.'[5] In fact the Rivetts' separation was mutual, and the Hensbys had taken on the care of Sandra's son.

Nor was it entirely true to say that Sandra was 'lonely'. Rootless, perhaps; but she was a very good-looking woman, and she had plenty of male friends, with whom she drank in the local pubs on her nights off. She was, wrote David Gerring, 'receptive to their advances'. One of these, a married man, was intensely embarrassed to be questioned after her death. At the inquest, Veronica was asked: 'Did you know whether she had many boyfriends?', to which she replied: 'I know of two, she talked to two.' Veronica also knew that Sandra had had a son adopted by her parents, although she was unaware of the second child.

The question was then put: 'Had any men friends come to your house?'

'No.'

'Had she asked if a man could come?'

'No.'

One of Sandra's boyfriends may have been a mysterious 'Norwegian seaman', now mentioned by the former officer Graham Forsyth (the Norwegian embassy was in Belgrave Square). Another was said to be named 'Ray'.[6] Recently a statement, made to the police in November 1974 by Sally Gibbs, was uncovered by a BBC journalist.[7] Sally recounted a conversation in which her niece Camilla had referred to a man who was living at Lower Belgrave Street, or who stayed 'on the odd occasion'. Frances, when told of Sandra's death, also instantly mentioned her 'boyfriend'.

'There was always this thing about Sandra's boyfriend,' says Christina. 'The children said that Sandra had a boyfriend who used to come in a big Mercedes. No idea who it was at all. She had had a row with him, and the affair had ended.' The police did indeed say, without making much of it, that Sandra had broken up with an unnamed man just a few days before the murder.

It seems unusual for a child as young as Camilla to have been aware of boyfriends; but she was highly intelligent and doubtless very alert. And there is evidence that she had mentioned them on another occasion. Frances's police statement also drew attention to Sandra's love life: 'During the last weekend we spent with Daddy on 2nd and 3rd Nov 1974, Camilla told Daddy that Sandra had boyfriends and went out with them.'

There were, in fact, more than two boyfriends. But only one became a known quantity: John Hankins, a twenty-six-year-old Australian barman, who came forward to the police of his own volition. He was introduced to Sandra at the Plumbers Arms some six weeks before her death. She would visit the various pubs in which he worked and sometimes spend the night with him. Hankins told the *Daily Express*: 'Sandra and I had talked about her returning to Australia with me in a few years' time. We might have got married.' Sandra had phoned Roger Rivett to discuss the possibility of a quick divorce, it is assumed on account of Hankins. Rivett replied that he would do what she asked if she provided evidence of adultery, to which she never responded.

The relationship with Hankins was occasionally fiery. The pair had rows, one in particular on Sunday 3 November. They made it up, however, and went out together on the 6th. Hankins rang Sandra on the evening of the 7th. In another interview with the *Express*, he said: 'We spoke for about fifteen minutes. We talked of going out next week. I was probably the last one, apart from her killer, to speak to her on the telephone last Thursday.' According to Roy Ranson this call took place at 8.00, although he claimed that the conversation lasted just five minutes. He may have been aware of a possible discrepancy here. In her statement, Frances told the police that she had entered her mother's bedroom at about 8.05pm after watching *Top of the Pops* in the nursery. 'We all', she said, meaning that Sandra was there also, 'watched the TV in Mummy's room.'

Another minor point arose as to why Sandra was at Lower Belgrave Street on the night of 7 November. Thursday was her usual day

off. At the inquest, Veronica said that she had changed it on account
of Hankins: 'Her current boyfriend had his day off on Wednesday,
and she asked if she could change hers to Wednesday as well so
that she could go out with him.' Ranson gave another explanation,
that Sandra had felt unwell and thought she might have glandular
fever. His account has Sandra actually saying this to her mother
on the night she died. The *Daily Mirror*, however, reported a different conversation. Mrs Hensby told the paper that Sandra rang
her 'shortly before the murder. She told us she was fine.' The time
of this call is unclear. Frances says that Sandra was already in her
mother's bedroom at 7.20pm, when she herself went to watch *Top
of the Pops*. If one accepts the phrase 'shortly before the murder',
Sandra probably rang her mother just before the call from Hankins.

Mrs Hensby made no mention of suspected glandular fever. Possibly Ranson, conscious of any prejudice against Sandra's active love
life, was seeking to stress the innocence of her reason for staying at
home. In the first days after the murder, and despite the emphasis
upon Lucan, newspapers were inevitably casting about for details
about the victim. The *Express*, which had particularly good police
access, reported a visit by detectives to the flat in Kenley, where they
found a 'huge colour magazine picture of a nude man' above the
bed. Hankins was also described in a way designed to arouse interest, although there was no mention of any other boyfriend.

'One thing I want to make clear', Hankins stated firmly, 'is that
Sandra was a very nice girl.' Similarly, Veronica would later say:
'As a young and attractive woman she did have boyfriends, but
not a large number. She did not give me the impression of being
promiscuous.'[8] Nevertheless rumours about Sandra had begun to
circulate among Lucan's friends, around the world of the Clermont.
As Stuart Wheeler says: 'One of the people that definitely was in the
Lucan circle said of the nanny, oh well, there were God knows how
many men in her book, the implication being that she was involved
in prostitution – which perhaps illustrates a willingness to put a
gloss on things.'

In other words, it was being suggested by those who sought to exonerate Lucan that there were alternative suspects within Sandra's life: that she, in fact, had been the intended victim. The idea that she was killed in error, which the official version of the case has never questioned, was, in the end, only an idea. In the world of the fictional detective, where the question of *what really happened* is the only one that signifies, the answer would be: *Sandra died.*

Yet her love affairs would soon be of scant interest to the press. There was only Lucan, Lucan, Lucan. An inevitable rumour arose that *he* had been having a fling with the nanny; by no means unknown, but also not his style, and as a lead it led nowhere. The police interviewed the men in Sandra's life (although the Norwegian, if he existed, remained elusive), but only as a matter of form. Roger Rivett, who has always maintained a gentlemanly silence about his wife, had an impregnable alibi. John Hankins, who on the night of 7 November was working at the Kings Arms pub in Buckingham Palace Road (at the bottom of Lower Belgrave Street), was also eliminated. He talked freely to the police about Sandra's situation, saying that she had appeared to be friendly with Veronica, but wanted little to do with Lucan. Veronica herself later made the strong assertion that Sandra was wary of Lucan. Against this, however, is testimony from Sandra herself. As recalled by her son Stephen Hensby, she had written to her parents saying that 'she had this good job in a lovely house and that both Lord and Lady Lucan were very nice to her'.[9]

Lucan was certainly pleased with Sandra, whom he met when he collected the children, and at birthday parties held for them at Elizabeth Street. And Veronica liked her very much. 'They used to go out together a bit,' says Christina Shand Kydd. 'For a drink.' Sandra, whose warm good nature brought ten weeks of relative happiness into the house at Lower Belgrave Street, had possessed a gift for life, something that the couple for whom she worked had lost along the way.

*

Can it possibly be true that, when interviewed by the police, one of Lucan's friends said of Sandra's murder 'What a pity! Good nannies are so hard to find'?

It has become the defining epigraph of the myth, yet according to David Gerring, who would doubtless have loved to claim it for a member of the Lucan circle, it was actually said by a complete outsider. The remark was made during house-to-house inquiries by an elderly resident of Belgravia. By degrees rumour did its work and attributed it much closer to home. There it sat very comfortably. Even if it hadn't actually been said by somebody that Lucan knew, it might as well have been. That was the kind of people they were.

It was further claimed that the Lucan camp completely ignored Sandra's family, at the inquest and at all other times. This, too, is not entirely accurate. Both Lucan's sisters, Sally and Jane, wrote to Eunice Hensby. Veronica did not do so. She did speak to Mrs Hensby on the phone, and Sandra's parents publicly wished her luck with her claim from the Criminal Injuries Compensation Board (their own failed, but Veronica's succeeded). Nevertheless Sandra's sister Charmaine told the press that 'some of the family were hurt that Lady Lucan had not sent a letter of sympathy'; she also said that when her aunt had gone to Lower Belgrave Street to collect Sandra's clothes, 'they were bundled in a paper bag and Lady Lucan handed them over'.[10] This may, of course, have been straightforward discomfiture on Veronica's part. It was also perhaps understandable that she sent a wreath, rather than attend Sandra's funeral at the Croydon Crematorium on 18 December 1974: Lord Lucan's fortieth birthday.

The *Sunday Mirror*, grinding its political axe on the wheel of the Lucan case, wrote that it was

Lucan's aristocratic family and gambling friends who dominated the London inquest. What an ugly real-life performance of *Upstairs, Downstairs*. Sandra Rivett, the Little Miss Nobody, was firmly kept in her lowly place by his chums: downstairs (where, indeed, she was slaughtered). If words of sorrow or compassion for her were spoken by the Upstairs Crowd, they were very few and far between.

The 'Upstairs Crowd', in this context, did not include the then Countess of Lucan.

And there was truth in what the *Mirror* said, but it was not the whole truth. In the same way, there is truth in the belief that Lucan's friends obstructed the police inquiry; but only some truth. That they behaved in this way is so central to the myth that it is difficult to deconstruct the image of the circle, the ring of people who sought to protect one of their own kind. Yet as with the Clermont gamblers, the notion of a single entity is a false one. These were individuals, and they differed from each other. Even the police later admitted as much; although more often it suited their purposes to lament the powerfully united wall of silence that confronted them. '[The police] were under pressure from above to find John,' says Daniel Meinertzhagen. 'So they blamed us.'

Forty years on, the same tune is still being played. The police remained extremely sore over their failure to bring Lucan to justice. David Gerring wrote defensively of the criticism hurled at the 'nob squad'. The very human desire to excuse themselves was displayed as recently as 2012, when a former detective said:

> I don't think a great deal of pressure was placed on Lucan's friends. Britain was more class-conscious than it is nowadays and they did have a pull. I wouldn't say that hindered us a lot but I don't think Roy Ranson got the assistance and honesty he should have got from witnesses.
>
> If the Lord Lucan case had happened today, I think he'd still have been helped, except that it would have been a little more diffi-cult for his friends.[11]

There are two separate accusations made against the Lucan circle. The first is that they were deliberately unaccommodating to the police when questioned; the second is that they aided a murderer in his flight from justice. Although obviously connected, one accusation is infinitely more serious than the other, and the two have been far too casually conflated.

Lucan had three very full address books, and the police contacted everybody in them. Within that large number of people were those who had known him very well, and others – a majority – who were acquaintances, often of the merely fleeting kind. Some of this second group were unhappy about being interviewed in connection with a murder inquiry. They did, undoubtedly, show it, in that testy, cool-eyed, God-what-a-bore way that the upper classes tend to adopt as a default mode. Lady Amabel Lindsay, whose husband sold the Lucan family silver, batted away police questions by saying (and how one can hear it): 'Now, what do *you* think happened?' 'We're not paid to think, madam' was the stolid reply. People would suggest a chat when they returned from a skiing holiday, or treat the police as funny little servants. 'If they behaved as arrogantly as they may have done,' says Stuart Wheeler, 'the police probably had good reason to hate them. I mean one man I knew from the Clermont – when the police came to interview him, one of them said to him, Lucan was a very good backgammon player, wasn't he? And apparently this chap replied: "No. He wasn't. Well, all right, he might have been the eleventh best in England." So there was all that sort of stuff...'

Soon the press, who were drinking cosily with the police in the Duke of Wellington or (the favoured ones) in Ranson's office, were playing to the gallery. Just a week after the murder, the *Daily Express* wrote of the 'masonic-style bond which links that certain breed of men whose "stud book" lines mostly lead back to the same stables – privileged prep schools, Eton, Oxford, the Household Brigade'. The article concluded: 'The honour code binds their silence' and warned that this 'may mean the police's work will now be just that more difficult'.

The press knew perfectly well what its readership thought of Lucan and his merry band. 'What can one say', wrote the *Daily*

Mail, 'but that a man is judged by his friends?' It knew that, in an age of austerity and privation, their way of life would both titillate and enrage. The idea that these people were also attempting to thwart the plods was too good to resist. But the truth is that, as with the Lucan marriage, the war was on both sides, and this time it was a class war. The police fell into cliché as well; even by calling themselves the 'nob squad'. Alert to accusations that they would be too deferential in their questioning, that they would bow and scrape, they often went too far the other way. Gerring was a self-consciously hardened policeman straight out of *Life on Mars*, known as 'Buster' because he had busted gangs, including the seriously villainous Richardsons. Although Graham Forsyth, a kindly man in his own right, now describes Gerring as 'very nice, lovely', he was surely not the right person to handle this inquiry, which required anything rather than his style of lairy bombast. He talked about the Lucan case being a 'nice little earner' (meaning overtime). He deployed a provocative idiom, hoping to offend the upper-class eardrum by saying 'was John a crumpet man?', when it would have been just as easy to ask if he had had girlfriends. In his book he stated airily that he 'liked the aristocracy',[12] but there was not much sign of that in his dealings with them.

There was also quite a lot of aggression, not physical, but designed to intimidate. 'I spent six hours at Gerald Road [police station],' says Daniel Meinertzhagen. 'It didn't bother me. But they were threatening. They wouldn't believe that I didn't know anything! All that nonsense about the circle...' Greville Howard's former wife Zoe says he was given a particularly rough ride.

> I think Greville had quite a hard time with the police, because of course they were all meant to be having dinner together that night [at the Clermont on 7 November]. We were split up by then, but I remember him ringing me up, it must have been early in the morning, and he said, I've just come out of the cells, or whatever... I think he had a horrid time.

Today, infinitely greater cynicism about the police allows the belief that they, too, were motivated by prejudice; anybody who has ever had an officer take against them will know what it feels like to be trapped within a force-field of legalized bullying. With people of the Lucan kind, however, there is probably a counter-belief that they deserved whatever they got. Nevertheless a man like James Goldsmith, a bully in his own right, was treated with a very light touch; with him they wouldn't have dared.

They resented the fact that these people did not play the police's game: the police like power, just as much as the aristocracy ever did, and they like it when even the innocent are just a little bit frightened of them. What they also liked, very much indeed, was moving and shaking within the Belgravia world. They used the Elizabeth Street flat; they obtained warrants to search a large number of houses, including Warwick Castle and Charlton Park; they visited the Clermont, and had it bugged. The ex-bunny girl receptionist, who had been present on the day of the murder, recalls how the staff were called into the middle of Berkeley Square and interviewed there (on the principle that walls have ears). She also remembers one officer getting hopelessly drunk at Annabel's: 'I had to call a police car to take him away.' And the police positively relished their closeness to Veronica Lucan, a *bona fide* countess who was nonetheless on their side, a 'good old girl', as Forsyth says. Her sister Christina visited her at St George's Hospital, where DS Forsyth was in attendance.

> He was her absolute shadow throughout the entire thing. I remember, I went to see her the next day – and she was extremely aggressive – well, she'd had a nasty crack on her head. But she was spoiling for a fight, cold as ice, absolutely... And I said to her, how are you? He was very much sitting there, and I was very much treated by him as an evil person, you know, that I was not nice. That came across very clearly. The sort of condescending rich sister, I think he looked upon me as – that's how he made me feel – he didn't even know me! Veronica was extremely difficult, and I said is there anything

Bill and I can do to help you? What can we do, just tell us? And she said something like, what do you ever do?

I mentioned money. And she said, I can assure you I've got plenty. Those were her exact words. So I said, oh I see. And then she just didn't speak anymore, I sort of tried to make some sort of conversation but it was made perfectly obvious that I was not required there. So I left.

Graham Forsyth also remembers that incident at the hospital. 'She walked in, the sister, and said, what have you done now? I had a lot of sympathy with Veronica. She seemed so isolated.'

Christina says:

The police disliked posh people [again, Veronica herself was made an exception to this particular prejudice]. And they made that absolutely clear. They came to talk to us, they searched our house – they assumed we were all posh people who had closed ranks to protect a friend. But as Charlie Benson said, whether you're posh, or whether you're a teacher, or whether you're a miner, you always protect your friends, it's nothing to do with being posh. It's friendship. And no one was lying for John. No one was saying he's not in my house when he was in the attic.

In fact the Shand Kydds and DS Forsyth got along amicably, away from the hospital. And Roy Ranson, says Christina, was 'a perfectly polite, nice man. It was Gerring that was so ghastly. Chippy, vaguely sort of louche.' David Gerring would later be dismissed for insubordination to his superiors. 'He was a disgrace,' says Bill Shand Kydd.

Ranson later claimed to have become intensely frustrated by 'the attitude of some of these people, trying to put one over on us, to take us on and beat us'. In the words of James Fox: 'It was as if, day after day, Ranson and Gerring were chasing the guests at some nightmare charity ball.'[13] Very soon this attitude was attacked not just by the press, but in Parliament: thus far had the notoriety spread of the Lucan circle. On 16 November, Charles Benson wrote to *The Times*, saying:

> I object to the suggestion by Marcus Lipton MP that some people are 'being a bit snooty with the police' over the search for Lord Lucan.
>
> As a still close personal friend of Lord Lucan, could I make my own position clear. As far as I know, all his friends have made themselves available to the police at all times. I personally rang the department concerned on the Friday morning following the murder, giving my name and address, and also offering other names, all of whom were in full agreement. I may add that we were not contacted for some days. Is this obstruction or non-cooperation by us?

Benson might just as well not have bothered: the image of the circle was already immovably in place.

It was later said that, when news of the murder was disseminated among Lucan's friends, 'a curious grouping process began to occur. People were dragged out of poker games and dinner parties, summoned from bars and clubs. Phones were taken off the hook; factotums were instructed to shoo the police away.'[14] It all sounds very orchestrated, very MI5. In fact it was a good deal more chaotic and directionless. Certainly the news spread among Lucan's friends like a fire catching dry straw; but then, it would. 'I was working in a jewellery shop in Beauchamp Place,' says the then girlfriend of one of the circle. 'And I remember the buzzer went – and Dominick Elwes came in and said, "The most terrible thing has happened. Lucky Lucan's nanny has been murdered, and he's disappeared" – and you know, I'd never been part of a world like that before. Little did I know that it would turn into this huge thing.'

The Shand Kydds were first given news of the murder by Kait Lucan, in the early hours of 8 November. A friend of Stephen Raphael's saw the police breaking into the Eaton Row mews, and rang to tell him that something was up. Raphael, whom Lucan might reasonably have contacted that night, but who in fact clearly knew nothing, rang Benson and Daniel Meinertzhagen on the morning of

the 8th. As recounted in his letter to *The Times*, Benson then contacted the police. Around the same time John Aspinall learned what
had happened; the myth has it that he knew already, because Lucan
had seen him after the murder, but this is almost certainly untrue.
It is possible, of course, that Lucan rang Aspinall from Uckfield. If
so, however, he would probably have rung other friends also; which
their actions do not suggest.

On the afternoon of the 8th, Aspinall hosted a lunch at Lyall
Street for some of Lucan's friends. Later Benson, a professional
bon vivant, would say rather mournfully: 'It wasn't really a lunch,
you know. It was just a few sandwiches.' This occasion has acquired
a mythic status: some have gone so far as to liken it to a counsel of
war. It was alleged that the circle of men agreed to tell the police
as little as possible about Lucan's marriage, his children, his state
of mind. There is some truth to this. A far graver allegation is that
they also agreed upon a plan to help him escape. This, it was said
during James Goldsmith's libel action against *Private Eye*, was to
suggest that 'those who were present were parties to a conspiracy
to obstruct the course of justice'; effectively, that these men were
criminals, the aiders and abettors of Muriel Spark's novel about the
Lucan case.

Accounts of the lunch, by those who actually attended it, are
naturally very different from the accepted version. What was discussed, essentially, was not how to get Lucan away, but what to do
if he turned up.

'That lunch did take place,' says Bill Shand Kydd, 'and I was
there. I was really the outsider of the group. And I said, if he turns
up we must get the police. Afterwards it was said that we'd helped
him escape. No.' Also present were Benson, Meinertzhagen, Elwes,
Stoop, Raphael and Aspinall. Both *Private Eye* and the *Sunday
Times Magazine* (who got away with it) stated that James Goldsmith
had attended the lunch, although this allegation was withdrawn
by *Private Eye*: Goldsmith was indubitably in Dublin at the time.
Inevitably a lot of boys'-own-adventure nonsense was spoken.

'It was all a lot of talk,' says Bill, mainly by Dominick Elwes, who was pacing about and 'doing a Hamlet'. Meinertzhagen recalls his urgent, excitable demand: 'Now what are we going to do about Lucky?' Elwes suggested smuggling Lucan away on a banana boat to South America. Bill replied that 'there was certainly no question of helping him flee. I said I certainly didn't think he'd done it and I wanted to get hold of him as soon as possible before he did something silly like killing himself or pissing off.'[15]

It is actually unclear how much Lucan's friends even knew, at this point. An obvious assumption is that Susan Maxwell-Scott told somebody of the visit to her house. If so, this was not generally discussed at the lunch. Certainly Bill Shand Kydd, who did not know that Lucan had visited his own home, and was of the unwavering opinion that Lucan's only option was to go to the police, would have moved straight into action had he heard that Lucan had been at Uckfield. He contacted the police as soon as he did know, when he saw the postmark on his letters on the morning of the 9th. Indeed the very fact that Lucan wrote letters at all implies that he did not speak to anybody thereafter.

Later Ranson said: 'They told me they were there to discuss ways of helping Lucan if he surfaced, and I believe them.' This is disingenuous; not untrue, but not quite true either. What in fact emerged was a consensus behind Bill Shand Kydd, the most sensible of Lucan's friends. As Daniel Meinertzhagen puts it, 'I would have helped John: to turn himself in.'

'The only one who would have helped him', says Bill, meaning in the other, more lawless way, 'was Aspinall.'

Aspinall, again: that showman, who hated Veronica, who adored a bit of trouble and friction, and who would soon say:

> If a close friend of yours came in covered in blood, having done some frightful deed, the last thing that would have occurred to you is to turn him in. It goes against every last instinct of human loyalties, and to hell with the law or the common norms of civic

behaviour or something. If he had begged asylum he would have had it. I would have helped him...

What a loss Aspinall was to the stage! Not that his gigantic personality would have suited the theatre of his own times; he did far better to create his own dramatic arenas, his clubs and his homes; but he would have made a truly fabulous actor-manager in the days of Garrick. He continued:

> If he had turned up at Howletts [Aspinall's house in Kent, where the police search was watched over by a gorilla] I would have taken him aside and had a long talk and looked at the problem. It may have involved him giving himself up or getting him funds to go to Costa Rica. He could certainly have had a lot of money. I had many people calling me and saying, if Lucan wants money, he can have it.

Aspinall would have thought that getting Lucan out of the country was *fun*. He would have relished the notion of striding about in a sphere of his own, somewhere above the law. And he would have loved the idea of getting back at Veronica, who had sat like a tiny ice statue inside his club and chilled its atmosphere with her unnerving gaze. Nevertheless it is quite a leap to say, as it would be later, that he was 'the self-appointed staff officer for the great escape'.[16]

After the lunch, Dominick Elwes went to see Veronica in hospital. Inevitably, this visit has been presented as something sinister. 'It was agreed that someone should try to find out what Veronica had told the police. Dominick Elwes, as the nicest person present, was chosen for this task.'[17] A further suggestion, made by *Private Eye*, was that Elwes had been sent under orders from Goldsmith. This seems unlikely, given that he was out of the country, and indeed the allegation formed part of his libel action.

Elwes was accompanied to the hospital by Christina and Lucan's brother Hugh. As he entered Veronica's room, she fixed him with a black eye and said: 'Well, now who's mad? Now who's the one with *paranoia*, eh?'[18]

It may have been straightforward (if reluctant) courtesy that lay behind this visit from Elwes; if he had indeed been sent, this was probably because he was judged to be the person least inimical to Veronica. A similar suggestion was made the following week. On Monday 11 November, Lucan's uncle John Bevan held a gathering for some twenty-five people, mostly family, at which the situation was discussed in detail. Also present was Lucan's old friend from Eton. 'And halfway through John said, you know, someone's got to make contact with Veronica. She's in hospital, and all. Somebody has got to say, we're all thinking of her. And it can't be a relation, it just can't be.' The person selected was a cousin of Sally Gibbs's husband, who took the precaution of asking a neighbour to listen as a witness to what was said. Veronica's first words were: 'All Gibbses are evil.' The reason for her saying this, says Lucan's friend, was that 'everybody was sort of involved in it, and not being supportive of her. The girl listening in was very surprised – that I do know.'

Veronica's words to Dominick Elwes sprang from the same source. He reacted by bursting into tears, and it was later asserted that 'unusually among Lucan's friends, Elwes was certain of Lucan's guilt from then on'.[19] This appears to contradict Elwes's own words to the *Daily Express* in June 1975: 'We are all prepared to accept his alibi and help him in any way possible', although that may, of course, have been a confused attempt to say the right thing. Actually, if Elwes did believe Lucan to be guilty, he was far from alone. In reference to the lunch at Aspinall's house, Christina says: 'I think they all considered that he'd done it, didn't they?' Bill responds: 'Oh, absolutely.'

'I could understand what he did,' Daniel Meinertzhagen now says, 'but I didn't approve of it.'

Christina reiterates:

They all thought that he'd done it. But remember that everybody knew the true reasons for anything going wrong, things that we've told you, and you can imagine there's a great deal more. That was the main closing ranks, you see. We didn't say to the press or police what we really felt. To protect the children, as much as anything. And so the press put it that we just didn't like Veronica.

Indeed the newspapers were strident in their assertion that Lucan had been protected for two reasons; not merely because he was 'one of us', but because Veronica was not. 'She didn't fit,' as Graham Forsyth puts it. Thus the sympathy for her continued to grow. On 21 November her 'minder', Mary-Geraldine O'Donnell, told the *Daily Mirror*: 'Not one nice thing has been said about Veronica. Not one of her so-called friends has come to her defence. She feels hurt – hurt that her family and friends have been against her during the last two years.' The *Sunday Times Magazine* article, published in June 1975, wrote of how 'her detractors had the monopoly on the gossip, which intensified after the disappearance of Lucan. Even her close family provided little support.' Two weeks later, after the inquest, the *Daily Mail* wrote of the 'mounting campaign by [Lucan's] friends of innuendo and vilification'. Veronica, who 'despite her efforts did not hit it off with her husband's circle', was being destroyed by gossip, a grotesque escalation of the rumours that had circulated the Clermont since the late 1960s. 'Doubts have even been cast about her mental state, which is in fact sound.' Yet the police, 'who are concerned only with facts', held her in the highest regard. 'If the detectives had not been neutral professionals, some of them would have sent a bouquet of roses out of admiration for the way she stood up to the strain and hostility.'[20]

It was, the press suggested, an irrational victimization. Like Mr Justice Rees before them, the police – and thus the press – placed such an absolute trust in Veronica, in her version of every aspect of her life with Lucan, that the logical obverse was to mistrust everybody who supported him. Nothing that they said could be believed; indeed, it never really has been.

'Some time,' wrote Bill Shand Kydd, in an ice-cold letter of response to the *Sunday Times Magazine*, 'the whole story must be written, exposing the misleading allegations made in the Press.'

'Nobody's ever wanted to understand it,' says Christina. 'But the police – they bought the whole thing. They looked at one side, and they listened to everything she said, and from that minute on he was finished. It was just such an appalling time. The frustration. You wanted to get up on the rooftops and yell.'

The police, who tended the image of the circle as if it were a precious orchid, at the same time undermined it continually when it was broken into separate components. 'I thought a lot of John Aspinall,' says Graham Forsyth, a fellow animal-lover. Gerring, who wrote tersely that 'if Lucan had been from the underworld the gangsters would soon have shopped him', went on to describe James Gold-smith, of whom he himself was slightly afraid, as straightforward, helpful and 'irritated to be involved at all' (you bet he was). He also referred to Dominick Elwes, who had informed the police about the lunch on 8 November, visiting Gerald Road and talking very freely. Ranson praised Bill Shand Kydd as 'a most helpful and forthright man', and described others who had attended the lunch as 'courte-ous, charming and helpful', which leaves: who?

The word 'helpful' recurs in these descriptions. Nevertheless the press continued to be fed criticisms of the tight-lipped and obstruc-tive circle. Lucan's schoolfriend says:

> The day after it happened, I was summoned by Chief-Inspector [sic] Ranson to Gerald Road police station, and I spent two and a half hours with him. He said one of the people he'd interviewed that day was the most unpleasant individual he'd come across in his police career. He said, you know, we had John Lucan's diary – endless names – and this chap, he happened to be available, and I got him in. [It is not known who this man was, although the implication is that he was not a close friend.] We got to know each other, talking that day. And Ranson ended up by saying, 'I've met some of the nastiest and nicest people I've ever met in my police career.'

This remark by Ranson, which has an air of absolute honesty, is a long way from his public portrayal of an indistinguishable gaggle of upper-class monsters. During the interview Ranson also offered the view that 'obviously John Lucan had two lives. One touched the worst side of the gambling world, and the other side was, you know, the most charming, thoughtful, kind, lovely fellow. It was extraordinary.'

Even more extraordinary is the gulf between this frank analysis and the way in which Ranson, some twenty years later, described his anger at the 'platitudes and praise heaped upon Lucan'. He was, says Lucan's friend, 'much more fair-minded in private'.

Meanwhile Graham Forsyth, who unlike Ranson and Gerring has never publicly endorsed the myth of the bond of silence, now destroys it entirely. 'The idea is that aristos don't grass, they don't like to be seen to be saying things... They talked all right! Most of them anyway. They just didn't want it *known* that they had talked.'

Greville Howard, for example, had the police rubbing their hands in glee when he revealed that Lucan had confessed a desire to murder his wife. As his former wife Zoe makes clear, Howard had been questioned very closely at Gerald Road, possibly more so than on any other of Lucan's friends. He told the police that he had been drinking with Lucan not long before the murder, and that Lucan had confided in him about his financial worries. Howard suggested a declaration of bankruptcy. Lucan said that there was another way out: killing Veronica. He mentioned dumping her body in the Solent, off Southampton. Howard's reaction, naturally, was that Lucan was being absurd, and that it would be infinitely worse for his children to have him arrested for murder than to be made bankrupt.

Lucan had, of course, said something like this to his old school-friend, with his remark that Veronica would be better 'off the hill'. People do say these things. If everybody who had ever longed for another person's death actually acted upon their wish, the murder rate in Midsomer would be quite accurate. Later the columnist Taki, who gambled at the Clermont, made merry in print with his inside knowledge of Lucan's plots. One version had Lucan making 'two trial runs to Newhaven before the murder, one in the company of a friend of his who is very much with us today'.[21] Other stories were more elaborate: Lucan had bought a speedboat, gone fitness training in Hyde Park, taken a sack weighing eight stone on his dummy runs, travelled to the deepest part of the Channel where the body could be lost forever. 'A lot of people wanted to climb on the bandwagon afterwards,' says the girlfriend of one of the set. 'They probably liked lots of publicity.' Although Taki's words about Lucan are sometimes quoted as damning fact, it is quite difficult to take them other than with a cellarful of salt.

Later it would also be said that Lucan told John Aspinall's mother, Lady Osborne, that he wanted to kill his wife; to which she replied that 'he must do whatever he thought was right'.[22] Again, it is hard to take this terribly seriously.

What Greville Howard said, however, was taken very seriously indeed; certainly by the police. During the week of the inquest Howard was laid up, receiving back treatment at the Nuffield Clinic. Counsel for the police requested that his statement be read in court. Michael Eastham, for the Lucan family, objected strongly that this would be 'devastating and prejudicial', and his argument was upheld by the coroner. Subsequently it was alleged by *Private Eye* that Howard, who then worked for James Goldsmith, had been coerced into staying away from the inquest.

Howard never spoke again about the case. Some of Lucan's friends did later talk to the press, and, contrary to myth, they did so in a manner not entirely loyal to him. Aspinall made frequent proclamations over the years. Charles Benson, himself a journalist, told the *Sunday Times* that Lucan was 'very Right-wing and he never compromised in front of people. He would talk about hanging and flogging and foreigners and n*****s equally to shock and get a reaction.' Dominick Elwes, who shifted uneasily between camps, said that Lucan's obsession with his wife and children 'was the dark side of the moon. It wasn't the Lucky I knew. It was perhaps a classic case of paranoia' (a damning choice of word, given Lucan's use of it in his letter to Bill Shand Kydd). Benson and Elwes were men who thrived on popularity; it was their *raison d'être*. It was natural that they should have felt uncomfortable as hate figures, and have shifted position closer to that of public opinion. They had their own skins to save, although Elwes proved unable to do so.

Yet there *were* people who did not tell things; whose loyalty to Lucan, or unwillingness to get involved, compromised the inquiry. Probably this is usual in any murder investigation. Michael Stoop did not reveal a letter and two envelopes. Others withheld details of Lucan's private life, leaving Veronica's version to become the only one that was accepted. But what was unusual, and deeply so, was that Susan Maxwell-Scott did not contact the police to say that Lucan had been at her house.

Gerring gave her a very hard time when he visited Uckfield (en route to searching the house of another friend, Algy Cluff, who was rumoured to be sheltering Lucan in his wine cellar). He accused Susan of lying about the state of Lucan's clothes. He questioned her about Lucan's mysterious overcoat, and suggested that she had burned it. He expressed disbelief when she claimed that she had not known, on 8 November, that Lucan was being sought by the police. He asked why she had not contacted Bill Shand Kydd about the letters that Lucan had written to him, but had left it to Bill to perceive their significance.

Susan remained unmoved. If Gerring had thought that he could frighten her, he was wrong. 'I don't care what you believe,' she said. 'I'm telling you the truth.'

Gerring then asked Ian Maxwell-Scott to attend at Gerald Road, and questioned him with equal ferocity. He got little that was new. Ian, who undeniably displayed all the arrogance with which the image of the circle was tainted, told Gerring what the rest of them would have dearly loved to say: 'I don't like your attitude.'

Later Susan would write a letter to the *Daily Star*, which reads slightly drunkenly, in reply to one of Ranson's periodic attacks upon Lucan's friends. She said:

I fully and truthfully answered all questions. I also gave permission to search the house and the grounds. Later still, I allowed police forensic science experts to examine my chairs for blood stains – they did not find any! I cannot imagine in what way I could have helped Ranson more! Friends have loyalty to each other – else they are mere acquaintances NOT friends. Loyalty among friends is, in my opinion, the highest morality in life. Without it friendship could not exist – only acquaintanceship.

The police concluded, among other things, that Susan was half in love with Lucan. 'She was a very loyal friend,' says Christina.

On 12 November, the day that a warrant was issued for Lucan's arrest, Bill Shand Kydd made a public appeal on ITV's *News at Ten*. Here, at least, was somebody facing the situation with appropriate realism. Of course the Shand Kydds were closely concerned with those half-forgotten victims, the children. Lucan's schoolfriend says:

> The evening before, on the Monday, Bill, Christina, Caroline Hill and I had dinner, and we discussed tactics. I knew Sandy Gall [then an ITN newsreader] very well, and Bill knew him slightly, and so we got hold of him. He said he would certainly make sure it was in *News at Ten* next time. And we had a bit with Bill on the news. He was saying, John, whatever the rights and wrongs, come forward.

What Bill also said, very decidedly, was that Lucan should contact him and that they would go with a solicitor to the police. This constitutes further evidence that the Lyall Street lunch, at which Bill had been present, had not in fact concocted a plan to enable Lucan to flee justice. So too does Dominick Elwes's desperate plea, made through the *Daily Express*: 'If Lucky is still alive, as I believe he is, would he please contact me?... I would tell him to go to the police and sort this whole bloody mess out.' Elwes was not in a condition to be disingenuous; he really did not know what had happened to Lucan.

'We were just thinking, where could he be?' says Lucan's old schoolfriend. 'We thought, maybe Robin Hill had him hidden away in a tunnel...' Hill, the future 8th Marquess of Downshire, lived at Clifton Castle in North Yorkshire. He and his sister Caroline were good friends of Lucan; Robin Hill was a rich man, and he could have helped a flight from justice; except that he didn't. 'But at first, yes, we thought John was alive. He said he was going to lie doggo for a bit...'

Again, this suggests ignorance of Lucan's whereabouts. It also, of course, suggests that very willingness to help him of which the circle was accused.

'I think they would have done it,' says Christina. 'I'm sure that people would have helped him. But Bill was right. – Bill is always right. He should have gone to the police. If he hadn't run...'

It was John Aspinall, beyond doubt, who inspired the myth that Lucan had been spirited away by a daredevil gang of plotters, led by himself. Take Aspinall out of the picture, and what is left is a sense of disparate people, most of them co-operating with the police, some not, some of them believing that Lucan was innocent, most not, stunned by the situation in which they found themselves, united only by Bill Shand Kydd's iron insistence that Lucan should return to confront the matter. Put Aspinall back into the picture, and immediately the circle regroups in all its outlandish aspect: the people who believed that the life of a young woman was a bagatelle weighed against the freedom of their noble friend.

When the police turned up to search Howletts, Aspinall pranced about mockingly, suggesting that they might like to lift the floor-boards. Asked if he was proud to call Lucan a friend, he pounced. 'I said, if she'd been my wife, I'd have bashed her to death five years before and so would you. I said, don't come that line with me...' As Bill Shand Kydd puts it: who needs a friend like Aspinall?

To the *Sunday Times Magazine* Aspinall boomed on, saying:

Lucan was really a leader of men. In fact he wasn't – but in more rigorous times he would have found a better role in life. In other words, in a time of war Lucan would have been a valuable acquisition to a country. He wouldn't have had any difficulty in getting loyalty from his men. He was a warrior, a Roman. He was quite capable of falling on his sword, as it were.

Beneath the bombast was a kernel of acuity, as well as contradictory hints as to Lucan's fate. He could have commanded enough loyalty to help him flee, but equally he might have committed suicide. You decide.

Aspinall's most famous comment was made when Ludovic Kennedy, a distinguished analyst of murder cases who believed in Lucan's innocence, asked what he would do if Lucan were to reappear. 'I would embrace him.' The remark would later appear on the wall of Aspinall's casino, inscribed under a relief of Lord Lucan (the date of whose death was left tantalizingly open).

'Quite right, too' was a later reaction in the *Guardian*. 'If you're going to forgive your dumb, four-legged friends for their violent actions, you might as well forgive your dumb, two-legged ones as well.'[23]

Reading Aspinall's words about the Lucan case, the overriding impression is of a man conducting a gigantic tease. He was completely unafraid of the police, indifferent to public opinion in a way that is very rare, amusing himself by making people think that he was harbouring all sorts of priceless knowledge. 'I formed a view he was secretly laughing at us,' David Gerring later said.

When asked directly about Lucan, Aspinall could suddenly revert to caution: 'He was very skilled at motor-boat racing,' he told the interviewer Lynn Barber in 1990, 'and I think he had a boat there at Newhaven, where his car was found, and I think he jumped into one of his little motor boats, went out to sea, put a big weight round his body and jumped overboard. And scuttled the boat. That's what happened.'

Later in the conversation, however, he said:

I'm more of a friend of his after that than I was – though I haven't seen him – because if he wanted me to do something, I'd do it for him. Because he needs one and, like everyone else in life, I like to be needed. What's the use of a friend who, because you make one mistake, suddenly... I don't believe in that.

Understandably, this left Barber with the sense that Aspinall 'more than anyone held the key to the Lucan mystery'. His own friends admit that he would have helped Lucan escape, that temperamentally this would have appealed to him. Indeed one is reminded of a novel, Agatha Christie's *The Hollow*, in which members of a dangerously charming upper-class family, aware of who has committed murder and seeking to shield the person, embark upon a half-amused, half-serious campaign of misdirection. 'I recognized fairly soon', says Hercule Poirot to the leader of this campaign, 'that it was *your* ingenuity that I was fighting against, and that you were being aided and abetted by your relations as soon as they understood what you wanted done!' This sounds very much like the popular solution to the question of what happened to Lord Lucan after the murder. John Aspinall, says the myth, designed a web of mystification, of stiff-upper-lipped silence obfuscated by outbursts of rhetoric, and behind it lay the truth in which he took such secret, laughing delight. He had outwitted the flat footed police and the news-hungry press. He had saved the nobleman from the lower-class fate of Wormwood Scrubs and the dismal one of becoming crab-fodder in the English Channel. Like the daredevil he was, he had gambled for Lucky, and the pair of them had won. A last repayment, as it were, for the earl's inheritance that was squandered at the Clermont.

The belief in this scenario is enduring: extraordinarily so. 'Confirmatory' stories have occasionally emerged, such as the one offered by Aspinall's former secretary, Shirley Robey, in which she told of obtaining passports for the Lucan children so that their father could observe them in Africa. Rumours still persist that Lucan was flown out of England in a plane, possibly belonging to the racing driver Graham Hill (Ranson strongly suggests this in his book); that he was given plastic surgery; that he has been sighted here, there and in almost every country on earth. The circle had effected Lucan's escape and, such was their class loyalty, they had also bankrolled it. Perforce: how else was Lucan to live?

Muriel Spark wrote in *Aiding and Abetting*:

His source of cash was here in Britain. Nowadays, he came twice a year to collect it from his old friend, the rich Benny Rolfe [an invented character], who always, since Lucky's operation to change his features, had a fat package of money ready for him on his visits... Most of the cash came out of Benny's own pocket, but there was always a certain amount contributed by Lucan's other old friends and collected by Benny Rolfe.

'Aren't you disgusted, ever, by what I did?' Lucan had asked Benny on one of these occasions. 'Aren't any of you horrified? Because, when I look back on it, I'm horrified myself.'

'No, dear fellow, it was a bungle like any other bungle. You should never let a bungle weigh on your conscience.'

'But if I'd killed my wife?'

'That would not have been a bungle. You would not have been the unlucky one.'

'I think of Nanny Rivett. She had an awful lot of blood...'

Aiding and Abetting is a gorgeous novel, but it has little to do with what really happened. It is a fable; a meditation on evil, identity and, of course, class. Anybody who sees it in terms of reality will encounter, immediately, a problem with the notion of 'Benny Rolfe' collecting money from the Lucan circle. It is the same problem that undercuts the whole alluring myth: which is money.

Soon after Lucan's disappearance it was reported that he was carrying £100,000 in cash, a figure that two days later had dwindled to £20,000, and subsequently to zero.[24] As for his friends: although they have been excitably portrayed as 'rich and powerful forces', which frankly sounds like something from a sub-Bond film script, the truth, as would later be said, is that they 'had no real links with power'.[25] It is also true that most of them were flat broke. Few people had much money in 1974, but these men had been cleaned out by Aspinall, who himself lost pretty much everything he had taken from them in the 1973 stock market crash. Altogether they could probably have spared enough to maintain Lucan on the run for about a fortnight. To take the most extreme example: Ian Maxwell-Scott, who left the Clermont in 1974, would soon have his house sold by mortgagees and be living off state benefits. For Aspinall to say, as he did, 'I had many people calling me and saying, if Lucan wants money, he can have it', was yet another tease. It flattered Lucan by implying that he could command faithful friendship; but it was also insidiously damning, designed to press the buttons that set off class prejudice. Who *were* these people, anyway, who had money to spare? Bill Shand Kydd was rich, but he wanted nothing to do with any lawless flights from justice. Nor did any of the other sensible, highly respectable figures in Lucan's life: his uncle John Bevan, his best man John Wilbraham, his old schoolfriend and the like. Later these people bought back some of Lucan's auctioned silver and contributed generously to his daughters' education. That was the way in which they showed their loyalty: to the children. The idea that they would have subsidized a criminal act is beyond belief, nor has it ever been suggested. Lucan did know some indestructibly rich people, like Selim Zilkha, Gordon White[26] and the Brady Tuckers. Again, however, one would have to be positively insane to suggest that anybody of that kind would have endowed a fugitive fund. Lucan also had a brother, Hugh, who moved to Johannesburg six months after the murder and who, not unlike Aspinall, has occasionally tantalized the press with contradictory remarks. 'There are lots of rumours and lots of outcomes,' he said in 2012, when asked about Lucan's fate. 'There are all sorts of possibilities and lots of things puzzle me but I am not sure I want to share them with anyone.' Yet Lucan's older sister Jane, who is in regular contact with Hugh, is still patently and movingly distressed by her ignorance of what happened to Lucan. The same was true of his younger sister, Sally Gibbs, who remained bewildered by these events until her death in 2002. The idea that Lucan lived in Africa, that Hugh suspected as much and said nothing to his sisters, is utterly ridiculous.

Therefore the focus is back on that wretched circle: the infamous lunchers.

How, then, was this new life of Lucan's to be financed? Not by a bunch of hedonistic paupers, that was for sure. Which means that one possibility remains: James Goldsmith. 'Men like Goldsmith and Aspinall saw themselves as outlaws,' it was said, 'and the murder of Sandra Rivett gave them a rare chance to live out that fantasy.'[27]

In 1997, when Goldsmith was safely dead, David Gerring let loose with a near-obsessive belief that 'the Golden Man', as he called him, had been the money behind Lucan's alleged escape.

> I don't believe he would have been involved in the nitty-gritty: he was too clever to have put Lucan on to a boat across the Channel himself. But I do believe he was involved in the planning from a safe distance. Think about it; Lucan has just committed murder, so who does he go to? His friends. They see he is in no fit state to organise his own escape, so they do it for him. He had many influential friends and Goldsmith was among the most influential and wealthy.[28]

A few years later, Gerring would go further. By this time he was landlord of a pub in Kent, and he sounds downright intoxicated in conversation with the author and former playboy Jeremy Scott, who was writing a book about what happened to Lucan after the murder. 'That wouldn't be clever,' Gerring warned. '*You can't upset the Golden Man.*' He then made a vague allegation that Lucan, having been helped in his escape, had become so much of a nuisance that he himself was murdered. 'If one of their mates gets into trouble they help him. The *once*! But if he then gets to be an embarrassment *they have him taken care of*, know what I mean?'[29] The belief that Lucan was shot dead, even possibly in the driveway of the Maxwell-Scott home, is still given some credence, supremely idiotic though it is.

Having formerly praised Goldsmith for his 'helpfulness', Gerring later said that he had avoided an interview for some weeks, and that when he finally spoke it was only to reveal 'name, rank and number'.

It is perfectly true that Aspinall expressed the desire to put Lucan beyond the reach of justice, and that Goldsmith had the means to effect this. The only question, and one that never seems to have been asked by those who believe in Goldsmith's involvement, is *why* he would have done such a thing. Does not a man with a business empire, plus a deeply engrossing love life, have more pressing matters to deal with than paying hush money to Lord Lucan's plastic surgeon?

'They had', Gerring patiently explained, 'this weird idea about being superior beings. The law did not apply to them. Like most of Lucan's friends, they gave the impression that we were making a lot of fuss about nothing. Sandra Rivett was only a nanny, after all. But Lucan, with his aristocratic background, was one of them. They would not have deserted him.'

To which one yearns to say: change the record, Dave. His argument, in sum, was that James Goldsmith, a wildly successful tycoon with ambitions to become a newspaper proprietor and acquire a knighthood, engaged upon a fraught and expensive enterprise that could have landed him in jail because he believed that Lucan was a superior being.

'The idea that Goldsmith would have risked his freedom in that way...' says a contemptuous Daniel Meinertzhagen. 'Ridiculous. He guaranteed one loan. That was it.'

'Neither Jimmy nor I at any time believed he was still alive,' his wife Lady Annabel would later write.[30]

In fact the two men were not even particularly close. Goldsmith spoke loyally about Lucan at the *Private Eye* court case in 1976, saying that they used to see each other relatively seldom, but adding: 'I do not want to look as though I am in any way reneging on Lord Lucan. I was a friend and I am sorry...' They *were* friends, and spent time together when Goldsmith was keeping 'open house' (as in the Mexico holiday, photographs from which later appeared in the *Sunday Times Magazine*). But they belonged to fundamentally different worlds: one was defined by ambition, the other by inanition. Goldsmith was not attracted by losers, which Lucan, superior being or not, had clearly become. He lived close to the edge, both in business and in private, but his daring was directional: he did it to make money, to pull a beautiful woman. He didn't need to get his thrills from aiding and abetting. And, as Meinertzhagen says, he would never have taken this particular risk. He had far too much to lose. The truth, very simply, is that he was a highly convenient figure to the myth. He was a hated figure among much of the press. His almost mystical wealth made him credible casting for the police in the role of Lucan's devilish fairy godfather. It was nonsense; just as it is nonsense to suggest that a popular, well-known man like Graham Hill would have risked his career to fly Lucan out of the country; or that children who were wards of court would have been mysteriously transported to Africa so that their father could watch them at a distance.

In fact, almost everything that has been written about the circle is nonsense. 'There was no such thing as the Lucan circle,' Goldsmith told the court during his libel action. He was probably pretty much right.

Yet the idea touched upon prejudice in a way that still resonates. It is prejudice, really, that has sustained belief in Lucan's great escape. That is what people like him do, and what people like his friends help him do. And there is a folkloric power, a literary allure, in the myth of the earl who moves like an ageing lion among the empty spaces of Botswana, drinking vodka martinis in bars shuttered against the sunlight, dreaming of the white island of Belgravia, his life vanished but his demeanour still tremulously in place. Could it really, by some magical means as yet unknown, have happened that way?

The girlfriend of one of the set says:

One read the rumours that he was spirited away. This thing that the friends were holding something back... I can't *believe* we wouldn't know by now. Someone would have talked. Particularly someone like Dominick Elwes. Charles Benson blurted *everything* out. I don't think there's any way that the secret would have been kept all these years. Someone would have spilled the beans by now. They were such big mouths!

There was another question: that of *time*. Remembering that this was not what was meant to happen, that if Lucan had indeed intended to kill he had also intended to make a success of it, nobody was expecting to have to construct a masterly off-the-cuff stratagem to deal with his failure. It was just before 10pm on the night of 7 November when Lucan left his house, and 10.05pm when the police arrived. From that time onwards, he was on the run. To get away was one thing, but to do so as instantly and definitively as Lucan did, if he did, was another thing altogether.

This is where Susan Maxwell-Scott, decidedly not a big mouth, re-enters the picture. An obvious implication of her silence through 8 November, her steadfast wait to be contacted by the police, is that she was allowing Lucan time to formulate his plans. She was giving him a day's grace.

In 1995 newspapers carried the story of a former babysitter for the Maxwell-Scotts, Mandy Parks, who claimed to have seen Lucan drinking with her employers in the early evening of the 8th. Suit-cases were in the hall at Grants Hill House. Lucan was wearing a blue suit that presumably belonged to Ian. It is unclear why Mrs Parks did not come forward at the time. 'It's not my place to question people like them,' she said, twenty-one years later, 'but it's not right that the truth should not come out.'[31] David Gerring's reaction was to restate his belief that Susan had kept something back. 'The car went to Newhaven,' he said, 'but Lucan didn't. It was a decoy to put us off the scent.'[32]

The Maxwell-Scotts' former nanny, who by the time of Lucan's disappearance had left the job, raises a practical objection to Mrs Parks's story. In 1974, four of Susan's six children were at boarding school. 'I doubt she would have needed a babysitter just for the others,' says the nanny.[33]

The Maxwell–Scotts' driver says:

> Why would they have a babysitter? I can't tell you that there wasn't someone, but it rings no bells. If she was female I'd have known her. Well, it wasn't a very big town. She wasn't stupid, Susan – she wouldn't let him stay there and let the babysitter see him. She was a very intelligent lady. How the police managed to get as much as they did out of her, I don't know. I know she didn't tell them the truth in the first place.

The driver has more to say on the subject of Lucan: an entirely new story, in fact, as to what happened in the early hours of 8 November. At this time his family ran the taxi firm that 'did the whole of Uckfield. Mother ran the taxi business from her shop. My father drove Aspinall – London mafia, I'd say he was. Dad used to carry the royal family, Vivien Leigh, loads of celebrities. 1968 I started, until 1976. I drove the royal family at seventeen, and I remember Princess Margaret because she gave me a cigarette. We all had security clearance. So we didn't talk about things.'

Part of what they did not talk about, until now, is information that the driver says was told to him by his father in 1987. 'He's dead so it can't hurt him now. They're all dead, so it can't do any harm. And I know it's true, because he told me some other things that I was shocked by. He was a bad man, my father. It's because we were sitting there doing nothing, and he told me lots. Why would he lie to me?'

According to the driver, his father said that in the early hours of 8 November he received a call to go to the Maxwell–Scott house. He then picked up Lord Lucan and drove him to Kent.

> There's a little airfield near Headcorn. He didn't actually say he went to an airfield – just near to Headcorn. In one of our cars. He never

said what time this was. Some nights he didn't come home anyway, so my mother would never have questioned anything.

I think Dad said Lucan went to France – which to me is logical, because I don't think you'd do it in one go. France, Spain, Africa. He had no passport. You've got to remember there was smuggling all the time, though that was usually Essex. But Kent's not far across at all.

Lucan got cleaned up, changed his clothes – had some of Ian's, though they were slightly large for him. That's what my Dad told me. And the gardener told me he got rid of Lucan's clothes.

The suggestion, of course, is that the clothes were bloody; which reopens all the old questions about the problematical forensic evidence.

The driver then claims that he himself received a call to go to Newhaven. '"A person" took that Ford Corsair to Newhaven, and I picked them up. I brought them to Uckfield. The next day, in the morning, in daylight.' Did this not seem an odd request? 'Why would I think it was odd – why would it be unusual somebody being in Newhaven? Why is anyone anywhere? That was what I did, I was a taxi.' The police, he says, never questioned him or his father.

How could you, if you were running the investigation, not ask the local taxis who were doing the work for the Maxwell-Scotts? The newspapers did. They came down, every weekend for about two months – I was quite happy to take their money off them and run them round. I was told to tell them any rubbish.

Now if the police had done a proper job, they would have been able to find out who Lucan rang – it was manual in those days, it's possible it went through an operator. Local you could dial – but if you wanted London... Uckfield was quite late with a phone system.

Anyway, Dad wouldn't have said anything to the police. You've got to remember a taxi cab was almost a sanctuary, a confessional. If we talked about what we did or what we didn't do, nobody would use us. They'd say to Dad, George, do us a favour... You can doubt me if you want to, but what I'm trying to tell you is that we all knew each other, and some things were acceptable and some things weren't. Why would we say anything? People weren't like that in those days. It was just part and parcel.

It is very difficult to know what to make of this story. The former driver has never tried to make money out of it, nor offered it to a newspaper. He has no obvious reason to invent what he says. Undoubtedly he did know the Maxwell-Scotts and some of their friends; details of their lives are identical to those given by the nanny. There are problems, however. The first is the thirteen-year time gap between his own alleged drive to Newhaven and the conversation with his father. He himself would have known, as soon as he read the papers, precisely why he was asked to pick up the 'person' from Newhaven. Even if he chose to say nothing to the police, why not discuss it with his mother, who passed on the order, or with his father?

To another question, why Susan herself did not drive Lucan to Kent and keep the plot in the family, as it were, he replies: 'I can't ever remember seeing Susan drive. I've been racking my brains – I never remember actually seeing her at the wheel of a car.'

There is also the problem of how, if Lucan did fly out from Headcorn, a plane was commandeered. 'Aspinall was the brains. You wouldn't know what he had.' True enough. He certainly had a country house in Kent. Nevertheless a private plane, which he did not have, not least because he was broke at the time, presented a huge logistical issue; particularly if one exonerates Goldsmith and Graham Hill from collusion, as common sense suggests that one should. And a further question arises. If Susan Maxwell-Scott had really been privy to some escape plan, why were the letters to Bill Shand Kydd allowed to carry the Uckfield postmark? Without that, nobody need ever have known that Lucan had visited Susan at all.

Lastly there remains the stubborn, and essentially unanswerable, question of money: how, once out of the country, Lucan was to live.

Although the driver's story hangs together in several ways, and he is a bright and amiable man, some of his theories on the case are harder to accept. He suggests, for instance, that the 'establishment' looked the other way with regard to Lucan, and did not actually want him brought to trial.

> When was the last peer of the realm convicted of murder? The establishment expected him to do the proper thing [in other words, kill himself]. That is what they wanted. The faceless ones, the ones who run this country. Ranson wouldn't have been in charge, there'd have been someone above him pulling the strings. Sussex police didn't want it. They didn't have the resources. If they wanted to find him they would have found him. He's probably in Africa.

Africa, the resting place of the myth. If Lucan did indeed make it to this particular place of safety, as the driver appears to suggest, then he and his friends had pulled off one last great winning coup; against the odds, and against the forces of justice.

Yet the driver then goes on to describe how, in the aftermath of Sandra Rivett's murder, the Maxwell-Scotts' life at Grants Hill House came quickly to an end. So too, by extension, did the life of the Clermont: of that world in its entirety.

'Everything stopped. People stopped coming. They went to Wales. Everything went downhill – the cars went, the house went, the friendships seemed to come to an end. I think it tore all their friendships apart. Everything went wrong after Lucan died.' Except, of course, that according to this story he did not die.

The probability remains that Lucan did die, on or soon after Friday 8 November.

In 1974 Roy Ranson said: 'I think he would rather die than let his children see him humiliated in court on a murder charge... I think the strain of murder on top of everything else has probably been too much for him. I think he may have parked the car and then got on board a ferry and thrown himself off halfway across the Channel.'

Twenty years later Ranson wrote an account of his search for
Lucan in Africa, in which he proclaimed his absolute conviction
that his quarry was alive. So had he really changed his mind about
Lucan's fate? Perhaps, perhaps not. It must have been great fun for
ex-policemen and journalists to go hunting in Gaborone, or Windhoek, or Maputo, or better yet in the Seychelles: a Lucan sighting
meant a bit of a jolly, a story to sell. As a former pressman wrote: 'I
spent three glorious weeks not finding him in Cape Town, magical
days and nights not finding him in the Black Mountains of Wales and
wonderful and successful short breaks not finding him in Macau,
either, or in Hong Kong or even in Green Turtle Cay in the Bahamas
where you can find anyone.' He also said, with a wise flippancy: 'The
game would be spoilt if he ever turned up.'[34] Lucan would now be
nearly eighty. But the family is long-lived, on the whole. He could
still, theoretically, be 'found'; only when a few more years have
passed will that faint possibility die.

Would he have wanted to live, or to die? That is the question. Those
who believe that he escaped cite his gambler mentality. He would not
have thrown in his hand, they say. He would have tried his luck.

Convincing though this ought to be, somehow it is not. Why?
Because Lucan was not that *kind* of gambler. His gambling, although
bold, was essentially an act of weakness, of evasion. It was an alternative to reality. It was also, of course, part of the earl's façade. In
1836 the Honourable Berkley Craven, who had lost £8,000 on the
Epsom Derby, shot himself like a gentleman rather than default on
his debt. That was the aristocratic exit route: the pistol, the glass
of whisky raised to one's forebears, the locked drawing room. For
Lucan, appallingly conscious of the tainted legacy that he was
bequeathing his children, facing a future that held only bankruptcy
and a murder charge, brought up hard at last against stony reality,
this was surely the natural way out. His life had gone wrong. He
had, as would be written of Edith Thompson, convicted of murder
in 1922, 'come to the place where dreams fail'.[35]

'Lucan was not an honourable man,' wrote Roy Ranson. But he

was Earl of Lucan still. It was all that he was; pretty much all that he had ever been. He may not have thought this consciously, but it was there in him, that mysterious sense of caste that had directed and misdirected his life. Psychologically, therefore, suicide is infinitely more likely to have been the chosen fate.

'I am sure he is dead,' Veronica said. 'My husband was a noble-man and he would behave in a noble way. That is why I call myself dowager, because I am a widow.'

Kait Lucan said, very simply: 'Everyone meets their Waterloo.'

The idea that Lucan was alive, said James Goldsmith, was 'absurd'.

'He is dead, you know,' says Daniel Meinertzhagen.

Victor Lownes, the man who took over the Clermont, says: 'He embarked on a cross-Channel ferry and jumped off. Oh yes, I'm sure. Lots of bodies don't get washed up. He was very recogniz-able. It would be very difficult to hide, looking as he did': a very valid point. It would have been like trying to hide the thoroughbred Shergar in a field of horses. Really, it could not be done.

Lucan's sister Jane says:

> At this point one just brushes off all the stories, and says oh, it's one more crazy — like the drunk Englishman in Goa [when Lucan was mistaken for the folk singer Barry Halpin]. As far as what happened to him, I don't know. In a way I can't imagine that he would commit suicide. Because his curiosity... I think he would have wanted to stay on so he could hear what was happening to his children. But he probably never did. There was the drink, of course — he was a heavy drinker. And a much heavier drinker at the end, when he was distressed.

'I've absolutely no idea if he died that night,' says Bill Shand Kydd, 'but I would have thought it likely. If a fisherman catches a body in their nets, they spike it — otherwise the whole catch is con-demned. They just put a boathook through it.'

'He had some drink with him, didn't he?' says Christina. 'And he got in the ferry and took a whole lot of pills and drank a bottle of whisky and dropped off the side – that's what we think. The police don't. All this rubbish about seeing him abroad...'

'There was certainly a lot of despair,' says Bill. 'And drink.'[36]

'Three of us swore an affidavit,' says Lucan's schoolfriend. 'I suppose it was eight or nine years after. Bill, me and another, saying that we believed, or we were convinced, that he was dead. Because he was so inquisitive, he loved to know what was going on. He couldn't have resisted getting in touch with someone. So I'm convinced, yes, that he went overboard.'

A problem remains: no body. Explanations for this are possible. If he had gone in the sea, he could have been spiked by a fisherman, eaten by crabs or, as Michael Stoop suggested, caught in the propellers of the ferry. As Victor Lownes says, not all corpses are washed up. 'When they dug the Channel Tunnel,' says Graham Forsyth, who does not espouse a belief in Lucan's mythical escape, 'they found lots of bodies down there, even from the war.' If he had gone into the undergrowth of the South Downs, the theory of Charles Benson, the body could have been natural prey to wild animals. Bones of other long-missing persons, including a judge, were found incidentally during the search for Lucan around Newhaven.

There is also a suggestion that Lucan drowned, went down with his boat, in the place where he had planned to dispose of his wife; possibly the Solent, or the River Hamble close by (which Forsyth believes to have been the intended site). Lucan had definitely sailed in those areas off Southampton, and knew the waters very well. The Solent has complicated tidal patterns; the Hamble, which is part-tidal, is extremely deep in parts. If he had indeed had the idea of sinking Veronica's body in a particular place, for which there is incidentally no proof at all, this meant two things. Firstly, Lucan knew of an area where a body could disappear. Secondly, he had access to a boat. There is no evidence whatsoever that he did, but this plot assuredly required it. If he then took over the plan and used it for himself, it means something else as well: that he did kill himself, but not on the morning of 8 November, at Newhaven.

Although there is psychological sense in the idea that Lucan died earlier rather than later, he himself wrote to Bill Shand Kydd that he would 'lie doggo'. Bill did not believe, when he received Lucan's letters, that he was dead. 'Oh lord no.' If, however, he had stayed for a day or so to see how the land lay, that would only have increased his certainty that there was no point in going on.

'Yes,' says his schoolfriend. 'It's possible that he waited. But I think he would have said, circumstantial evidence was such that he was in trouble, and he didn't want his children to go through their father being tried for murder.'

The problem with the Newhaven death is very simple: that this physically striking man was not more remarked upon, either during the half-mile walk to the sea, boarding the ferry, or taking out a boat. Although security was lax, one does come up against the sheer *noticeability* of Lucan. He might not have cared, if he was going to die; nevertheless the fact is that one would expect somebody to have seen him.

Against this are a couple of other indications. It was dark; it was very early; it may well have been raining. And there was the evidence of two trawlermen, who later reported a 'distinguished-looking gentleman' on the pier, who 'stuck out like a sore thumb'[37] and whom they thought was perhaps a customs officer or court official. Was this the one true sighting among the thousands of fakes, like the woman who claimed to have seen Agatha Christie in Harrogate in 1926, and whose true account was lost amid the theorizing folly?

There is also the question of who drove the Corsair to Newhaven. Lucan knew where it had been left, because he wrote the street name to Michael Stoop. He could, of course, have been given this information. But there is one fact that suggests, very clearly, that he went there himself. His letters to Stoop were written on a pad kept in the Corsair and posted in unstamped envelopes. In other words, Lucan wrote them in the car. Why would he have done this, if he had not driven himself away from the Maxwell-Scott house? If he had written to Stoop during the journey *towards* Uckfield, why not borrow stamps from Susan? Anyway his own words suggest a later hour. The letters to Bill Shand Kydd are not quite suicide notes; the letter to Stoop, the one that was read at the inquest, is hard to interpret as anything else. The tone is slightly different, as of somebody who has given up on everything except the club courtesies ('I won't bore you...') and the children for whom this had all happened. 'I no longer care except that my children should be protected.' If Lucan did spend several hours alone on the road to Newhaven, if he slept in the Corsair, awoke to the clammy interior and the sharp memories of what had happened, drank yet more alcohol and perhaps took more pills, the combination was already one from which it was impossible to be roused. If he were innocent, he knew that he would be accused. If he were guilty, then he had not only done a terrible thing, but he had done it in error. 'I said to the police,' says Daniel Meinertzhagen, 'I'm sure that nobody regrets what happened to Sandra more than Lord Lucan.'

It is possible that Lucan did hole up for a day or so before moving on elsewhere. Certainly this would be the definitive explanation of why no body was found near Newhaven. Yet the facts, so enigmatic in this case, so resistant to a pattern, nevertheless do point most firmly to Newhaven as the journey's end. Susan Maxwell-Scott, with her delaying tactics, and Michael Stoop, with his concealment of his whereabouts, may have believed that they were giving Lucan time to effect some sort of escape. The likelihood is that he simply wanted a few more hours in which not to be caught, so that he could die.

'If he'd had the guts to remain,' says Christina Shand Kydd, 'I don't think that they could have convicted him. They might have wanted to, but there were plenty of holes in it. The point was, if he'd stayed – it was all circumstantial, the evidence.' David Gerring admitted to concern at the time that, if Lucan returned, 'the rapscallion could get a split-points decision in court'. And it is quite true to say that, with regard to forensics, the evidence was inconclusive. The real case against him was, in essence, the same as it had been at the custody hearing: the word of his wife.

The fact that he ran away, rather than staying to put his word against hers, is of course entirely damning. Why run, if there truly was another side to this story? Christina says:

> Well, he answered that question in his letter to Bill ['*V. has demon-strated her hatred for me in the past and would do anything to see me accused.*'] He knew he wouldn't get justice. By that time I think Veronica had intimidated him to an extent that he just couldn't believe... You know, she always won. Always, always won, because she played the little girl lost card, and she could pull herself together if she had to. And he thought she'll say it was me, and the children will have to go through some ghastly court case.
>
> If he had come back he could never have had a fair trial. By that time the media and everybody had completely hanged him already. Some people say they would not have been able to try him, because of it. [Lawyers did, indeed, express this concern.]
>
> I can promise you, Veronica in the box would have been... [as convincing, is the unspoken implication, as she had been in the custody case]. And he would have looked so stern and cold – because he would have been so nervous and upset and things. I can quite see why he would run away, when I think about it.

Some of Lucan's friends, the so-called circle, did try to do their best for him thereafter. At the end of 1974 a firm of private detectives was hired in an attempt to clear his name. Kait Lucan hired Michael Eastham to do the same for her son at the inquest. None of this had any effect; in fact it backfired. These people, it seemed, would go to any lengths to defend an aristocratic murderer. They were bad losers.

Yet misgivings about the inquest were by no means confined to Lucan's supporters. A bill to limit the power of coroners' juries was introduced just a month later. Lucan was not, as is often said, the last person to be named guilty in a coroner's court; another man, Lee Ford of Brighton, was named as a murderer just a week later;

but the very public controversy of the Sandra Rivett verdict helped to bring this legal oddity to an end. The law finally changed in 1977.

It had been, says Christina, 'a farce'. 'You can't really have an inquest without a person, can you?' says the girlfriend of one of Lucan's set. Certainly the coroner, Gavin Thurston, had had a very difficult job. A trial remained a technical possibility, so there was the danger of prejudicing it. Veronica was neither 'compellable nor competent' to testify against her husband with regard to the murder. Yet the tradition that a witness could not be discredited in a coroner's court worked so much in Veronica's favour that it was, in itself, prejudicial to Lucan. In July 1975, as the debate about the powers of the courts continued, *The Times* published a letter from the Coroner's Society of England and Wales. This defended the conduct of the Sandra Rivett inquest, explaining that whereas at a trial the accused alone is allowed legal representation, at an inquest 'every person affected by the death may be legally represented'. Justice had to be 'accorded to all the persons who were interviewed or otherwise involved or named in connexion with [Sandra's] death'.

But in practice this had proved a near-impossibility. Because of the nature of the Lucan marriage, whose private battles raged on in the public sphere, Michael Eastham was unable to defend Lucan without attacking Veronica. His cross-examination of her was halted after two questions. In conference with the coroner, her counsel Bruce Coles said that it would be an intolerable infringement of Veronica's rights if she were subjected to verbal attack or innuendo in the witness box.

When Eastham asked Veronica if she had 'entertained feelings of hatred' for Lucan, and objections were instantly raised, he went on to cite the letter to Bill Shand Kydd, in which Lucan said that he was not the attacker but that Veronica was 'deliberately making it look as though he were'. Therefore, said Eastham, the relationship between the Lucans was pivotal. Exploring it would help the jury to decide whether Veronica's testimony 'is an honest recollection of Lady Lucan's, or whether it is a fabrication'.

The coroner, who disallowed this line of questioning, said in his summing-up:

> It is fairly clear from Lucan's letters that there is existing in the family animosity, tensions and matters which if heard could only be prejudicial [albeit only to Veronica]. They would cause pain to the persons concerned if aired. The airing of family tensions would not benefit this inquiry. If it could benefit this inquiry then I would have taken a different view. But simply to turn this into a forum for airing family tensions would be a wrong thing.

The judicious air with which this was said masked the fact that 'family tensions' were not, in this case, a frivolous froth of scandal: they were the stuff of the matter.

Eastham also submitted that the letter's reference to 'the dream of paranoia' needed elucidation. The coroner turned him down. Had Bill Shand Kydd been allowed to offer an explanation of the phrase, it would have led to revelations about Veronica's history of instability. This was alluded to only briefly. After a wrangle between counsels, Graham Forsyth attested that Kait Lucan had described Veronica as a 'manic depressive'. Then Kait herself recounted telling Christina Shand Kydd that Veronica was in hospital, to which Christina asked if her sister had 'attempted to kill herself again'. The implication of previous suicide bids,[38] about which no details are in the public arena, drew an objection from Veronica's counsel. He asked that the press should not report what Kait had said, but of course the remark appeared anyway. Bill Shand Kydd also referred to suicide attempts, and again questioning was halted. Sensitive though this undoubtedly was, it was a highly relevant line of inquiry. As a commentator would later write: 'A suspect could not probe the credibility of his accuser, a basic right of English justice.'[39]

Meanwhile Lucan's witnesses were attacked repeatedly, in particular his mother and Susan Maxwell-Scott, so the 'tradition' of not discrediting them was clearly one that could be overlooked as and when. Furthermore, while Eastham represented the Lucan camp, Veronica effectively had two counsels on her side: her own man, Bruce Coles, and Brian Watling for the police.

The coroner was an experienced man, but not a worldly one. He had led the inquest into the death of the boxer Freddie Mills, who was shot through the eye in 1965, and had failed to address the fraught issue of Mills's gangland connections. A verdict of suicide was brought in, but it has always been disputed. Doubtless the verdict was a convenient one. As much as anything, Gavin Thurston was a man who did what was expected of him.

The jury was less amenable. On the third day of the inquest, the foreman said: 'We heard about Lady Lucan going to the barman at the Plumbers Arms and saying to him, "He has murdered my nanny." How did she know the nanny had been murdered?'

It was a damn good question; a better one than the coroner had been prepared to answer. 'Quite right,' he said, as to a particularly bright pupil. Later, after a private conference, he told the jury that they should not speculate as to why this was said. 'The difficulty is that in law Lady Lucan is barred from giving evidence other than that concerning an assault.'

Although the inquest was prevented from offering enlightenment, the jury's question had in fact been answered, very publicly, some five months earlier. Veronica gave a long interview to the *Daily Express*; or, as David Gerring put it, broke her 'dignified silence'. Although the article was assiduous in not mentioning Lucan's name, this was of course meaningless. It pictured Veronica standing in the breakfast room 'at the spot where Sandra's body lay'. During the interview, which according to Gerring must have been hated by Lucan's supporters because Veronica came across so wonderfully, she described how she had asked her assailant: 'Where is my nanny?' The reply came: 'She is dead.' The question of whether this newspaper article was prejudicial never arose.

'He wouldn't have told her,' says Christina. 'Nobody would, would they? They wouldn't admit to it. So how did she know? She never went into the basement!'

Incidentally, the assertion that Lucan told Veronica of Sandra's death is in direct contravention of Susan Maxwell-Scott's evidence. This stated the complete opposite: that it was Veronica who told Lucan. 'She told him', said Susan, 'that the man had killed the nanny and had attacked her.'

Lucan's alleged confession to murder was deemed inadmissible at the coroner's court; quite rightly, since it was wholly uncorroborated. Clearly there were other possible answers to the jury's question. Veronica could, for example, have gone into the basement and seen Sandra's body. Yet despite the blood on her shoes, it was gospel that she had never done so. 'If the blood came about through walking in the basement that would not be compatible with what Lady Lucan has told us,' said the coroner, firmly. In his final address to the jury, he maintained his air of supreme fairness as he outlined the case against Lucan, as told to the police by Veronica, as enshrined in myth ever since.

> You have seen Lady Lucan for yourself. You have had her sitting there in the witness box for over two hours. You have heard her give evidence. You have had the advantage of seeing her for yourself and of observing her demeanour, of the way she answered questions. She answered very carefully and gave each question a great deal of consideration.
>
> As regards motive, there is the question of Lord Lucan's financial situation. There is no doubt that, as a result of the separation, he was having to keep two establishments with all their outgoings. It could have eased his financial situation if he had only one establishment instead of two. [He was also] obsessed with his children.

The coroner then moved on to Lucan's behaviour towards his wife after the attack. 'If – as Lord Lucan says – he was only trying to help his wife and give her succour – why did she then run out into the street screaming "Murder! Murder!"? What is an instinctive reaction for someone in that situation? Would an instinctive reaction be to do what the barman of the Plumbers Arms did, when he telephoned at once for an ambulance and the police?' In fact, as Mr Whitehouse testified, he had not done this 'at once'. First he had acted exactly as Lucan did: he laid Veronica down and fetched a cloth for her wounds.

'The circumstances are quite clear,' the address concluded. 'If you are satisfied on the evidence that you have heard that there was an attack by another person, then your verdict will have to be murder. And you've got to decide on the evidence whether you can name the person responsible.'

The jury was out for thirty-one minutes. The guilty verdict came at 11.45am on Thursday 19 June. One has to think that Lucan did, perhaps, do the right thing in running away.

The witnesses emerged into the sunshine of Horseferry Road, where huge crowds had gathered, and some of them spoke briefly to the press. Susan Maxwell-Scott said she believed 'implicitly' in Lucan's story. Christina also asserted his innocence. Kait Lucan, holding Bill's arm, remarked in characteristic fashion: 'No comment. It is a useful phrase and I shall be having a record made of it.'

'I don't know that my mother allowed herself to think too deeply about it,' says Jane now. 'Although I say that, she must have, because she was a very thoughtful person.'

Kait's son-in-law, William Gibbs, said: 'This is not British justice. To me, it is frightening and amazing that a man can be named in court as a murderer without the jury hearing all the relevant evidence, and without being given a chance to defend himself.'

'It was certainly true', wrote a later commentator, 'that the verdict represented a breathtaking breach of contemporary legal etiquette.'[40] A great deal of evidence had been suppressed or obfuscated. The inquiry was innately flawed. At the time, Roy Ranson remarked that Lucan had only to have turned up, and 'I would have been delighted to have given him the full trial that his supporters were demanding.'

But the inquest had been tainted with prejudice, the prejudice that is so hard to avoid, that once worked so gruesomely in favour of murderous earls, and that had now swung so firmly to the other side: being an earl was the worst thing that Lucan could possibly have been. As for his supporters: 'On that professional stage they were made to appear selfish, heartless, antediluvian, dangerously close to being unworthy of respect, dangerously close to being ridiculous.'[41] The prejudice flooded over Lucan's family, his mother and sisters, as well as his friends. There was nothing to be done about it. Prejudice has its own logic, against which no argument is possible.

Now that a form of justice had been done, the wreckage of lives was horribly apparent. Sandra's mother said: 'I have prayed for three days and three nights that this would be the verdict', but the comfort must still have been cold as ice. She and her husband returned to Stephen, who the following year would discover that Sandra was not his sister but his mother, and that she had been horribly murdered. It seems peculiarly spiteful that compensation was not awarded by the Criminal Injuries Board, for his sake at least.

After the change in law limiting the powers of coroners' juries, Kait Lucan tried very hard to have the verdict on her son retrospectively removed, but failed. From the age of seventy-five, until her death in 1985, she had not a clue of what had happened to him. Like almost all the people who had been close to Lucan, she would suffer grievously for having known him. Lucan had escaped, but they never would. Only John Aspinall and James Goldsmith dealt with the taint of the case, as tough people can, and sailed on to greater fortune, rather as the 3rd Earl of Lucan and the 7th Earl of Cardigan had done after the Charge of the Light Brigade.

Outside the inquest, Veronica's solicitor spoke on her behalf. He said that she was 'neither pleased nor displeased with the verdict', but had been 'only concerned with establishing the facts'. Now she hoped to 'continue to lead a family life'. The irony is that just a few years later she did lose her children.

'My husband knew I'd won,' Veronica later said. Certainly if Lucan had indeed intended to destroy her, what actually happened is that she destroyed him. 'He was a bad sport. I'd won. He knew when I escaped and ran down the road: "She's won."' That, she suggested, was why Lucan wrote the letter to Bill Shand Kydd, expressing the desire that he should have care of the children. It was his final attempt at revenge. 'He didn't like being beaten by a woman. Even at the last moment he undermined me.'[42]

After Lucan's disappearance, his sister Jane sought to maintain contact with her nieces and nephew.

> We would go, and try and be civil, you know, call Veronica and say will you come and have a cup of tea, or something. And we did, a couple of times, my husband and I. And my brother Hugh... Hugh almost befriended her, in a way. Not necessarily because he thought that she was guiltless, but I think he just felt very sorry for her. And she maybe thought that he was safe.
>
> We went once to a club – Hurlingham, I think. My family, Veronica and her children. The idea was the children would swim and play tennis together. It was as it always was... Very awkward.

In 1976 the trustees sold 46 Lower Belgrave Street for £42,000. This now seems an unbelievable sum. 'Wicked,' Veronica later said. 'It was worth far more than that.' Quite true. It was worth at least £100,000; although perhaps not everybody would have wanted to live there.[43] Veronica and the children moved to the Eaton Row mews, where Jane visited, although she says: 'Many many times, you would call and you couldn't get... Like the children, they would knock on the door, and no answer. Veronica was incommunicado, a lot of the time.'

In 1980 Veronica gave an interview in which she claimed that she had 'been shunned by her husband's former friends and [was] estranged from her mother and sister'. She also said that 'family and former friends have tried to have her committed to a mental home'.[44] She was again receiving treatment, and by 1982 the Shand Kydds had assumed *de facto* care of the children. 'They were pretty well living with us,' says Christina. 'We were beginning to look after them. Frances was older, of course [eighteen, with a place at Bristol University]. And they were very, very loyal to their mother. Very protective of her.' Discussing this subject with a journalist in 1998, Veronica would say: 'I was very hurt when my son aged fifteen said he preferred to live with his uncle's family rather than me. I don't think George or my elder daughter Frances was ever very keen on me.'[45]

In 1983, Veronica was found wandering in Belgravia and taken to hospital.[46] 'There were reports of seeing her pretty wild, walking round Eaton Square,' says Jane. She spent seven months in a mental institution at Banstead Hospital in Surrey. Christina visited twice a week, but Veronica refused to see the children if they came to Banstead chaperoned by her sister. From that point, the loss of their custody was inevitable, and this was formally awarded in 1984. 'It was hard work,' says Bill. 'But we got there eventually.'

In 1986 Veronica gave an interview, stating that she had gone to Banstead for a rest: 'I am not undergoing psychiatric therapy.'[47] Twelve years later she spoke more openly about her stay. She contrasted the behaviour of her children with that of 'lots of other mothers who'd been involuntarily addicted to prescribed drugs, as I had been, and who visited them nonetheless'.

> I just used to think, 'What have I done? Where did I go wrong?' These children were younger than my children. They gave up long evenings to stay with their mothers in this ghastly Victorian place with no television, just to get them better. I was so frightened and alone. Not one word... they were going to get rid of me in that place, believe me.[48]

Later, again in reference to her children, she said: 'They were carted off to bum off some rich relations. That's a vulgar way of putting it but that more or less sums it up.'[49]

In fact, as George would make clear, the children tried many times to contact Veronica after the stay at Banstead, but by her own admission she was not inclined to forgive the fact that they had gone to a stable life with the Shand Kydds (whose home they already knew very well, from prolonged previous stays). In 1984 it was reported that although Christina regularly visited Eaton Row, and kept in touch with the police station at Gerald Road, Veronica remained unreachable. 'All attempts by the family of the Countess of Lucan to maintain contact are being shunned and when her younger daughter, Lady Camilla Bingham, 14, went to see her mother during the last school holidays, she was told from an upstairs window: "Go away, I'm busy."'[50]

In an interview in 1998, Veronica said:

They had to suffer for what they'd done. It would have been wrong to let them turn up whenever they felt like it saying 'We're off to France next weekend... I've just passed sixteen examinations into Oxford and I'm terribly bright!' and you've got to say 'How clever you are' and sit back with no role, nothing. You would be foolish to put yourself in such a situation and it's better for them to know that I'm a strong person.

The article in which these words appeared stated that Veronica had

never recovered from the loss of her children, Frances, George and Camilla. Custody was transferred from her to the Shand Kydds, fulfilling her husband's wish, in 1982. To Lady Lucan, it was the ultimate betrayal. But the whispers about her mental condition started by her husband have persisted and, she believes, have been used by his supporters to 'write her out of the picture' and undermine her evidence that he was the killer...

Her anger towards her son was sealed in 1994, as the twentieth anniversary of the murder approached. Two books, written by the investigating officers, were published and there were three television programmes and a radio play. 'People who were interviewed were personally abusive of me. One said "She wasn't fit to be a mother." Through all that agony in 1994 I had no support, not even a lawyer.

It was appalling, but there was nobody to protect me or stand up for me. My son, if he had called himself Earl Lucan, which he could have in 1992, as his father was presumed deceased in 1992, could have said these people were writing trash. Why didn't he say, "Even though I haven't been close to her for a number of years she was a very good mother before that"? Even if he didn't think so. After all, as a boy of 15 you may be made to do things which you feel are not quite right, but as a man of 30-odd there's no excuse for it.'[51]

'George had once just seen her in the street,' says Jane. This was in 1995, when George was twenty-eight, had taken his degree at Cambridge, and was working as a banker. 'And they walked around for a bit, and then she said goodbye and I'll probably never see you again.' Of this meeting Veronica would later say. 'I thought "How sad that nothing of his father had been transmitted to him." I had hoped that I would see or hear his father again. But his father had gone.'[52]

In 1998 Veronica was seen outside St Peter's Church in Eaton Square on the day of her younger daughter Camilla's marriage. It was reported that she had not been invited, although Christina made it clear that she had. 'No, I was not invited to Camilla's wedding whatever anyone may say,' Veronica told a journalist, while admitting that Camilla, who later became a QC, had written on the occasion of her engagement.

> She may have a double first in classics from Oxford but she certainly hasn't got any manners. I think it's absolutely disgraceful behaviour not to invite me. But then what do you expect, having been brought up by those people?

'Sometimes I feel', she said, 'that nothing more can happen to hurt me.'[53]

The following year it was reported that Veronica planned to sue her son. She told the press that he had removed family documents and photographs from her home while she was in Banstead, and that some of the photographs had been sold to a newspaper (including one taken by Veronica herself: 'My son is using my intellectual property'). George had also stated that he believed Lucan to be innocent of murder, which according to his mother was defamatory in the light of the evidence that she had given at the inquest. She did not want to see her children, she said, because she feared that they would persuade her to change her account of the events of 7 November 1974.

> I don't trust them. I don't want to hear that I am a liar or a bad mother. If I was a bad mother, too bad. I am so disgusted with them that I feel ashamed to be their mother. To be loyal to your own family is paramount. To be loyal to another family is despicable, especially as they know how I had suffered. I am not sentimental about children. They are just a hotchpotch of genes: me, my ancestors and him [Lucan] and his ancestors. I am just the birth mother. I have no feelings of wanting to see them.[54]

Yet upon Lucan himself, who by her own account had tried to kill her, Veronica bestowed a kind of absolution. Her feelings towards him were kindly, if anything. 'There was no bitterness on my side. I have always called it a tragedy, a misunderstanding.'[55] At times she could describe him with something like adoration. 'A very good-looking man,' she said, referring to a photograph that she had offered to the press. 'Look at the way his collar fits – perfection.'[56] Throughout their marriage Veronica had sought to turn a sense of inferiority into dominance, and had done so with extraordinary success. But the pride in having married him remained. Lucan's portrait by Dominick Elwes,[57] the paintings of his ancestors Lavinia Bingham and the 3rd Earl, the backgammon cups that he won at the Clermont, were still in her house. She still wore her wedding ring. 'Even now', she said, 'I have a feeling of devotion to him in some way.'[58]

She also said, in a long interview given in 1981: 'Three years ago I woke in the night with the conviction that he was in my bed with me... I could feel his physical presence beside me, and I was suddenly full of happiness.

"Everything will be all right now you're back," I told him. "I've missed you so much."'[59]

'She always said she still loved him,' says Christina. 'And she has always said, in all those strange outbursts, that she would have stood by him.'

After Lucan's disappearance, the force of Veronica's anger was directed, not at the husband for whom she felt such a complexity of emotion, but at those around him; in particular the sister who fulfilled his wishes for their children. 'It is easy', she said, 'to forgive someone who can no longer torment you, but it is not so easy to forgive people who are still a threat to you.'[60]

'It sounds very strange,' says Christina. 'But I am, in my way, still extremely fond of her. And I really do believe that she did love the children.'

'You have to give her some credit for those children,' says Lucan's schoolfriend. 'They're wonderful, all of them. They're a very good lot.'

'It is totally extraordinary, I always felt, how they turned out,' says Jane. 'I just wish John knew.'

Solutions

'I have known crimes that were artistic – they were, you understand, supreme exercises of imagination. But the solving of them – no, it is not the creative power that is needed. What is required is a passion for truth.'

AGATHA CHRISTIE, *The Hollow*, 1946

BUT IMAGINE THAT Lord Lucan did get away by plane from the airfield at Headcorn, and that by some means he lived on. The facts are against it, but it *could* be true. Imagine that for reasons of cowardice or daring he had thought it preferable to continue, despite exile from his country, habits, rituals, friends, family, children. That it was still possible to be oneself, even though one's self no longer existed. That one would be able to live half one's years as a half-life, a kind of unending *purgatorio*. At first there would have been the thrill of escape, the anxiety of the fugitive. Then perhaps a sense of freedom that is beyond our comprehension.

Imagine, too, a scene in which somebody entered the dusty bar in Gaborone, with the shutters against the heat, fell into conversation with a remote, patrician, elderly ex-pat, and by degrees realized who he was. Imagine that during the course of an evening this person, this old Englishman, conceived the desire to do the thing that was most forbidden to him: talk. Imagine that he felt compelled to empty his head, to tell his side of the story, while he still could. This, of course, is the fundamental allure of the belief that Lucan is alive. He could tell us *what really happened*.

The Lucan story is about many things: class, marriage, lies, prejudice. But even to call it a 'story' is misleading. There is no one story in this case. Instead there are versions, theories, myths. It is a case that breeds stories, and these have acquired more substance than the elusive thread of actuality, which imagination grasps and loses by turns.

Only two people know what happened on the night of 7–8 November 1974, and only one of those people has been heard. Veronica Lucan has told her story. It is officially accepted as the truth, although the contradictions within it have led to variations upon its essential theme; yet it is in fact only one side of the story, just as it was only one side of the custody hearing, and indeed almost everything else to do with the Lucan marriage. Truth requires that the other side is also heard. Otherwise the solution, however much of truth it contains, can only ever exist in the realm of fiction.

There is, of course, the version that Lucan offered at the time, about the fight seen through the blinds in the basement, the man who ran off into the night. But even he would admit that this is insufficient. Again, although it may hold something of the truth, it remains a story. So what would Lord Lucan say, if somebody were there to listen to it all? What images would be inside his head? Most are unknowable. A few are not. There would, for instance, be a memory of Belgravia, which on the night of 7 November is a discon certing place: the unnatural stillness, the spacious empty streets, the great stucco houses that loom like icebergs, with the cold and unforgiving separateness of wealth. Black sky slanted with watery floodlights; white shapes fretted with black porticos, punctuated by narrow black cobbled mews, gaping with dead black windows. A soft, shadowy, chiaroscuro gleam as he approached Lower Belgrave Street, like walking through a giant silent film. And then?

The unsolved, or even partly solved, murder case holds this painful fascination: one will never know for certain what really happened. Nevertheless, and despite the near-certain knowledge that Lucan has been dead for forty years and thus can never tell his story, it should still be possible to do as the fictional detectives do. If there is a story into which all the facts fit, then logically this is *not a fiction*

In real life, of course, facts are not immutable. They slip and slide like eels. 'We want proofs. We want facts. How? How? How?' says Lord Peter Wimsey; and he gets them, because the genre demands it.

The facts in this case are remarkably few. The identity of the assailant is assumed to be known, but is actually unproven. The weapon is assumed, but not definitely stated, to have been the length of piping found at the house. The extent and accuracy of the forensic evidence is very far from certain. The timings of events are imprecise, because the statements of Veronica and her daughter contradict each other.

Their statements can, however, be conflated to form a timeframe, thus:

> At some point between 8.35pm and 8.55pm, Sandra Rivett went downstairs at 46 Lower Belgrave Street and entered the basement.
>
> At some point between around 8.50pm and 9.15pm, Veronica Lucan went downstairs.
>
> At some time after 8.35pm, Sandra was killed in the basement.
>
> At some time after 8.50pm, Veronica received blows to the head, delivered in the area between the ground-floor cloakroom and the basement stairs.
>
> At some point before 9.05pm, Lord Lucan entered the house.
>
> At 9.50pm, Veronica Lucan entered the Plumbers Arms: this is corroborated by the barman in the pub.

There is then the conflicting testimony from the Lucans, thus:

> Lord Lucan told a story of passing the house, seeing his wife being attacked in the basement, and going in to interrupt the fight. He ran into the basement. His wife's assailant ran away. His wife accused him of hiring a hitman, and told him that Sandra had been murdered.

Veronica Lucan told a story of going to find Sandra, hearing a noise in the cloakroom and being attacked at the top of the basement stairs. The assailant was her husband. He told her that Sandra had been murdered.

There is also the evidence at the house:

Blood from Veronica's A group was found in the kitchen and on the mailsack containing Sandra's body.

Blood from Sandra's B group was found on Veronica's shoes and on the back of her skirt.

Blood from Sandra's B group was found in the back garden.

Blood from A and B group was found on the piping, in the cloak-room, and on both the driver and passenger sides of the Ford Corsair abandoned at Newhaven.

The door to the garden was found unlocked.

The chain on the front door was left off that night.

From which the following possible inferences can be made:

Sandra Rivett was killed before Veronica Lucan was attacked.

Veronica Lucan entered the basement. This has been denied so vigorously that it cannot be stated as fact. Nevertheless there is evidence to imply it. There are two obvious possibilities: first, that the attack on Veronica began in the basement, where she stepped in Sandra's blood and left small amounts of her own; and that it continued as she ran up the stairs, making contact with Sandra's blood on the stair wall, spraying her own blood on the wall above the third step. The second possibility is that Veronica went downstairs *after* she herself was attacked, with or without the assailant. In *The Times* on 9 November, and again on 11 November, it was stated that the killer of Sandra Rivett had been discovered by Veronica in the basement. 'Police have been told that Lady

Lucan disturbed a man as he was attempting to carry Mrs Rivett's body from the basement to a waiting car.' It is unclear where this rather precise image came from; but it suggested that Veronica *had* gone into the basement, and the attack upon her had begun there. On 14 November, the *Daily Express* reported Veronica as having participated in a 'reconstruction' of the crime in the presence of detectives. The article, written by a journalist who was particularly close to the police, described the attack on Veronica as having begun 'halfway down the basement steps': not in the ante-room.

Somebody unlocked the back door, went into the garden and dripped Sandra's blood. There is a faint possibility that, as the police said, the door could have been left unlocked inadvertently; also that the blood in the garden could have been transferred accidentally, although dripping implies that it came from a heavily bloodied source.

Lord Lucan entered the house, either because he was passing and saw something through the basement window; or because he was intent on murder; or for some other reason that is unknown.

So much that is unknown; one is cast adrift from the consolations of fictional omniscience. Nevertheless it is possible to assemble theories, facts and suspects in a metaphorical library, and test them.

> *'The crime was not committed so –*
> *M. Poirot must know that perfectly well.'*
>
> AGATHA CHRISTIE, *Murder on the Orient Express*, 1934

The first theory is that the attacks on Sandra Rivett and Veronica Lucan were incidental. What had been attempted at 46 Lower Belgrave Street was not murder but burglary, possibly arranged by Lord Lucan.

This seems psychologically bloodless, in the face of all the passionate motives that were flying around: it is rather like the suggestion by

Hercule Poirot that the murder on the Orient Express was committed by an outsider, a character who does not appear in the book, a nameless assassin who skipped on to the train disguised in a *wagon-lit* uniform. This is *solutionus interruptus*. It lacks the catharsis of true resolution. But it could have happened that way. Sometimes a solution is not an epiphany.

Similarly, when one comes down to cool-headed fact, it must be said that what Lord Lucan needed more than anything in the world was money. Veronica herself would later say that his motivation was 'purely financial':

> He decided that he was about to go bankrupt and he had to save the reputation of the family. The only way he could do that was either to win a terrific amount at the tables – which obviously he couldn't – or to get hold of the house and sell it as fast as he could. Since I was firmly in place at the house he had to get rid of me. It was a calculated act. There was no personal feeling involved.[1]

It is quite true that Veronica was immovably stationed at 46 Lower Belgrave Street. Could Lucan have told the courts that he needed to sell the house? The former lawyer, who commented on the custody case, says: 'He had the right to ask. He couldn't force it. Because she is resident in the house. They would look at the overall finances of the family, and say is the house in Belgravia of disproportionate value in the circumstances? It's simple arithmetic.'

The fact that Lower Belgrave Street had been handed unquestioningly to Veronica, as if it were her inalienable right to live in a six-storey house off Eaton Square, would have caused agony to Lucan. Nevertheless the idea that he planned his wife's death in order to get control of the house cannot be true. The lease was in the hands of a family trust, set up by Pat Lucan as part of the marriage settlement for his son.

Lucan had already tried to get Coutts bank to release capital from one of the trusts, but had backed off because this might have reflected badly in an appeal against the custody judgment. He knew, therefore, that 46 Lower Belgrave Street could not be sold simply because Veronica was no longer there to live in it. The terms of the trust would not permit it.

He could, however, have dreamed up the idea of an insurance scam. The auction of the family silver was imminent at Christie's, but estimates did not cover Lucan's liabilities, and anyway he may have been reluctant to go through with it: the loss of those beautiful, irreplaceable things. He could, therefore, have been attracted by the thought of a staged burglary. Alternatively there could have been a genuine burglary, carried out by parties unknown and independent of Lucan, which ended in violence.

For all that Lucan was flirting dangerously with the prospect of bankruptcy, he had a family house full of valuable items. In the basement, close to where Sandra was attacked, was a large safe. Somebody may have intended to get into that safe. There were also heirlooms and jewellery in the property. A sapphire and diamond necklace was around Veronica's neck at the time of the attack.

In support of this theory are two small points. The first is the American mailsack, which the police found impossible to trace. David Gerring wrote in his book that it had probably come from the Clermont, but this typically casual statement was unsupported even by Ranson; actually the sack is most easily explained if the killer was a professional. The second point is that the Lucans had been burgled before. In 1964 there was a mysterious theft of £2,000 worth of jewellery, although it was reported that 'no sign of forced entry to the house was found'.[2] In such circumstances, two explanations are likely: either somebody connected to a member of the Lucan household had cut a key, or Lucan himself was behind the theft.

The same explanations hold, ten years on. In the intervening period, particularly the sixteen months leading up to the murder, a large number of people had been employed by the Lucans. The antecedents of some of these were unknown. Any one of them might have seen and talked about what was in the house, and had access to a key. Many burglaries are, of course, carried out in these circumstances.

And a burglar could have attacked the two women who surprised him. Veronica described her assailant putting his hands around her throat, which was encircled by a valuable necklace. 'At one point', read the *Daily Express* interview that she gave in January 1975, '[she] felt her assailant grabbing at it. Surprisingly she found the composure to demand: 'What are you doing with my necklace?' The sound of her voice seemed to make him stop...' This account is at odds with the story given to the inquest, where Veronica stated that the attack stopped for an altogether different reason: she had grabbed her husband's testicles. Perhaps modesty prevailed in what was then, in some ways at least, a more decorous press.

The burglar, who had entered the house with a key that had been previously cut or loaned, could have fled when Lucan arrived. The police expressed downright scepticism about any such 'second man', saying that nobody saw a blood-stained person in Belgravia on the night of the murder, but the same objection applied to Lucan himself. And if Lucan could be said to have made his getaway in a car, so too might anybody else have done.

In 2004 Channel 4 broadcast a documentary entitled *The Hunt for Lord Lucan*. In it Lucan's son, George Bingham, suggested that Sandra Rivett was murdered by a burglar; Lucan was waiting outside the house, and went in when he sensed that something had gone wrong. 'I suspect', said George, in defence of his alternative theory, 'that the original investigation into this matter fell well short of what a reasonable general public might expect of the police. And I think on that basis alone the case merits a further investigation.'

This is incontrovertible: the investigation was little short of pathetic. Nevertheless Veronica reacted fiercely in the press, accusing George of impugning her evidence, and insisting that there was nothing of value in the basement safe.

It is true that most of the silver was at Christie's, but a silver regimental dagger was actually found in the safe after the house was sold, and it has been suggested that there were other items kept there.[3] The bloody footmarks mentioned at the inquest by Graham Forsyth, which could not have been transference as he was so early on the scene, led to the area of the safe. It 'appeared to be locked', Roy Ranson wrote carefully. Of course the safe may not have been the target of this hypothetical burglary. A thief who wished to steal items upstairs might wait in the basement until Veronica was asleep; although it is a moot point whether jewellery, for instance, was in fact Lucan's to claim on insurance.

If Lucan were behind such a burglary, he would clearly have chosen to stage it on Sandra's night off. Hence his question, as recounted by his daughter: 'Daddy asked me when Sandra had her days off. I said her day off was Thursday.' It is possible, just, to interpret this in a favourable light: Lucan's concern for his children meant that he wanted to know when his wife was home alone with them, and accordingly checked on the house to ensure that all was well. Nevertheless the more obvious interpretation, that Lucan sought confirmation of when his wife would be the only adult in the house, constitutes extremely damaging evidence against him.

A burglar could have made the bloody footprints that led to the back door, and shed the group B blood in the garden. Susan Maxwell-Scott, in her account of the conversation with Lucan, told the inquest: 'He said the man made off. In my imagination it was probably out of the back door.' If the intruder failed to escape that way, he could then have left the house by the front door when the Lucans went upstairs.

Susan was leaving the exit route deliberately unclear; but it may be that the back wall was not as difficult to scale as has been implied. It was six feet high, with a three-foot trellis on top and some handy creeper to climb. At the inquest, Veronica said: 'It would have been a prickly business': not an impossible one. The police claimed to have found no evidence of anybody climbing the wall, but they were not looking for it. They had their man.

There was also a third means of entry: the door at the bottom of the steps that lead down from street level to the basement. The police, who dismissed any idea that this door had been opened on the night of the murder, stated that it was found locked. According to Pierrette Goletto, however, who had a key to the basement door while she worked for Veronica, it was in frequent use. Therefore, although a less certain means of access than the front entrance at Lower Belgrave Street, the door cannot be completely overlooked.

The burglary scenario goes some way to backing up Lord Lucan's own story. This has him passing the house for no other reason than that he liked to keep an eye on it; particularly, it might be said, on the nanny's night off. He was on his way to Elizabeth Street, to change for dinner, and so he took the route past the house. It is perfectly credible that he would do this, given his anxieties about his children; people do stare at houses when they are fixated on their inhabitants.

The problem, however, is that given the effort that is required to see into the basement, Lucan must have looked *deliberately* through the window. For what reason? Why would he have peered and stooped? He might have done so if he had *heard* something untoward. Yet he did not say this.

It could be, however, that Lucan, having arranged a burglary, was hanging around and on the alert, as his son George suggested. He might, then, have looked through the basement window. But the only way in which he could have 'interrupted a fight in the basement', as his mother told the inquest, was if Veronica received most of her injuries on the ground floor, then ran downstairs, followed by her assailant. If that is untrue, and it certainly seems most unlikely, there remains the possibility that Lucan looked through the window and glimpsed evidence of violence; that he saw blood on the floor, or even the mailsack; and realized that something had gone very wrong. Nevertheless his story remains problematical in the extreme.

The most difficult question of all is why a hypothetical burglar should have committed acts of such tremendous violence. If he had come armed with the piping, why not simply use a knockout blow?

One can stretch possibility to its fullest extent and say that the man may have been an unsuspected psychopath. In the 'A6 Murder' of 1961, the petty criminal James Hanratty pulled a gun on an adulterous couple, drove around with them through the night, then, in the early hours, shot the man dead and left the woman paralysed. It was suggested that he had been paid to frighten the pair into ending their affair, although his motive may simply have been theft; either way the extreme violence was out of character. Nevertheless, it happened.

This, then, is the first theory: not impossible, but far from satisfying.

> 'I said to myself: "Let us be simple. What has really happened?"
> And I saw that what had really happened was that Maggie
> Buckley had been killed. Just that! But who could want Maggie
> Buckley dead...?'
>
> AGATHA CHRISTIE, *Peril at End House*, 1932

The second hypothesis, which is more interesting, is that Sandra Rivett was the intended victim all along.

Why did Sandra go downstairs that night? To make tea, say Veronica and the police. Yet Veronica also said, at the inquest, that it was unusual for her nanny to offer to make tea.

There was a Baby Belling on the third floor, which Veronica has subsequently stated was 'disconnected'. There is no reason to doubt the truth of this, although the facility to make tea was presumably there for the convenience of the Lucan nannies. If Veronica liked to drink tea in the evening, it was for her convenience also. Why, then, should it have been disconnected? It is hardly desirable to have to go down three or four floors to a darkened basement, in a house where the light bulbs were frequently blown out, to make tea at night. In fact it would be downright unnerving to many women. Ranson knew this, and sought to counter it. Sandra, he wrote, was 'settled in comfortably to this friendly, family home. The creaks of

the stairs and the dark of the waiting kitchen held no fears for her.'
Nor was she bothered when the light failed to switch on at the top of
the basement stairs. She continued down, 'undaunted by the darkness', despite the fact that she was wearing dainty little court heels
and carrying teacups.

There is another oddity about the tea, contained within the evidence given by Frances. Her statement was not always convenient
to the police; and Michael Eastham objected to its inclusion at the
inquest, probably because of Lucan's question as to when Sandra
took her night off. Yet the words of a bright ten-year-old, who
had the clarity of mind to report facts but not the adult ability to
interpret them, nor to bend or elide them to any particular end, are
peculiarly trustworthy.

In her recollection of the evening of 7 November, Frances said
that she watched *The Six Million Dollar Man* with her mother, sib-
lings and nanny in the second-floor bedroom.

> When the programme finished at 8.30pm, I went back upstairs to
> the nursery and played a little more with my game. Sandra brought
> George and Camilla upstairs and put them to bed...
>
> I stayed in the nursery for about five minutes only, then I went
> downstairs again to Mummy's room. That would have been about
> 8.40pm. I asked Mummy where Sandra was and she said she was
> downstairs making some tea. I didn't see her go downstairs so I
> don't know if she took any empty cups with her.

At the inquest, Veronica gave a different version of these events,
which shifted the timeframe of the attacks forward by some twenty
minutes. Sandra, she said, had looked into the bedroom at around
8.55pm and asked if she would like a cup of tea.

'Where were you', asked the coroner, 'when she said she would
get you some tea?

'I was lying on the bed.'

'And your daughter also?'

'Also.'

'You can place the time from the television programme at about five to nine?'

'Yes.'

In direct contradiction, Frances said: 'The last time I saw Sandra was when she took George and Camilla upstairs to bed.' In other words, if Sandra *had* looked in on Veronica, it was at around 8.35pm, while Frances was briefly in the nursery. If anybody noticed the discrepancies between these statements at the inquest, nothing was said. Once Frances's statement became admissible, Eastham might have made use of it to quiz Veronica about the accuracy of her own, but his cross-examination was halted after two questions. Twenty years later Veronica gave another, again slightly different version of the half-hour between 8.30 and 9.00pm. She said that Sandra had phoned her parents, then gone upstairs and done some ironing in her room, before making the offer of tea.[4] This is impossible if one accepts Frances's statement.

As some crockery was found dropped close to Sandra's body, it would be absurd to say that she did not go down to make tea. But if the offer to do this was unusual, did she have another reason for going downstairs? The first reaction to the murder of the former nanny, Lilian Jenkins, whom Veronica had sacked in late 1972, was that Sandra had gone to let somebody into the house.

There are indications that Sandra was a possible victim in her own right. Women who enjoy a fun, sexy freedom arouse strong emotions in those who do not: puritanical disapproval, envy, spite. In men they can arouse anger. How dare they live as they please? Among Sandra's male friends there could have been one who turned nasty, a misfit beneath the charm. Her 'official' boy-friend John Hankins, to whom Sandra spoke that night, and who was working near to the house, was cleared by the police. But there was the man with whom she had broken off a few days before the murder; presumably the same man as was mentioned by Christina, whom the children described as driving a Mercedes. There was, too, the mysterious Norwegian seaman, whose existence is only a rumour but such a particular one (would anybody invent the fact of him being Norwegian?) that it carries conviction. At the time, there was definitely a vague swirl of opinion that Sandra had been killed by design rather than in error.[5] Wishful thinking within the Lucan camp may have been the origin of the idea. Yet there was something to it, a small fire within the smoke.

Supporting it was the statement made by Lucan's sister Sally. This alluded to a man who sometimes stayed at Lower Belgrave Street. It is likely that Sally was piecing together scraps of information in the hope that, when assembled, they would create an alternative culprit. She was a pleasant, sincere woman, liked even by the police, but insistent upon her brother's innocence. Indeed she was so desperate to exonerate him that she fell for the tale of a punchy ex-boxer, Michael Fitzpatrick, who claimed that a friend had seen a man, definitely not Lucan, leaving the house on the night of the murder. Later Fitzpatrick would admit in court that the story was an invention, although rumours persisted that there was substance to it. Sally was not the kind of person to invent stories, although she may have exaggerated. And if the man who allegedly stayed at Lower Belgrave Street had been in the house on the night of the 7th, one has to think that Frances would have mentioned it. 'She was muddying the waters,' says Graham Forsyth, of Sally's statement. 'But I admit, we weren't looking elsewhere.'

That is not to say that this man, or another, did not come to the house. 'I always thought there was a third person there, according to blood types,' says Lucan's other sister Jane. 'But of course one's memory does funny things.' Jane's reference is to the AB group blood that was found on the mailsack, in the cloakroom basin, on the back of Veronica's skirt, and on the lead piping. The assumption has always been that the AB blood was a mixture of Veronica's and Sandra's groups, and given the general blood patterning this is almost certainly correct, although it could have come from a person belonging to the AB group. But the forensic truth can never, now, be determined.

The suggestion that Sandra admitted a man through the front door, then went down into the basement with him, is an intriguing one, but it confronts an instant problem. According to the police, the working light bulb had been removed from its socket at the bottom of the basement stairs. In other words, the killer was *in situ* before the victim.

Therefore whoever Sandra met in the basement was already inside the house. Perhaps she let a man in when she made her phone calls, before going upstairs to put the children to bed, then returned downstairs with the teacups. Or, just possibly, this person had a key. If Pierrette had had a key to the basement door, presumably so too had Sandra. And although David Gerring stated at the inquest that only the Lucans were known to have keys to the house, it seems likely that Sandra had a key to the front door, for use on her nights off when the chain was left down.

One can hypothesize that, after killing Sandra, her murderer heard Veronica calling for her. He fled into the garden, there shedding some of Sandra's blood. Then, realizing that he could not quickly escape that way, he went back into the basement and attacked Veronica as she ran away up the stairs. During the assault, Lucan entered the house. The killer ran out through the front door. And Veronica, whose unknown assailant had been replaced in the dark ante-room by the figure of her husband, believed that the man who had attacked her was Lucan himself.

Could it have happened this way? It is possible. Sandra's stay at the house lasted just ten weeks, but it contained a complexity of relationships. And there is a powerful argument in support of the theory: the nature of the assault. The impression given by the police is that Sandra was struck down instantly, in the pitch dark, by a blow to the back of the head. 'She died quickly and without a sound,' wrote Ranson.[6] But the poor girl did not die quickly. The pathologist Keith Simpson told the inquest that she was heavily bruised in three areas: on her face and shoulders, as if the weapon had missed its target of the skull; on her upper arm, as if it had been gripped; on her hand, where it had been raised in an attempt at self-protection. Her left eye and mouth showed evidence of having been slapped or punched. These were not injuries inflicted upon a semi-conscious person. They were the result of a prolonged and terrible fight.

And the basement was not pitch-dark; the slats in the blind above the sink were open at forty-five degrees. The murder took place in line with the kitchen window, where a stream of light was coming in from the street lamp directly opposite. A very dim light, it is true. But enough to glimpse shapes, features.[7] Keith Simpson would later state his opinion[8] that the attack had begun when Sandra and her murderer were face to face. For Ranson to say, as he later did, that when Sandra was lying on the ground 'it is likely that the murderer... still did not realize whom he had killed' is utterly extraordinary.

Furthermore, four of the splits in the scalp were sited as if Sandra had been facing her attacker. They lay above the right ear, towards the eyebrow. Only the last two splits, above the nape of the neck, would have landed when Sandra was on the ground. So too, possibly, did the bruising blows to the shoulders, which may have been delivered as she tried to roll out of reach. This was not just a grotesque attack, it was a grotesquely inefficient one.

Given that Sandra was a small woman, with what was later described as a 'thin skull', the ferocity needed to kill her is a little surprising. Either the murderer or the weapon was poor at their unspeakable job. There is the very faint possibility that the piping used to attack Veronica was not the same piece that killed Sandra, as none of her hairs were found on it; there was group B blood, but that could have come from the killer. A lighter, sharper weight of piping would explain why the assault was so prolonged and bloody. Logic suggests that the same piping was used on both women, but the facts do not, at least not unequivocally. There is, however, the possibility that the forensic analysis was not as thorough as it might have been. The piping looked like the weapon, and probably was the weapon; there was no need to put every last molecule under a microscope.

There is one further small point in defence of this theory: it would explain how an assailant entered the house without being seen. The difficulty of doing this has never really been questioned; but if, as the police say, the means of entry was the front door, there was a considerable risk. Sandra was buzzing about that evening. She rang her mother. She received a phone call from John Hankins. Of course if Lucan were the assailant, he would not have expected Sandra to be there: but she was. If one accepts Frances's timings, the only safe period for getting into the basement was the half-hour between 8.05pm and 8.35pm. If the assailant were known to Sandra, the risk recedes.

In truth, were it not for the weapon and the sack, it would be very easy to believe that Sandra was the intended victim: that she was killed, after a prolonged struggle, in a ghastly *crime passionnel*. But the weapon means premeditation, and that is less convincing. A current lover, who might have committed the impassioned manslaughter, would have been unlikely to come armed for murder. And Sandra would have been unlikely to admit to the house a rejected lover, particularly the one with whom she had just split up: the kind of man who might, logically, have committed this murder. Therefore the explanation that best supports the theory is that a former boyfriend, burning with a grievance, had somehow obtained possession of a key to 46 Lower Belgrave Street. It is also possible that Sandra's killer was somebody who appeared to be a friend but was, in fact, mad.

The sense remains that what happened on the evening of 7 November was all about the Lucans, the playing out of the last act in the absurdist tragedy of their marriage. For Sandra to have been engaged in a drama of her own that night does, indeed, seem like the 'unbelievable coincidence' described by Lucan. It is so hard to rid oneself of all that *a posteriori* knowledge, which says that the violent events of that night were an inevitability, and that Sandra was the collateral damage. Actually this may not be true. The inevitable often only seems so after it has taken place. On 6 November

1974, Sandra Rivett probably seemed as likely a murder victim as Veronica Lucan.

> 'How convenient if you could ring up Harrods and say
> "Please send along two good murderers, will you?"'
>
> AGATHA CHRISTIE, *The Pale Horse*, 1961

But the third hypothesis does have Veronica as the intended target. It suggests that the attacks were carried out by a hitman, paid by Lucan to kill his wife. The police dismissed this theory, which gives it instant appeal.

Psychologically, it is extremely convincing that a man like Lucan would have asked a hitman to do the job for him; that was the nature of his class. And it is not particularly hard to find a hitman, although they vary in quality. If Lucan did employ one, then his man was a hopeless amateur, not least in choosing a weapon whose only virtue was its silence. Lucan would not have known how to judge what he was getting, and the chain that led to the man would probably have been quite long. But he could have found somebody, most likely through John Aspinall. Without actually making the introduction, Aspinall was in a position to make oblique suggestions. He had mixed with low life when he staged his peripatetic gambling parties, and perforce, as a one-man casino business, would have continued to do so (especially if the story is true that he was operating occasional bent chemmy games, as suggested by the mobster Billy Hill). If he had had some idea of what Lucan was up to, this would sit quite convincingly with the strange, show-off game of grandma's footsteps that he played with the police. He taunted them with the possibility that he held a secret, going so far and no further. The secret might have been that he had helped Lucan to escape. But it might, far more credibly, have been the belief that Lucan had paid somebody to kill the vexatious wife.

Of course Lucan did not really have the cash to pay such a person, but he was in so deep as to make no difference. The visit to the moneylender, two months before the murder, could have been made for just such a purpose.

The hitman hypothesis appeals for another reason. It removes perhaps the strongest objection to the police case: that Lucan apparently did not know his own wife.

'If you think about it,' says Christina, 'if you've been married to somebody for quite a few years, how do you mistake them for somebody else? The papers tried to say that they [Veronica and Sandra] were similar, but they weren't.'

This is confirmed, oddly enough, by the person who endorsed the mistaken identity theory: Veronica herself. 'He said "shut up" and then I knew it was him,' she would later tell a newspaper. 'I knew his voice and I could tell it was him from the way he smelt. A wife knows her husband's smell. I know it was him.'[9]

It could be said that Lucan was so overwrought, so full of alcohol, that he simply fell upon the woman who came down the stairs because he assumed that it *was* his wife. And this is possible. Indeed it must have been that way, if the police and the coroner's jury got it right. Sandra resembled Veronica sufficiently in essentials not to set off an immediate alarm. She was small, albeit fuller of figure than Veronica, and her hair was longer, more like Veronica's, than in the familiar, smiling picture taken four years before her death.

But the attack upon Sandra was not the swift cosh-to-the-head of myth: seven blows were inflicted when she was facing her killer. The intimate nature of this assault raises serious questions, which are answered if the man who murdered Sandra did not know that she was not Veronica.

A hitman would have turned up for the job in more appropriate clothes than Lucan's 'gentleman's casual'. He could have had access to the exotic mailsack and prepared the weapons with his hacksaw. He could, of course, have been given a house key; either to the front door or the basement. He could have driven to the house in the Ford Corsair that Lucan borrowed from Michael Stoop, and have left the second piece of lead piping in the boot. After the attacks he could have made his getaway in the Corsair. It is an incidental oddity that blood was found on *both* front seats of the car. A possible explanation is that it was parked with the passenger side against the kerb at Lower Belgrave Street, that the assailant used that door to minimize the risk of being seen in the road, and that as he slid into the driver's position both seats were smeared with blood. It is also possible that a bloodied garment was placed on the passenger seat.

There is something more in defence of the theories that Lucan did not, himself, commit these crimes. Billy Edgson, the linkman at the Clermont, told the police that Lucan had spoken to him outside the club at 8.45pm. If that information is correct,[10] then the plain fact of the matter is that the man named as guilty has our old friend: an alibi.

This is pretty seismic, really. It is as if, back in 1910, somebody mentioned in passing that Dr Crippen had been on holiday at the time that his wife was buried in the cellar. The police were perturbed by this statement, of course, but they overcame it admirably.

Nevertheless Edgson, together with Frances, knocked annoying little holes into the watertight case against Lucan. They were the human equivalent of that deeply irritating blood evidence. Frances stated that Sandra went downstairs before 8.40pm, and her mother at about 8.50pm. Edgson stated that Lucan was outside the Clermont at 8.45pm. Therefore Lucan did not commit the crimes. Simple as that. The police sought, in an avuncular way, to dismiss Frances as a witness. 'The evidence of Frances was always slightly muddled,' wrote Ranson; in fact it was notably precise. Frances, he wrote, was 'half asleep' as she lay on her mother's bed watching television: there is no evidence for that at all. She had not even been to school that day, so was probably very much awake (another small contradiction here was Veronica's statement, in her 1975 *Daily Express* interview, that on the day of the murder 'the children were home from school on time'). David Gerring described Frances as 'highly intelligent', not 'horror-struck', possessed of the 'amazing resilience' displayed by her grandmother. He too was aware of the problem that she posed, contradicting as she did the gospel according to Veronica, and sidled up cunningly to address it. 'Time', he later mused, 'is a funny thing in murder enquiries, and people have different ideas about it. In most enquiries timing is terrible, people can't remember times even though they think they can. The timing was marked on the working copy [of Veronica's police statement] as needing tightening up but no great significance was attached to it.'

This all reads very reasonably. But Frances, in her statement, wasn't making confident guesses. If she did not know what time something happened, she said so. Otherwise she referred to an accurate corroborative source: the television. She was quite right to say, for instance, that *Top of the Pops* began that night at 7.20pm. She was probably right to say that her mother had gone downstairs before the start of the nine o'clock news: a good, firm, memorable marker. Veronica, however, said that she left the bedroom at 9.15pm. 'The BBC news had been on for fifteen minutes,' wrote Ranson, doggedly parroting this version of events as if no other could ever have existed.

And yet: even if Veronica's timings were the right ones, and Sandra did not go down to the basement until 8.55pm, if Edgson's statement is accepted, then it was *still* well-nigh impossible for Lucan to have committed the murder. Lucan had to drive to the house from the Clermont, a journey of at least seven or eight minutes. He had to enter without being seen, remove a light bulb and conceal himself. And he had less than ten minutes in which to do it all. In other words, for Lucan's alibi to break, Edgson had to have been mistaken. Possibly he was. He may have got the wrong time, the wrong night, the wrong everything. Nevertheless his testimony placed a giant question mark over the official solution to this case; the way in which it has been batted away is alarmingly casual. Surely it was men like Lucan who dismissed the words of a servant?

If, however, Edgson's evidence was reliable, and Lucan did indeed drive past the Clermont at around 8.45, this was a slightly odd and flagrant thing to do. In fact it constitutes a further support to the hitman theory. It has the distinct air of a deliberately created alibi: look at me, doing something innocent! Furthermore, Edgson stated that Lucan was almost certainly driving the Mercedes, which if true creates an additional difficulty for the official theory, with its insistence upon the role of the Ford Corsair. The police believed that Veronica was to have been stowed in this car, probably after the sack had been placed in the basement safe. It is usually said that the Corsair was borrowed because it had a capacious boot, as if a Mercedes does not; its real advantage would have been its insignificance. According to Edgson's timings, Lucan could not possibly have swapped cars. But a hitman could have used the Corsair, transported the body into its boot, then left the car near to Lucan's flat in Elizabeth Street. Lucan would have been summoned by Sandra, when she returned from her night off and found Veronica gone; or perhaps he would have found a pretext for ringing the house. At some point thereafter he would, if the police theory is correct, have driven to the south coast and effected his wife's 'disappearance'. In fact the body could just as easily have been thrown from a Thames bridge in an appearance of suicide. The blows to the head would today be identified as murderous, but in pre–*Silent Witness* 1974, when the average person was far less forensically clued–up, Lucan may not have thought that way. He may also have thought that one blow would be enough to kill, and that post–mortem it would seem to have been caused in the water, effectively as if self–inflicted.

There is, however, something rather nonchalant in the belief that Lucan intended to dispose of a body in this way, particularly to load it into a car on a London street with nobody the wiser. This was also pre–CCTV, of course, so much more could be done under wraps; even so, the moment of hauling the burden out of the house and into the boot would have been a nasty one. As ever, the police shift their words to suit their argument. Gerring, who theorizes that the body would have been removed via the basement door, also says that Lucan had earlier parked the Corsair directly outside the house. In flat contradiction Ranson says that there were cars all along Lower Belgrave Street that night, which means that the body would have been carried almost into the middle of the road before being placed in the boot. Not very discreet, but Ranson had been too busy making another point to worry about this: he wanted to underscore the fact that Lucan, if he had been driving past the house, could not possibly have seen anything through the basement window. Therefore it is unclear how close the car would have been to number 46, had the plan been enacted.

For Lucan himself, bundling a body into a sack and taking it out into the street would have been unspeakably terrifying; almost as alarming as murder. For a hitman it was all in a night's work. And if one believes that Veronica was the intended victim, this *must* have been Lucan's plan. It would seem that she had simply wandered off into the night, that there had never been a murder at all. Her history of instability would make this a feasible scenario; the visit to the chemist that afternoon, in which Lucan asked about some of his wife's pills, may have been intended to support it. Anyway Lucan would never have left Veronica lying dead in the house. Nicholas Boyce, who in 1985 would kill the other nanny, Christabel Martin, in a violent rage, nevertheless went to grisly lengths in disposing of her body so that it would not be seen by his children.

Taken all in all, the hitman hypothesis has a great deal in its favour. Certainly it permits an explanation for the blood anomalies. For example: Veronica could have surprised the killer in the basement, as was suggested in *The Times*; he could have begun his attack upon her there, then continued it on the ground floor; he could have tried to exit through the garden, either before or after the second assault. The theory also explains the minimal blood on Lucan, the fact that he was wearing a coat (having just come in from the street), the blood in the car, the mailsack.

It can explain pretty much everything, in fact; which makes it all the more vexing that it has one gigantic flaw. It is the same problem that sits at the heart of the other theories, but in this case it is near-impossible to overcome. Why in the name of heaven, if he had employed a hitman, did Lucan go to Lower Belgrave Street that night?

The obvious, the sane thing to do would have been to stay as well clear of the house as possible. Not merely to be seen driving past the Clermont at 8.45pm, but to be sitting blamelessly at the tables, gambling away, while the proxy did his murderous work. One could say that Lucan did not actually *need* an alibi, given that the plot was to suggest that Veronica had disappeared, not that she had been murdered. Nevertheless, once the police were notified, the estranged husband would have been an object of some suspicion. It would have been sensible, to say the least, to be visibly elsewhere throughout the evening of the 7th.

It is possible, just, that Lucan was not sensible enough to do this. That he lurked outside the house, perhaps out of concern for his children; looked through the window, saw Veronica in the basement; and realized that the plan had gone amiss. That he then entered the house, as Susan Maxwell-Scott told the inquest. 'She [Veronica] cried out to him that someone had killed the nanny. And then, almost in the same breath, she accused Lucan of having hired the man to kill her, not Sandra.' These words are echoed in one of the letters to Bill Shand Kydd. 'When I interrupted the fight at LB St. and the man left Veronica accused me of having hired him...' This could have been an elided version of the truth.

There are other possibilities. Did Lucan go to the house because he had been left the job of putting the body in the car? Did he himself launch the attack on Veronica as the hitman fled, like Macbeth in the guise of Third Murderer? Were there, in fact, two assailants: the hapless psycho who bludgeoned Sandra, and the incompetent raging aristocrat who could not kill a wife half his size?

What nonsense it all sounds. One does not, as they say, buy a dog and bark oneself. If Lucan had taken the fantastic step of finding a hitman, the last thing he would logically have done was turn up and pitch in himself.

So the theory, which in so many ways resembles a solution, becomes a flawed hypothesis.[11] Perhaps the least explicable thing about it is why Veronica was left alive at the end of it all. But then the same conundrum applies to the fourth hypothesis, the one that is generally believed to be not a hypothesis at all but straightforward fact: that Lord Lucan, *solus*, is guilty.

'A murderer is always a gambler'

AGATHA CHRISTIE, *The ABC Murders*, 1936

It is quite extraordinary, given the weakness of the case against Lucan, how strong is the general assumption of its truth; how a story that is circumstantial and partial is viewed as resoundingly complete. One can pick the thing apart, arguing to and fro about blood here and alibis there, loosening the bonds that appear to tie it all up. It makes no real difference. Everybody still believes that he did it. Is that simply the myth, exerting its power? Is it prejudice? At the trial of Edith Thompson, scarcely a jot of real evidence suggested that she had colluded with her lover to plot the death of her husband; yet she was convicted, because the judge didn't like her, and public opinion distrusted her adulteress's allure. Yet the lover of Dr Crippen, Ethel Le Neve, was acquitted of a similar count of conspiracy, because people thought she looked fragile and innocent and incapable of dissimulation. Ninety years after Edith Thompson's execution, the bias that condemned her is terrifyingly apparent. One would say that it could never happen now. But of course it could, if the accused triggered a different, contemporary prejudice.

In Muriel Spark's *Aiding and Abetting*, the psychiatrist treating a patient who claims to be Lucan says:

'You would be tried for murder if you are indeed Lord Lucan.'

'Are you sure?'

'Yes, I am. And you would be found guilty on the evidence.'

But that is not really so. A good defence counsel could have pulled the evidence to pieces, picked remorselessly at the loose threads in Veronica's story. Almost certainly Lucan would still have been found guilty, and what would have convicted him is prejudice.

In the battle of his word against his wife's, he would have lost. He would have stood there like a waxwork, spluttering in his cut-glass accent, enraging everybody with his talk of debts, of loans, of bets, of trust funds, all computed in sums that exceeded the average annual wage; none of which in itself made him a murderer. After the custody case, he knew what was ranged against him. The phrase in the letter to Michael Stoop, 'judging by my last effort in court no one, let alone a 67 year old judge, would believe...', is incoherent but clear in import. In the eyes of many, the strongest evidence of Lucan's guilt is that he ran away. Yet those who knew the story of the custody hearing understood why he did.

Veronica *did* persuade: the High Court judge and the police and the coroner. Everybody says how convincing she could be when she chose. 'She could win over anybody,' says Zoe Peto. 'Yes, she could twist everyone round her little finger,' says Pierrette. 'She was very, very, very persuasive,' says Christina Shand Kydd. None of these women, incidentally, believes in Lucan's guilt. Nor did his counsel at the custody hearing, the highly esteemed James Comyn, who had seen the prejudice against his client in action.

It is a dangerous game to question Veronica's version of the events of 7 November 1974, except as pure hypothesis. She has been believed for forty years, but she remains alert to any hint of criticism. In 1999 she threatened to sue her own son for alleged theft of private papers, and gave an interview condemning him for suggesting that his father was semi-innocent. The following year she issued a public warning to Muriel Spark, saying that the concept of *Aiding and Abetting* was 'absurd and insensitive' and that Spark should have spoken to her before writing the book. 'I am not only thinking about me but also my son.' Yet *Aiding and Abetting* was essentially on her side: it was a brilliant spin on the story, but it still took the official line. Spark wrote that the police believed Veronica. 'They had every reason, with so much corroborative evidence, to believe her.' When Veronica said, in 1998, 'I am the one who has been vilified', one has to wonder what on earth she meant. Nothing she has ever said about her husband has been doubted, except by the people who knew him; for which crime they are the ones who have been dismissed and excoriated.

Some who knew Lucan believed in his guilt, while accepting a theoretical defence of provocation. 'He did do it,' says Daniel Mein-ertzhagen. 'He talked about doing it. I saw him getting obsessive.' This echoes remarks made by Charles Benson, Dominick Elwes, Greville Howard and John Aspinall. The girlfriend of one of the set also says: 'Obviously he became completely obsessive, and it pushed him over the edge. I definitely saw that in evidence. I suspect he tried to get custody back and failed, and in the end he was so obses-sive he took that step – which is quite a step to take. No one thought it would go to that extreme, no one. People were amazed, shocked.' Stuart Wheeler says:

> I could sort of see, if he thought, this needed to be done. My wife's mad – I'm not saying she is, of course, I'm saying that's what he thought – and I want to get the children... There's only one way to do it, so that's what I'm going to do. No, I wouldn't have thought that especially surprising. I don't mean to say I expected it. I was astonished.

Unnamed friends were also quoted, after the event. 'Very occasionally one did see a flash of temper, and then it was quite unpleasant. He would get very tensed up and shake – the classic bellicose effect. He would get angry with golf caddies who wouldn't listen, and so on.' This is in contrast to the character portrayed by Lucan's old schoolfriend, but one has the sense that Lucan was at his best with this relaxed, kindly, level-headed man. What was also made much of were Lucan's right-wing politics. 'We used to have long heart-to-hearts about the dreadful political situation,' said Michael Stoop. 'His remedies were fairly drastic. Liberal solutions were no good any more.'[12] Today, of course, this is almost worse than murder. Yet one must place it in the context of the early 1970s, when Britain was in a state of fairly frightening disarray and, like

Lucan himself, essentially bankrupt. 'He felt we were on the edge of an abyss,' said Stoop. He was not alone. Stoop himself had joined the private army organized to keep Britain going in the event of anarchic breakdown.

Lucan's sister Jane, who is staunchly on the left, is naturally repelled by this; but nevertheless does not take her brother's politics wholly seriously. She views his hysterical outbursts as an expression of the angry misery that possessed him at the time, an exaggerated by-product of his fascination with money, a stubborn stiffening of the Conservative tradition that the family, before Pat broke free of it, had followed for centuries. 'A lot of it was talk. Like friends we all have, who try and get your goat.' Fear, which was in Lucan's nature, extended to fear about what was happening to the country. Nevertheless he did have recordings of the Nuremberg rallies in his flat at Elizabeth Street, later falsely described as a 'shrine to Hitler'.[13] 'I don't think necessarily you have to be a great fan of Hitler to be *interested* in the Nuremberg speeches,' says Stuart Wheeler. 'On the other hand, it's possible that he was.'

There is no doubt that Lucan had areas of extreme oddity. The very tautness of his demeanour implies twists of tumult within, as first evidenced in childhood. At the same time he could be kind, generous, wryly amusing; a devoted father; a sensitive soul, with a private love of playing Bach and Scott Joplin. The portrayal of a cold, dull, vicious throwback is simplistic in the extreme. It bears no relation to the man as described by those who knew him. It may have been the mask that he wore when he felt inadequate, which was surprisingly often. Without wishing to deny all evidence of his dark underbelly, one has the sense that much of it came from hangers-on, people looking to chuck in their ha'porth of gossip.

But Lucan's marriage, an odd thing in itself, sent him the wrong way: as marriages can. His qualities began to drain into nothingness. His gambling, at first a hopeful, would-be shrewd dream of 'making my pile', became a reality that only delusion could hide. Lucan was weak, *au fond*, and he masked a lack of inner substance behind the impeccable marvel of his appearance. He was the perfect thorough-bred that did not know how to race. He was 'alien and unhappy; he felt that the enormous apparatus rank required a gentleman to erect around himself was like the massive armour that had been the death warrant of so many ancient saurian species'.[14] He certainly had not a clue how to live in a world that had once belonged to his ancestors, who had been free in a way that he could only pretend to be, thus tightening the trap ever more closely. He *was* trapped. If there were ways out, then he could not see them. All he could see were the red bills, the chemmy table, the cards, the chips, the impregnable white house at Lower Belgrave Street, containing all that should be his; the constricted little maze within the sacred postcodes, without an exit.

Did all this mean that he was also a killer? Was that where the trap naturally led him, to the escape of violence? Did he, who had lost the battle of his marriage, seek to win the war with a show of strength?

Was he that kind of man? It is not true to say, as detective fiction has it, that everybody is capable of murder. What this means is that everybody is capable of the emotions, the motives, that lead to murder. Lucan certainly had motives enough. Resentment; anger; hatred; self-hatred; wretched agony over the children; ineradicable creeping shame at the accusations thrown at him in the custody case; urgent need to stop paying for two establishments; the knowledge that Veronica had won, and would go on winning: in sum, the classic domestic murder motive, which sees the removal of the disruptive element as the only way to restore life to its equilibrium. 'He had a motive – he had twenty motives!' says the former nanny Pierrette Goletto, who nevertheless believes him to be innocent. 'He was a guy who could shout, and this and that, but he was not strong. He was shouting, but not violent. He was too weak. I know he went through hell.

'But he wasn't the type to kill.'

It is interesting that a worldly Frenchwoman perceived Lucan in this way, and that the bright Maxwell-Scott nanny, whose sharp eyes missed not a trick, also saw straight through the façade. The weekends that he spent at Grants Hill, with the time in the nursery playing with his children, left an impression of softness, vulnerability, rather than aggression. 'I think because I didn't have a dad, I was drawn to that side of him. No, I didn't believe it when I heard what had happened.'

These are outsiders. Their testimony is valuable. Yet so too is that of the people who really knew Lucan: Bill and Christina Shand Kydd, the old friend from Eton, the sister. It has been so easy, so convenient, to dismiss Lucan's defenders simply because they are upper-class, and therefore to say that they stick to their own kind (but Veronica, too, was of that kind: nobody placed more importance upon breeding than she). Some of them were not, strictly speaking, likeable. Ian Maxwell-Scott comes across as a drearily self-destructive snob; his wife as something of a Lady Jekyll and Mrs Hyde, an intellectually frustrated woman who became volatile in drink: *they* were the Lucans of myth, far more than the Lucans themselves. John Aspinall, for all his outlandish charm and his miraculous rapport with animals, was a complicated personality with a moral code all his own: or so he liked people to believe. His style has infected this story, and turned Lucan's world into an image of archetypal arrogance. But it is not that simple. Only a fool would be so reductive as to say that all members of the working class are the same; logically, therefore, this should not be said about the upper classes; yet it *is* said, and without compunction.

It is necessary, therefore, to emphasize that the people still alive who knew Lucan best, and who forty years on still seek to offer a different view of him, are nice people. They are remarkably open and straightforward. They command respect. They have no reason now to say the things that they do of Lucan: to portray him, also, as a victim of his marriage. Saying this does not help their own cause: they would do better to toe the familiar line, and say that he was a swine. Forty years on he is not going to be brought to trial, given a hearing. Yet a hearing is what they want him to have, because they believe that he has been portrayed unjustly, and they liked him

353

enough to mind about it. There is, too, the fact that his children have been obliged to grow up with the Lucan myth, which these people mind about even more.

That is not to say that they think him blameless in this story. It is not that simple, either. What they think is that too much has come from one side only, and that the truth is therefore incomplete. They think that Lucan did have motives, but that these sprang from something real, not from some crazed construct of feudal entitlement. They think that what happened is an appalling sadness for the Lucan family, and a tragedy for Sandra Rivett and her family. To them, it is not a myth.

Yet such is the strength of the myth that it is almost shocking to hear it spoken about as something real. Even to hear the name 'John' is a jolt. To be told about the Clermont, or the marriage, or the lunch at Aspinall's house, or the letters written at Susan Maxwell-Scott's house, induces a sense of dislocation: as if actuality has made a sudden sidling entry into a hazy filmic image, dark with the accretions of years of story-telling.

For the people who really did know Lucan, there is a different kind of disbelief. 'No, I can't believe it all happened,' says Jane. She is still, touchingly, distressed by the fact that it did. Yet her view is clear-eyed. 'He could be very kind to people – but I think he might have been capable of being deliberately unkind. Which is a bad side to him. But he could, yes, be wonderful.'

Christina Shand Kydd says:

This is the thing that's always upset all of us most, the way the press have portrayed him as the cold-hearted gambling aristocrat. He was a gambling aristocrat, but he was far from cold-hearted. I liked him very, very much. When our son was ill, with leukaemia, he was just so touchingly concerned and sweet. I remember Caspar lying on the sofa at home and he'd gone to sleep, and John just said that he would carry him up to bed. And I always remember, he picked him up and he had tears in his eyes, he was so upset and worried.

I don't know – I just find it absolutely incomprehensible that John did it.

'No question,' says her husband.

His schoolfriend says:

We were very, very close. My parents particularly liked John. They were pretty effective people, and they really liked him. And he had some very high-quality friends – when I say high-quality, I mean proper people. You know, they rated him.

I would have done anything for him, you know. What went wrong, I just don't know. I think about it quite a lot, and I just think, well, hell of a waste. And the tragedy of the nanny. Terrible. That, I can't... I mean, there's no way he could have mistaken her for his wife, and there's no way he would have done that. Physically, I mean.

Zoe Peto, who also came to know Lucan well and was fond of him despite her complicated friendship with Veronica, says cautiously: 'My first thought was not that John had done it.' She also takes a sensible, sceptical view of Lucan's conversation with Greville Howard, in which he confessed the desire to kill:

I don't think, if he really was going to do it, that he'd say it! I mean – the worst scenario is he blew up. It *could* have boiled up in him over those fifteen months. After losing the children, he may have got very, very upset, and into such a state... But I just can't believe... I don't know what it was, but definitely something wasn't right about what was said.

It is a fascinating test, to consider who among one's acquaintance might be capable of murder. Those who pass have either a streak of sudden unaccountability, a hint of darkly glinting deviousness, or an unnatural air of polite self-control. Lucan had this last quality, of course: the mask, behind which his life was crumbling. He could have snapped, broken out. Jane says:

I just thought that he was so deranged that he could have wanted to remove her. But I didn't think he'd have the ability to do it himself. Sally was adamant that he hadn't done it. My brother Hugh – I don't know what he actually thinks about who did it. I think he would probably say what I'm saying, which is that I didn't think it was possible for him to have done it.

For there is not merely the fact of murder; there is the way in which the murder was carried out. The attacks were not just evil. They were clumsy, lumbering, thuggish. It would take a lot, to wait in the dark and batter a woman to death. The bludgeon is a bungler's tool, at odds with Lucan's physical fastidiousness. The remorseless blows, the punches to Sandra's face, were the actions of somebody used to violence.

'If you'd known him – the first thing that we've always said to everybody,' says Christina, 'it was always a joke how squeamish John was. So the idea of him actually bludgeoning somebody, is sort of laughable, really.'

In the past Bill Shand Kydd has stated that it is impossible to imagine Lucan wielding the piping. He even left the room when his dog scuffled with another. The former nanny Lilian Jenkins recalled him wincing at the sight when she cut a finger, and asking her to cover it with a plaster.[15]

'I couldn't imagine that he would have done such a bloody thing,' says Jane, 'because he was very squeamish. I was in medical school, and he didn't like the thought of anything to do with the body, really. Those things can go by the board, I guess, when the mind does something... But it would be there, still, the squeamishness.' This is a repeated emphasis: the fact that drawing blood, inflicting wounds that would visibly and audibly damage, was inimical to Lucan.

There is also the laconic comment of his brother Hugh: 'You can't plan to go berserk.' This is extraordinarily to the point. Because the oddest thing about this murder, or failed murder, is that it falls somewhere between a planned crime and an uncontrollable impulse.

Lucan might have lost his temper during a row, and launched an attack upon Veronica that might then have turned lethal. Indeed she stated that he had done exactly that in the past (*pace* her remark that he was 'not a violent man'). But that is not what happened on 7 November. If Lucan was the man with the bludgeon, then he had thought hard about what he was doing. He had planned, as Hugh Bingham says, to go berserk. So the only explanation is a kind of madness. He was lost in the dream of his own violence, which lasted through the planning and many minutes into the execution, and only ended when his wife broke the spell: by inflicting a literal version of the low punch that she had laid on him during the custody case.

Yet nobody who knew him well, except his wife, believes that Lucan could ever have entered that state. His *desire* to do violence is not denied. His sister, in particular, who saw his guard right down, speaks of his hatred and anger towards Veronica. Jane is not the sort of person to defend her brother out of sheer sentiment; she is plain-speaking, and does not shirk the truth about him. If she thought that Lucan had planned and committed the attacks, she would almost certainly say so. But she cannot, quite, picture it.

If Lucan did do it, however, the plot must have gone like this. He had learned from his daughter that Sandra was away from the house on Thursdays. He also knew, somehow, that Veronica went downstairs to make tea at around 9.00pm. 'After eleven years of marriage he knew her routine,' wrote the faithful Ranson. In fact during the marriage (only nine years of which were spent in the same house), there would not have been much evening tea-drinking: Veronica was at the Clermont, having a dreadful time. The tea came later, post-separation. How, then, did Lucan know about it? Bill Shand Kydd took the robust view that he could have stood in the basement every evening for a week before somebody came down to make a cup of tea. Could Lucan, however, have learned the routine from the children? Frances did not mention this to the police, but it is possible that her father asked a question along these lines. Veronica herself suggested that if somebody had watched the house 'they would have known about my habit of going down to make tea at about nine o'clock on a Thursday evening';[16] a remark that gives rise to a couple of thoughts. First, it implies that she did not make tea on any night other than Thursday. Did this mean that tea was usually made by a nanny, or perhaps not made at all? Either way, if Veronica had been observed, then Lucan must have been looking into the basement of the house at a very specific time: effectively, the time of the murder. He must have been doing pretty much what he claimed in his story, the one that was so ridiculed by the police at the inquest.

There are, in fact, small indications that Lucan had slightly more to do with his wife than was generally assumed. Pierrette Goletto, who worked for the Lucans in 1974, says that they spoke on the phone, and had frequent arguments in a ground-floor room when he turned up to collect the children. Veronica told the inquest that she last saw her husband 'to speak to' at George's sports day, around 18 July 1974, and that her last sighting of him was on 24 October, when he was parked outside the house. Nevertheless he must, somehow, have got hold of the pills that he showed to the chemist on the afternoon of the murder: a minor mystery. Also, if Lucan entered the house by the front door on 7 November, he must have known somehow that the chain was left down when Sandra had her days off.

The police usually cite the front door as his means of entry, although David Gerring did say that the outside basement door would have been used for the removal of Veronica's body. In fact the basement door was also a better way in. Lucan could have locked the door from the inside, or more likely after he left the house.

One then has to accept that Lucan waited in the dark for a woman to come down the basement stairs; that he began his assault unthink-ingly and that, once it became clear that his victim was not Veronica, was compelled to continue it; that he placed Sandra's body in the mailsack because he did not know what else to do with her; and that he then attempted to murder his wife, presumably thinking that he would shroud her in a monogrammed sheet and remove two bodies from the house: or perhaps not thinking at all.

According to Veronica, Lucan was in the ground-floor cloak-room when she looked down into the basement for Sandra. He had, wrote Ranson, walked 'calmly' upstairs. Why? What was he doing in there? Rinsing the blood from his leather gloves, and perhaps from the piping? Sponging his trousers? Grey-blue fibres were found on the towel and basin. It would have made more sense to do all this in the kitchen, although the cloakroom was also in darkness. Perhaps he had gone in there to wait for his intended target, who at any minute might come in search of her nanny. Or did Veronica's opportune appearance simply impel him to go berserk again?

Veronica told the inquest that she heard somebody behind her in the cloakroom. 'I walked towards the sound, or at any rate moved towards it.' Then: 'somebody rushed out and hit me on the head.' There is an oddity here. The blood was said to have been trajected 'backwards' on to the ante-room ceiling and the cloakroom door. Yet one would think that, if Veronica had been moving towards her attacker, thus facing him, the blood would be trajected backwards on to the wall *behind* her: the area at the top of the basement stairs. Nevertheless it is beyond question that blows did land on Veronica's head in the vicinity of the ante-room, so the remark about moving 'towards the sound' is not overly relevant.

Again, however, there is the vexed question of the blood anom-alies, so blithely dismissed by the police: the group A blood in the basement, the group B on Veronica's clothes. As other commenta-tors have suggested,[17] there is no reason why Veronica should not have innocently entered the basement. Her denials exonerate her from any implied involvement in Sandra's death (she later said, in reference to the inquest: 'It was only then I realized that I myself was suspected of murdering her'[18]). They also destroy Lucan's story of seeing a fight through the window. This was obviously desirable from Veronica's point of view; but it was a bizarre story anyway, so why worry about it? Theoretically, it is *possible* that the attack on Veronica began in the basement. It is also possible that she entered the basement *after* the attack. She could have gone to see for herself what had happened to Sandra. Again, this is an entirely innocent thing to have done.

According to Frances's timings, Veronica was attacked just before 9.00pm.

> Mummy said that she wondered why Sandra was so long [Frances has Sandra going downstairs at about 8.35pm]. I don't know what time this was but it was before the news on the television at 9pm. I said I would go downstairs to see what was keeping Sandra but Mummy said no, she would go. I said I would go with her but she said no, it was okay, she would go. Mummy left the room to go downstairs and I stayed watching TV. She left the bedroom door open but there was no light in the hall because the bulb is worn out and it doesn't work.
>
> Just after Mummy left the room I heard a scream. It sounded as though it had come from a long way away. I thought maybe the cat had scratched Mummy and she had screamed. I wasn't frightened by the scream, and I just stayed in the room watching TV. I went to the door of the room and called 'Mummy?' But there was no answer so I just left it. At about 9.05pm, when the news was on television, Daddy and Mummy both walked into the room.

Later Veronica said that it was 'utterly incredible'[19] that Frances had blamed the scream on the cat, and had continued to watch television. It is perhaps surprising that the scream was all that she heard, but the site of the attack was two floors away.

By Frances's timings, Veronica and Lucan were downstairs for approximately ten minutes. Of course the attack itself would not have lasted very long. Nevertheless there was not much time for the halted colloquy on the stairs, during which Lucan supposedly confessed to murder.

Veronica's account, on the other hand, in which she went down-stairs at 9.15pm, and upstairs at a time unspecified, easily allows for the confession on the ground floor. It also minimizes the mysteri-ous period when the Lucans were alone together in the bedroom. Having fought with her husband, gone to the cloakroom and talked on the stairs, there was then time for little more than what Veron-ica told the inquest: going upstairs, lying on the bed, escaping at 9.50pm. In the account supplied by Frances, however, the Lucans spent some forty-five minutes together in the bedroom.

Factually there are things that do not make sense, if Lucan were indeed guilty as named. There was blood at the sites of attack, but in no other part of the house where he was that night. There was nothing to say that he was blood-boltered, as he undoubtedly would have been, except the possibility that he covered himself afterwards in a coat: a circumstance that his wife is likely to have mentioned. There was blood in the garden, where he had no reason to go, and an inexplicably unlocked back door. The smears and smudges of blood in the car, on his trousers, on the letter to Bill Shand Kydd, on Mrs Florman's doorstep, were in minimal quantities given the violence of these crimes, and could have been present for reasons that were innocent as well as guilty. Lucan had undeniable contact with Veronica, who was covered in blood. And he admitted having entered the basement, whose floor and walls were similarly bloody. Grey-blue fibres, presumed to have come from his trousers, were found in the cloakroom and the car. Those can be legitimately explained. There were also fibres on the lead piping, which could have been briefly examined for an innocent reason; although their presence more strongly suggests guilt. Yet no fibres were left on the mailsack into which Lucan must have forced Sandra's body, despite the fact that the police would certainly have wanted to find them there. This, if he was guilty, is a near-impossibility.

At what point did he enter the basement? This is difficult. He told his mother that he had seen 'something terrible': the body in the mailsack. It could be, of course, that he saw it because he had put it there. Assuming that he did not, however; assuming that he entered the house after Veronica was attacked: he could have gone down to the basement before taking her to the bedroom. It would have been natural to do this, to see what had happened to Sandra. The problem is that no blood was reported on the upper floors of the house, yet was found on Mrs Florman's doorstep. Logically, this implies that Lucan went down to the basement *after* taking Veronica upstairs, and before leaving Lower Belgrave Street. He had time to do this; just. It is possible. It may seem a good deal more probable that Lucan entered the basement in order to commit murder, but again one returns to the conundrum of the forensic evidence.

There are other things. Lucan had an alibi; albeit an imprecise one. Furthermore, after Veronica ran from the house he lingered in the area and rang the doorbell in Chester Square, whereas a guilty person would surely have scarpered as fast as possible. He managed to raise the piping over his head in the ante-room, despite the fact that he stood six feet two and the ceiling was only four inches higher. Taking an overview, there was a sheer lack of logic to the whole enterprise. Did he not think about the practical problems of, say, cleaning up the blood in the basement? Would it not have been better to murder his wife in some other way, less susceptible to the vagaries of chance; possibly even when his children were staying at Elizabeth Street (although it would have been necessary for Sandra also to be out of the house)? And why, if what he wanted was his children, would he have taken even the slightest risk of being arrested for the murder of their mother? He could so easily have been seen that night; the dangers were very considerable.

If this had indeed been Lucan's plan, it was not a good one. It is said that he was sufficiently stupid to think that it was, but that is not true. Only in moments of lunacy would he have believed such a thing. There were times when he did behave like a madman; when he rushed towards the endgame, as though the future could be won or lost on a throw of the dice. At other times he pulled back and was himself again. For the police, it was precisely these displays of good-humoured normality that proved Lucan to have been planning murder. In other words, he was in his right mind. Like the aristocratic killers of old, the only lunacy in Lucan was that of unconscionable arrogance: the sense of entitlement that said, away with my unbearable little wife.

Except, of course, that this was not that kind of murder. It was domestic murder. Not sudden and sword-flashing, but secretive, stealthy. Planned and plotted. The sort of thing that Lucan might have dreamed up, in his lonely flat, when he receded into the black holes of his life: a story that he told himself.

Veronica's own story is said to have been immutable. Roy Ranson wrote that she 'never varied from the essential facts of her account of that night'. In fact some inconsistencies did later arise, most notably in a long interview with the *News of the World* given in 1981.

For instance: although Veronica had previously stated that Sandra Rivett made her offer of tea at around 8.55pm, to the newspaper she was more precise. 'Sandra put her head round the door just as Big Ben came on the screen.'[20] Veronica then described going downstairs, being attacked by her husband and sitting with him on the stairs. According to the police story, it was at this point that Lucan confessed to murder. Here, however, the account was rather different.

'Where's Sandra?' I asked. It was in my mind that if she were in cahoots with him, like the other nannies,[21] I was a goner. They were going to be able to do away with me without any difficulty.

In reply to his wife's question, Lucan did not confess but simply said: 'She's down there. But don't look. It's an awful sight.' He then started to complain that Veronica's solicitor had been demanding more money. 'I'm fed up with it. It's getting me down.' After a long rant about lawyers and his financial situation, he said suddenly: 'I'll have to go away... Will you come with me? The children will be all right with your sister.'[22]

The implication of these remarks, which were never publicly reported by the police, is that if Lucan committed the crimes then he did so for monetary reasons; and that, far from being obsessed with his children, he was willing to parcel them off casually to Christina Shand Kydd.

In 2008 Veronica offered another version of this post-murder conversation, claiming to have suggested to Lucan that they cover up Sandra Rivett's death. 'I offered to help him conceal her body.'[23] Four years later, she would say something similar when she told a newspaper:

> If I could have helped him I would have done. I wouldn't have given him money, I would have said, 'Go away, I will handle it from here.' But I was too badly injured to try to help him. I had to have my injuries seen to. If he had not attacked me I would have said, 'Get out. I have not seen you.' I would have protected him.'[24]

Veronica had brought up this theme as early as January 1975, in her long interview with the *Daily Express*. At that time, however, she portrayed the offer of protection as a ruse, a diversionary tactic. 'I pretended to be helpful. I said that as Sandra had no friends or relatives [sic] no one would miss her...' Veronica then described sitting on the stairs with her attacker, who demanded to know if she had any sleeping pills. 'When I replied that I had some he asked me if I would take them. I suppose to finish the job! I said I would. Then he took me up to my bedroom.'

This story does give an answer of sorts to the imponderable question: why, despite having every chance to do so, Lucan did not actually kill Veronica. She stated a couple of times that he did make a second attempt, but with pills. On or around 15 November 1974,[25] Veronica related the story of that night to Christabel Martin, her nanny, in a long telephone call. When Christabel returned to work at Lower Belgrave Street, the two women talked further. Christabel then wrote up the account in a diary, 'based on eighteen hours of conversations with Lady Lucan',[26] and revealed after she herself was murdered in 1985. It recounted:

She fought with him like mad. Eventually he gave up and sat on the stairs. They talked. V bleeding badly. He admitted killing Sandra. Was going to put V's body in safe. V persuaded him to go up to the bedroom. She said she wanted to lie down and wash her face. She said they would hide the body to calm him down.

They went upstairs and Frances came down and saw them both. He was covered in blood. He told Frances to go back upstairs. She did. In the bedroom he said they must go away together and would she bring her sleeping pills to take an overdose. Yes, yes. She got up and ran like hell downstairs... I hope they catch the bastard Lucan. Dead, I hope.

Although this story is familiar in essentials, there are discrepancies; most notably the strong hint at a suicide pact. There is, too, the reference to Frances coming down to the bedroom, whereas in fact she was there already; and the description of Lucan as 'covered in blood', which Frances did not say to the police. She said that she could not see if there was blood on his clothes. It is possible, of course, that the child had sought to protect her father. But would she really have done that, given that he had apparently attacked her mother?

It was natural that Veronica and Christabel would have discussed these events. That does not mean that the diary recorded them wholly accurately. When Christabel left Lower Belgrave Street for the last time in early 1975, it was reported that 'among her plans is to write a book'.[27] There was no suggestion that her subject was to be the Lucan case, but it does imply that she was capable of embellishment: the Mayerling touch.[28] Did Lucan really make this highly remarkable suggestion that they both take sleeping pills? Did he, as Veronica previously stated, suggest that she alone should take them? Veronica does not consistently mention it in her accounts.

She did not mention it in the *News of the World* interview, which gives a different, detailed version of the post-attack period. The police do not mention it at all. But if Lucan did believe that he could induce somebody to take an overdose, then he was truly as mad as a hatter. His daughter, one of the people for whom he had supposedly committed these crimes, had just seen him with Veronica. What did he think he would do with his wife's battered and drug-filled corpse? And what, if the two of them were preparing to go away together, was to become of the children?

It frankly beggars all belief that Lucan, having killed once, and having at his mercy a tiny woman close to the oblivion of uncon-sciousness, did not finish her off there and then, but instead started trying to ply her with sleeping pills. Why, if he was her assailant, did he not kill her during the attack? Yes, she had put up a fight, but he was still twice her size. He may have been crying with the ordeal, as she later said (although later still she would say: 'My husband did not cry on my shoulder or break down and weep during our con-versation sitting on the stairs following the murder of Mrs Rivett'[29]). But she herself was bleeding from the head. She was, as she told the *Daily Express*, 'weakening physically'. If Lucan was the killer, he should have killed her. Otherwise, what had been the point of it all?

'The moment had passed, I think they would argue,' says Chris-tina. 'The adrenalin had gone.'

'He was worn out,' says the former detective-sergeant Graham Forsyth. 'He's killed someone. That's a shock to his system. I think that really would have drained someone.'

And that argument might hold; were it not for this rigmarole of the sleeping pills. Lucan was too exhausted to strike or to strangle, but he was prepared to perform a Svengali-like hypnosis to compel his victim's self-destruction.

What went on between the Lucans, in the aftermath of the attacks, is a mystery: perhaps the deepest in this story. Such is the nature of marriage, even in its death throes. As Christina said, there was a bond between them. Even their hatred was a kind of bond.

The police would say that Veronica was playing for time when she suggested to Lucan that they conceal his crime. 'You know, saying, "let's talk this over",' says Graham Forsyth. 'Thinking, "if he gets me upstairs he's going to finish me off." She was fighting for her life.'

If Frances's timings were correct, however, Lucan *did* get Veron-ica upstairs quite quickly, where he did *not* finish her off. Nor did he call an ambulance. One or the other, surely, would have been logical. What they talked about, if anything, is entirely unknown. A pact? If so, Veronica broke it when Lucan went into the bathroom and she ran to the pub; and yet, more than thirty years on, she was still expressing her retrospective desire to have helped her husband. When the police entered the bedroom, they found just one lamp switched on and Veronica's blood on a towel spread over her pillow. A strange scene, darkly intimate, a Sickert set in Belgravia.

Equally strange is this remark, made by Veronica in 1998: 'If I had known how to do it I would have hired a hit man and got him first. But I didn't know what to do and I hadn't got £2,000.'[30]

What does this mean? Was it, perhaps, an expression of Pier-rette Goletto's analysis: 'She wanted to destroy John. I cannot have you so I'm going to kill you'? In other words, hell hath no fury. Lucan had walked out on the marriage, and nobody really finds it forgivable to be left. Veronica later repeatedly insisted that she had wanted Lucan to come back to her, and that he too had wanted to return. This is contrary to all other evidence, in particular Jane's recollections, as Veronica must surely have known.

Yet in the face of this she said:

> He didn't hate me and I certainly didn't hate him. He was my husband. There wasn't even an official separation between us and there was certainly no talk of divorce. There was a battle to get the children, of course, but I felt then and I have always felt that we were soul mates and the feelings we had for each other transcended those difficulties.[31]

Another remark was made in a BBC television interview, when Veronica said that it might have been better if she had, in fact, been murdered.

These profound oddities cannot really be explained, except, just possibly, in a fictional retelling of the events of 7 November 1974.

Fiction would allow that something far stranger went on that night than contradictory, inconvenient reality can accept. It would dip beneath the facts, into the subliminal waters of the unconscious. It would suggest that Lucan was seeking to escape from the immaculate absurdity that his life had become, and that his wife, with whom he shared a mysterious bond, understood that desire. That the murder of Sandra Rivett was the unintended culmination of the *folie à deux* that was the marriage between these two: the real endgame.

It would say that Veronica, in a fugue-like state that mirrored her husband's, was trapped in that endgame; that when she left the chain off the front door, when she followed Sandra down into the darkness, she was caught up in her husband's destructive impulse; that he fell into that temptation, then, at the last moment, when they were fighting together, resisted it. That they discussed the possibility of concealing his crime, finding a way together out of the trap. That when he was no longer with her she ran out of the house, and that after sitting in the pub for a minute, lost in silence, she broke the bond and denounced him: ended his life, as he had sought to end hers.

This is fiction only. Yet it might contain psychological echoes of the truth.

The most powerful inconsistency in Veronica's story came in the *News of the World* interview, when she seemed suddenly to give way to doubt about the identity of her attacker.

> What is extraordinary is that there was no blood on Lord Lucan. Our daughter confirmed this... There is a theory that someone else was in the house and that it was he who killed Sandra and hit me and knocked me unconscious. Some people don't believe I could have withstood such heavy blows and it does seem strange that I did.
>
> I only know that at the time, I thought my husband had hit me. I didn't think I had fallen. Maybe I did. Maybe he had lifted me to my feet when I recovered consciousness.
>
> There could quite easily have been someone hiding downstairs

or in the cloakroom. Our house was heavily carpeted and I would not have heard them if they had kept still.

I simply don't know.[32]

Christina Shand Kydd says:

She admitted to us that she couldn't be absolutely certain that it was John who attacked her on the stairs. And I said, well, you should tell the police that. You should tell them you couldn't swear to who it was on the stairs.

But you don't know whether she just decided to say that. You know, it's something she could just suddenly say, to make you interested in her, and then deny it three hours later. And you'd say, you said so and so, and she'd say no, I didn't.

In fact there is something oddly poignant about Veronica's words to the *News of the World*. It is as though her desire to put the case for the defence is motivated, not just by an instinct to play fair, but by a kind of wishful thinking: it was not he who wanted to kill me. 'He could have finished me off at any time and it would have been to his advantage to do so,' she said. 'But he didn't.'

Nevertheless – and whatever the reasons for making it – the admission of uncertainty, of confusion, opens up a possibility. It suggests that Veronica could indeed have been attacked, in the darkened hall, by a man who was not Lucan; and that when Lucan himself arrived at the house she believed that the attacker was him.

The people who knew Lucan best all say the same thing, that he was incapable of wielding that piece of piping: that he could not have planned to go berserk. The Shand Kydds believe him to have been entirely innocent, and hold to the theory of a second man connected to Sandra.

Lucan's schoolfriend also believes in a second man, but thinks that this man was connected to Lucan himself. 'He could have, I suppose, hired someone to do it. Which is not a nice thing to say about your great friend.'

Lucan's sister Jane, who perhaps saw most clearly his state of mind, and can still conjure its lurching anguish, says:

> I think it is an unlikely scenario, that he planned something when the children were in the house. But when you've got to such a point, and off the rails – which I think he was very close to – almost anything is possible.
>
> He was so desperately paranoid, and taping all of her conversations on the telephone – there was a real sort of a violent outlook, I think. He'd become not rational. He just sounded so... He visited us shortly before – he came two or three times every year. And he was very anxiety-ridden, pacing the floors – very upset. Because he really adored those children, and saw that they were in bad hands.
>
> I found it impossible that he should have done... But he might have hired somebody, that was always an option. I could imagine that John might have hired a hitman, yes.

Yet the hitman theory presents its own conundrum: why was Lord Lucan at the house that night? And it does not supply a satisfactory answer.

There is, however, this.

It was always apparent that Susan Maxwell-Scott, that loyal sphinx, was hiding something. The police suspected different things: that Lucan had told her about the murder, that she was implicated in his escape, that she had driven the Corsair to Newhaven, lent him her husband's clothes, what you will, and that she kept silence partly because she was half in love with him. One could hardly blame Susan if she had preferred sleek, courteous Lucan to the dishevelled and bad-tempered Ian; but that, even if it were so, is not really relevant.

The police came closest to the truth with their first assumption. Susan gave Lucan sanctuary for a few hours and, in between ringing his mother and writing his letters, it seems that what he mostly did was talk. Knowing that she would not give him away, that this might be his last chance to say it all, he told her what really happened that night. Not the story of walking past the house and seeing a fight in the basement. That was the public version, the one that could be said out loud; a story full of holes, but the best that he could come up with. He was compromised, after all. He had been at the house. He had blood on his hands. The story told to Susan in private was not so very different, in a way, from the story that she told on his behalf at the inquest. In another way it was different altogether.

Susan died thirty years after the murder, having lived for some years as a widow in Battersea. During that time she talked, occasionally, about the events of that night. Her former nanny, who remained close to the Maxwell-Scotts, was told this story by a member of the family.

In the absence of the ex-pat with the nobleman's profile, drinking martinis in the bar in Gaborone, it must suffice as his testimony.

The nanny says:

So Lord Lucan arrived at Susie's. They had several drinks, and he told her this. He said he'd had enough of Veronica. He was losing control, he'd lost access to the children and he felt desolate – he couldn't live with it. And so he hired a hitman to kill her. He did that. Whether it was done in a drunken stupor or not... Anyway.

At the last minute, at the eleventh hour, he panicked. He changed his mind – came to his senses. He didn't want it to happen, and he tried to call it off. Then he went round there. He rushed round to the house, and it had already happened, and the guy had killed the wrong woman.

Susan Maxwell-Scott, in her later life, did speak more openly about the Lucan case; and not always very cogently. But this story has never before been told. There was no reason for Susan to invent it. What would have been the point? As a Roman Catholic, she would have known that a mortal sin exists in its intention, as well as its commission. So the story did not exonerate Lucan. Nor does it have the air of invention: it is too straightforward for that. The tendency, therefore, is to believe that Lucan did tell Susan exactly this.

It can only ever be a hypothesis. Nevertheless the story is the one into which the facts do fit. It takes on the theory of the hitman, by far the most convincing solution to the case, and at a stroke resolves the central problem: why Lucan himself was at the house. It explains the 'plan to go berserk', because the man who planned, and the man who went berserk, were two different people. It explains the testimony of Lucan's mother at the inquest: he did go into 46 Lower Belgrave Street to 'interrupt a fight', although (as Kait may or may not have been told) it was he who had instigated the fight in the first place. It explains the remark made to Kait, which has the pleading sound of absolute honesty: 'Oh mother, there was something terrible in the basement. I couldn't bring myself to look.' It explains the letters that he wrote: their references to a man who had been 'hired', to a 'night of unbelievable coincidence'; and their odd obliqueness of tone, as if something were being implied that was not quite a confession, but could not quite be said.

It accommodates the belief of those who knew Lucan best, who say that he could not have planned to commit those acts himself. It reflects the waywardness of Lucan's moods, the energetic resentment and violent despair that could shift, quite suddenly, and give way to a sane acceptance. It suggests a delusional state from which he awakened into sobriety: too late. This was how his life had been, after all. A series of dreams, of a magical deliverance from traps of his own making, that were not always his fault.

Above all the story explains Lucan. It makes him guilty, and not guilty. Which he always was, in truth.

But myths are not so easy to kill.

I was in Belgravia on the same night, at the same time, thirty-nine years later; an uneasy walk, that made the events of 7 November 1974 both more and less real to me; and a strange thing happened as I walked down Lower Belgrave Street. An oldish man came lumbering towards me. He had the fuzzy appearance of one slightly drunk. He was tall, straight, dressed in a suit and coat, an upper-class type, one would have said, who had fallen on difficult times. In the unset-tling light he gave the impression of being dusty grey: his face and hair, as well as his clothes. He was muttering as he walked. As he approached me, outside number 46, his eyes glanced into mine, askew yet direct. There was an aggression in the look; as if I had trespassed upon his territory; and there was something else, a kind of half-amused knowingness.

I turned the corner into Chester Square and rang a friend. I said: 'I've just seen Lord Lucan.'

I had believed it, for a moment.

APPENDICES

Appendix I: Aristocratic Murderers

Appendix II: Domestic Murderers

Appendix III: The Lucan Family

Appendix I:
Aristocratic Murderers

A summary of the eleven titled murderers referred to on page 3.

1541 9th Baron Dacre, found guilty. Five years earlier he had been a member of the jury at the trial of Anne Boleyn. During a boys' night out he and his friends decided that it would be a great wheeze to go poaching on a neighbour's estate; a fight ensued with the landowner's servants, in the course of which a man named John Busbrigg was killed. Although Dacre had no malicious intent he was hanged at Tyburn, 'strangled as common murderers are'.

1556 8th Baron Stourton, found guilty. After a long campaign of intimidation against his mother's steward, William Hartgill, with whom he had argued over money, he ordered four of his servants to kill both Hartgill and his son. Probably the only aristocrat to have been hanged with the traditional silk rope, he was buried in Salisbury Cathedral.

1615–16 1st Earl and Countess of Somerset, found guilty and pardoned. The couple were accused of poisoning Sir Thomas Overbury, secretary to the earl and formerly his close friend. Overbury had opposed the Somerset marriage and made an enemy of the countess's powerful family, the Howards. His removal thus became politically desirable. The countess, although clearly guilty, was pardoned immediately. Her husband's guilt is contested, but having fallen from his previous high favour with King James I, he was not pardoned until 1624.

1666 15th Baron Morley, found guilty of manslaughter and pleaded privilege of peerage. He killed a man named Hastings during a drunken brawl at the Fleece Tavern; or, as the testimony at his trial put it, 'ran Mr Hastings through the head'.

1678 3rd Baron Cornwallis, found not guilty. After a night out with a friend, Mr Gerrard, both were 'somewhat distemper'd with drink', and fell into an argument with a sentinel at the Palace of Whitehall, which seems to have revved them up for indiscriminate violence. Gerrard put his sword into a young man named Robert Clerk, who simply happened to be in the wrong place at the wrong time. The degree of Cornwallis's complicity is uncertain.

1678 7th Earl of Pembroke, found guilty of manslaughter and pleaded privilege of peerage. He killed a man named Nathaniel Cony in a tavern brawl, and later that year became chief suspect in the death of Sir Edmund Berry Godfrey, found stabbed in a ditch on Primrose Hill. Godfrey had prosecuted him for the Cony crime.

1680 7th Earl of Pembroke, found guilty and pardoned. Charles II, whose mistress Louise de Kérouaille was Pembroke's sister-in-law, accepted a petition on his behalf after he killed a nightwatchman, William Smeeth, during a drunken spree at Turnham Green. Pembroke was frankly out of control, and committed any number of maniacal assaults during this period. Like any good thug, albeit one with a very large house, he also owned a menagerie of fighting animals: 'fifty-two mastives', 'some beares, and a lyon'.

1692 4th Baron Mohun, found not guilty. A character straight from a thunderous Restoration comedy, he went on an all-night rampage through Covent Garden with a friend named Hill. The pair were in howling pursuit of the actress Anne Bracegirdle; eventually Hill stabbed an actor, William Mountfort, whom he had decided was his rival for her affections. Mohun was technically innocent. Nevertheless his acquittal caused much disquiet.

1699   4th Baron Mohun, found not guilty. This was one of the rare duelling deaths resulting in prosecution for murder: a man named Captain Coote died after a duel with Mohun in Leicester Square. Mohun's obsession with duelling, which was to kill him in 1712, is described by Thackeray in *The History of Henry Esmond*.

1699   6th Earl of Warwick, found guilty of manslaughter and pleaded privilege of peerage. He had participated with Mohun in the Leicester Square duel.

1760   4th Earl Ferrers, found guilty. He used his own carriage to drive from the Tower of London to Tyburn, and wore his wedding clothes to his execution; it was, he said, 'at least as good an occasion for putting them on as that for which they were first made'. His request to be beheaded was denied. He then asked to be hanged with a silk rope. This, too, was almost certainly refused him. Instead he became the first person to be hanged with the 'new drop', a platform that came apart beneath the feet. 'Am I right?' he asked the hangman, as he positioned himself on the trap.

1765   5th Baron Byron, found guilty of manslaughter and fined. He had killed his cousin, William Chaworth, in a darkened room, after a table-thumping argument over which man had more game on his land. Chaworth died, very slowly, complaining that if there had only been more light he would have seen what was happening to him. Later Byron shot his coachman and slung the body on top of his wife, who was sitting in the carriage, then casually took over the reins.

Additional to this list is the Italian peer the Marquis de Palleotti, an obsessive gambler, who was hanged in 1718 for the murder of his servant.

Appendix II: Domestic Murderers

A summary of the domestic murderers referred to on page 7.

1886   Adelaide Bartlett was acquitted of the 'Pimlico Mystery', although it is generally assumed that she did poison her ghastly husband with chloroform. What could not be explained, and helped her defence immeasurably, is why this corrosive substance did not burn Edwin Bartlett's throat on its way to his stomach. A commentator observed: 'Now that she has been acquitted for murder and cannot be tried again, she should tell us in the interest of science how she did it!'

1928–9   In the unsolved Croydon case, three members of the same family died from arsenic poisoning. The deaths took place in two respectable houses in neighbouring streets. The chief suspect was Grace Duff, whose husband, sister and mother were the victims, although there was scant evidence against her, and the confused forensic evidence has even led to suggestions that the three died from natural ingestion of arsenic, then a substance present in many household preparations.

1876   The poisoning of Charles Bravo at the Priory in Balham also remains an unsolved case. His wife Florence fell under suspicion, as the marriage was an unhappy one; so too did Florence's much older former lover, Dr Gully, and her friend-companion Jane Cox. The book *Death at the Priory* by James Ruddick (Atlantic, 2001) presents a well-researched and very convincing solution.

1857   Madeleine Smith, a young woman living in the Glasgow home of her socially prominent family, was accused of poisoning her lover Emile L'Angelier. She was said to have plied him with arsenic-laden cocoa after she ended the affair. Her love letters, full of magnificently pagan declarations of passion, were viewed as even more shocking than the crime. Miss Smith was acquitted on the Scottish verdict of 'not proven'; her guilt seems overwhelmingly likely. F. Tennyson Jesse's essay in *Famous Trials*, volume 1 (Penguin, 1941) is superb.

1889   American-born Florence Maybrick was convicted of poisoning her much older husband at their home near Liverpool. James Maybrick has occasionally been named as a Jack the Ripper suspect. He was an arsenic eater, and his wife's conviction was unsound, but although the death sentence was commuted she remained in prison until 1904. Kate Colquhoun's *Did She Kill Him?* (Little, Brown, 2014) gives an excellent account of the case.

1910   Dr Crippen poisoned his nagging wife, the failed music-hall singer Cora, then cut her up and buried her beneath his cellar in Camden Town. He might have got away with it had he not behaved idiotically. He dressed his mistress, Ethel Le Neve, in Cora's jewels, paraded her in front of Cora's friends, suddenly took fright and absconded with her. The pair were apprehended on board ship. Ethel was disguised as Crippen's son. Both were tried; Crippen was hanged.

1912–14   George Joseph Smith, the 'Brides in the Bath' killer, was a multiple bigamist who exerted a mysterious spell upon women who were otherwise sensible but deemed to be 'on the shelf'. Smith met them on his prowls around seaside towns and murdered them for their savings. He married Bessie Mundy, Alice Burnham and Margaret Lofty in quick succession, then drowned them in their boarding-house baths. He was hanged in 1915.

1931   The insurance agent William Wallace was found guilty of clubbing his wife to death in the sitting room of their Liverpool house, but the conviction was quashed on the grounds that the evidence did not support it; effectively, that the jury got it wrong. Wallace offered a strange alibi, stating that he had been telephoned and asked to call at the house of a prospective client, but that the address given did not exist. P. D. James, a student of the case, wrote a fascinating article positing Wallace's guilt (*Sunday Times*, 27 October 2013).

Appendix III: The Lucan Family

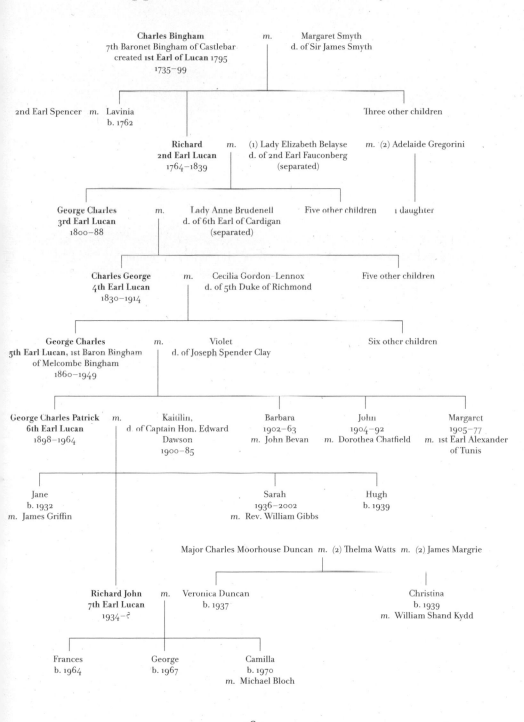

Charles Bingham
7th Baronet Bingham of Castlebar
created **1st Earl of Lucan** 1795
1735–99
m. Margaret Smyth
d. of Sir James Smyth

2nd Earl Spencer *m.* Lavinia
b. 1762

Three other children

Richard
2nd Earl Lucan
1764–1839
m. (1) Lady Elizabeth Belayse
d. of 2nd Earl Fauconberg
(separated)
m. (2) Adelaide Gregorini

George Charles
3rd Earl Lucan
1800–88
m. Lady Anne Brudenell
d. of 6th Earl of Cardigan
(separated)
Five other children 1 daughter

Charles George
4th Earl Lucan
1830–1914
m. Cecilia Gordon-Lennox
d. of 5th Duke of Richmond
Five other children

George Charles
5th Earl Lucan, 1st Baron Bingham
of Melcombe Bingham
1860–1949
m. Violet
d. of Joseph Spender Clay
Six other children

George Charles Patrick
6th Earl Lucan
1898–1964
m. Kaitilin,
d. of Captain Hon. Edward
Dawson
1900–85

Barbara
1902–63
m. John Bevan

John
1904–92
m. Dorothea Chatfield

Margaret
1905–77
m. 1st Earl Alexander
of Tunis

Jane
b. 1932
m. James Griffin

Sarah
1936–2002
m. Rev. William Gibbs

Hugh
b. 1939

Major Charles Moorhouse Duncan *m.* (2) Thelma Watts *m.* (2) James Margrie

Richard John
7th Earl Lucan
1934–?
m. Veronica Duncan
b. 1937

Christina
b. 1939
m. William Shand Kydd

Frances
b. 1964

George
b. 1967

Camilla
b. 1970
m. Michael Bloch

Notes

INTRODUCTION

1. This information comes from James Fox's *White Mischief* (Cape, 1982), as does the account of the crime.

2. When the body of Courvoisier's victim was discovered, he said: 'My God, what shall I do? I shall never get a place again.' His execution was described by William Thackeray in the essay 'Going to See a Man Hanged'. 'I feel myself ashamed and degraded', wrote Thackeray, 'at the brutal curiosity which took me to that brutal sight.'

3. The legend was always that Webster had dropped her victim's head into the Thames from Richmond Bridge (it was also said that she sold dripping to her neighbours, concocted from the corpse). However, during excavation works at a former pub beside the home of Sir David Attenborough, who lives close to the murder site, a skull was uncovered that was almost certainly that of Mrs Thomas.

4. From Volume 5 of *Old and New London* by Edward Walford (1878).

5. For example in the *Daily Express*, 11 November 1974.

6. Quotation from V. S. Naipaul.

THE LUCAN MYTH

1. Quotations respectively from: *Guardian*, 9 September 2003; *Sunday Mirror*, 22 June 1975; *The Times*, 28 October 1999; *Observer*, 3 May 1998; *Sunday Mirror*, 22 June 1975; *Observer*, 3 May 1998; *Guardian*, 2 November 1994.

2. *Daily Express*, 20 November 1974.

3. Stuart Wheeler, in conversation with the author.

4. Roy Ranson, *Looking for Lucan: The Final Verdict* (Smith Gryphon, 1994).

5. In conversation with the author.

6. In James Fox's article for *Sunday Times Magazine*, 8 June 1975.

7. Ibid.

8. David Gerring, *Lucan Lives* (Robert Hale, 1995).

9. Fox, *op. cit.*

10. In conversation with James Ruddick, in his book *Lord Lucan: What Really Happened* (Headline, 1995).

11. According to legal opinion this is the most likely estimate, although some sources, for example Gerring, put the cost as high as £40,000.

12. James Fox, revisiting the case in *Sunday Telegraph*, 10 October 2004.

13. Fox, *Sunday Times Magazine*, 8 June 1975.

14. Patrick Marnham, *Trail of Havoc* (Viking, 1987).

15. Both Marnham and Ruddick espouse the hitman hypothesis in their books.

16. Marnham, *op. cit.*

17. In the *Daily Mirror*.

18. *Daily Express*, 14 November 1974.

19. This phrase came from the journalist Richard Ingrams. In the *Independent*, 7 January 2003, he recalled an article written for *Private Eye* soon after the murder, which included 'a sentence that went something like: "From the beginning, the police have met nothing but obstruction from the circle of boneheads and gamblers who are friends of Lucan."'

20. Patrick Marnham in the *Daily Telegraph*, 19 September 2000.

21. Marnham, *Trail of Havoc*.

22. In conversation with the author.

23. Gerring, *op. cit.*

24. In 2014 much publicity was given to the fact that John Bingham, MI5 operative and Lucan's distant cousin, had been the inspiration for John le Carré's George Smiley. It was suggested that during the 1970s Bingham had been interested in the right-wing activities at the Clermont Club. Be that as it may, one can imagine that there would have been more useful places to observe.

25. *Sunday Times*, 3 July 2005.

26. *Sunday Mirror*, 22 June 1975. The royal meeting was afflicted that year by a strike for higher pay by stable lads.

27. *Daily Mail*, 20 June 1975.

28. In September 2014, it was reported that an author named Russell Edwards had in fact identified Jack the Ripper. DNA found on a shawl, said to have belonged to the fourth victim Catherine Eddowes, appeared to correlate

with that of Aaron Kosminski, a Polish barber who died in an asylum, one of the six men commonly named as a suspect for the murders.

29. *Daily Express*, 27 June 1975. Lady Lucan stated that her husband would never pass for a Frenchman and spoke the language 'like a sixth-former'. On the same day, however, the *Daily Mirror* told her that the sightings had been dismissed by Lucan's friends, who had cited her own argument that his French was not fluent enough. Her reaction was: 'Oh my God, how could they? How could they?', implying that she herself wanted to believe the report. This may, of course, have been journalistic licence. Nevertheless Lady Lucan's attitude did shift publicly, and not only in 1975: in 1981, for instance, she told ITN's *News at Ten* and the *News of the World* that she believed her husband to be alive, but in 1994 told ITV's *GMTV* that he was dead.

30. The encounter between Lucan and Brian Hill was cited by Richard Ingrams in the *Guardian*, 14 August 1994. In the same article Ingrams wrote: 'It has always been my hunch that if Lucan is alive (as I believe him to be), he is lurking somewhere in this part of the Dark Continent...'

    There were further sightings in Mozambique. It was suggested that Lucan had lived there with a German woman (his German was certainly better than his French). In 2002 photographs were passed to Scotland Yard of a man using the name John Crawford and bearing a resemblance to the earl.

31. *Daily Mirror*, 27 April 1976.

32. In 1982 a convicted murderer on the run saw Lucan in a Harare hotel: 'I called him Lucky, like people used to, and he didn't even raise an eyebrow' (*Daily Mirror*, 1 March 2012). In 2001 the former detective John Stalker said that he, like 'the cops in charge of the case', believed Lucan to be living in Africa. 'One of them went to, I think it was Zambia, or Zimbabwe, and is absolutely sure he came within a day of laying a hand on him.' (*Daily Mail*, 25 February 2001)

33. In 2012 a former secretary to John Aspinall named Shirley Robey claimed that she had been asked to organize passports for Lucan's two elder children, Frances and George, to visit Kenya and Gabon. She also stated that she did not know Lucan had been named as a murderer: 'The last thing I would look at would be scandalous news.' As reported in the *Daily Telegraph*, 20 May 2012, her story detailed arrangements between Aspinall and his then business associate, Sir James Goldsmith (both men were safely dead by this time). 'It suggests', the article stated, 'that John Aspinall, the casino owner who died twelve years ago, was in prolonged and regular contact with the peer. It also implicates Sir James Goldsmith, who in the 1970s sued *Private Eye*, the satirical magazine, over claims he had helped Lucan after his disappearance.

'They were talking about John Bingham [Lucan],' Miss Robey says. 'The conversations were, "What are we going to do?"; "Have you been in touch?" I was just making notes. At the end of the meeting, John Aspinall was saying, "Quite definitely, we need to do something about this" and there was a bit of a disagreement between him and Sir James Goldsmith.

'"No we mustn't do anything; causes too much trouble, we just wait," and then the end of that meeting closed with James saying, "You speak to him", and it was then said, "You only speak to him on that phone don't you?" gesturing to the private phone.

'He [Goldsmith] looked at me, he didn't even know my name, and said, "What does she know about anything?" And Mr Aspinall said, "She knows a bit, I'm going to bring her in on it".'

The plan, enacted in both 1979 and 1980, was to fly Frances and George to Gabon, where Aspinall had a gorilla centre, then to Kenya. Miss Robey also stated that Aspinall was convinced of Lucan's innocence. 'I'm not saying, and I can't say, whether he would have covered up for him if he thought he was guilty but I think he's made of better stuff than that.'

Some years after Aspinall's death in 2000, when according to her best belief Lucan was still alive, Miss Robey contacted the police. 'They said to me, everything you've said, we're already aware of.' She also wrote to George Bingham, who did not acknowledge her letter and later firmly refuted the story. 'The trip to Kenya was much later,' he said, 'I think nearer 1985. I was nearly 18. Both my sisters were present as were two other families, neither of which had any connection to John Aspinall.' This was confirmed, surely unanswerably, in a statement from his mother Lady Lucan. 'The children were wards of court, at boarding school. I was their carer. I would have known if they had gone to Africa. I can guarantee they didn't go to Africa. I had to get permission from the court to take them abroad.'

In 2000, Lucan's children Frances and George visited a 'luxury holiday lodge' near Windhoek. An investigator named Ian Crosby later seized upon these holidays as suggesting that Lucan had been in Namibia at that time. The story was reported in the *Daily Mail*, 10 March 2012: 'We do not doubt that he [George] has not knowingly set eyes on his father since 1974. However, who is to say that his father was not watching him on a visit to Namibia?'

34. *The Sun*, 28 February 2012. The 'links to Botswana' cited in the article are unknown. In 1993 Lucan was sighted once more in Gaborone, at the Cresta Riley's hotel.

35. An article in the *Daily Mail*, 3 February 2013, examined the findings of the BBC1 *Inside Out* documentary broadcast in December 2012. The programme was presented by Glenn Campbell, who had uncovered new evidence regarding the hunt for Lucan, as well as a hitherto unseen

police statement given by Lucan's sister, Lady Sarah Gibbs (see p.272). The *Daily Mail* wrote:

> Lord Lucan's brother has told the BBC that the fugitive aristocrat died in 2004 and is buried in Africa. Hugh Bingham is said to have made the startling disclosure in an 'unguarded moment' after an interview at his Johannesburg home. When the cameras stopped rolling, he was pressed by a journalist on the *Inside Out* programme about whether Lucan – accused of murdering his children's nanny, Sandra Rivett, in 1974 – was 'dead or alive'. Mr Bingham, 72, replied: 'I know for a fact my brother died in 2004 and that his grave is in Africa.' The alleged admission – which would mean Lucan was 70 when he died – was revealed by Mrs Rivett's 46-year-old son, Neil Berriman.

None of the facts about this 'revelation' has ever been corroborated.

36. It was revealed on *Inside Out* that Scotland Yard had considered sending an undercover detective to the Hebridean island of Eigg. Lucan was rumoured to be hiding near the ruins of Kildonan monastery, having used a powerboat to cross from the Scottish mainland. 'That explains a lot,' was a comment on Facebook. 'It's rural and isolated. I'm from Mull and even we don't visit Eigg.'

37. An ex-SAS bounty hunter named John Miller, who had previously found the escaped prisoner Ronald Biggs (a member of the Great Train Robbery gang), claimed that Lucan had been captured and was being held by employees of Miller's security company. This story was revealed to be a hoax after a television reporter paid Miller $4,000 for the story and took a boat to Caracas in search of Lucan. A former drug dealer had been paid to act the part of the vanished earl.

   There was also a police report suggesting that a British citizen, living on Barbados, had been sending money to Lucan in an unidentified South American country. This rumour has echoes of a 1974 story that a telegram had been found at Lucan's Elizabeth Street flat, sent by an unidentified relation, offering him the use of a property on Haiti.

38. Quoted in *The Times*, 6 March 2012.

39. Quoted in the *Daily Mail*, 27 October 2004.

40. Many of the facts in this section come from Dominic Sandbrook, *Seasons in the Sun: The Battle for Britain 1974–79* (Allen Lane, 2012).

41. Martin Amis, *The Pregnant Widow* (Jonathan Cape, 2010).

THE STORY: THE LUCANS

1. His nephew and heir, Robert, married one of the Turbervilles, whose name – as d'Urberville – was appropriated for the aristocratic ancestors

of Thomas Hardy's Tess Durbeyfield. With Lucy Turberville, who unlike Tess retained her birth privileges, came the manor of Melcombe Bingham in Dorset.

2. Richard's nephew, Henry, became the 1st Baronet Bingham of Mayo in 1634. Henry's brother John was the progenitor of another family line: his great-great-great-grandson was created 1st Baron Clanmorris of New-brook in 1800. The MI5 operative John Bingham was the 7th Baron.

3. This was Anne Vesey, whose grandfather William Sarsfield had married Mary Stuart, an illegitimate daughter of Charles II and Lucy Walter. The Vesey family held senior posts in the Irish church. Coincidentally Anne Vesey's aunt, who bore the same name as her niece, married one of the Clanmorris Binghams.

4. Horace Walpole, that supreme aesthete, who would have revelled in bitchiness had Margaret been in the usual run of amateurs, wrote to a friend in 1773 that 'Lady Bingham is, I assure you, another miracle. She began painting in miniatures within these two years... She allows me to point out her faults, and if her impetuosity will allow her patience to reflect and study, she will certainly very soon equal anything that was ever done in water-colours.'

5. Amanda Foreman's biography of Georgiana, Duchess of Devonshire, sister to the 2nd Earl Spencer, suggests that Lavinia displayed a tight-lipped jealousy towards her glamorous sister-in-law. 'She looked well and healthy but is so coarse I hardly knew her,' was Lavinia's report to her husband in 1788, when Georgiana was out and about campaigning for the Whigs. (*Georgiana, Duchess of Devonshire*, HarperCollins 1998)

6. A contemporary account gave a shrewd, gossipy description of the 2nd Earl's parting from his wife. 'It was more from disagreement of temper and extreme absurdity on both sides than any other cause. How extraor-dinary, after giving up the world for each other and living happily near ten years! At the end of that time they went to Brighthelmstone [Brighton] where he had the gout. She took to racketing and neglecting him, he grew low spirited and scolded her... This continued for near two years!' The stay at Brighton was glittering, despite the gout: the Lucans were listed in *The Times* as guests of the Prince of Wales at the Royal Pavilion.

7. The Irish lords were elected, but only by each other, so there was no wide democratic principle in play. The system came to an end in 1922 with the creation of the Irish Free State.

8. Only rich men could afford, for instance, the £1,190 that it cost to buy a lieutenant's position in the cavalry in the 1830s. After that, officers could keep climbing the ranks by paying the difference. Naturally there was a black market; some commissions were sold to pay off a debt (from

gambling, most likely), and in 1806 a mistress of the Duke of York was found to be doing a roaring trade in them. In the 1850s Lord Cardigan paid £40,000 to become Colonel in the 11th Hussars, which had previously charged so calamitously with the Light Brigade during the Crimean War. It was this hapless campaign that helped to draw attention to the deficiencies inherent in the system, and it was abolished in 1871.

9. Nobody really knew how many people lived on these poor little fields. One landlord, who requested famine relief for what he estimated to be around sixty tenants, received more than 600 applications.

10. What Lucan wanted, in fact, was for the British government to deal with the Irish famine. The government thought that the responsibility lay with the landowners, whom it blamed not just for the suffering but for the alarming torrents of half-dead people disembarking at Liverpool. Rescue funds for Ireland were ineffectually deployed, although some £8 million was contributed by the British taxpayer. In 1851 a correspondence was published between Lord Lucan and the prime minister, Lord John Russell, regarding the repayment of this money. True to form, Lucan made endless difficulties. 'Great care', he lectured, 'should be taken in the collection of a tax so onerous.' Russell, keeping his temper, nevertheless concluded his reply with a cool coda: 'I must again ask your Lordship, yourself a member of the Legislature, to withdraw your plea of setting yourself above the law.' In the end, the government was obliged to write off about half of its debt.

11. The description is from William Forster, a Quaker philanthropist and later Chief Secretary to Ireland under Gladstone. During the famine he was involved in distributing the Friends' relief fund.

12. In 1842 Lucan had been seriously enraged by an incident that began at the Castlebar Petty Sessions, where he had accused Mr St Clair O'Malley, a Mayo magistrate, of hunting and 'sporting' on his land. 'This is', O'Malley declared, 'a mean and malicious prosecution, and I entertain the most utter contempt for it and Lord Lucan and everything emanating from him.'

   Lucan thundered: 'I call on you to commit that miscreant to the dock,' but O'Malley was equal to him. 'If it were not for where you are,' he replied, 'I would be licking you with this stick [a giant shillelagh] until I would break every bone in your body.' After their ludicrous brawl both men were excluded from the magistracy. Lucan raised the matter three times in the House of Lords, and in late 1843 was restored to his position; but so too was O'Malley. Lucan, who declined to be reinstated and, strictly speaking, had right on his side, bore a deep grudge.

13. Although history has found the 3rd Earl of Lucan peculiarly guilty in the ghastly affair of the famine, he was by no means unsupported in

his attitudes. It was quite true that the farming of Ireland needed to be reformed; Lucan was not the only landowner doing this, albeit his methods were notably ruthless, and some (not all) of his fellow peers took the same view as the *Times* correspondent. The fact was that, despite its status as part of the United Kingdom, Ireland was still regarded by many as separate, alien and intensely annoying. 'The real difficulty', wrote the lord-lieutenant of the country, Lord Clarendon, in 1847, 'lies with the people themselves – they are always in the mud... their idleness and helplessness can hardly be believed.'

14. As recounted by William Russell, first of the great war reporters, in *The Times*.

15. Lord Raglan said, very damningly, that Lucan had made 'some misconception of the order'. Lucan said that Raglan's order had been extremely imprecise. Lord Cardigan accused not only Lucan but also Captain Louis Nolan, who had delivered Raglan's order, of relaying the instructions incorrectly. Lucan pleaded that he could not have disobeyed Raglan 'without any reason than that I preferred my own opinion to that of my General'.

16. At first Lord Cardigan had returned to a hero's welcome and tea with Queen Victoria; this despite the fact that he was seen to have galloped away from the charge before hand-to-hand combat began. He airily stated that he had done his duty by leading his men and had not wanted to 'fight the enemy among private soldiers'. Having emerged without a scratch, Cardigan 'calmly returned to the yacht on which he lived, had a bath, dined, drank a bottle of champagne, and went to bed'. (from Volume IV of Winston Churchill's *A History of the English Speaking Peoples*, 1958)

17. In 1675 Charles II bestowed the title of Duke of Richmond upon his illegitimate son by Louise de Kérouaille. The Lucans were also descended from Mary Stuart, his daughter by Lucy Walter (see note 3, above).

18. The 1901 census records a list of nineteen servants at Laleham, including three ladies' maids, three housemaids, two kitchen maids, two footmen and two grooms. In addition there were three gardeners, an undergardener, a 'seedsman' and a carpenter.

19. At the July auction the Duchess of Albany's Surrey seat was also up for sale; so vast was its acreage that it realized £51,000.

20. This quotation by the Liberal politician C. F. G. Masterman is taken from David Cannadine's *Decline and Fall of the British Aristocracy* (Yale, 1990), as are many of the facts in this section.

21. Two years later, Leverhulme had the house pulled down. It was re-erected, like Dorchester House, as a hotel.

22. The calm, mysteriously atmospheric river path leading to Laleham House had been a favourite walk of the poet Matthew Arnold, born in the village and buried close to the Lucans in All Saints' church. 'I could', he wrote in 1848, 'make out the wide sheet of the gray Thames gleaming through the general dusk as I came out on Chertsey Bridge...'

23. Respectively: Companion of the Most Honourable Order of the Bath; Knight Commander of the Order of the British Empire; Privy Counsellor; Territorial (Officer's) Decoration; Deputy-Lieutenant; Justice of the Peace; Knight Grand Cross of the Victorian Order.

THE STORY: JOHN BINGHAM

1. A British social research organization founded in 1937, a rich resource from a panel of some 500 untrained volunteers who commented on everyday life, either through diaries or questionnaires.

2. From an interview with the *News of the World*, 8 November 1981.

3. The remark about Kait's clothes was made by her brother-in-law, John Bevan; the description of her hair came from Jonathan Miller, in an interview for James Fox's *Sunday Times Magazine* article, 8 June 1975.

4. These recollections come from Kate Bassett, *In Two Minds: Jonathan Miller* (Oberon Books, 2012).

5. *The Spectator*, 28 November 2009.

6. This interviewee, whose contributions appear throughout the book, requested anonymity.

7. *Sunday Times Magazine*, 8 June 1975.

8. In an interview with the *Daily Telegraph*, 31 March 2001.

9. The quotations and facts about National Service are taken from Peter Hennessy, *Having It So Good: Britain in the Fifties* (Allen Lane, 2006).

10. Quoted in Ruddick, *Lord Lucan: What Really Happened.*

11. *News of the World*, 8 November 1981.

12. *Daily Express*, 21 January 1975.

13. An unnamed interviewee in *Sunday Times Magazine*, 8 June 1975.

14. Tic-tac, now pretty much defunct in the era of computerized on-course betting, was the sign language whereby bookmakers' prices could be conveyed across the track.

15. *The Times*, 12 May 2001.

16. The reference is to Alfred, Lord Tennyson's 1854 poem 'The Charge of the Light Brigade', whose first stanza runs:

> Half a league, half a league,

Half a league onward,
All in the valley of Death
Rode the six hundred.
'Forward, the Light Brigade!
'Charge for the guns!' he said:
Into the valley of Death
Rode the six hundred.

THE STORY: THE CLERMONT

1. Vincent Orchard, *Tattersalls: Two Hundred Years of Sporting History* (Hutchinson, 1954).

2. The present Chancellor of the Exchequer, George Osborne, is the grandson of Lt-Colonel Sir George Osborne, 16th Baronet, who married John Aspinall's mother in 1938. She was previously married to Dr Robert Aspinall, a British Army surgeon.

3. *Daily Telegraph*, 31 March 2001. The duke's description of Lucan's demeanour is well supported by those who attended the Clermont, although in the *Mirror*, 9 August 1998, Lady Lucan offered a very different view. 'Speaking of their life prior to the killing, she said: "He was easily stressed and he used to drink and gamble, that was his life. When he gambled you could see the sweat pouring down his face and I often thought I'm going to be a widow."'

4. The description is by Thormanby, the pseudonym of a renowned Victorian racing writer.

5. Lilian Pizzichini, *Dead Men's Wages* (Pan Macmillan, 2003).

6. The story of the 'Big Edge' came to light in 2007, with the publication of Douglas Thompson's *The Hustlers: Gambling, Greed and the Perfect Con* (Pan Macmillan). The charming Irishman Burke had been a longstanding associate of Aspinall, dating back to the days of the itinerant chemmy parties, although the partnership ended rancorously.

7. John Burke made a silky response to Lady Annabel in the *Daily Mail*, 14 August 2007.

    > Choosing his words with great delicacy, Burke, who once dated model Sandra Paul, now wife of ex-Tory leader Michael Howard, says of Lady Annabel: 'She seems to have had a lapse in memory.'... Protecting Aspinall's reputation, Lady Annabel dismissed Burke as a mere employee. But Burke, now in his 80s, tells me: 'I was a founding director of The Clermont Club. There were two of us – the other was John Aspinall.' He alleges that before the club was established, Annabel, then married to Mark Birley, lent him and Aspinall their home in South Kensington 'where we hosted

one of our illegal games... If her memory is going, I have all the records. I know how much she won and lost. I have all the paperwork about that and my days at The Clermont.' He says he has furnished the book's publishers with certified copies.

8. This story is told in *Heroes And Contemporaries* by Jonathan Aitken, Continuum 2006.

9. Lady Annabel Goldsmith, *Annabel: An Unconventional Life* (Weidenfeld & Nicholson, 2004).

10. Ibid.

11. For example in Gerring, *Lucan Lives*.

12. David Spanier, *Easy Money: Inside the Gambler's Mind* (High Stakes, 2006). Interesting that Aspinall did not claim that Jagger had joined the upper classes.

13. Ibid.

14. Quotations, respectively, from the *Independent*, 12 November 2004; *Independent on Sunday*, 4 September 2005; and *Sunday Times* 3 July 2005.

15. This phrase was used on the ITV news and is quoted in Dominic Sandbrook, *Seasons in the Sun: The Battle for Britain 1974–79*. I am again indebted to the book for many of the facts in this section.

16. MI5, which installed bugs at Downing Street in 1963, even harboured a theory that Hugh Gaitskell, Wilson's predecessor as leader of the Labour Party, had been murdered by the KGB.

17. Sarah Curtis (ed.), *The Journals of Woodrow Wyatt*, Volume I (Macmillan, 1998).

18. The knighthood was part of the so-called 'Lavender List', Wilson's resignation list, comprising some fifty names written by his secretary Marcia Falkender on lavender-coloured paper. In 2007 Lady Falkender won a BBC settlement against the suggestion that the list was her work. Recipients alongside Goldsmith, with whom Lady Falkender had become friendly, were David Frost, James Hanson and Joseph Kagan. In his diaries Tony Benn wrote of Wilson: 'That he should pick inadequate, buccaneering, sharp shysters for his honours was disgusting.'

19. Quoted by James Fox, *Sunday Telegraph*, 10 October 2004.

20. Curtis, *op. cit*

21. *Independent*, 7 January 2003. In reference to the *Private Eye* case, to which Ingrams had alluded in his obituary of Goldsmith in the *Guardian*, this letter (not from one of Lucan's friends) was published 22 July 1997: 'Richard Ingrams leaves out of his obituary the reason for Goldsmith's "sudden passion for litigation". *Private Eye*'s accusation was that he was

a criminal, who had helped Lord Lucan escape a murder rap. Had the *Eye* had solid evidence to support this claim, Goldsmith would have gone to jail. Since it didn't, it repeated the claim ad nauseam, and Goldsmith issued writs with the same frequency. Why Ingrams regards this as the *Eye*'s finest hour is beyond me.'

22. From his obituary in *The Times*, 19 June 2002, which described him as a 'large, ebullient man with a quick, caustic wit', and wrote that 'the Saturday night dinners he gave with his second wife, Carolyn, made their house in Trevor Square, a stone's throw from Harrods, probably the greatest sporting "salon" ever assembled. There one might meet sporting legends such as Dennis Lillee, Allan Border, Vitas Gerulaitis, Ilie Nastase, John McEnroe or Jackie Stewart alongside Albert Finney, Diana Rigg, Bryan Ferry, Lord Hanson and Sir David Frost.'

23. 'Like a dart' was Bill's own description in an interview with the *Daily Telegraph*, 20 January 1997. 'There is not a lot you can do about it, really,' he said. 'You just have to kick on and make do with what you have got left. I was not intensely depressed about it because it seemed to me a pointless emotion.' An interview with the *Daily Mail*, 26 January 1999, quoted him saying that he had never done things 'by halves', and referred to his projected parachute jump in aid of the International Spinal Research Trust. 'I told my anaesthetist that I was going to have a champagne reception in the ambulance after the jump. He advised me to have the reception before the jump.'

24. Marnham, *Trail of Havoc*, op.cit.

25. Although other sources put Elwes's fee at £200, James Fox himself stated that the figure was £500 (*Sunday Telegraph*, 10 October 2004).

26. *Daily Express*, 21 January 1975, carried photographs from 'Lucan's Family Album', including one from 1968 captioned 'Skipper Lucan cruising off Sardinia', in which he was pictured smiling broadly with a drink in his hand.

   Daily Mail, 12 September 1980, showed photographs of Lucan on holiday in Venice; he was described as 'looking like the doomed composer Mahler'.

   Daily Mirror, 17 August 2008, also printed photographs, and wrote: 'In one Lord Lucan enjoys a fun bout of "après ski" in the posh Swiss resort of St Moritz – the sort of privileged world the average member of the public would never have seen back in the early 60s. Others show him relaxing on holiday or enjoying happy days at home with his wife Veronica and children in London's exclusive Belgravia. Veronica opened the private family album as part of her bid to set the record straight about what happened to the Irish peer after he disappeared in November, 1974.'

In *Sunday Telegraph*, 10 October 2004, James Fox stated very clearly that the photographs illustrating his article had come from Veronica: 'Lady Lucan sold us rights to her family albums.' Fox also explained that he had been unaware of the accusations against Elwes as he was then out of the country.

> I regret it badly. Had I known about Elwes's predicament I would certainly have revealed the source of the Acapulco pictures at the time. Twenty years or so ago, in exasperation at the continuing myth that Elwes was to blame for them, I did reveal the source in the letters page of the *Spectator*, but nobody seemed to notice – except Lady Lucan.
>
> The pictures had been lying about in Lady Lucan's house and I had taken them along with her photograph albums, with her consent. She left a message on my answering machine after this revelation saying: 'You know what we do with foxes. We break their necks and break their backs.' She didn't leave her name, but I would recognise her voice anywhere.

27. *Daily Telegraph*, 9 September 2000.

THE STORY: MARRIAGE

1. Her daughter Lady Barbara Bevan died aged sixty-one on 17 December 1963, Pat Lucan on 21 January 1964.
2. *Daily Mail*, 19 September 1998.
3. This was said by an unnamed source in *Sunday Times Magazine*, 8 June 1975, although James Ruddick attributes the remark to Dominick Elwes.
4. *Daily Mail*, 19 September 1998.
5. Goldsmith, *Annabel: An Unconventional Life.*
6. *News of the World*, 8 November 1981.
7. Ruddick, *Lord Lucan: What Really Happened.*
8. In an interview with the *Sunday Telegraph*, 11 October 1998.
9. *Daily Express*, 20 January 1975.
10. *Daily Mirror*, 9 August 1998.
11. In 2000 the robes were sold at auction for £3,290.
12. In *Lord Lucan: What Really Happened*, Lady Lucan told James Ruddick: 'It might seem very grand to have someone who is always there to look after your children, to wash the nappies and change the beds and generally take them off your hands. But then you ask yourself: what is there for me to do? They're *my* children, after all.' With regard to the sacking of Lilian Jenkins, Ruddick wrote: 'Perhaps it was a conscious cry of anger, a determination to take charge, in spite of what her husband demanded.'

13. *Sunday Times Magazine*, 8 June 1975.

14. Norman Lucas, *The Lucan Mystery* (W. H. Allen, 1975).

15. *Sunday Times Magazine*, 8 June 1975.

16. Ibid.

17. *News of the World*, 8 November 1981.

18. In an article on the Lucan case for *Vanity Fair*, Dominick Dunne wrote that Lady Lucan had been dubbed an 'NOC, darling' [not our class].

19. Part-quoted in Ruddick, *op. cit.* Most of the remarks were originally made in the *Daily Express*, 20 January 1975.

20. Ruddick, *op. cit.*

21. *News of the World*, 1 November 1981.

22. In conversation with Ruddick, *op.cit.*

23. *Sunday Times*, 20 September 1998.

24. *Daily Express*, 20 January 1975. Lady Lucan's contract with the newspaper was referred to by James Fox in the *Sunday Telegraph*, 10 October 2004.

25. *Daily Mail*, 19 September 1998.

26. The 'shocking outbursts' are mentioned in Ruddick, *op. cit.*; the phrase 'aggressive and unbalanced' is from James Fox, *Sunday Telegraph*, 10 October 2004.

27. Ruddick, *op. cit.*

28. The suggestion that the drugs were 'partly' to blame for the paranoia and hallucinations comes from Marnham, *op. cit.*

29. As attested in Lucas, *op. cit.*

30. Dr Ann Dally, who died in 2007, was a supporter of the methadone treatment for heroin addicts. Although found guilty of professional misconduct for 'over-prescription' of methadone in 1983 and 1987, she continued to criticize conventional drug policies.

31. *News of the World*, 1 November 1981.

32. *Sunday Times Magazine*, 8 June 1975.

33. Ibid.

34. These rumours were cited, with additional baroque elaborations, in a *Daily Mail* article entitled 'The Vicious Campaign of Hate that is Haunting Lady Lucan', 27 June 1975. A friend of Veronica's named Peter Langley spoke out against the 'evil untruths'.

35. Quoted in Marnham, *op. cit.* He wrote that Aspinall at such times sounded like 'a violent version of Mr Micawber'.

36. *Sunday Times Magazine*, 8 June 1975.

37. Quoted in Ruddick, *op. cit.*

THE STORY: HOUSE BLUE

1. Antonia White, *The Sugar House* (Eyre and Spottiswoode, 1952).

2. Nick Peto, *Peto's Progess* (Long Barn Books, 2005).

3. In a letter to Robert Conquest of 5 January 1989; from Zachary Leader (ed.), *The Letters of Kingsley Amis* (HarperCollins, 2000).

4. In *Trail of Havoc*, Patrick Marnham wrote of Lucan: 'The judge considered him arrogant and untruthful and, on his own admission, lawless.'

5. In *The News of the World*, 1 November 1981, Lady Lucan spoke of having fallen 'into the trap of taking up some of my lonely life with doctors who would talk to me.' Lucan, she said, 'used this against me. He went to court without my knowledge and on the evidence of two doctors was granted temporary custody.'

6. Along with much of the evidence given to the inquest, Kait's testimony was widely published in newspaper reports: for example the *Daily Express*, 18 June 1975.

7. Lawrence Stone, *Road to Divorce: England 1530–1987* (OUP, 1990).

8. This information was also cited in a 2012 television documentary, *Fred Dinenage: Murder Casebook*, which contained interviews with James Ruddick and a former police officer on the Lucan case.

9. *News of the World*, 1 November 1981.

10. *Daily Mail*, 19 September 1998.

11. *Daily Express*, 31 October 1975.

12. *News of the World*, 1 November 1981.

13. Sally Moore, *Lucan: Not Guilty* (Sidgwick & Jackson, 1987).

14. Ruddick, *op. cit.*

15. Moore, *op. cit.*

16. Ruddick, *op. cit.*

17. As posited by James Fox, *Sunday Telegraph*, 10 October 2004.

18. This was reported by James Fox in the *Sunday Times*, 22 June 1975.

19. *News of the World*, 1 November 1981.

20. *Sunday Times*, 1 November 1998.

21. Quoted in Marnham, *op. cit.*

22. Later, Veronica herself would say that her husband had actually paid the nannies to leave. 'He would take them out to expensive dinners, and the

more they drank, the more they talked and he would persuade them to go. The intention was to make it look as if I could not keep staff' (*News of the World*, 25 October 1981). This suggestion seems never to have been made elsewhere.

23. The *Daily Mail*, 10 October 1985, reported that Christabel had 'escaped death at the hands of Mrs Rivett's killer that night in 1974 only to be killed herself and hacked into more than 100 pieces... Mrs Boyce escaped at the Lucans because she and 29-year-old Mrs Rivett, who were colleagues, swopped shifts at the last moment.' There is absolutely no corroboration for this fascinating allegation.

24. In an interview with the *News of the World*, 25 October 1981, Lady Lucan said: 'He still had keys to the house – I never stopped hoping he would come home'.

25. Ruddick, *op. cit.*

26. In *Trail of Havoc*, Patrick Marnham suggests that Lady Lucan also walked regularly past her husband's Elizabeth Street flat, in the same way as he patrolled Lower Belgrave Street: 'In a thoroughly sensible move she responded to this harassment in kind.'

27. *Daily Mirror*, 9 August 1998.

28. Lucas, *The Lucan Mystery*.

29. *News of the World*, 1 November 1981

30. In Ruddick, *op. cit.*

31. This letter was revealed by Dennis Gilson, the accountant who in 1975 was appointed Lucan's bankruptcy trustee. He sold it to the *News of the World* in 1979, with the £1,000 proceeds going into the bankruptcy fund.

32. Goldsmith, *Annabel: An Unconventional Life*.

33. *Daily Express*, 12 November 1974. The cover story, together with a photograph of Miss Colquhoun, was headlined 'Deb's Plea to Hunted Earl'.

34. This version of events is from David Gerring. To the *News of the World*, 25 October 1981, Lady Lucan gave a slightly different account in which her husband did speak to the headmistress. '[She] was sarcastic with him. Our troubles over our children were well-known. She told him she had not the faintest idea why Frances was not at school, and hung up.'

THE INVESTIGATION: MURDER

1. In a 1968 letter to Francis Wyndham, then editor of the *Sunday Times Magazine*.

2. In the *News of the World*, 25 October 1981, Lady Lucan explained that she had been rushing that night with the children's supper: 'In our haste we forgot to put the chain on the door.'

3. *Daily Express*, 20 January 1975.

4. *Daily Express*, 17 June 1975.

5. In the *News of the World*, 25 October 1981, Lady Lucan claimed to have guessed that her husband would have driven to the Maxwell-Scott home: 'I'd tried to mention this the night before [7th] but the hospital wouldn't let me speak to the police until I was stitched up... Next morning, the policeman was there to ask me questions and I told him where I thought John had gone. I was right.' This notwithstanding, the Maxwell-Scotts did not enter the police investigation until 9 November.

6. In Sally Moore, *Lucan: Not Guilty*.

7. Moore, whose research is formidably detailed, describes the blood thus: right shoe, toe and upper; left shoe, sole and upper; blood inside the arches of both shoes. All blood from group B.

8. As said to Ruddick, *op. cit.*

9. *The Sun*, 5 November 2004.

10. To Sally Moore, *op. cit.*

11. *The Sun*, 1 December 2012.

12. Ruddick, *op. cit.*

13. Aspinall's magnificent pink house stands just two doors away from the former home of Thomas Cubitt, chief architect of Belgravia.

14. *News of the World*, 25 October 1981.

15. Marnham, *op. cit.*

16. In *The Times*, 21 June 1999, Bill explained: 'He rang me just after the event but the bedside phone was turned off and when the girl answered the phone downstairs she thought I wasn't in.'

17. Marnham, *op. cit.*

18. *Sunday Telegraph*, 10 October 2004.

19. Quoted in Marnham, *op. cit.*

20. Marnham, *op. cit.*

21. *News of the World*, 8 November 1981. Lady Lucan claimed only to have learned about this hearing through a paragraph in the newspapers: 'When I showed it to Detective-Sergeant Graham Forsyth, the policeman guarding me, he got up and said: "Come on"... the Sergeant took me home to change, and then rushed me to the court in his Panda car.'

22. In the *News of the World*, 1 November 1981, Lady Lucan stated that she had returned unaccompanied to 46 Lower Belgrave Street after the murder. 'I let myself into the dusty, dimly-lit hallway of the big, old house full of apprehension...I spent that night there completely alone and I was very frightened. My bedroom door didn't lock and I heard every creak during the night. But I got through it.'

23. This remark was recalled in the *Daily Mail*, 29 April 1998.

24. *Sunday Times Magazine*, 8 June 1975.

25. *Daily Mail*, 19 September 1998.

26. Miss O'Donnell also attended the auction of the Lucan silver, and was pictured at Christie's in the *Daily Express*, 28 November 1974. She was said to be 'keeping a watching brief for Lady Lucan', who had opposed the sale.

27. Agatha Christie had written to her brother-in-law, the playwright Campbell Christie, telling him that she was going up north to a spa town. Eleven days later she was discovered where she had said she would be, at the Hydro hotel in Harrogate. Her confused intention had almost certainly been for Campbell to act as an intermediary between herself and her husband, whose love she was seeking to reclaim; and for her 'disappearance' to remain a private incident.

THE INVESTIGATION: THE CIRCLE

1. 20 January 1975; the necklace had belonged to Lucan's great-aunt. Similarly, on 18 June 1975 the *Daily Mirror* printed adjacent photographs of Veronica and the 'millionaire's wife' Christina.

2. *Daily Mirror*, 20 June 1975.

3. *Daily Mail*, 3 June 2007.

4. These must have been addresses loaned by friends. Egerton Gardens is directly opposite the Holy Trinity church.

5. *Daily Express*, 20 January 1975.

6. Mentioned in Moore, *Lucan: Not Guilty*.

7. Glenn Campbell, presenter and researcher of BBC1's 2013 *Inside Out* documentary.

8. *Daily Mail*, 3 June 2007.

9. Stephen Hensby was interviewed by the *Daily Mail*, 23 October 1999.

10. *Daily Mirror*, 20 June 1975.

11. *Daily Mirror*, 8 March 2012. Former Detective Chief-Superintendent Drummond Marvin asserted the belief that Lucan was in Africa, having had plastic surgery paid for by his friends.

12. Gerring also referred to the tradition, which in fact happened on only one occasion, of hanging aristocrats with a silk rope – 'That would have been something to see' – suggesting that in an earlier century this might have been Lucan's fate.

13. James Fox quoted in Ruddick, *op. cit.*

14. Ruddick, *op. cit.*

15. Moore, *op. cit.*

16. Marnham, *op. cit.*

17. Ibid. Patrick Marnham wrote that 'Veronica, who knew exactly why he had come, was not particularly impressed...'

18. Quoted in Ruddick, *op. cit.*

19. Marnham, *op. cit.*

20. *Daily Mail*, 27 June 1975.

21. Taki wrote this in *The Spectator*, 23 October 2004.

22. This remark, much quoted, was originally made in Brian Masters, *The Passion of John Aspinall* (Cape, 1988).

23. *Guardian*, 20 November 1994. The article began: 'Some of John Aspinall's best friends are killers. For a start, there are his animals "whom I love more than people". Balka, the tiger which savaged a keeper to death last week; Zeya, the Siberian tigress who killed two keepers in separate attacks; Bindu, the Indian bull elephant who crushed a keeper to death. And there's Lord Lucan, the English bull elephant who bludgeoned his children's nanny to death...'

Aspinall wrote a rather superb letter in reply, published 27 November 1994, in which he stated: 'There is no such thing as a dumb animal. In your allusion to Lord Lucan as a "dumb human", I must here take issue and also challenge your assumption that I hero-worshipped him [as the article had suggested]. John Lucan was a good friend of mine. I enjoyed his company and found in him qualities that I admire. By no stretch of the imagination could it be said that I "hero-worshipped" him. The concept is a baseless journalistic conceit and without merit...

'I don't know where you got the opening quote of your article that I "love animals more than people". This is a misconception. I love my animal friends and intimates in the same manner and to the same intensity that I love my human friends. For some mysterious reason, some journalists find that extraordinary. My fortune, such as it is, was built upon the success of my human relationships and then deployed in the protection of wild species.

'Your writer carefully lists the various tragedies that have afflicted us at Howletts and Port Lympne over the last 35 years. I suppose it is too much to ask of him to juxtapose a credit column. Failing to mention the 400 tigers we have bred and the 50 gorillas, seven black rhinos, 40 snow leopards etc etc merely devalues the human lives that we have lost. It is a crude injustice to Trevor Smith, who was killed by Balkash, to ignore the positive side of his work.'

24. *Daily Express*, 13 and 15 November 1974.

25. *Sunday Times Magazine*, 8 June 1975.

26. Later Lord White of Hull, the multi-millionaire financier Gordon White was co-founder of the Hanson Trust conglomerate.

27. Patrick Marnham in the *Daily Telegraph*, 19 September 2000.

28. *Independent*, 3 August 1997.

29. Jeremy Scott, *Fast and Louche* (Profile, 2002).

30. Goldsmith, *Annabel: An Unconventional Life*.

31. *Daily Mail*, 27 October 2004. The article stated that Mrs Parks 'claims to have later received a note from a friend of Susan Maxwell-Scott warning her that what she had seen should remain absolutely confidential. As a teenager she kept her counsel, telling only her mother. But years later, and by then married, she watched Susan Maxwell-Scott on TV talking about Lucan's disappearance. Mandy was so incensed at what she heard that she rang Scotland Yard. She insisted to police: "What she said was not the whole truth." To this day, Scotland Yard officers believe that Lucan's car was taken to Newhaven as a decoy while he himself was spirited off to a new life.'

32. *Evening Standard*, 10 August 2007.

33. At the 1975 inquest into the murder of Sandra Rivett, Mrs Maxwell-Scott confirmed that she was at home that night with her two youngest children.

34. Garth Gibbs, in an online article headlined 'Looking for Lucky'.

35. F. Tennyson Jesse, *A Pin to See the Peepshow* (William Heinemann, 1934), a fictionalized retelling of the Thompson-Bywaters case.

36. In an interview with *Sunday Telegraph*, 11 October 1998, Bill stated his conviction that Lucan was dead: 'Some people can act their way through life, taking on other personas. But you have to be extrovert; he was cripplingly introverted.'

37. *Daily Mirror*, 15 November 1974.

38. *Daily Mail*, 1 March 1982, reported that Lady Lucan had been admitted to Westminster Hospital after an apparent attempt to kill herself.

39. Ruddick, *op. cit.*

40. Ibid.

41. Marnham, *op. cit.*

42. *Sunday Times*, 20 September 1998.

43. The purchaser had the house exorcised by the Queen's Chaplain.

44. The interview with *Woman's Own* was cited in the *Daily Mail*, 1 April 1980.

45. *Daily Mail*, 19 September 1998.

46. As reported in *The Times*, 5 December 1983.

47. *Daily Mail*, 22 April 1986.

48. *Sunday Times*, 20 September 1998.

49. Quoted in the *Guardian*, 1 November 1999.

50. *Daily Mail*, 9 November 1984.

51. *Sunday Times*, 20 September 1998.

52. Ibid.

53. *Daily Mail*, 19 September 1998.

54. *Sunday Telegraph*, 31 October 1999.

55. In a television interview with ITV's *GMTV*, November 1994.

56. *Daily Mail*, 12 September 1980.

57. Lady Lucan also painted her husband: her unfinished portrait was pictured in the *Daily Express*, 20 January 1975, and described as a 'bold amalgam of blues, reds and slashing yellow'.

58. *Sunday Telegraph*, 31 October 1999.

59. *News of the World*, 25 October 1981.

60. *Sunday Telegraph*, 31 October 1999.

THE INVESTIGATION: SOLUTIONS

1. Ruddick, *Lord Lucan: What Really Happened.*

2. *The Times*, 5 December 1964.

3. Notably, by Sally Moore in *Lucan: Not Guilty.*

4. Ruddick, *op. cit.*

5. In 1974 my father was working in Hill Street, around the corner from the Clermont, with a business associate who was an acquaintance of Lucan's.

Many years later we discussed the murder, and he recalled that gossip at the time had centred upon the idea that Sandra was the intended victim.

6. In the *News of the World*, 25 October 1981, Lady Lucan said of Sandra: 'She had been given one blow on the back of the head, and died instantly.'

7. Lady Lucan half-confirmed this herself, in conversation with James Ruddick, when she described sitting with her husband on the anteroom steps and staring at the front door across the hall. 'The corridor was very dim. There was only the streetlight coming in through the glass over the door.'

8. To Sally Moore, *op. cit.*

9. *Daily Mirror*, 9 August 1998. To the *News of the World*, 25 October 1981, Lady Lucan said: 'Perhaps he mistook Sandra for me. But she had a lot of hair, mine is finer. She was the same height but broader-hipped. She used different scent.'

10. The Edgson sighting is cited in James Fox's *Sunday Times Magazine* article of 8 June 1975, although no time for it is given. Lucan, wrote Fox, had 'switched to his Mercedes' after giving Hicks-Beach a lift home.

11. Both James Ruddick and Patrick Marnham espouse the hitman hypothesis in their books, *op. cit.* Ruddick suggests that Lucan went to the house himself to ensure that 'his masterplan was progressing smoothly', and that he did not ask the hitman to dispose of Lady Lucan's body because 'that would have entailed exposing the code of the safe' (given that her body was to have been concealed inside it). It was Lucan, says Ruddick, who told the hitman to use the lead piping, which was inadequate but had the virtue of being silent. 'It will be remembered that Lucan was adept at telling people how to conduct their business.'

    Marnham's theory is that Lucan hired a hitman and told him to enter the house through the back door, via the mews at 5 Eaton Row (in fact no access is possible that way). Marnham then suggests that the original hitman was replaced by a deputy, 'not a specialist', thus explaining the ineptitude of the crime and the failure to kill Lady Lucan (the badly chosen weapon having been distorted by the attack on Sandra Rivett). Marnham also posits that the plan required Lucan himself to remove the body from Lower Belgrave Street.

12. Quoted in the *Sunday Times Magazine*, 8 June 1975.

13. *Daily Mail*, 10 March 2012.

14. John Fowles, *The French Lieutenant's Woman* (Cape, 1969).

15. Moore, *Lucan: Not Guilty*.

16. *Daily Express*, 20 January 1975.

17. Sally Moore, who argues for Lucan's innocence, constructs a theory in which the attack upon his wife began in the basement; Patrick Marnham says that Lady Lucan 'must either have come into contact with the man who was covered with Sandra's blood or herself been into the basement'. He adds carefully: 'She made no mention, of course, of going into the basement.'

18. *News of the World*, 8 November 1981. Lady Lucan was referring to the bizarre question as to whether her wounds could have been self-inflicted (see p.222).

19. Ruddick, *Lord Lucan: What Really Happened*.

20. *News of the World*, 25 October 1981. Another minor discrepancy arose in this interview when Lady Lucan said that, after making the offer of tea, 'Sandra gathered up some other cups and went back downstairs'. At the inquest she had said that she did not recall Sandra taking any cups: 'She may have had them in her own room'.

21. See note 22 (House Blue), p.398.

22. *News of the World*, 25 October 1981.

23. *Daily Mirror*, 17 August 2008. In the same interview Veronica said that after the attack 'she overheard Lord Lucan telephoning his mother, Countess Kaitilin Lucan, telling her about "blood and mess in the basement".' This was the first suggestion that the call to Kait had been made from Lower Belgrave Street; which it cannot have been. Kait did not return to her own home that night until around 10pm, some ten minutes after Veronica entered the Plumbers Arms.

24. *Daily Telegraph*, 20 February 2012.

25. This was the day that Lady Lucan regained custody of her children at the High Court. She had returned to Lower Belgrave Street two days previously.

26. *Daily Mail*, 10 October 1985.

27. *Daily Mail*, 4 February 1975. Christabel, it was said, had left her job: 'She is telling friends that she has had enough and wants to get back to her old life.'

28. Mayerling is the name of the Austrian hunting lodge where in 1889 Crown Prince Rudolf, the drug-addicted heir to the throne of the Austro-Hungarian empire, shot his lover Baroness Mary Vetsera before turning the gun on himself.

29. *Daily Mirror*, 17 August 2008.

30. *Daily Mirror*, 9 August 1998.

31. Ruddick, *Lord Lucan: What Really Happened*.

32. *News of the World*, 25 October 1981.

Acknowledgements

Although, quite understandably, there were people whom I approached who did not want to talk about the Lucan case, those whom I did meet – including several who have never spoken before – could not have been more generous and frank, and I am extremely sensible of this given the difficulty of the subject matter. For legal reasons it has not been possible to reveal all that they told me, but despite restrictions their contributions were invaluable in shaping my thoughts. My deepest gratitude goes to Bill and Christina Shand Kydd: it is impossible to thank them enough. I also greatly enjoyed my time with Dr Jane Griffin, sister to Lord Lucan, whom I met in New York. Victor and Marilyn Lownes, Pierrette Goletto, Graham Forsyth, Daniel Meinertzhagen and Stuart Wheeler were extremely charming and helpful to me, as were Nick and Zoe Peto; I was very sorry to learn of Zoe's recent death.

I extend additional warm gratitude to the people who, in return for their contributions, wished to remain anonymous. Chief among these was Lord Lucan's schoolfriend, who has never spoken before about these events and was a delight to meet.

Further help was given by Tim Thomas, Max Hudson, Jenni Day and John Penrose. The Clermont Club extended a kind welcome, and The Print Place in Leighton Buzzard enabled me to send the text when my internet connection died on the day that the book was completed. The staff in the newsroom at the British Library, and before that at Colindale, were marvellous as always.

My thanks to Val Hudson, and to Charlie Viney, who took the proposal to Head of Zeus. I could not have had better publishers, and I am hugely grateful to Anthony Cheetham, my lovely editor Richard Milbank, Amanda Ridout, Becci Sharpe and indeed everybody at Head of Zeus for their support and unceasing kindness. Georgina Capel has been wonderful in helping me through the final stages towards publication. Finally I give love and thanks to my mother and my brother John, who listened with exemplary patience and made many contributions; and to Milo.

Selected Bibliography

Firstly: this is by no means the first book about the Lucan case (such is its fascination) and I should like to acknowledge a huge debt to the other people who have written about it. I am chiefly grateful to Sally Moore, whose *Lucan: Not Guilty* is a brave, highly readable masterpiece of research. James Ruddick's *Lucan: What Really Happened* contains long interviews with Lady Lucan, which were extremely useful to me. Patrick Marnham's *Trail of Havoc* is a brilliant book, an immensely stylish portrait of the era, while Norman Lucas's *The Lucan Mystery*, written soon after the event, is full of interest. The books by the two policemen who led the investigation, Roy Ranson's *Looking for Lucan* and David Gerring's *Lucan Lives*, were valuable sources. I am also much indebted to the writings of James Fox: chiefly the famous *Sunday Times Magazine* article of June 1975, which gave such an incisive picture of Lucan and the Clermont Club, as well as a 2004 piece in *The Sunday Telegraph*.

Other books that were enormously helpful include:

Barrow, Andrew, *Gossip*, Hamish Hamilton (1978).

Bassett, Kate, *In Two Minds: Jonathan Miller*, Oberon Books (2012).

Cannadine, David, *The Decline and Fall of the British Aristocracy*, Yale (1990).

Chenery, J. T., *The Law and Practice of Bookmaking, Betting, Gaming and Lotteries*, Sweet & Maxwell (1963).

Fallon, Ivan, *Billionaire: The Life and Times of James Goldsmith*, Hutchinson (1991).

Flanders, Judith, *The Invention of Murder*, Harper Press (2011).

Foreman, Amanda, *Georgiana, Duchess of Devonshire*, HarperCollins (1998).

Goldsmith, Annabel, *Annabel: An Unconventional Life*, Weidenfeld & Nicolson (2004).

Hennessy, Peter, *Having it So Good: Britain in the Fifties*, Allen Lane (2006).

Kynaston, David, *Austerity Britain 1945–51*, Bloomsbury (2007).

Masters, Brian, *The Passion of John Aspinall*, Jonathan Cape (1988).

Mosley, Charlotte, ed., *The Letters of Nancy Mitford and Evelyn Waugh*, Hodder and Stoughton (1996).

Peto, Nick, *Peto's Progress*, Long Barn Books (2005).

Sandbrook, Dominic, *Seasons in the Sun: The Battle for Britain 1974–1979*, Allen Lane (2012).

Scott, Jeremy, *Fast and Louche*, Profile (2002).

Spanier, David, *Easy Money: Inside the Gambler's Mind*, Secker & Warburg (1987).

Spark, Muriel, *Aiding and Abetting*, Viking (2000).

Stone, Lawrence *Road to Divorce: England 1530–1987*, Oxford University Press (1990).

Index

surveillance of wife and children
191–2, 197, 208
taping wife's conversations 189–90
wedding day 145
wife seen as victim of 146–7
Personal Life
appearance and demeanour 24, 26,
86–7, 94, 200
attributes 351
bank career 26, 87–9, 90–1
bankruptcy 148, 208, 209–10
birth 69
bobsleighing 98
borrowing money from friends and
relations 202–3, 206–7
cars and driving 95
character traits 92, 143, 198, 351
childhood and upbringing 25–6,
81–2, 143
and Clermont Club set 18, 27–8, 29,
30, 98, 119–20, 144, 200
daily routine 171–2
death theories 40–1, 259, 305–10
debts and finances 16, 19, 30, 170,
173, 200–1, 201–2, 209–10
disappearance and search for 34–5,
38, 39
drinking 209
education and schooling 26, 80–2
at Eton 81–4
evacuated to America during Second
World War and stays with Brady
Tuckers 76–9
family background 53–68
girlfriends 93, 200
and golf 95–6
greyhound racing 89
High Court declaration of death of
(1999) 211
horseracing 26, 27
insecurity and lack of self-
confidence 144
last weeks before murder 206–9
leaves William Brandt's bank 90–2
lifestyle and social life 92–3, 95
living in Botswana hypothesis 42–3
myth of 23–49
and National Service 85–6
no body found and explanations for
308
non-existent status of 40
offered film role by De Sica 24, 94,
156
pet dog 199

powerboat racing 96
rebellion against parents 84–5, 92, 93
relationship with mother 80
right-wing politics 350–1
selling of family silver to pay for
debts 149, 202, 207, 211, 330
sightings of 41–4, 295–6, 309
skiing and bobsleighing 95, 98
squeamishness of 356
suicide hypothesis 306–7
value of estate in 1999 211
view of women 141
White Migrant yacht 78, 96–7
Lucan, Elizabeth, Countess of 8–9, 138
Lucan, Kaitilin, Dowager Countess (*née*
Dawson) (Lucan's mother)
appearance 75
attempt to have inquest verdict
retrospectively removed 317
burial 74
car accident 69
defence of son 76
denial of world of privilege 75
dislike of gambling 84
and education of son 81–2
family background 73
police statement and evidence given at
inquest 175–6, 246–9, 247, 248, 251
political beliefs/career 74–5
and son's custody case 178
telephoning of by son after murder 33,
226–7, 239, 247, 251
upbringing 72–3
and Veronica 162
Lucan, Margaret, Countess of 56, 138
Lucan, Veronica, Countess (*née* Duncan
(Lord Lucan's wife) 27, 137, 175–6
allegations against Lucan of physical
abuse 167, 197–9
appearance 137
Aspinall's dislike of 27, 152, 168–9, 284
attempts to keep in contact with by
Lucan's family 319–20
behaviour 147–8, 164–5
birth of children 149, 166
childhood and upbringing 139, 144
and custody battles 29, 177–85, 262–4
Daily Express interview after murder
159, 268, 314, 331, 343, 364, 366
education 139
entering pub after murder covered with
blood 221–2, 231
evidence given at inquest 32, 176,
267–8, 312–13, 314–15, 335–6, 359, 361

Picture credits

1. John Bingham, 7th Earl of Lucan, by Bassano, 24 January 1973 (© National Portrait Gallery, London).
2. Laleham Abbey (Wikimedia Commons).
3. The 3rd Earl of Lucan (Universal History Archive/Getty Images).
4. The Lucan Memorial (Laura Thompson).
5. Lord Lucan's parents' wedding (Planet News Archive/SSPL/Getty Images).
6. Lucan at St Moritz (Topfoto).
7. Lucan in a powerboat race (Topfoto).
8. Lucan and Veronica announce their engagement (Topfoto/UPPA).
9. The Lucans' wedding day (Douglas Miller/Keystone/Getty Images)
10. Aspinall, Burke and Lady Osborne (Paul Popper/Popperfoto/Getty Images).
11. Dominick Elwes and Tessa Kennedy (REX/Associated Newspapers).
12. James Goldsmith in France (Central Press/Getty Images).
13. Veronica with Frances (Topfoto).
14. The Clermont Club (Topfoto).
15. The Shand Kydds, 23 February 1971 (Popperfoto/Getty Images).
16. Lucan and Zoe Howard at Portofino (Daily Mail/REX).
17. Lucan at a gambling club, 30 April 1973 (REX/Associated Newspapers).
18. Lucan's mews home in Eaton Row (Laura Thompson).
19. Lucan's flat at 72a Elizabeth Street (Topfoto).
20. Andrina Colquhoun in Hyde Park (Len Trievnor/Express/Getty Images).
21. Sandra Rivett (Topfoto).

22. 46 Lower Belgrave Street, 8 November 1975 (Mirrorpix).

23. The Plumbers Arms (Topfoto).

24. Grants Hill House, Uckfield (Mirrorpix).

25. Susan Maxwell–Scott (Keystone/Getty Images).

26. The Ford Corsair in Newhaven (East Sussex archives).

27. The police hunt for Lucan (Mirrorpix).

28. Ranson and Gerring (REX/Ken Towner/Associated Newspapers).

29. Veronica returns to Belgravia (Frank Barratt/Keystone/Getty Images).

30. *Daily Mirror* front page, 14 November 1974 (Mirrorpix).

31. Kaitilin Lucan (REX/Graham Morris/Associated Newspapers).

32. Roger Rivett, 16 June 1975 (Central Press/Getty Images).

33. Frances, George and Veronica (REX/Geoffrey White/Associated Newspapers).

34. Lord Lucan in a West End club, 30 April 1973 (REX/Evening News).

35. 46 Lower Belgrave Street today (Wikimedia Commons)

36. 'Jungly' Barry in Goa (Topfoto).

Endpapers: 1967 London Premier Map, reproduced by permission of Geographers' A–Z Map Co. Ltd. Licence No. B6916. © Crown copyright and database rights 2014 Ordnance Survey 100017302.